LAIRDS

LAIRDS AND LUXURY

The Highland Gentry in
Eighteenth-century Scotland

Stana Nenadic

JOHN DONALD

First published in Great Britain in 2007 by
John Donald, an imprint of Birlinn Ltd

West Newington House
10 Newington Road
Edinburgh
EH9 1QS

www.birlinn.co.uk

ISBN 10: 1 904607 71 3
ISBN 13: 978 1 904607 71 7

Copyright © Stana Nenadic 2007

The right of Stana Nenadic to be identified as the author
of this work has been asserted by her in accordance
with the Copyright, Designs and Patents Act, 1988

All rights reserved. No part of this publication may
be reproduced, stored, or transmitted in any form, or
by any means, electronic, mechanical or photocopying,
recording or otherwise, without the express written
permission of the publisher.

British Library Cataloguing-in-Publication Data
A catalogue record for this book is available on request from the British Library

Typeset by Hewer Text UK Ltd
Printed and bound in Britain by Bell & Bain Ltd, Glasgow

To the memory of Leah Leneman
and
Leslie Walker

Contents

Preface and Acknowledgements   ix
Prelude   xi

Introduction: Transforming the Highlands   1

PART ONE
Gathering and Spending   17

1   Families and Estates   19
2   Children   40
3   Gentlemanly Careers   65

PART TWO
The Luxury Trap: Officers and Gentlewomen   87

4   Military Men   89
5   Gentlewomen   112

PART THREE
Consumer Behaviour, Houses and Sociability   135

6   Consumer Behaviour and the World of Goods   137
7   Houses   159
8   Sociability and Hospitality   183

Conclusion: From Luxury to Loss in Five Generations   205
Notes   212
Bibliography   243
Index   254

Preface and Acknowledgements

This book has evolved from a number of parallel interests. The first was my research on consumer behaviour among the eighteenth-century urban middle classes, which provoked a curiosity to know how much the consumerism of towns could also be found in the most impoverished and inaccessible parts of Great Britain. The second was my longstanding wish to form a better understanding of the Highlands, and the Highland gentry in particular, since the latter have not had a good press as far as assessments of the state of eighteenth-century society and economy are concerned. The third was sparked by a much loved novel, *Kidnapped*, by Robert Louis Stevenson, published in 1886, which revolves around a real event, the Appin Murder of 1752, and which I was reading at much the same time that I stumbled across the remarkable inventories and correspondence of Colin Campbell of Glenure, the 'gentleman consumer' who features prominently in this study and happened to be the unfortunate victim of that infamous political murder. I have also, it must be admitted, cultivated an interest in the subject of this book because it gave me a good excuse, if excuse be needed, to visit the Highlands and to see the beautiful places in Argyll, Perthshire, Skye, Sutherland and Caithness where 'my' Highland gentry lived.

My research has been undertaken over a number of years in conjunction with other projects and it is hard to call to mind all of the people who have been helpful along the way. Since the book itself has been written during a period of sabbatical leave, my first thanks are to my employer, the University of Edinburgh, and to the School of History and Classics for allowing me this time. I am also indebted to my colleagues and research students in the departments of Economic and Social History, Scottish History and the School of Scottish Studies for their stimulating collegiality and many helpful insights and suggestions. Over the years, there have been many undergraduates who took my honours course, 'Scottish Economy and Society, 1745 to 1832', and more recently my masters course 'The Material Culture of Gender in Eighteenth Century Britain', who unwittingly, through their questions and enthusiastic debates, have increased my understanding of these fascinating topics.

Elements of this book, making parallel but separate arguments, have been published in an earlier form as the following articles: 'Experience and expectations in the transformation of the Highland gentlewoman, 1680–1840', *Scottish Historical Review*, 80 (2001); 'The impact of the military profession on Highland gentry families, 1730–1830', *Scottish Historical Review*, 85 (2006); 'The Highlands of Scotland in the first half of the eighteenth century: Consuming at a distance', *British Journal for Eighteenth Century Studies*, 28 (2005). I am grateful to the publishers of these journals for permission to reprint excerpts from the articles here.

In 2001, at about the time I started to work seriously on the Highland gentry, I was appointed as a commissioner of the Royal Commission on the Ancient and Historical Monuments of Scotland (RCAHMS). This was a rare honour as well as an opportunity to get to know the scholarly work of that wonderful organisation, founded in 1908. My understanding of Scotland's past has been immeasurably deepened by staff and fellow commissioners at RCAHMS, and I owe them many thanks, not least because an important part of this study is based on the Argyll survey that was undertaken by RCAHMS staff in the 1970s–80s, and published in seven volumes between 1971 and 1992. *Argyll: An Inventory of the Monuments* is a truly remarkable undertaking.

It is usual, in writing such acknowledgements as these, to give thanks to funding bodies for grants to cover the costs of research visits. I have no thanks to give, for I am in the happy situation of having my principal archives and research libraries quite literally on my doorstep, mid-way between my home in Edinburgh's New Town and my office in the University. I am, however, very grateful to the courteous and efficient staff of the National Archives of Scotland, the National Library of Scotland and the University of Edinburgh Special Collections for helping me in my work among their collections. I also wish to thank the staff in the Argyll and Bute Archives at Lochgilphead for their help, and a cup of tea, when I turned up, unannounced, to see the Poltalloch papers.

Mairi Sutherland and Jacqueline Young for Birlinn have been unfailingly helpful and efficient.

Finally, many friends, including my daily dog-walking companions, have shown a lively (and tolerant) interest in my research and offered much-appreciated support. This book is dedicated to two dear friends (one also a colleague) who died while I was working on this study, and who, in their different ways, loved the Highlands.

Prelude

Gentlemen Consumers: Colin Campbell of Glenure, Hugh Mackay of Bighouse and John Campbell 'of the Bank'

On 15 January 1752, Hugh Mackay of Bighouse wrote from Tongue in the north of Scotland to his son-in-law Colin Campbell of Glenure, who was visiting Edinburgh, requesting him to purchase some goods for his house. 'I know you can do it as well and as frugally as anybody,' he wrote.[1] Mr Gray, an Edinburgh lawyer, was instructed to give Colin the money he needed, and Charles Ross, 'merchant below the Tron Church', was to arrange for everything to be sent by boat to Thurso. Most of the things that Campbell was to buy were for fitting out a dining room: looking-glasses, 'strong and showy, without being dear . . . I would have frames of walnut [or] mahogany plain', and 'the grates I want just of the kind I saw with you'. He wanted 'chairs of the same kind [I saw with you,] something genteel, and to be covered . . . of cotton'. He also wanted some pictures for the wall.

> Buy me a dozen prints, set in black frames, done in the same way I have already. The heads to be of our present King and Duke, late and present Dukes of Argyll, Lord Stair, Mr Pope, Prince of Orange, his Princess, her Majesty the late Queen and any other three you please. This costs but a trifle, and yet are showie.[2]

Colin Campbell spent eighteen days in Edinburgh in early 1752, lodging with John Gibson, a merchant, who provided his breakfasts and organised his laundry.[3] It was a typical visit of the sort he had been making several times a year since early manhood. He visited Edinburgh on legal business connected with his estate, or to oversee the education of younger siblings, or to see one of his illegitimate children who was fostered in Edinburgh.[4] Sometimes he went there on a shopping trip. Hugh Mackay's letter suggests that the men had been shopping together in Edinburgh not that long before, which was likely, since Colin Campbell had only recently married Janet Mackay, eldest daughter of Bighouse. The couple had met in Edinburgh, the wedding took place in Edinburgh in 1749 and it was from Edinburgh that Campbell had purchased most of the things necessary for his new married status and his new house in Argyll. These had included silverware, glass and chinaware – the latter purchased from John Gibson, his landlord in 1752 – a set of 'best Dutch tiles' for a dining-room fireplace, and eight black frames with gilt edges for a set of engraved portrait of the type that his father-in-law had asked him to buy.[5]

At about the same time that Colin Campbell and Hugh Mackay were comparing notes about the furnishings for their houses, another Highland gentleman was having his portrait painted in Edinburgh. John Campbell, the illegitimate son of Campbell of Ardmaddie, was chief cashier for the Royal Bank of Scotland. He was painted by William Mosman, a fashionable portrait artist, in a full Highland dress of tartan belted plaid, with a sword, dagger and pistol, along with some banknotes on the marble table, a pile of books on the windowsill, and a Highland scene in the background glimpsed through the window.[6] Portraits such of these were luxury items displaying fine clothing and a fashionable presence, normally for hanging in a gentleman's dining room, such as the rooms that Colin Campbell and Hugh Mackay were furnishing.

These three men were connected in numerous ways by ancestry, marriage and the lives of their children and grandchildren. They had something else in common, for notable Gaelic poets memorialised all three in bardic tributes. In Sutherland in the 1740s, the great Robert Donn Mackay wrote a celebration of traditional deer hunting when Hugh Mackay moved from the west of the lands of Reay (owned by his elder half-brother) to take up residence on the Bighouse estate in Strath Halladale in the east. The poem commemorated the laird's love of the land, his attachment to the people and his regrets on having to leave.

> Take my farewell and good wishes
> To the other end of the country
> Where I used to be joyful
> Between Tongue and Cape Wrath
> At the time when I climbed the brae.[7]

John Campbell 'of the bank', who was a financial 'fixer' for several Campbell noblemen, commanded a glowing account in poetry from Duncan Ban Macintyre, a celebrated Argyllshire bard. This also evoked the Highland landscape and the gentleman's love of kin. It even praised the banker's fashionable appearance, with 'hat and wig in the mode'. And the poet suggested, in a sentiment that mirrored Mossman's portrait, that if Campbell had not been a banker, 'Thou couldst be an army commander / In time of warfare or stress / As a man of courage and valour, / Versed in all tactics'.[8] Duncan Ban Macintyre also celebrated the third man in this trio of gentleman consumers, Colin Campbell of Glenure, in a lament on his death.

> Wretched is each of thy kinsfolk
> Since thy dear body entered
> The cramped, narrow, close-jointed coffin,
> And the new linen shroud.
>
> Handsome, stalwart, trim, hale;
> Thou wast gentle, serene and pleasant,
> Noble, humble, benignant,
> Kind, clannish and friendly,
> With no fault to be added thereto;
> Thou wast full of wisdom and vision,
> Bold, courageous and valiant.[9]

Colin Campbell of Glenure was murdered one May evening in 1752, three months after his last Edinburgh jaunt. He was shot while riding along a forest path in the Appin district of Argyll, just a few miles from home. He was forty-four years old, a tall, vigorous, good-looking man. He was going about his everyday business as a crown factor on forfeited Jacobite estates. He was mourned by his family and revenged by the great Campbell lords of Scotland. The Appin Murder, as it soon came to be known, was an act of Jacobite defiance.[10] The aftermath was an exercise in aggressive reassertion of Hanoverian control that called into action in various ways Colin's immediate kin in Argyllshire, his father-in-law Hugh Mackay in Sutherland and his distant cousin in Edinburgh, John Campbell the banker. The murderer was never identified for certain, but a scapegoat was found in a local tacksman called James Stewart, who was put on trial in Inverary and suffered a showcase execution. Stewart's body was hung in a cage on a hill above the Ballachulish ferry as a warning to other Jacobites. Colin Campbell was buried secretly at nearby Ardchattan Priory in an unmarked grave to avoid desecration by Stewart's supporters. Such tragedy and barbarity seemed to inhabit a different world to that of polite shopping in Edinburgh.

Yet at the time of the murder Colin Campbell was typical of men of his background at a point of transition in the character of the Highland gentry. He embraced the fashionable world of urban consumption, but, as the bards reveal, he and his contemporaries were also fully embedded in the traditional world of clanship. He belonged to the last generation of his family that was part of the everyday Highland scene. He was bred there and lived there, despite regular visits to Edinburgh. He fully understood the ways and customs of the Highlands. He dressed in the clothing of the Highland gentleman farmer, spoke the language of Gaeldom and served for a while as an officer in a Highland regiment. He was married to a woman who was a native Gaelic-speaker and a practical housewife. His father-in-law, weighing up Colin's suitability as husband for his eldest daughter, concluded with approval that 'he does not want of the Highlandman in him'.[11]

The death of Colin Campbell had massive implications for his family. He owned land and was in the process of completing a new house. He was recently married, and had a wife who was barely out of her teens and two baby daughters. He also had three illegitimate children that he supported, all girls. He was desperately hoping for a son. His wife was pregnant when Colin Campbell died, and her future and the future of his estate depended on the birth of a son. In the event, the baby was another girl. Widow and children left Argyll for Sutherland, and Campbell's brother, a lawyer in Stirling, inherited Glenure. Colin Campbell had assets and debts, responsibilities and commitments, hopes and ambitions. Up until the moment of his death he was nothing more than a very ordinary minor laird. And like many another Highland gentleman, he kept detailed records of what he purchased, what he wore and the things that he had in his house.

Introduction: Transforming the Highlands

This book is about a group of people who were responsible for much of the change that took place in the Highlands of Scotland during the 'long' eighteenth century from about 1680 to 1830. It is focused on a series of landowning families and their evolving relationships through five generations with luxury consumption.

This may seem a like frivolous subject. The eighteenth century was, after all, an age that witnessed many great events of national and international importance in the Highlands, from the Jacobite uprisings to clearance and mass migration. Political oppression, economic collapse, militarisation and population loss are some of the weightier themes of Highland history. Yet many historians, in pointing to the transformative and ultimately disastrous changes that took place in the Highlands, have blamed much of the ills of the age on the luxury and financial fecklessness of lairds. Here is a typical example, taken from what is probably the most widely read history of Scotland of the past thirty years.

> Highland landowners were often greedy and short-sighted . . . They seem to have creamed off a larger proportion of the total profits [of their estates] into their own hands than did the Lowland lairds . . . Clanranald never ploughed anything back into the Uists . . . He was content to spend the kelp money on conspicuous consumption and adding to and servicing the heavy debt charge on his estate.[1]

The theme is echoed in a recent influential survey of modern Scotland.

> Among the aristocracy and gentry the eighteenth century was an era of conspicuous consumption . . . the atmosphere in elite circles was one of competitive display . . . this was the world now inhabited by the highland landowners, one which was a constant drain on the purse

and in which they could not well easily survive on the paltry returns of traditional agriculture.[2]

It appears again in a social history of the period, which draws attention to some of the sources of profit from late eighteenth-century Highland estates and concludes that much of what was earned by landowners was 'dissipated on conspicuous or non-productive consumption', resulting in spectacular bankruptcies by the early nineteenth century.[3]

It is not surprising that historians should take such a view, for there were many bankrupt Highland estates in the early decades of the nineteenth century, and many contemporary observers were similar impressed by the scale of modern consumerism. A Highland laird, William Macintosh of Borlum, writing in the early eighteenth century, highlighted what he called an 'epidemic' of spending, 'in very little houses, and as little estates to supply them'.[4] In 1773, when Johnson and Boswell took their famous tour of the Highlands in search of the ancient life of the clans, they were disappointed to find that southern 'politeness' and the metropolitan 'world of goods' had greatly eroded what they had come to observe, and that those elite Highlanders who still lived a life embedded in the social practices and material culture of the past yearned for the comforts and conveniences of 'modern refinement'.[5] Indeed, Boswell reveals evidence of modern consumerism on even the remotest islands, and though this did not reach the lives of the very poor, it certainly shaped the experience and expectations of the middling sort of people and the gentry.

Gaelic poets, representing the voice of the ordinary people, charted the new interest in commercial wealth and its trappings with a growing sense of dismay. Here is Rob Donn Mackay, writing mid-century on the rising generation of Sutherland gentlemen.

> They are within the letter of the law
> And they are sharp over debts
> And they are punctilious in paying
> What they owe one another,
> But for the rest, it will be stowed away
> Though it's hard to hoard against hospitality;
> And their purses and their eyes
> Are equally shut to the man in need.[6]

Rob Donn also composed a poem to his patron, Hugh Mackay of Bighouse, when the latter purchased a new suit of clothing and wore it for the first time. The tone was not complementary. 'There is not a button nor a button-hole in it / That hasn't taken money off a poor man.'[7]

By the early nineteenth century, the popular condemnation of Highland elites was often couched in the moral language of the Presbyterian evangelical, as in the following verse by Mary MacPherson of Badenoch, celebrated Gaelic poet and pious widow of a local schoolmaster.

> Dangerous is the effect upon mankind
> Of everyone determinedly seeking wealth,
> Travelling near and far to find it
> With war and strife to bring it home.
> Many a person spends his labour
> Whose wealth have given him no pleasure.
> Cursed be the one who robs the needy
> In order to enrich himself.
>
> And because we all must travel on
> To the holy ground from which we rose at first,
> Into the grave in which we'll speak not of wealth
> And in which we'll have no need to spend,
> Vain is each fashion and fine clothing,
> Thin is the shirt in which this body goes.[8]

Historians of recent times have continued to use a moralising tone when describing the consumption habits of the eighteenth-century Highland gentry. Foolishness and venality are the usual accusations. But such reasoning offers no real insights into why so many lairds and their families behaved in this way, for surely not all were fools. We know little about the underlying reasons for the 'epidemic' of spending among those with 'very little houses' and 'very little estates' to supply them. And we know less about who was doing the spending and what it was that they actually bought. This book is intended to offer some answers. Yet to find the roots of eighteenth-century conspicuous consumption, which was a distinct form of social behaviour vested in longstanding cultural beliefs and complex relational practices, we have to start in the century before, when agencies outside the Highlands sought to encourage change.

ECONOMIC CHANGE

There is a popular assumption that change in the Highlands only happened after the rebellion of 1745 with the systematic assault on Gaeldom, and that up until the final defeat of the Jacobites an Arcadian form of clanship had prevailed, uniting rich and poor in common interests.[9] But as with so much of Highland history, this narrative is flawed. Recent studies have shown that clanship was in decline by the early seventeenth century, had only existed for a few hundred years and was an inherently unstable system of economic and social organisation.[10] Some changes were autonomous, but various devices were also used, largely at the instigation of central government, to bring clans under control and to shape the character of the Highland gentry. The events of the eighteenth century did not happen in a vacuum. They were grafted onto earlier endeavours in economic transformation and cultural civilisation in this the poorest, most remote and unmodernised part of Britain.

There can be no doubt that the seventeenth century witnessed profound changes in the uses of land in the Highlands and in the nature of personal wealth among elites, giving rise to new attitudes and significant departures from many earlier forms of behaviour.[11] Chiefs became commercial landlords and as landlords they regarded their land and the products of their estates as private property and as commodities for market exchange. Several important studies have sought to chart these predominantly economic developments through the intimate details of land use within the townships,[12] through exploring the broader compass of estate policies as determined by professional factors,[13] or through charting the impact of external political forces.[14]

Most accounts of the early modern Highland economy highlight the strategic use of commerce as an agent of civilisation in a policy of state control that was used throughout the developing British Empire.[15] The eastern counties of Scotland, with their many connections with Europe and England, were peaceful and prosperous, but much of the rest of the country was perilously poor and existed in conditions of near lawlessness as far as central government was concerned. Poverty and disorder were intimately connected in contemporary thinking, and they were dangerous. Though half-hearted attempts were made to address the issue in the sixteenth century, the Highland problem moved up the political agenda with the Union of 1603, when much of the machinery of Scottish government moved south to London and the contrast between Scotland and commercial England became more apparent and less acceptable.[16] In attempting to commercialise and civilise the Highlands, the lower layers of landed society were targeted. The lairds were resident on their estates and in daily contact with the ordinary people and everyday ways of conducting life. They were also linked to the government and nobility through family connections and powerful chains of patronage.[17] If the middling layers of landowners could be reformed, then the influence would flow downwards and the whole of Scotland would benefit.

The most famous commercial injunctions to be imposed on the Highlands were those contained in the Statutes of Iona, enacted in 1609, designed to promote good conduct among chiefs in the most lawless part of Scotland, the western isles, and supplemented in following years with additional legislation.[18] Though the statutes were hard to police, and the impact remains a subject of debate, the official expectations were clear.[19] Lairds were required to cultivate a home farm and improve the amenities of their estates through such activities as tree planting in order to be 'exercised and eschew idleness'.[20] Aspects of personal consumption were curtailed, particularly heavy drinking of costly imported wines, because it 'draws numbers of them to miserable necessity and poverty'. The retinues of leisured gentleman maintained by lairds in their households were limited to reduce the 'intolerable burden' on estates. Other measures were also introduced. Large numbers of baronial burghs were founded, mainly for the purpose of trade through fixed markets and fairs. Many were on the southern and eastern Highland fringes, close to the modern market economy of central Scotland.[21] And official initiatives were matched by those from the aristocracy, which included an attempt by the earl of Seaforth in the 1630s to establish a Dutch trading 'colony' on the Isle of Lewis in the hope of introducing economic modernisation to this remote island.[22]

Encouraged by the state and noblemen, who were also increasing demands for taxes and dues paid in cash, the primary agents in bringing the introduction of market relationships to the Highlands were not the lairds but their tacksmen and senior clan servants, who now had opportunities to develop as successful middlemen in trade. The area of commerce to which the traditional middle layer of Highland society directed its energies was the cattle trade. On Skye, for instance, the cattle trade was first introduced in the 1650s by one of the warrior bards and cadets of clan MacDonald, who had farmed the island of Eriskay as a tacksman, and late in life, having fallen on hard times, turned to cattle droving, much to the initial disgust of his higher kinsmen, who found the idea of trade beneath their dignity. But the financial reward of this first enterprise in taking a herd of cattle to market in Crieff was so great that others soon followed.[23] It was men like this, with little land of their own but close connections with clan superiors and some available capital, that were best able to exploit opportunities to develop trade. It was men like this, inspired by profit, who were soon familiar with social life outside the Highlands and had the opportunities for spending their profits on modern consumption.

Skye, as with many of the islands, was late in entering the sphere of modern commerce. Long before, lairds and tacksmen on the mainland were involved in cattle trading and were putting into place the means whereby their lesser tenants could also market their own cattle and other produce.[24] Cattle rearing and droving was an attractive form of commerce because it could exist side by side with established systems of tenure and land use. In some ways it allowed traditional Gaeldom to flourish among the ordinary people and added a new and a widely celebrated macho droving culture onto that which already existed. But the cattle trade had additional implications for the gentry. It promoted money-based relationships with tenants, it elevated a culture that saw the profits from land as the primary purpose of landownership, and it gave the gentry large sums of cash to spend elsewhere.

With the commercial cattle trade well established, but problems of lawlessness and political threat still endemic, the eighteenth century witnessed further initiatives in the longstanding policy of commerce as an agent of civilisation. Though property forfeited by Jacobite rebels in 1715 was simply returned to the market, those estates that were forfeited following the '45 were brought under state control to be run as models of modern efficiency.[25] Gentleman factors such as Colin Campbell of Glenure were appointed to manage them under instruction from an Edinburgh office. The mid- and late eighteenth century saw the creation of several government and quasi-government agencies with unprecedented rights of intervention in the Highland economy.[26] The Highland Society under the patronage of the duke of Argyll was founded in London in 1778 to promote the development of the Highland economy whilst simultaneously preserving the best of Highland culture – an ambiguous agenda, needless to say, when the 'best' was represented by the poetry of Ossian.[27] Thereafter, many societies with similar aims took root in the Scottish cities. Britishness and loyalty were now identified with commercial improvement, and the patriotic Highland gentleman was expected to modernise his property and his tenants, as well as himself, or risk social censure and political exclusion. Since cattle no longer made a profit, other products were sought, including sheep and the more efficient use of such coastal resources as fish and kelp. This new patriotic agenda was particularly responsible for the push for economic change during the warfaring years of the later eighteenth and early nineteenth centuries, and gave rise to some of the first brutal clearances.[28] The patriotic commercial agenda was also connected with many aspects of conspicuous consumption among the gentry.

MILITARY CONTROL

Government initiatives to encourage a commercial spirit in the Highlands changed the mental habits of lairds and their families. But there were other areas of outside interventions. In addition to economic backwardness, early modern Highland society, and the gentry in particular, were militarised in ways that threatened the British state. Cultural practices were imbued with military preoccupations. The military generated a rich material culture in clothing, weaponry and hospitality. Displays of physical valour fuelled traditions of feuding and violence between families. Conquest was a well-established device for gaining land, and systems of blackmail and threat relied on a well-armed military element within clans. Government measures were taken from the late sixteenth century to suppress disorder, prevent the outbreak of violence and break the 'brutall custome of deadlie feadis.'[29] One of these was the creation in 1609 of a network of justices of the peace to prosecute criminal violence. Another was seen in the requirement under the Statutes of Iona that the carrying of arms be restricted. Neither had an immediate impact, but gradually the military rationale of clans was undermined.

Yet the military culture of the Highland gentry was sustained through a widespread engagement in mercenary service in the European theatres of war.[30] This was a useful source of foreign earnings and it kept military men out of the way and out of trouble at home. Those soldiers who served in states that were politically sympathetic to Britain were sometimes deployed in Scotland. This happened in 1689 when Dutch regiments, under the leadership of General Hugh Mackay, joined Scottish troops loyal to William and Mary to fight the Jacobites. They lost at Killiecrankie, but won the war.[31] Seventeenth-century governments sought to channel the Highland military to their own ends if they could. Strategic state patronage was deployed with those clan elites who had the right politics and religion to act as a quasi-policing presence in the Highlands. Under instruction from government officials in Edinburgh, short-term regimental formations such as those of clan Campbell were used as local occupying forces to threaten Highlanders into compliance. Sometimes the policy went badly wrong, as the Massacre of Glencoe and its bitter aftermath reveal. In other less infamous cases the policy seemed to work.[32] Loyal clans were overtly attached to the interests of the centralised state, but they also maintained strong allegiances to traditional military Gaeldom in their culture and practices.[33] Even in the late seventeenth century, some were engaged in predatory military activity for their own gains. Lord Glenorchy, a graceful courtier when it suited him, waged bloody battle in Caithness in 1680 against Sinclair interests, to gain land and title in that part of Scotland. The dispute rumbled for twenty years before it was settled by the crown and due process of law.[34]

Highland militarism was manipulated by state agencies in the seventeenth century, creating a longstanding relationship with profound implications for elites. The early eighteenth century was not a good time for Scottish officers. Mercenary services had declined in Europe and there was a strong aversion to a large standing army in Britain. But after 1750, with the growth of empire and demand for regiments abroad, the government was able to tap into a surviving culture of militarism that was sustained in the Highlands through a 'world of symbols and representations'[35] long after the reality of clan warring and mercenary service had ended. This was one of the reasons why so many Highland gentlemen joined the army.[36] There were new links between the British military establishment and the economics of Highland estates through recruiting.[37] The military could be a major source of revenue for lairds. The reinvention and romanticisation of Highland culture around the concept of patriotic military Highlandism – looking backwards to the supposed traditions of clanship whilst simultaneously looking forward to new colonial glories – was also part of a modernisation agenda, directed from outside the Highlands, to further the process of civilisation and economic transformation in this part of Britain.[38] One way or another, the military Highlands were sustained by the state. And, as we shall see, military men and the military cultural agenda were profoundly implicated in the conspicuous consumption of the Highland gentry.

CIVILISATION THROUGH LAW AND ITS PRACTICES

In seeking to civilise lairds, the state and its agencies sought to shape their beliefs and values. An assault on religion and language was begun through seventeenth-century initiatives to promote Protestantism and oblige the gentry to speak English.[39] In common with the rest of early modern Europe, the British government also encouraged the gentry and nobility into state service to maintain their status, and it promoted value systems and sources of identity that privileged individual ability and merit over lineage and wealth.[40] The military profession became an avenue for state service that rewarded the able individual. The legal profession was another.[41] Indeed, just as lairds were being transformed into landlords, they were also seizing the opportunity to become lawyers, with all the attendant mindset and culture this entailed. As Rob Donn in Sutherland rightly observed in the mid-eighteenth century, the new elites with their new preoccupations with wealth were 'within the letter of the law'. They knew the law, they understood it through written formulations and they used that knowledge to further their individualised advantage.

In England and Lowland Scotland, early modern gentleman landowners were closely aligned with the legal profession and judicial service.[42] Systems of law in Highland Scotland were not as 'lawless' as a many monarchs believed, but they were subject to different rules and traditions. Oral culture and tenacious hereditary rights came to be associated with arbitrary justice, which had to change if Scotland was to be governed with any uniformity by a centralised state. The assault on local practices in the Highlands began in earnest with the Statutes of Iona and later 'Regulations for Chiefs', which included the requirement that the eldest sons of lairds be educated in the Lowlands and in English in the standard gentlemanly way. Lowland and English gentlemen placed a high value on the acquisition of the sort of legal knowledge that was likely to be of value to a landowner who viewed his estate through the lens of commerce. The campaign against Highland lawlessness was furthered by the state's requirement for documentary evidence of right of ownership and written legal undertakings for good conduct by lairds. Since Highland commercial activity was fragile, a command of the technicalities of the law ensured easier transactions. For this reason the cattle trade came to be associated with sophisticated systems of legal contract and monetary exchange. The state legal system also offered careers for non-inheriting sons.

It is not surprising that throughout Britain and Europe, lawyers were mostly recruited from the ranks of small-scale landowners. Knowledge of the law enhanced the power base of minor gentry families and furnished technical devices for maximising the value and productivity of estates. The legal profession was also a gateway to a wide range of patronage positions. An early education based on legal study, with some sons entering the legal profession as a lifelong career, had become a feature of successful and expanding Highland families by the start of the eighteenth century, with significant implications for cultural practices and attitudes. This introduced the Highland gentry to higher levels of urban living than before, and was paralleled by another very effective device for getting lairds out of the Highlands and into the city.

ACCOUNTABILITY IN EDINBURGH

Scottish monarchs prior to the seventeenth century maintained control over their fragmented nation through annual tours around the country designed to impress the gentry and nobles with the power of the king and the benefits of royal patronage.[43] This system of government, which prevailed elsewhere in Europe, was physically demanding and politically risky. James VI repeatedly spoke of making such a tour, but never did, and his departure for London in 1603 brought greater urgency to the search for more centralised and bureaucratic systems of government.[44] One device, instituted in the early seventeenth century, was the requirement in law that the gentry and nobility, along with set numbers of supporters, make an annual visit to the seat of government in Edinburgh to give formal accountability for their behaviour in the previous year and signal loyalty and conformity to the laws of state. This accountability, the reverse of the annual royal tour, was put under the control of a court official, the Lord Lion at Arms, and employed the visual power of heraldry and written genealogical records to effect control.[45] The Lord Lion's primary duty was to create and maintain an archive of heraldic emblematic devices showing family connections and lines of descent, along with privileges and rights to property. He also stage-managed the annual procession of nobles and gentlemen in Edinburgh. Ordered according to rank and connection, participants were required to carry their full heraldic colours and devices to signal to one another other, and to the population at large, the relationships among them. It was a dazzling spectacle.

Heraldry and genealogy were powerful tools for civilising the gentry in the lawless parts of Scotland and for developing their role in government.[46] The Lord Lion maintained an impressive network of regional officials, an informal civil service drawn from among the lesser landowners, who maintained a watching brief over matters of law and inheritance in local areas and were especially important in organising and monitoring the funerals of the great. Elaborate and strictly controlled funeral processions, designed to display the order of relations among nobles and gentlemen through their arms and heraldic emblems, provided the state with a means of controlling the disputes and disorder that often followed the death of a landowner. Calling on an army of device painters and heraldic costume makers, the Lord Lion or one of his regional deputies would ensure that the burial was conducted with propriety and in a manner that allowed participants and observers to see lines of family connection and lawful inheritance. Though long abandoned in other parts of Scotland, elaborate and expensive funeral ceremonies were maintained in the Highlands well into the eighteenth century.

Sir James Balfour of Denmilne and Kinnaird (1600–57), Lord Lion in the 1630s and a minor Fifeshire laird, was typical of the new breed of government bureaucrat[47] The most important single event that he organised was the great funeral procession for his patron George Hay, earl of Kinnoul, in Perthshire in 1635. Hay was an important figure at court in London, but when he died he was buried in his home territory in what was a major statement of order and government control. It was also a ruinously expensive exercise in the conspicuous consumption of liveries and mourning clothes.[48] James Balfour's father was a courtier both before and after the Union of 1603, and several of his many brothers pursued careers in government and law. Balfour was educated in Scotland and London and on the continent. He had wide scholarly interests. But he was also involved with practical projects to establish a map record of Scotland through the work of Timothy Pont, the cartographer, and the map publisher Bleaeu of Amsterdam. This was another form of government control through print culture. He owned a large library and was a prolific author. He also gathered together a vast collection of official documents, many from the libraries of pre-Reformation monastic establishments. Much of Balfour's collection was acquired by the Faculty of Advocates in Edinburgh to form the core of that institution's new library at the end of the seventeenth century.

Though he was interested in genealogy as a field of scholarly study and a process of bureaucratic control, gentleman officials like James Balfour were individualists and they were well embedded in a material culture of luxury and consumption, partly as a consequence of urban living. Though not a rich man and possessed of only modest estates, Balfour commissioned his own portrait, which was unusual for someone of his status in Scotland. It is full of telling details: a finely decorated lace shirt; expensive books and manuscripts; and a table covered with a sumptuous oriental carpet, with seals and coins and compass on it, invoking officialdom, commerce, map-based knowledge and the merit of the individual personality.[49] It is a visual representation that would doubtless have appealed to that most famous of book-learned, aspirational, late seventeenth-century Highland gentlemen, Martin Martin (c.1660–1718). Born in Skye of lesser-gentry background, Martin was educated in Edinburgh and Leiden and often traveled to London and the continent on business for his clan patrons. He was part of a growing group of elite Gaels who as soldiers, lawyers and scholars were eager to be part of mainstream metropolitan society, while maintaining their Highland contacts and credentials. Though not employed in any bureaucratic capacity, Martin's published antiquarian and geographical research was partly Treasury-funded. His intellectual agenda looked to the past, but he also had an eye to the future betterment of the Highlands through trade and the founding towns and by encouraging the people 'to acquire mechanical arts and other sciences'.[50]

THE UTILITY OF BENEFICIAL LUXURY

For Martin Martin and his contemporaries, the term 'mechanical arts and other sciences' was shorthand for manufacturing; and most of the goods that were manufactured at this time were for personal consumption. Martin identified glass and earthenware, both part of a growing industrial sector in Britain, as areas for future investment in the western isles.[51] In raising the possibility of commercial manufacture in the Highlands, Martin hinted at a further characteristic of changing belief systems among the gentry when they adopted, in common with most British elites, what has been called the 'theory of the utility of beneficial luxury'.[52]

Some seventeenth-century government initiatives to control the Highland gentry were targeted at dangerous levels of luxury consumption, particularly of alcohol, which seemed to be linked to excessive feasting and fighting and also generated balance-of-payment concerns.[53] But most of the state's civilising agenda was designed to encourage beneficial luxury through the provision of markets and the channelling of consumption habits into durable and domestic forms that would generate employment and taxes. This was not a straitforward matter in post-Reformation Scotland. The ambiguities of luxury in a Calvinist context are best articulated through the seventeenth-century Dutch example, where an 'embarrassment of riches' gave rise to a form of bourgeois consumerism that was underpinned by a constant moralising critique.[54] Calvinism bred a culture of austerity that went hand in hand with luxury, as many a seventeenth-century Dutch merchant could demonstrate. But from the late seventeenth century the moral and religious anxiety was gradually undermined by enlightenment theories of the social good or utility of certain types of consumption.

'Beneficial luxury' was an economic argument with cultural and behavioural implications. Adam Smith in his *Wealth of Nations* of 1776 – when he stated that 'consumption is the sole end and purpose of production' – was the most famous advocate, but the idea had been in common currency since the 1680s and was particularly associated with the Dutch-born London-based philosopher Mandeville.[55] The basic principle was that economic growth and the associated social benefits could only take place through personal demand for domestically manufactured goods, or through foreign imports that could be taxed. Such demand would stimulate industry, promote skilled employment and generate wealth. Beneficial luxury was in the interests of the nation. So too was 'improvement' – of land, houses, manufacturing processes and personal behaviour, which meant industriousness for the poor and politeness for the rich. Industriousness generated the goods of consumption; politeness was connected with the purchase and uses of such goods.

Beneficial luxury and the parallel concept of improvement were both associated with modernisation and progress in Scotland, and they were closely linked to patriotism. A succession of political initiatives both before and after the Union of 1707 was designed to encouraging luxury manufacture and consumption. The Board of Trustees for Fisheries and Manufacturers, founded in 1727 with public money arising out of the Union settlement, had an interest in developing the consumer goods industries and even established a design school in Edinburgh to improve the quality and appearance of Scottish-made goods.[56] Plans for Edinburgh's New Town in 1752 were explicitly directed towards more luxurious styles of living for the Scottish elite, in order to keep that elite in the Scottish capital, where they would spend their wealth for the benefit of the country as a whole.[57] The Board of Trustees was active in the Highlands in seeking to improve the quality of locally manufactured goods and the Forfeited and Annexed Estates Commission, established in 1752 to run Jacobite estates, adopted the same modernising commercial agenda.[58]

LAIRDS AND LUXURY

With their increasingly British and European orientation, the Highland gentry were as much a part of a luxury culture as were other elites in Scotland or England. They could hardly be otherwise given the numerous efforts to transform the beliefs and behaviour of lairds and their families. Yet the contours of luxury and consumption in the Highlands did assume a very particular and ultimately dangerous form, and this book seeks to explain why that was so. It begins by looking at families and family formation in order to understand the often complex characteristics of lairds and their relationships with estates and with the other people who lived in the Highlands. There were female heirs, bachelor lairds and growing numbers of landowners who took their primary incomes from employment elsewhere, and these all influenced consumerism among the gentry. The second chapter explores the experiences of children through their changing education, which included a sophisticated introduction to the cultures of urban consumption. The third chapter is about how men of Highland gentry background made and used their incomes – what Rob Donn called their 'gathering and spending' – both through their estates and, just as important, through the careers they were obliged to adopt to supplement estate revenues, or because they were non-inheriting sons. The concept of 'knowledge practices' is important here, for it suggests that what people knew and believed and the way in which that knowledge was created through education and work had implications for behaviour in the sphere of consumption.

The middle part of the study is focused on two groups of Highland elites who shaped to a disproportionate degree the changing mental habits and consumer behaviour of lairds and their families – military officers and gentlewomen. Although the changing character of the Highland gentry was influenced by an urban professional culture of lawyers, the occupation that had the greatest impact was that of the soldier. Young gentlemen who were trained as farmers or merchants flocked to join the army when military opportunities began to rise in the 1750s. By the late eighteenth century, most of the sons of the Highland gentry were sent into the army, often in their early teens. It was a short-term route for disposing of surplus males in a gentlemanly fashion that put responsibility on the individual to make his own way in life. But it had negative implications for families, for it caused the loss of practical and useful kin in farming or trade, and introduced young men to levels of conspicuous consumption unknown elsewhere. Soldiers were members of a luxury profession. Soldiers were also romantics. Luxury and romanticism spawned a cultural legacy of nostalgic regret for what had been lost and a cultural blindness to debt and its implications, as well as blindness to the brutal realities of life for ordinary Highlanders by the early nineteenth century.[59]

The Highland gentlewoman was also painfully locked into a culture of romanticism and luxury by the early nineteenth century. The history of the Highlands has been written as if almost no women ever lived there. Yet women were of enormous importance in defining the character of gentry experience – a fact that was recognised in 1609 when the Statutes of Iona included provision for the Lowland education of the eldest daughters of Highland lairds, as well as sons. Women brought in resources to families and estates, and they cost resources to maintain, and the balance between the two changed over the eighteenth century alongside a changing social experience and cultural expectation among gentlewomen. Put briefly, in 1680 the wife or daughter of a laird was born, lived and died within the Highland counties without once venturing into the Lowlands or beyond. She was illiterate, largely Gaelic-speaking and her daily routines were built around the practical affairs of household management, dairy work, cloth production and child rearing. By 1820, the Highland gentlewoman was born and mostly raised in the Lowlands, particularly in Edinburgh. She was a book-learned woman whose knowledge of Gaelic was limited and whose familiarity with her family estate was mostly restricted to summer holidays. Her daily routines were defined by leisure and were mostly conducted indoors. Such women were consumers, not producers, as their great-grandmothers had been.

The final section of this book explores the material culture of the Highland gentry as represented through their consumption habits, the purchase of 'things' and the social life involved once things had been acquired. It looks at housing and the decoration of houses both in the Highlands and elsewhere as lairds increasingly found it necessary to live in towns. It also looks at the changing social life of the Highland gentry as defined by a new preoccupation with gentility and politeness.

The approach to this study is informed by collective biography and is focused on the Campbell family of Barcaldine and Glenure from Argyll and their many connections through marriage, which included the Mackay family of Bighouse in Sutherland. It uncovers the lives and experiences of both men and women, lairds and their ladies, and also the tribes of younger sons and unmarried daughters who were a part of all gentry families and deeply attached to Highland life but had no hope of land ownership, or even marriage in many cases, and were often obliged to live outside the Highland counties. These people were an abiding cause of interest and concern within families and it was their experiences that that gave rise to many of the new consumption habits of the Highland gentry.

The Campbells of Barcaldine have left an unusually extensive, rich and continuous body of family correspondence and estate papers that reveal the behaviour, aspirations and disappointments of a middling landowning family over five generations from the later seventeenth to mid-nineteenth centuries.[60] The other families and individuals that figure in this book are less well served by surviving records, but by plotting their more fragmented lives against the experience of the Campbell family it is possible to show that although local conditions and values shaped some aspects of consumer experience, most of what is described here was witnessed throughout the Highlands.

Part One
Gathering and Spending

1 Families and Estates

INTRODUCTION

The front page of the *Scotsman* newspaper of 14 August 1839 carried the following advertisement for a 'SPLENDID DOMAIN AND VALUABLE ESTATE IN ARGYLLSHIRE', to be sold by auction in the Old Signet Hall, Royal Exchange, Edinburgh. The Campbell family of Barcaldine had owned the property for almost 200 years.

> THE BEAUTIFUL AND EXTENSIVE ESTATE OF BARCALDINE, lying in the parish of Ardchattan, about 12 miles north-east from the thriving Royal Burgh and Sea-Port of Oban and about 25 miles south-west from Fort-William, and the like distance north-west from the county town of Inverary. It is situate [sic] on Loch Creran, an arm of the sea, branching from the Linnhe Loch, through which the Glasgow and Inverness Steam-Boats pass, and comprehends the whole of the Southern Bank of Loch Creran, a stretch of about twelve miles of coast, while at one point on the south it nearly reaches Loch Etive.
>
> The Estate contains, by a survey and plan drawn up in 1801, 10,741 acres Scots, or 13,546 imperial; but this being horizontal or plan measure, a large addition may be made on account of the great inequality of surface throughout the Estate, particularly on the hills and woods, so that the true extent of surface measure may fairly be taken at upwards of 15,000 imperial acres.
>
> The present Rental including the value of the Sheep Farms and Low Grounds, and the Wood Cuttings, as estimated by an experiences valuator in 1835, may be stated at nearly £2700 and the rental might be greatly increased by a moderate outlay.

The public and parish burdens amount to about £95. The estate holds of a subject superior for a payment of a trifling feu-duty, and the Land-tax is redeemed.

BARCALDINE possesses peculiar recommendations and attractions as a singular fine and most desirable RESIDENCE; and with regard to natural beauties few anywhere can vie with it.

Game of all sorts, with the exception of Pheasants, is found on the Estate. Large Herds of Wild Fallow Deer roam over the grounds and Roe abound in the sequestered thickets. During winter, Red Deer, occasionally come from the upper forests.

The Exclusive Right of Salmon Fishing in one side of Loch Creran belongs to the Estate, which affords a constant supply of the finest Fish. Salt-water Fish of all sorts are also found in abundance in the Loch; and, besides, Trouting on the Estate, there is capital Fishing in the Streams and Lochs in the neighbourhood. Loch Creran is particularly favourable for Boating, for which the beauties of the scenery and the opportunities of Fish hold out every inducement.

Lithographical copies of the plan, with a report by Mr Henderson, land-valuator, in 1835, rental and further particulars will be supplied by James Brown and Charles Pearson, acommptants in Edinburgh (who have power to conclude a private sale), or by John Archd. Campbell, WS, Edinburgh; and Hugh Sinclair, at Barcaldine Lodge, will point out the estate.[1]

Barcaldine was on the market because of the pending bankruptcy of Sir Duncan Campbell and was sold as a sporting and leisure estate, in common with many similar Highland properties. The potential purchasers comprised wealthy businessmen from the Scottish Lowlands or industrial north of England, the occasional nabob with an East India fortune and fashionable English gentleman.[2]

The sale of Barcaldine was a tragedy for many Campbells and their connections in the area and beyond. Though the family was scattered across the globe, the 1839 advertisement gives a hint of the kin network that was still held together by such an estate. John Archibald Campbell, a descendent of John Campbell 'of the bank', was one of many generations of an Argyll family that had made their careers in the Edinburgh legal profession and provided legal services and advice for the Campbells of Barcaldine. He was also Sir Duncan Campbell's first cousin. Hugh Sinclair, a factor, was probably connected to those Sutherland–Caithness families that were the product of three generations of Campbell marriages since the mid-eighteenth century. Yet these fleeting glimpses of a family network give little idea of how the estate had functioned in its earlier history. The Campbell family of Barcaldine had lived in the Benderloch area of northern Argyllshire since the early seventeenth century. Part of the kin and patronage connections of the earls of Breadalbane, they were typical of the middle and upper laird class. Through a combination of astute political judgement, good professional and commercial links, advanced estate policies and strategic marriages, the family had experienced a sustained increase in wealth throughout much of the eighteenth century, and the head of the family saw his status rise from farming laird and chamberlain to the earl of Breadalbane (*c.*1700) to leisured gentleman and baronet by the early nineteenth century. Their independent landholdings in 1688 were modest. By 1751 the family was sixteenth in the league table of Argyllshire landowners, and tenth in 1802.[3] Reflecting their rising status, a cadet branch of the family, known as Campbell of Glenure, was created in the 1740s. But after nearly a century of economic success, a gradual decline set in. Mounting debts resulted in the sale of the Glenure property in 1815 and the Barcaldine estate was finally lost in 1842. The head of the family in the mid-nineteenth century was landless and most of his brothers were in India. He was employed as agent to the marquis of Breadalbane and died in retirement in Wimbledon near London. His eldest son emigrated to Australia.[4]

Highland gentry families in the early eighteenth century were synonymous with their estates. Land provided the social space on which ties of kinship were forged and maintained, and land provided the economic resources to support a kin network.[5] Most lairds were originally established as landowners by their clan chief, who granted land to a vassal or tacksman. There were various devices whereby lairds acquired further land to advance the interests of their families. Conquest and crown charter were common in centuries past, but purchase was increasingly likely with the commercialisation of land. The processes of property accumulation were also linked to family and family formation. Individuals acquired land that had belonged to their forebears, and thus ancestry was important, but they also gained lands through gifts from their clan superior and through marriage settlements. A large extended family living locally was essential for maintaining the viability of an estate, and most lairds measured their status through reference to the scale of their kin connections. Members of an extended family were the usual tenants of the laird, and relationships within a family were controlled in such a way as to keep as much of the family resource under family control as was possible in order to maximise production and regulate consumption. Managing family

22 *Gathering and Spending*

resources through the hazardous stages of marriage, births and deaths was an essential skill for Highland lairds. Such management could only be accomplished through carefully orchestrated face-to-face relationships, where everyone involved operated with the same objective in mind. Those elements within a family with potentially competing interests – particularly women from other families who were connected through marriage – were tightly controlled. An illustration of how such relationships were successfully managed is provided through a detailed dissection of organisational responses within the Campbell family of Barcaldine to the death of one of their important kin tacksmen.

FAMILY AND PROPERTY AT DEATH

Colin Campbell of Invernan, a farm on the Barcaldine estate that was held on tack, was the fourth and youngest son of Alexander Campbell of Barcaldine and brother of Patrick, the laird. He died at home in February 1731, aged about thirty-five, leaving a widow, Isabell, daughter of John Campbell of Torinlink, and two young sons, Alexander and Mungo.[6] His property and finances, along with the responsibility for the future well-being of his wife and children, were left entirely in the hands of his kinsmen – an uncle, three brothers, two cousins and two nephews – reflecting the trust that he had in these men and the fact that his affairs in death as in life were intimately linked to the family and estate. To mark his status and theirs, his kinsmen organised a big and expensive funeral in the Highland manner.

When Colin died, Patrick Campbell took immediate charge of the boys, who were removed from their mother and sent to lodge at nearby Ardchattan Priory, where there was a clergyman who was closely connected with the family through marriage and who ran a school for the sons of the local gentry. The priory was adjacent to the ancient Campbell graveyard, where their father was buried. Isabell, the widow, who was still a young woman, returned to her own family with an annuity of 100 merks, provided by the Barcaldine estate in accordance with her dowry. There may have been daughters of the marriage, but these were not mentioned. Isabell had little further communication with her sons, and she probably later remarried to advance the interests of Campbell of Torinlink through some other connection.

Colin Campbell did not own land, but as a senior tenant he did own a significant stock of animals, particularly cattle, and his immediate relatives purchased most of these. Patrick Campbell acquired eight 'quays', or heifers, for £106 12s. 4d. James Campbell of Clachanseyle, who was an uncle, a senior and respected figure in the family and also a Barcaldine tacksman, purchased twenty-five 'yell' cows – that is, cows in calf – for £504 3s. 4d. And John Campbell younger of Barcaldine, a nephew who had recently married and established on a farm of his own, acquired fourteen 'tydy' or milking cows with their calves for £340 13s. 4d., and eleven 'stirks', or bullocks, for £122 16s. 5d. With the sums raised from the sale of two horses and their 'furniture', along with quantities of timber planks in the house and byre, farm equipment and modest household goods, a total sum of £1,222 17s. 8d. was raised. The widow and children were also due a series of payments, amounting to £1,555 12s. 10d. from family members, including all of those noted above, plus other Campbell relatives and several members of the McIntyre family, a local landless service clan.

The legal business associated with the death was undertaken by Colin Campbell's cousin, the lawyer John Campbell of Inverary and by Patrick's third son Duncan, nephew to the deceased, a young man recently qualified as a lawyer. The funeral was organised by John Campbell, another brother, who was also a tacksman on the estate. Supplies for the funeral, which were mostly purchased from a firm called Murray & Co., were sent from Inverary by Alexander Campbell, also a cousin, who was a merchant in that town. Other than members of the McIntyre family, almost all of the names that are recorded in the extensive accounts of Colin Campbell's estate and affairs-at-death were male members of his close kin network. The single exception was a woman, Elizabeth Clark, spouse to John McInnes of Ardnaskroch in Muchairn (possibly a medical practitioner), who was owed £54 13s. And having died, Colin's assets and male progeny were absorbed back into the family and his tack was granted to another kinsman.

Such close connections, operating at multiple levels, meant that a kin tacksman was far more than just a convenient economic arrangement for lairds and estates. He was a figure of trust and a social resource in a system that was central to the stability of families and estates. The business of managing death and inheritance, or marriage and dowries, called kinship groups into conversation and action to reify their bonds of common interest. This is one of the reasons why the system was so difficult to break and why the breaking was so emotionally charged. Indeed, even when the tacksmen began to be removed by modernising landowners, the tenants that replaced them were often members of the same extended kin network.[7]

The system of family management that is revealed in this event relied on everyone involved being willing to put the collective family interest ahead of his own. In settling Colin Campbell's financial affairs, sums of money were recorded on paper for the purchase of 'stock and gear' and for debts owed. Yet little real money was exchanged, for bonds of kinship were paralleled by bonds of indebtedness, and demands for cash were destabilising. The one figure in this story that offered the greatest threat was the widow, whose marriage had brought in real resources from outside the family in the form of a dowry and who now expected her annuity in cash. She may have had little emotional connection with her husband or sons, since marriages in this level of Highland society were mostly political arrangements. That is why she was quickly returned to her own family. But annuities or jointures were often late, or reduced arbitrarily, or not paid at all, if lairds could get away with ignoring the burden.[8] As far as this or any other similar family was concerned, the best things that the widow could do were die or remarry and save them further expense. It was a brutal way of treating women, but one that was designed to preserve family resources.

MARRIAGE AND FAMILY FORTUNES

Patrick Campbell of Barcaldine, the laird who managed the affairs of his dead brother Colin, was a cleaver strategist as far as the maintenance of family property was concerned. His day-to-day existence was built around the farming routines and seasonal cycles of the estate and the people who lived there, and his evenings were spent in a tireless correspondence with a wide circle of men of similar status and Campbell interests who lived beyond the locality.[9] He will have recognised in the poetry of Lachlan MacPherson, a gentleman bard from Badenoch to the north of Barcaldine, who was a distant marriage connection, a reflection of his own daily preoccupations.

> Drinking and music and market-time,
> Baptism and marriage and death,
> King and church and physician
> And a thousand details thereafter.
>
> The dog and the thief and the guest,
> Mole and lost cattle and kinsfolk,
> Master, service, and offspring –
> Make sure you keep count of the wife.[10]

But overlaying the ordinary events and prosaic details of the Highland gentleman's life in the first half of the eighteenth century was a broader ambition to promote the interests of the family as a whole, particularly through advantageous marriages. As far as 'counting' wives was concerned, Patrick had two. Both predeceased him, which meant that his heir was not burdened with a widow's annuity. The first marriage, organised by his father, was within the clan, and his wife, Ann Campbell of Kilmun, died young in 1706, leaving him with two children, a boy and a girl.[11] His son John was destined to inherit Barcaldine, and his daughter was destined for an advantageous marriage, again within the clan, to keep her dowry under close family control. The second, more ambitious marriage in 1707 was brokered by himself with a family beyond the male clan connection but linked to his own mother. Lucy Cameron of Lochiel, who was Patrick's first cousin, was a younger daughter of John Cameron, laird of Lochiel, whose extensive estates lay to the north. Her mother and Patrick's mother were sisters, born into the family of Campbell of Lochnell, which was a wealthier estate than Barcaldine.[12] A wider horizon was opened for the children born of this second marriage than was usual for younger siblings, and Lucy Cameron's eldest son, called Colin, was destined to be a laird in his own right through the founding of a cadet branch of the family in the 1740s, based on a gift of land from his father to form an estate. The new family was known as Campbell of Glenure.

Established as a laird, Colin Campbell of Glenure, like his father before him, married strategically outside the clan to secure prestigious links with a powerful family in a more distant part of the Highlands. Janet Mackay of Bighouse in Sutherland was the granddaughter of a nobleman, Lord Reay, and connected by blood and marriage to a wide network of Sutherland–Caithness gentry and nobility. Her father, Hugh Mackay, the younger son of Lord Reay, was a senior military laird and cattle drover. This marriage between Sutherland and Argyll, celebrated in Edinburgh in 1749, should have been the foundation for a flourishing cadet to parallel and support the interests of the Campbell family of Barcaldine. The early death of Colin in 1752 without a male heir swiftly ended these plans. Yet a pathway into the north-east Highlands was established, and the next generation of the Campbell family of Barcaldine also married into a grand Sutherland–Caithness clan. Alexander Campbell, a military man and heir to the family estate, married Helen Sinclair of Ulbster in 1765. One of the daughters of this union married Sinclair of Mey, who became the twelfth earl of Caithness at the end of the century.[13]

Through several generations, successive strategic marriages brought increasingly elevated family connections to the Campbell family of Barcaldine, to complement and enhance their growing property holdings and rising wealth. Solid local linkages in Argyll were maintained through the marriages of younger daughters, but family ambitions and family fortunes were extended northwards and eastwards through the marriages of older sons into great families. Some of these connections were Jacobites – a cause that evoked some sympathy in Breadalbane circles – and caused political problems for the family mid-century.[14] David Campbell of Kethick, brother-in-law of John Campbell of Barcaldine, was said to have attended every Jacobite execution in Carlisle dressed in deep mourning.[15] Indeed, the Appin Murder of 1752 is partly explained by the strength of local feelings against a man who, though fiercely loyal to the Hanoverian state, was connected via his mother to a Jacobite clan that suffered badly in the post-'45 retributions. Archibald Cameron, a younger son of Lochiel, a cousin and exact contemporary of Colin Campbell of Glenure and a much-esteemed surgeon in Lochaber, was executed in London in 1753 as a result of his involvement in Jacobite plots.[16] The head of the family and his eldest son, both generous to young Colin when he was a boy, died in exile and many of their kin tenants were evicted.[17]

Marriages into the Mackay and Sinclair families took the Campbells of Barcaldine into safer waters. Of strong pro-Hanoverian politics and a fervent Presbyterian, Hugh Mackay of Bighouse had taken up arms against the Jacobites in 1745 and was a kindred spirit in many ways.[18] He certainly held his new son-in-law and the Barcaldine family in the highest esteem, for the marriage opened new horizons and gave him opportunities to socialise with some of the greatest noblemen in the land, including the duke of Argyll. This fact was not lost on the poet and celebrated commentator on the Sutherland social scene, Rob Donn Mackay, who was not altogether complimentary when describing his patron's ambitions.

> Play your hand, Hugh, as your good sense directs you,
> Make hay while the sun shines brightly . . .
>
> O you are in the great houses as you love to be . . .
> And you are increasing your knowledge
> Among all men, big and small.
> Now you are off to see
> Barcaldine and his wife.[19]

Hugh Mackay made strategic marriages for his younger daughters in the 1750s. Marion was married to the master of Reay, the laird's eldest son and a cousin, and Elizabeth, the youngest, became the wife of William Baillie of Rosehall, a local laird.[20] When Glenure was murdered, the widow, Janet, should have remarried to further her father's ambitions, but she eloped with the stepson of her youngest sister, causing a scandal in the neighbourhood and incurring Hugh's great displeasure. Both of Hugh's sons died young and unmarried, Marion died young in childbirth and Elizabeth was widowed when young. The Bighouse estate passed through two generations of female inheritance, with damaging consequences. In comparison with others, his was not a lucky family.

In the later eighteenth century, the marriage strategies of the Campbell family of Barcaldine continued to be driven by ambition but no longer confined to the Highlands or circumscribed by the older imperative of careful management of family resources and family consumption in the interests of the estate. Several sons travelled abroad and found their wives in other countries.[21] The heir to Barcaldine made an important marriage into the family of John Campbell 'of the bank' in the 1780s. John Campbell, chief cashier of the Royal Bank of Scotland, was rich, politically powerful and lived well in Edinburgh. But he was a businessman, not a laird. He had a Lowland wife, his eldest son was an Edinburgh advocate, his eldest daughter was married to David Dale – the great cotton merchant – of New Lanark and his youngest daughter, married to Barcaldine, was bred to urban comforts. The final generation, in the early nineteenth century, saw the laird of Barcaldine married to the daughter of a wealthy industrialist from Dumbarton. It was another grand connection into a high-living family, though not of a character that was likely to help the interests or fortunes of a Highland estate.

WOMEN AND PROPERTY

At no stage in the history of the Campbell family of Barcaldine did women inherit land in their own right. Daughters carried dowries but not land. Young widows, like Janet Mackay, returned to their own families, often to marry again. Older widows were sometime granted life-rented farms by their husband's will, but heirs were often quick to overturn such provisions in the interests of male kin.[22] In Britain as a whole, it was urban property that gentlewomen were most likely to inherit, but the Highland gentry did not own urban property before the late eighteenth century. There is scant evidence of female inheritance anywhere in the western Highlands at this time. Yet in Sutherland and Caithness and elsewhere in the north-east, there were many female heirs to important estates, and powerful widows were well-known. The family of Mackay of Bighouse furnishes an illustration.

George Mackay, the fifth laird of Bighouse, died in 1710 and the estate passed first to a son, who died unmarried, and then to the joint ownership of two sisters, Elizabeth and Janet. Elizabeth married one of the younger sons of Lord Reay, and her husband, Hugh Mackay – of whom we have heard so much already – became laird of Bighouse.[23] The husband of the second sister, William Mackay of Melness, who held land in his own right, contested the settlement but was satisfied with a lifelong financial compensation, an annuity on the property. After the death of Hugh Mackay's wife in 1769, their surviving children, both daughters, along with the several children of these women, became co-heirs to the estate. But Hugh, as younger son of Reay, still had ambitions that a son might inherit the chiefdom, which was also destined for female co-inheritance, and to this end he remarried in 1770. He was in his late sixties and desperately ill. He died within the year, without fathering a son. The Bighouse estate was saddled with expensive legal bills and many dependants, the inevitable consequence of contested female co-inheritance. It eventually passed into the hands of a lesser gentleman, George Mackay of Handa, who had married Louisa Campbell, eldest daughter of Janet Mackay and Colin Campbell of Glenure. A Barcaldine cousin, sending news from the north to his father in Argyll, described the complex family situation and resulting financial mess.

> I believe Ellan Handa gets the estate of Bighouse, Mr Baillie's eldest son [the son of Elizabeth Mackay of Bighouse, with an estate of his own] two thousand pounds, Colina [youngest daughter of Janet Mackay and Colin Campbell of Glenure] and Mr Baillie's younger children five hundred pounds each . . . I fear the widow [of Hugh Mackay of Bighouse] will not come in for the share she ought considering the sacrifice she made, and the care she took of him.[24]

This was more than country gossip, for the affairs of the Mackay family of Bighouse remained close to Barcaldine interests. Indeed, the laird of Barcaldine was trying to persuade Janet Mackay's youngest daughter, Colina, into a marriage with one of her Barcaldine cousins.[25] She refused, and who could blame her, for she was now financially independent, as were several other young women as a consequence of this settlement. The estate as a resource had remained within the family, but spread thinly over a wider group than would have happened with a single male heir. The widow, as an outsider, inevitably fared badly. Yet there was some sympathy for her plight.

There were other female-owned estates in Sutherland and Caithness in the second half of the eighteenth century. Ann Sinclair of Brabster, an only surviving child, was married in 1762 to a cousin, Robert Sutherland of Langwell, to create a new family and estate of Sinclair-Sutherland.[26] But the marriage did not flourish, and Ann secured her father's property in her own right in 1774 following a divorce that she instigated with her widowed mother's support.[27] The widow could only take such action because of her own financial independence, which included an ability to make land purchases in her own right to augment the family estate. She galvanised members of her Sinclair kin network to release her daughter, with two younger children, from near imprisonment on the Langwell estate. The eldest son, though young, was kept by his father and sent away into family fosterage, against the wishes of his mother. He died in youth, and the estate eventually passed to Ann Sinclair's second son, who was raised by mother and grandmother.

Further to the south, near Inverness, Elizabeth Rose of Kilravock was also married to a cousin prior to inheritance, and when her husband died in 1779 she successfully petitioned parliament to secure the property in her own right. Some elements of the family gave her their support while others favoured a male cousin, but she too enjoyed the assistance of a powerful and able mother.[28] She did not remarry and raised her only son in a mostly female household. The most famous instance of female inheritance in this part of Scotland was that of Lady Elizabeth Sutherland, the only surviving child of the earl of Sutherland, a minor and an orphan when her case was contested in the house of lords. Her maternal grandmother, Lady Alva, was one of the forces behind the inheritance. It was she who raised the young girl to her patrimony and brokered her subsequent marriage to the wealthy Earl Gower.[29]

It is hard to offer an explanation for this pattern of female inheritance in the north-east but not in the western Highlands. It may be mere coincidence, or it may have represented some part of a matriarchal culture of long standing flowing from connections with north-west Europe, where women had strong inheritance and property rights.[30] It may have reflected a less commercial and more professionally oriented form of clanship, in contrast to the aggressive form of military commercial clanship that prevailed in the west. What ever the reason, it certainly was not easy for a woman to run a Highland estate, and some preferred to live elsewhere and hand over the day-to-day management to a male relative or factor.[31] But where there was a strong network of independent women they could and did take control of estate affairs. Ann Sinclair of Brabster, with her elderly mother's guidance, was a hands-on estate manager for over three decades. Her domestic duties were largely given over to a spinster cousin, Wilhelmina Sinclair of the house of Mey, who remained a part of the Brabster family long after Ann had died and her children were grown.[32] But female inheritance, which usually meant co-inheritance by two or more sisters rather than a single heir, was draining for estates, irrespective of the management skills of individual women. And another type of estate owner, who was also more in evidence in the north-east Highlands than in the west, the bachelor laird, brought another set of problems for gentry families and their property.

BACHELOR LAIRDS

Most Highland gentry families secured the viability and well-being of their estates through marriage connections and carefully managed family obligations, directed in such a way as to maximise production and regulate consumption. It was difficult, though not impossible, for a female landowner to operate in her own right, and it was also difficult, though not impossible, for a bachelor to do the same. Not surprisingly, there were few bachelor lairds among the Campbells of Barcaldine. Colin Campbell of Glenure delayed marriage until his early forties, and had owned his estate for almost ten years before choosing a bride. But during much of that time he was abroad on military service. Others in the family tended to marry young, and none who were destined for land inheritance or tacksman status were lifelong bachelors. This pattern began to change in the second half of the eighteenth century, when sons left farming for professional employment.

One laird who was a lifelong bachelor was George Sutherland of Rearquahar, which was a small estate near Dornoch held on tack from the principal house of Sutherland.[33] The bachelor status of this military man, who entered the army as a youth in 1745 and remained in service for five decades, may well have been a function of his non-landed career, for many soldiers did not marry. Yet he managed his estate well enough through a network of female dependants and kin connections. He had a paid housekeeper living on the property and carrying out the normal wifely duties of household and dairy management. The husband of a niece, who was postmaster and sheriff clerk in nearby Dornoch, managed his estate affairs when he was away on military duty. George Sutherland also relied on a nephew called George Gun Munro of Ponyzfield, another bachelor laird, who worked in London from the 1750s to the 1770s as an insurance broker. The latter had inherited his estate from another military bachelor uncle. When George Gun Munro died in 1806, Ponyzfield passed to a bachelor brother, also in the army.

All of these properties were small and managed in old-fashioned ways. The lairds relied on personal earned income from other sources to get by in life.[34] Doubtless they hoped for sudden windfalls, but none came their way. Lesser kin and loyal servants managed the estates, but they allowed no avenues for ambition. Not one of these men could afford to marry and support a wife and children without compromising their standards of living as gentlemen.[35] Yet it was through fathering children and then brokering the marriages of these children that Highland lairds could extend their estates and influence. Another bachelor laird with a similar personal strategy for much his life – though this strategy changed completely when he unexpectedly inherited a major estate – was Dr William Sinclair of Thurso in Caithness. William Sinclair, like his father before him, was a medical practitioner.[36] His parents were of gentry stock, in common with many professionals in Highland areas, and connected in various ways to Sinclair, Sutherland and Mackay lairds. Hugh Mackay of Bighouse was a distant cousin and friend of his father. Ann Sinclair of Brabster was another cousin. Dr William Sinclair the elder left his son a good inheritance when he died in 1767, and William the younger purchased the small property of Lochend in 1778. Since the estate was at an inconvenient distance from Thurso, his sister, a soldier's widow, was installed as housekeeper, and his brother-in-law, an excise officer, acted as factor.[37] This was a good arrangement for a bachelor professional laird who now described himself as William Sinclair of Lochend but continued to live in Thurso and support himself and a couple of bastard children through medical practice.[38]

The circumstances of Dr William Sinclair might have remained much the same for the rest of his life. He lived comfortably enough, but the medical business was competitive, even in Thurso, and he was losing customers as the local gentry gravitated towards the cities for their medical advice. From time to time he thought about emigration or joining the army to raise his fortunes, but he did nothing.[39] His fortunes did change, however, but through an unexpected route, when in 1794 he inherited the old estate of Freswick in Canisbay from a distant relative, via a complex and contested entail.[40] Though middle-aged, he now embarked on marriage and the business of fathering children. By his first wife, who died in 1812, he had three children, and by his second – whom he married in 1816 when he was sixty-eight – he sired a further four. Both wives were the daughters of major lairds, which secured his position in genteel society. His family strategy and patterns of expenditure changed completely on becoming a landowner, but the Freswick estate struggled to support him in his new expectations, which included a house in Edinburgh and an English education for his children.

RELATIONSHIPS WITH 'SERVICE' FAMILIES

Gentry families sought to secure adjacent and upward family connections to advance their collective interests, but they also relied on lesser families to support them on their estates. Some of these lesser families were members of the extended kinship group, and some were connected through marriage. Other had no direct familial links with the local laird, but co-existed in a mutually beneficial 'service' relationship. These service families had often evolved over several generations from small clans and were mostly landless, relying on larger landed clans for their position in Highland society.

The Campbell family of Barcaldine, along with the broader clan connections of their chief, the earl of Breadalbane, enjoyed an intimate relationship with various members of the Macintyre family who were settled as small tenants and skilled estate workers in northern Argyll and Perthshire. Duncan Ban Macintyre, one of the finest of the mid-eighteenth century Gaelic poets, was born in Glenorchy and worked mainly as a forester and gamekeeper for the earl and for John Campbell of Killin.[41] In later life he lived in Edinburgh, where he was employed as one of the city guards (a ramshackle, rather elderly quasi-police force, much ridiculed by contemporaries) and where he also enjoyed the patronage of many of the Campbell elite. His elegy of the early 1750s to the virtues of John Campbell 'of the bank' gives an indication of how he viewed the gentry families on whom he and so many of his kin depended. Here is just a flavour of his sentiments:

> A flower thou art, in the midst of jet;
> nobility doth revel
> with ardour in they nature;
> humble, friendly,
> clannish and kind thou art.[42]

Much of Duncan Macintyre's considerable poetic output was committed to paper and published during his own lifetime as a result of Campbell patronage.[43] He was a valued figure in Campbell public relations. Other Macintyres also commanded esteem. Earlier in the century, when the affairs of Colin Campbell of Invernan were being settled, as detailed at the start of this chapter, several Macintyres were listed in the debt and credit network. They were a trusted element in the personal and financial affairs of the Campbell family of Barcaldine. On another occasion at about the same time, a nephew of Patrick Campbell of Barcaldine wrote of the recent illness of his brother, saying: 'Donald is now fully recovered and on foot . . . If Donald had continued any time unwell I believe there would be a necessity for getting a Macintyre wife to attend for when I was looking out for one to stay about him he earnestly recommended she might be a Macintyre.'[44]

The illegitimate children of lairds and their sons were raised in Macintyre households, including Isabel Macpherson, one of the daughters of Colin

Campbell of Glenure, who was fostered for four years in the mid-1750s by John Ban Macintyre, a cowherd in Calnish in Glenorchy, before moving on to a Campbell household nearby and later to a dressmaking apprenticeship.[45] One of Duncan Macintyre's loveliest poems is titled 'Song to a Foster-Child', and tradition has it that the child in question was the natural offspring of the house of Barcaldine. It may have been the same girl.

> Young Isabel of the yellow, golden hair,
> rose-like is thy cheek, and apple-sweet thy kiss;
> beautiful, tender and dainty thy mouth,
> from which one was favoured with tuneful, sweet songs.
>
> 'Tis the most charming damsel they had in the land,
> that chanced to be in my house, being nursed at the breast;
> when she takes her place some day at the King's Fair,
> many a landed gentleman will ask who she is.[46]

Macintyre was a good publicist for his Campbell patrons, but he also noted the changes that were under way in the western Highlands in the second half of the eighteenth century. Many who left Argyll for Edinburgh or for emigration abroad were part of the extended Macintyre family. They included the head of the family, James Macintyre of Glenoe, a Breadalbane tacksman and a talented poet who could no longer afford the rents and left for America in the late eighteenth century.[47] There were also lesser working men such as the Donald Macintyre, who petitioned Alexander Campbell of Barcaldine in 1783 for a recommendation to a Campbell kinsman in the East Indies.[48] Commercial pressures, the professionalisation of the gentry and increasing absenteeism gradually eroded the links of day-to-day intimacy and trust between the two families. Yet even in the early nineteenth century, members of the Macintyre family still held a privileged position in Campbell affairs. Several ministers in northern Argyll were Macintyres who corresponded with the laird, Sir Duncan Campbell, in Edinburgh on parish business, including cases of indigence within the clan. Whether Sir Duncan was interested in the pitiable condition of such a worthy local figure as Mrs Shaw, an elderly midwife and distant Campbell connection, now living in penury, is doubtful, since two Macintyre ministers, on separate occasions, mentioned her case.[49]

Just as important as the lower-status service families who provided the Highland gentry with practical support were the professional and middle-ranking service families that lived in Highland districts, including medical men and clergymen. These were often closely connected with lairds and were commonly descended from younger sons. In Caithness, with a home base in

Thurso, Dr William Sinclair the elder, the grandson of a laird, was a close confidante of Hugh Mackay of Bighouse and several other local landed gentlemen. He provided them with medical services as well as advice and gossip mid-century.[50] Dr William Sinclair junior occupied much the same role for the next generation of Sutherland–Caithness gentry families in the later eighteenth century, before he moved into independent landownership. Legal families were also closely connected with lairds. The Campbell family of Barcaldine made use of a series of Campbell lawyers based in Inverary before shifting their affairs to other members of the same extended kin network in Edinburgh. Highland commercial families were similarly important, including the MacPhersons – Glenfyne cattle drovers with business interests in Glasgow – who were connected by marriage and tutorage for children, and served the Barcaldine family well over three generations.[51]

In the Mackay lands of Reay, there was a strong connection in the 1730s–40s between the young Hugh Mackay of Bighouse and a local cattle drover and gentleman tacksman of the old school, called Iain Mac Eachainn. Rob Donn described the sense of loss among the ordinary people of Sutherland when the latter retired from business in old age, while his younger partner turned his ambitions to affairs beyond the Highlands.[52] Indeed, a great deal of the poetry describing Hugh of Bighouse was framed in terms of regret among the lesser country people as he abandoned his local connections. Another group that poet Rob Donn highlighted were the networks of clergy families living in the Highlands in intimate relationship with the gentry elite and with the country people that they served. And though he was not always complementary, Rob Donn and other Gaelic poets owed their survival in print to the energies of local ministers, or members of minister's families, often women, in writing the poetry down and seeking publication.[53]

Highland ministers were intimately connected by blood and marriage to the local gentry. This can be shown from the details that are listed in the *Fasti Ecclesiae Scotticanae*, which provides a biographical record of all established clergy since the reformation. In two presbyteries, Lorn in northern Argyll (which included the lands of Barcaldine) and Dornoch in Sutherland (which included the lands of Reay and Bighouse), there were seventy-nine ministers over the period *c*.1680–*c*.1820 for whom family details survive.[54] Of these, it is possible to identify the occupations or status of the fathers of sixty clergymen. Just under half (twenty-six individuals) had fathers who were also ministers, all in Highland parishes and in many cases in the same parish as their son. Here, as in other areas of Highland life, lines of patrilineal inheritance were important. However, almost a third of the ministers (eighteen individuals) had fathers with some sort of landowning status in the Highlands, mostly as modest lairds, and about a fifth (eleven individuals) had fathers who were tacksmen or substantial tenants with family connections into the gentry elite.

Those with a paternal interest in land dominated the Highland clergy. This was particularly marked in the first half of the eighteenth century but was sustained into the nineteenth century. One of the most famous was Colin Campbell of Achnaba, born in 1644, the son of Patrick Campbell of Innerzeldies, who was a forebear of the Campbell family of Barcaldine, and Bethia Murray, who was the daughter of Murray of Ochtertyre. After an education at St Andrews University, he became minister of Ardchattan, where he remained from 1667 until his death in 1726. He was a celebrated scholar in the field of mathematics and maintained a regular correspondence with such contemporary luminaries as Sir Isaac Newton as well as with his numerous relatives nearby, which included both Alexander and Patrick Campbell of Barcaldine, father and son, who were cousins.[55] He was noted for his medical knowledge and for his Gaelic scholarship, and he kept a school at Ardchattan for the sons of the local gentry. Each of these characteristics was commonly found among Highland ministers at this time. He was also a significant landowner, owning the properties of Coullandalloch, Scoull and Achnaba, inherited from his father, which he later exchanged for the lands of Drimvuick, which were closer to his parish. His wealth and status as a landowner ensured good and prosperous marriages. His first was to Mary, daughter of Sir Hugh Campbell of Calder, and his second was to Margaret, daughter of Colin Campbell of Blarantibbert. None of his four sons entered the ministry. The eldest was a laird.[56]

In addition to owning land, the Rev. Colin Campbell married wives who were the daughters of the landed. This was a strikingly consistent character-istic of Highland ministers throughout the eighteenth century, and in some respects it ensured that entry into this career for those of modest backgrounds could become a route to upward social mobility for themselves and their children. Of the wives of the ministers of Lorn and Dornoch, sixty-six women in all, over half (thirty-five individuals) were the daughters of lairds, and more than a quarter (seventeen individuals) were the daughters of ministers with landed connections. In almost all cases these women were long-term residents in their husbands' parishes, and the marriages were celebrated shortly after the clergyman was appointed. Many ministers' wives were the children of the previous parish incumbent, and it is likely that the widow, who may well have been a laird's daughter, continued to live in the same household. By marrying the successor, the family of the old minister at least ensured that the house, often built at the incumbent's expense, remained in the family.[57] The incoming minister also ensured that he had a good network of support from women who were intimate with parish life.

Ministers who married into the landowning gentry were usually wedded to younger daughters with limited dowries. There were always numerous candidates. The father of Donald Sage, minister of Resolis in Sutherland in the late eighteenth century, married, as his second wife, the daughter of George Sutherland of Midgarty, a military laird. His aunt, a clergyman's daughter, had married into the local gentry.[58] It was rare to marry an eldest daughter unless the minister enjoyed landowning status in his own right. An unusual exception was another minister at Ardchattan, Hugh Fraser. He was born in 1780 in Inverness-shire, with gentry family connections on both sides, but little inherited wealth. He was educated at Aberdeen University, and after serving in several parishes in Argyll for short periods under the patronage of Duncan Campbell of Lochnell, he was appointed to the Ardchattan parish in 1817. The following year, he married Helen Maria Campbell, the London-educated only daughter of Alexander Campbell of Barcaldine – to the great dismay and disapproval of her widowed mother and her brother Sir Duncan. The couple lived much beyond their means and went bankrupt in the 1830s, which was rather unusual for a clergyman.[59]

Though Highland ministers for the most part lived modestly in the eighteenth century, they were part of what might be described as a 'pseudo-gentry', with polite manners and tastes, and held privileged positions in Highland society. Many of their daughters married into the local gentry, and about a tenth of the sons of the ministers in Lorn and Dornoch became lairds in their own right as a result of inheritance via mothers of landed background. This pattern of connections through marriage on the female side gave these local 'service' families a greater importance in the lives of the Highland gentry than is commonly given credit for. Family correspondence gives little indication of this before the latter part of the eighteenth century because interactions mostly took place through frequent face-to-face contacts, particularly among women. But later clergy memoirs, including *Memorabilia Domestica* by Donald Sage, the son and grandson of Sutherland ministers with many family connections into the local gentry, give a good idea of the closely connected worlds of lairds and ministers, particularly during the period when lairds lived on their estates. Poets, including Rob Donn in Sutherland, with his eye for the intimacies of everyday life, also reveal the pivotal social role that ministers could play through their connections both up and down the social hierarchy. Of course, ministers were not always happy to receive the attentions of a social commentator like Rob Donn, who took a dim view of the social climbing and commercial activities of some ambitious clergyman. Donald

Sage described the first meeting between his father and the poet when his father first worked on the Reay estate.

> My father, when schoolmaster of Tongue, met with the poet. He invited him to dinner, an invitation which was accepted. The poet was pleased with his fare and still more with his host, and at parting offered to make his entertainer the subject of a poem. This offer my father declined, aware of those high powers of satire with which his guest was endowed, and which, like a razor dipped in oil, never cut so keenly as when intermingled with compliment and praise.[60]

COMPLEX FAMILY CULTURES

Highland lairds and their relationships with estates were more complex than is commonly believed, and this complexity and the intricate cultures it entailed helps to explain some of the patterns of conspicuous consumption in which the gentry engaged. To thrive in the Highlands, landowning families had traditionally relied on networks of support from other co-located families that were practical, sometimes spiritual or emotional and always based on trust and a recognition of conditions of mutual dependence. Connections with labouring families, personal service providers or medical, legal and religious professionals were built on frequent face-to-face contacts and an intimate knowledge of one another's affairs. The younger daughters of the dominant family often married into the middle-ranking service families. Indeed, women of high and low status were a central feature of these connected family networks. This was as true of those parts of Highland Scotland where women inherited estates as it was in Argyll, where there were more masculine family inheritance cultures.

But family formation among the Highland gentry evolved in ways that few could predict or control, despite the considerable efforts of many lairds and their kin to do just that. Patterns of gentry inheritance along different lines to the standard 'father-to-eldest-son' model occurred in most families and introduced a broader spectrum of cultural influences to bear on estates than most commentators on clanship and economic change have described.[61] The implications of marriage choices, strategic or otherwise, and the agency of women more generally in Highland society and in landowning families in particular, is largely uncharted territory.[62] Also uncharted is the influence on the use of land and other family resources of professional men who were lairds or the close relatives of lairds. Yet this short survey of a series of fairly typical families has revealed that men who were trained as ministers, doctors or lawyers did inherit estates, both large and small. And by the second half of the eighteenth century, large numbers of Highland gentlemen who were tacksmen or lairds were also army officers, a profession with distinct patterns of family formation. The Highland gentleman reared with no other purpose than to be a practical farming laird hardly existed by the end of the eighteenth century. Almost all lairds had been trained to some other employment, and even though, like Dr William Sinclair, they no longer practiced their profession, the cultural influences of professional education and careers shaped the evolution of their families and estates, and also determined their relationships with luxury.

Despite the varying patterns of family and estate formation in the different parts of the Highlands, and despite the changing fortunes of particular families and their properties, the one thing that most had in common was financial crisis in the first few decades of the nineteenth century. As we have already seen, the Barcaldine estate was put on the market in the 1830s due to the pending bankruptcy of Sir Duncan Campbell. This was not the first time the family had faced a crisis. Back in the 1770s, the estate was also on the brink of a disaster due to mounting debts, but the property remained in family ownership through sale from one brother to another. The new laird was a lawyer.[63] Other family properties of great antiquity were lost. The Reay estates, including Bighouse, were sold in the wake of Waterloo, in common with many other Highland properties.[64] The Sinclair-Sutherlands of Langwell and Brabster sold the Langwell estate in 1775 to pay off debts. Their lands and house at Skibo were poinded following legal action in 1785. The rest of the family property was finally sold to the earl of Caithness in 1863 for £16,500.[65] It might be asked how the earl could afford such a purchase, but aristocratic families with financial interests beyond the Highlands could draw on wider resources than those available to the gentry, particularly if they made the right sorts of marriage. Indeed, as Eric Richards has shown for both the Sutherland and the Cromarty estates, it was marriages into the English aristocracy with industrial wealth that secured these properties in family control.[66] As part of a long-running process of estate consolidation, it was the great aristocrats with non-Highland resources who fared best.[67] But even when smaller properties did survive in family hands, they were a constant cause for concern. Dr William Sinclair of Freswick wrote a detailed memorandum in 1819 on his mounting debts and the struggling capabilities of his estate. His inheritance late in life was fraught with disappointments.[68]

Another experience that these Highland gentry families had in common was a tendency to move away from the Highlands for permanent residence elsewhere, with only occasional visits to their estates. By the 1790s the

Campbell family of Barcaldine had a permanent townhouse in Edinburgh's New Town.[69] Dr William Sinclair and his ailing first wife set up home in the Lauriston district of Edinburgh in 1810. He built a fine new house in Thurso in 1816 when he married his second wife, who was the daughter of John Sinclair of Barrock, a Caithness laird. But just a few years later the Barrock estate was bankrupt and sold, and possibly out of embarrassment Dr William Sinclair and his family made a permanent move to Edinburgh. In great old age in the 1830s, he lived in Torquay on the south coast of England.[70] After the death of Ann Sinclair of Brabster in 1806, her family also gravitated southwards to Edinburgh. Her eldest grandson, who had been in India, retired to fashionable Blacket Place in the suburbs of Edinburgh.[71]

So these Highland families with their complex family cultures mostly ended up in much the same place in the early nineteenth century. The manner of their getting there had much to do with attitudes to estates. And at the heart of evolving relationships with estates were the changing experiences of children, as parents planned their futures in the hope that they would bring benefits to the family. Coupled with education, particularly for boys, were the career choices made by lairds for their many sons. These are the subjects of the next two chapters.

2 Children

INTRODUCTION

In the 1680s when Lord Glenorchy embarked on an illegal predatory raid in Caithness his retinue of gentlemen and advisors included a Dutch necromancer, supposedly skilled in the art of conjuring the dead to see into the future. Those who criticised the nobleman and sought to bring him to justice through the courts said that the Dutchman was a warlock, a dangerous judgement to have made of you in an age when witchcraft was still punished with death.[1] Martin Martin's *Descriptions of the Western Isles circa 1695* contains numerous references to magic and superstitious beliefs among the ordinary Gaelic people. He described, for instance, a valuable 'curiosity' called the Baul Muluy, a 'green stone, much like a globe in figure, about the bigness of a goose egg' that had long belonged to the Macdonald clan. The stone was said to have medical properties, it was used for swearing oaths by and it had served as a talisman in battle. The lady who kept it, 'preserves the globe with abundance of care . . . wrapped up in fair linen cloth . . . locked up in her chest, when it is not given out to exert its qualities'.[2]

As Martin observed, the ordinary people 'labour under the want of knowledge of letters and other useful arts and sciences'.[3] Yet sophisticated, Lowland-educated Highland gentlemen shared in some of their beliefs. Martin had faith in second sight, and generated ridicule among the metropolitan literati as a consequence.[4] Thomas Pennant the travel writer, visiting Caithness and Sutherland in the 1760s, cited several cases of mystical practices among the ordinary peasantry and also reported the case of a local 'gentleman' who professed the power of second sight. This was William Sinclair of Freswick, an educated man 'of ability and of considerable local note' whose son was an Edinburgh-trained lawyer.[5]

By the early nineteenth century this form of knowledge, if it existed at all outside the country people, was mostly in the domain of scholarly antiquarians, collecting fragments of a vanishing culture before it vanished for all time. Many antiquarians were local clergymen.[6] In some cases they were linked to magical beliefs by family traditions. The Rev. Donald Sage of Resolis, son and grandson of Sutherland ministers, was proud to record that his elderly grandfather Alexander Sage had seen a vision of his own funeral just before he died in the 1770s. As interpreted by the grandson, writing in the 1830s, this vision connected his grandfather with the ordinary people of the parish, who had 'become true and vital Christians through his ministry, and were themselves the primitive fathers of the spiritual generations that followed them'.[7]

So how did Lord Glenorchy and Martin Martin in the late seventeenth century, or William Sinclair of Freswick and the clergyman Alexander Sage many decades later, come to believe in the power of necromancers, or magical stones, or second sight and visions? They learnt such things in childhood, of course, through belonging to a society whose knowledge practices were constructed around a cultural understanding of the world and its processes that admitted the agency of magic and hidden spirits.[8] And although, unlike the ordinary people, all of these gentlemen were also exposed to alternative knowledge practices, the product of modern education, that disavowed the world of magic, they nevertheless continued to hold on to some of the 'traditional' beliefs of the Gaelic society into which they were born.

Enculturation – that is 'the process of learning a culture in all its uniqueness and particularity'[9] – is a complex and dynamic phenomenon. It begins at birth and in infancy, long before any systematic schooling, and is as much a product of informal interactions with those who are not responsible for any aspect of training or education, as it is of formal interactions with those who are charged with the business of schooling the young. The processes of 'enculturation' among the Highland gentry changed significantly over the period of this study. There was a revolution in print culture, there were shifts in religious practice and belief that accompanied the continuing advance of Protestantism, and there was new technical and professional knowledge. Some of this was put into effect in the seventeenth-century Highlands through state endeavours to civilise lairds and bring them into a more commercial relationship with their estates. Policies designed to 'regulate chiefs' also stressed the importance of childhood education.

> The principal cause of barbarity, impiety, and incivility . . . has proceeded from the small care the chiefs and principal clansmen have had in the education and the upbringing of their children in virtue and

learning. Careless of other duties, they keep their children still at home with them, where they see nothing in their tender years but the barbarous and ancient forms of the country; so that, when they come to years of maturity, they cannot be reclaimed . . . if they had been sent to the inland in their youth and trained in virtue and learning, and the English tongue, they would be the better prepared to reform their countries and reduce the same to godliness and civility.[10]

Lairds took note and were routinely sending some of their children to the Lowlands for some part of their education by the late seventeenth century. This had an impact on language, but changes were not dramatic since it was possible and commonplace to engage simultaneously in different knowledge practices according to the circumstances. So, while conversation and letters written in the laird's family were in English, the language of the farm, kitchen or dairy, all part of the daily life of the gentry, remained Gaelic. An ability to maintain a parallel location in two competing cultures is a feature of many communities in the past and present, particularly those with migrant tendencies.[11] Such dualism is possible where there are strong incentives and an ability to move physically between the two geographies that define the two cultures. Evidence of culture shifting among the Highland gentry occurred in numerous forms and in ways that were paralleled in other eighteenth-century European countries.[12] Language and participation in print culture offer one illustration, and another is seen in different forms of clothing, particularly for men. This may not seem an obvious case to illustrate an argument concerned with education, but it becomes more relevant when we begin to see how much of the formal and informal education of the children of the eighteenth century gentry was concerned with their appearance and deportment and their relationships with the material world of goods.

In an inventory of his personal possessions in 1740, Colin Campbell of Glenure distinguished his 'Highland clothes' from the clothing that he wore on his frequent sojourns in Edinburgh.[13] The differences were neither practical (country clothes compared with city clothes) nor traditional, since his Highland plaids, kilts and a short kilt-jacket were of a new fashion. We do not know how he felt when he donned these Highland clothes. Were they more comfortable, as some men claimed when forced into trousers following the post-'45 proscription of traditional clothing?[14] And did they change his manner of walking and his bearing from that of the polite Edinburgh gentleman, 'walking the streets',[15] to one that marked a more masculine presence as a Highland laird? Many contemporaries remarked on the distinctive manner of walking adopted by lairds in the Highlands as a means for commanding respect.[16] The chances are that Colin Campbell did behave differently when dressed in his 'Highland clothes', for this was part of his enculturation into a subtle understanding of what was proper for a laird.

The deeply embedded intellectual allegiances and cultural habits of a man like Colin Campbell, and those around him, are hard to uncover. The formal education and socialisation of children where it yielded a written record is more easily understood. Though it presents only a narrow window on the mental world of the Highland gentry, it hints at the informal world of children and parents that lies beyond.

SIBLINGS, PARENTS AND COUNTRY PEOPLE

The formal education of Highland gentry children was mostly determined by gender and a father's plans for their future. A child's place in the sibling hierarchy was also important. The eldest son would inherit the family property, and the eldest daughter would have the biggest dowry and the best chance of a good marriage, unless the girl was disadvantaged in some way by health problems or disability. Eldest children were educated into expectations that set them apart from their siblings, and they commanded more interest and attention from those about them. The eldest daughter was easily recognised, as Boswell noted in 1773 when visiting the laird of Rasaay. 'Miss Flora [the eldest] is really an elegant woman (tall, genteel, a pretty face) sensible, polite and good humoured . . . She alone has been at Edinburgh. All the rest were never farther than Applecross, a gentleman's seat in Ross-shire on the opposite coast.'[17]

The eldest son and heir to the laird of Rasaay was distinguished by the presence of an attendant in the form of Mr MacQueen, 'a genteel young man, his tutor'. There were ten daughters and three sons in the family. Both parents were in good health, which allowed them to make an input into the rearing and education of their children. Where a parent had died while children were young – which was often followed by another marriage and the start of a new family – it was common for the children of the first marriage to be raised elsewhere. Complex provisions were made between male kin for rearing orphaned sons to try to maintain their status and expectations. Orphaned daughters received less attention and often experienced a fall in social status on the death of a father, particularly if their mother remarried. The redoubtable Flora Macdonald was the victim of such a situation in her early life. Her father, a gentleman tacksman of North Uist, died when she was a girl in the 1730s, and when her mother remarried she was sent to live in the household of an elder brother. With neither education nor dowry, she was little more than a farm servant.[18]

Though a family crisis such as the death of a parent could derail the education and anticipated life course of children, particularly daughters, when things went to plan childhood and the processes of education and socialisation were roughly divided into three phases. The first, which was experienced by both boys and girls alike from birth to about seven years, kept children close to home and raised in a manner that was similar to the ordinary peasant children that belonged to the extensive households of lairds. According to Edmund Burt, a military administrator of forfeited Jacobite estates, commenting in the 1720s:

> The young children of the ordinary Highlanders are miserable objects indeed . . . nor are the children of some gentlemen in much better condition, being strangely neglected till they are six or seven years old: this one might know by a saying I have often heard, viz. that 'a gentleman's bairns are to be distinguished by their speaking English'.[19]

The link between the gentleman's child and the country people was reinforced in infancy by wet-nursing, which was a device to maximise the fertility of well-born mothers.[20] Wet-nurses normally lived in the laird's family, causing inconvenience for their own husband and children, but it was an honourable, well-paid role with many benefits for the woman and her family.[21] Even in the later eighteenth century, when Highland gentlewomen had their confinements in town to secure access to professional medical attendance, babies were sometimes sent to the country for wet-nursing.[22]

Laird's families were often large, since women married young and were quickly replaced if they died in childbirth. But mortality among children was also high, and it may have been the case that a high investment in the elaborate care of small children was not especially worthwhile when so many died in infancy.[23] Even in the later eighteenth century an older kinswoman could caution a younger against worrying about the health of her child, saying 'don't be too anxious about him my d[ea]r Mary, children are uncertain pleasures'.[24] Though not easily discernible to an outside observer such as Edmund Burt, allowing small children to run wild with local peasant children was a cost-effective system of childminding, and subtle social distinctions were preserved. Gentry children were better fed and better housed than the country children, though their everyday clothing in a rough-and-tumble outdoor existence was probably much the same. Their mother, though busy with the practical affairs of the household, was a constant presence to protect their interests. Father was more likely to be an absent figure, but the respect he commanded among the ordinary people would inform even a very small child of his or her own status. The family position relative to the rest of the clan will have been the daily subject of stories, songs and conversations among the servants who watched over children. Relationships formed between the children of the laird and servants, even at this early age, would have laid foundations for loyal service and reciprocal obligations in later life. When genteel families started to fix their permanent homes outside the Highlands, their children were no longer exposed to this early socialisation in the culture of Gaeldom. Though many lairds living in Edinburgh townhouses employed Gaelic-speaking female domestic servants, the cloistered and sparsely populated nursery of the city-raised child was a culturally impoverished environment when compared with the kitchen or byre where country children played.

EDUCATING AND SOCIALISING BOYS

Edmund Burt gave another illustration of the seemingly neglected character of young gentry children in the early eighteenth century when he wrote of a bird-catcher, employed by a laird, who told him that

> for three or four days after his first coming [to the laird's house], he had observed in the kitchen (an outhouse hovel) a parcel of dirty children half-naked, whom he took to belong to some poor tenant, till at last he found they were a part of the family; but, although these were so little regarded, the young laird, about the age of fourteen, was going to the university; and the eldest daughter, about sixteen, sat with us at table, clean and genteelly dressed.[25]

This hints at the distinctive shift in socialising practices that occurred among gentry children in their early to mid-teens, but it fails to take account of the fact that in mid-childhood many children, particularly boys, were fostered with other related families as part of a process of socialisation into adult kin culture. This was the second phase of childhood. The bird-catcher saw the younger children and the eldest (those in the third phase), now home from their formal education in the Lowlands, but not the ones in the middle. But Burt did remark on fostering practices elsewhere in his observations.

> When a son is born to the chief of a family, there generally arises a contention among the vassals which of them shall have the fostering of the child when it is taken from the nurse . . . The happy man who succeeds in his suit is ever after called the foster-father, and his children

the foster-brothers and sisters of the young laird. This, they reckon, not only endears them to their chief, and greatly strengthens their interest with him, but gives them a great deal of consideration among their fellow vassals; and the foster-brother having the same education as the young chief, may, besides that, in time become his 'hanchman' . . . a sort of secretary.[26]

Fostering was a complex and changing economic and social arrangement that sought to secure relationships within and between families. As Burt observed, it involved significant financial advantages to the foster parent and future patronage for his own children. It sometimes involved boys going to live with families of similar status to their own, but more often with the families in the middle layers of Highland society, particularly the tacksmen, where they would learn the ways of the clan or kin group at large.[27] James MacDonald of Sleat, born in 1742 and succeeding to his inheritance when still a young boy, was fostered from the ages of five to twelve, along with his younger brother, by Alexander MacDonald of Kingsburgh, later father-in-law to Flora MacDonald. In adulthood, the young man granted an annuity of fifty pounds sterling to the elderly Kingsburgh, 'for making his old age placid and comfortable . . . in return for the long and faithful service done and performed by him to my deceased father, and to myself during my minority, when he was one of my tutors and curators'.[28]

Learning the culture of Gaeldom was an important reason for placing James in the Kingsburgh household and necessary since James' mother was of Lowland background and not a Gaelic speaker. According to his father, commenting with some pride, 'son Jamie [was] getting more Gaelick at Kingsburgh than tongue can tell'.[29] Fosterage did not mean that children lost contact with parents. Margaret MacDonald, widowed mother of James, kept a regular oversight of her boys while they were living in the Kingsburgh household, and they often accompanied her to Edinburgh for the winter months.[30]

Through much of the seventeenth century, the training acquired by boys during the fosterage years stressed those practical and physical skills that were necessary for gentlemen whose status was maintained through bodily robustness and a capacity to command respect in fighting, or sport or at the feasting table.[31] Even in the eighteenth century, fosterage tended to focus on the cultivation of masculine attributes, but increasingly there was a shift in emphasis towards a formal book-based classroom education in English at the hands of specialist tutors with professional careers who acted as foster parents. These professional fosterage systems still engaged the middle layers of

Highland society, and the men involved may also have been tacksmen and fighting men. A transitional type of foster-parent arrangement, secured with a formal legal agreement of 1638, was that undertaken by Neil MacKinnon, minister of the parish of Strath in Skye. A graduate of Glasgow University, accustomed to wearing a kilt and sword when officiating in the pulpit to signal his senior clan position, Mackinnon had a foot in both professional and clan culture when he undertook to foster the third son, and eventual heir, of John MacLeod of Dunvegan, also called John.[32] The legal agreement mentioned the role of both MacKinnon and his spouse, highlighting the importance of a regular domestic establishment. The child was to be 'maintenet and upbrocht be thame ay and quhill he be apt for schoolis, God always spaireing him dayis and lyfe'. A thousand merks was transferred to the foster father to be invested in land on behalf of the boy, with certain benefits allowed to MacKinnon himself.[33]

Provided with a sophisticated book-based education as a result of this fostering and through his later schooling, the younger John MacLeod was a man of high culture. His own children were probably fostered when young, but were also educated at home by a tutor, the university-trained antiquarian and writer, Martin Martin, son of a tacksman. Martin's first employment in education seems to have been as tutor to Donald MacDonald of Sleat, whom he tutored until he was about twenty-one years old in 1686. From 1686 to 1692 he was 'governor' to the young MacLeods of Dunvegan. Martin was a cosmopolitan man who spent much of his own life living outside the Highlands.[34] He offered a modern classical and scientific education to the young men in his charge. He may also have been partly responsible for developing their taste for southern ways and fashions, for the heir to Dunvegan, Roderick MacLeod, a former pupil who succeeded in 1693, quickly abandoned the traditions of the house. According to one near contemporary, reflecting with bitterness, 'Dunvegan Castle was neglected, and the services of bard, harper, and piper were dispensed with to make room for grooms, gamekeepers, factors, dogs and the various etceteras of a fashionable English establishment'.[35]

The shift from clan fosterage to professional tutorships was presaged by early forms of education in some of the pre-modern Highland professions, notably in the field of medicine. Several members of the seventeenth-century Beaton family maintained peripatetic schools where they trained members of their own clan along with youngsters from elsewhere, including Ireland.[36] Boys began their schooling in traditional, mostly oral-based and practical medical skills from about the age of eight, and continued with their master, often travelling with him on his annual cycle of visits, until they were well into adulthood. The training involved transcribing significant medical texts in Gaelic, Latin and English for their own future use, in which they also recorded details about their life and education. These manuscripts reveal the close emotional bonds that often developed between a master and his charges. They also testify to the high levels of educational accomplishment that could be acquired in the early modern Gaeldom. But increasingly, even for boys who were destined for a medical career in Highland practice, the trend was towards a formal Lowland education.

By the early eighteenth century, the distinction between a foster parent and a tutor was becoming blurred in gentry families. Many boys still left home at about the age of six or seven, but often to join a household that allowed them to attend a local school, such as the minister-run school at Ardchattan Priory. Other boys were placed in the household of a professional 'governor', as in the case of the younger sons of John Mackenzie of Delvine. John MacKenzie was the younger son of a laird and was a lawyer by profession. He purchased the considerable estate of Delvine near Dunkeld in Perthshire in 1705 and had a large family of fourteen children.[37] Three of his sons, Alexander (b. 1695) and twins Kenneth and Thomas (b. 1699), were under the guidance of James Morice, described as their 'governor', from about the age of eight years. Morice was a university-educated man who later became a clergyman. He had previously been 'governor' to one of the sons of David Campbell of Kethick, Argyll laird and family connection of the Campbell family of Barcaldine. The pupils lived with Morice and his wife and children, often with one or more boys of similar age from connected gentry families. Morice, in effect, operated a small private elementary school. He occupied various houses, initially close to Delvine, allowing frequent visits by parents, but later relocated to the town of St Andrews, where the older boys attended university classes whilst the younger continued to be taught by Morice. The 'governor' reported regularly by letter on matters concerning education, domestic accommodation, food, clothing, health and discipline. The boy's mother was as concerned in these issues as their father, sending written instruction on her own account, particularly with regard to medical treatments for their various minor ailments and instructions about clothing. The boys could not write properly themselves (although they could read) until they were about eleven years old.

The education of the three Mackenzie boys was tailored to their individual needs and abilities. All were privately tutored by their 'governor' and also attended university classes, but the elder of the three was removed from St Andrews at the age of eighteen and sent to Edinburgh for a legal apprenticeship. The twins graduated and Kenneth continued his studies at Leiden. He later became an advocate and university professor, but Thomas died before establishing a career. Most of their classes were classical, mathematical and scientific. They also learned to sing, ride and fence and spent much of their time – too much, according to their 'governor' – playing golf. One was skilled at archery. They had access to small arms such as pistols for sport and made 'squibbs' out of gunpowder. Keeping control over his pupils was a constant strain for James Morice. The boys spent most of their time in the company of others of similar background and age. Theirs was a very masculine world. Elder brothers and cousins were as powerful a presence in their lives as their parents. Their sisters, of whom there were many, were rarely mentioned.

The Campbell family of Barcaldine further illustrates the role of Lowland education in the lives of teenage boys. Alexander Campbell of Barcaldine (1647–1720) had four sons, all fostered when youngsters. His own education is not known, though he was a cultured man with a sophisticated knowledge of law and business and wrote in the perfect English of the day. His eldest son, Patrick (b. 1677) was educated in Edinburgh through private tutors and university classes, and in 1693, when he was sixteen, recorded an account for his father of his varied expenditure on teachers and masters. There was a sum 'to be given to yr regent for candles' (a normal practice in schools and universities, where children provided direct payment for heat and light), plus money to buy a 'writing book' and a 'greek book'.[38] The boy lodged with James Urquhart, a writer in Edinburgh, along with his eldest sister Margaret, aged about fifteen, and younger brother Colin, who was fourteen. Colin died in Edinburgh in 1693 and James Urquhart made the funeral arrangements with funds provided through a relative, Patrick Campbell, also a writer in Edinburgh.[39] Patrick Campbell the writer was a regular correspondent and 'man-of-business' for the father. A third son, James, was apprenticed in 1708 to the writing office of a lawyer in Inverary.[40] A couple of years earlier, he had also been in Edinburgh, lodging with a widowed merchant called Sara Campbell, doubtless a relative, attending classes in the university and paying fees through the writing chamber of Patrick Campbell, his kinsman. James was trained for a legal career, but in later life he was also tacksman of the farm of Rarey on his elder brother's estate.[41]

To be educated in partnership with a brother of near age was a normal pattern for Highland gentry boys. By their mid and later teenage years, when 'finishing' their formal education in the Lowlands, it was also increasingly common to find a sister present as part of the family arrangement. This was particularly true of eldest sisters in conjunction with eldest sons. The girls were fifteen or sixteen years old, and their brother, under the guidance of an adult 'man-of-business', normally their father's lawyer, oversaw their financial affairs and well-being. This was a new and important part of a boy's training in family management and the control of female consumption practices. As an introduction to adult life, the presence of a sister had distinct social advantages, since the children together could attend such events as the closely chaperoned 'balls' that were held by dancing masters. An indication of the costs incurred in the education of a brother and sister in Edinburgh in 1690 is given below. The boy in question was Roderick MacLeod, Martin Martin's former pupil, who succeeded to the family estate on Skye in 1693 and died not long after, married but without an heir. His sister was Isobell, whose subsequent history is unknown. The account underlines the fact that Isobell's education was focused on elite accomplishments such as music and painting. Her accommodation, doubtless under the careful supervision of a gentlewoman, was more costly than that of her brother, who could get by with the rough and tumble of student lodgings. But the most expensive tutor was Rorie's fencing master.

> Scots Money
> Candle money to the class £4 6s.
> The Janitor of Edinburgh University £4 6s.
> His man £1 8s.
> To the Doctor and Schoolmaster £13
> Ane Schoolmaster of a half years fee £5 18s.
> A pair of compasses £0 16s.
> For painting Crystal glos for Isobell's picture £3 16s.
> Spirits for Isobell £1 10s.
> Specles [spectacles] for Isobell £1 4s.
> Rushes and tripella [lighting] £1 10s.
> Ane half years board for Rorie £66 13s. 4d.
> One quarters board for Isabell £60
> The writing master per term £2 18s.
> A fencing Master £29
> A dancing Master per quarter £5 10s.
> On a ball night (frequent entry) £1 9s.
> Plaiing to the book on the Virginal per quarter £17 8s.
> Ane quarter to the viol £12
> Ane quarter to the singing £6
> Violl strings per doz £0 6s.[42]

This range of education remained the norm through to the mid-eighteenth century. But in many families the education of younger sons was increasingly directed towards professional or commercial training, with the intention that they would make their adult careers in spheres outwith land. Patrick Campbell of Barcaldine had eight sons who survived infancy, and five daughters; an expensive family when it came to questions of education. All of the children spent some part of their teenage years in Edinburgh. Several also lived in less expensive towns on the fringes of the Highlands in their early teens, particularly in Stirling and Perth, where there were good grammar schools and tutors and numerous relatives to keep an eye on the children. As with their father's generation, they tended to move about in groups. In 1727, Colin, aged nineteen, along with younger brother Duncan and sister Mary, were in Perth, lodging with 'Mr William Murray's daughter'. Colin and Duncan were 'learning of Corace Titus, Livius and Virgil . . . we are not yet begun our Greek, but will begin within a fortnight or thereabouts'.[43] They moved to Edinburgh a few months later before Duncan, who was destined for a legal career, was sent to Glasgow for a formal apprenticeship in a writer's chamber

Their eldest half-brother John (b. 1700) had been in Edinburgh in his late teens and early twenties, attending the writing chamber of Colin Kirk, where his father instructed that he was to learn writing style, law (criminal and civil), book keeping, French, Latin and Greek, and also fencing. Although Kirk watched over the youth, John was responsible for finding his own masters. One of the books that he mentioned in a letter to his father was *McKenzie's Institutions and Criminals*, a classic legal text, and part of his training involved copying large sections of this book for his own private use. But John was also in Edinburgh to carry out commissions, mostly purchasing domestic goods and clothing on behalf of his stepmother, and he conveyed information, legal and political, on behalf of his father. He formed part of the circle of young men surrounding Lord Monzie, a senior member of the clan, a close connection of the earl of Breadalbane and his father's friend and patron. As a member of this circle, John advanced his informal education in politics and politeness and began to look for a wife.[44]

With so many sons to provide for, Patrick Campbell gave serious thought to their education and future careers. Only one, John, was heir to the estate and raised to be an elite gentleman in the courtly circle of a major Scottish aristocrat. His second son, Colin, known later as Colin Campbell of Glenure, was the eldest child by a second marriage and was eventually granted a small estate, but he spent most of his early adulthood as a professional soldier, serving in Britain and abroad in the 1730s and 1740s. The third son, Duncan, was a lawyer and trained to this from late boyhood in the 1730s. Alexander, the fourth, was destined by his father's wish to be a minister, and he lodged for a while in his early teens with a clergyman living near Inverary. But he objected to such a life, begged his father to allow him to become a soldier like his elder brother Colin and was eventually allowed to do so, only to die young. Archibald, the fifth son, was a merchant in Glasgow, and Robert, the sixth, was a merchant in Stirling. Both learned their respective trades through long apprenticeships in the 1730s. The youngest boy, Donald, was apprenticed in 1731 to Mr McPhelan, a 'cherurgeon' in Edinburgh. The conditions, as arranged by older brother Colin on his father's behalf, were that 'he is bound for three years and pays 700 merks the half when he enters and the other half against martinmas next, besides five guineas to his landlady; for which he has insight into cherurging and bed board but not washing'.[45]

Patrick Campbell's careful provision for his sons was mostly with the aim of providing them with alternative employments to those offered by land, in areas of work that would be of some benefit to the family. Until the middle decades of the eighteenth century, professional or commercial apprenticeships were commonplace among younger sons, even in aristocratic families. For instance, in 1741, Norman MacKenzie, a teenage son of Lord Cromartie, was bound apprentice for three years to Gilbert Gordon, a merchant in Inverness. The premium was £50 sterling, for which he was given board and lodgings and taught the trade of merchant.[46] But many younger sons were not so well furnished with a practical and potentially lucrative training as this, and in the second half of the century entry into a trading career had increasingly negative status implications. They still resorted to tenant farming, but this was hard work for which few with a Lowland education were fitted. James Boswell, travelling the Highlands in 1773, remarked on one young man that he met while visiting Dunvegan Castle in Skye.

> Mr Donald MacLeod, late tenant in Canna but now disposed of it, was still with us. He was an obliging serviceable man. His father was one of MacLeod's ministers; and the late laird educated him, and in particular had him several years at school near London. He was at present in that kind of wandering state that many a highland younger brother is . . . he was tall and a good sportsman.[47]

In short, he was well educated to be a gentleman, but was without the means of getting an income in the Highlands.

In the second half of the eighteenth century, a trend towards a teenage education in English schools provided the sons of the higher gentry with gentlemanly accomplishments that allowed them to participate on equal terms with national elites, but unfitting them for most employments. It also removed them from informal training in female consumption management. An English schooling was likely to be followed by an English university education, or even a European grand tour. The trend was resisted and resented by many in the Highlands, as is evident in the conflicts over the teenage education of Sir James MacDonald of Sleat in the 1750s. Sir James was fostered on Skye while his father was alive but was taken to London by his widowed mother and sister in 1754 to continue his education at Eton and Oxford.[48] The cost was a source of real concern for the 'tutors' who managed his affairs during his minority, which included his foster father, MacDonald of Kingsburgh. They and the widowed Lady Margaret and Sir James met in Edinburgh on 7 September 1759 to try to settle their differences. The tutor's case was put by the laird of Abercairny, who threatened to pull out of the further management of young man's affairs 'unless the Scheme of his Education were alterd'. He wanted him to 'receive his University Education in Scotland' for the following reasons:

> First, that an education pursued solely in England might give him ideas of expense, which are very improper for his fortune which is but moderate and considerably loaded with debt . . . 2ndly, by such a plan of education he becomes an entire stranger in his younger days to his own country and countrymen, and must contract habits and inclinations averse to residing at home in his more advanced years . . . by which means he cannot be supposed to apply his mind to the improvement of his estate . . . which should be the principal tendency of his life . . . he observes from experience that those young noblemen and gentlemen of this part of the country [Highlands] whose education is confined to England betwixt 12 and 20 years of age, their inclinations are also fixt there for the rest of their lives, which has proved fatal to their fortunes.[49]

Lady Margaret countered this argument with the superiority of the Oxford education, saying that 'a turn to reading and being a scholar' was her son's 'chief ambition', and with assurances that Sir James would visit Scotland every year 'to continue his acquaintance with his friends and countrymen'. The tutors were not convinced, and with good cause. Sir James kept his word and did visit Scotland, but he also travelled to Europe on an extended grand tour and died in Rome in 1766. His younger brother Alexander, who succeeded to the estate, was educated at Westminster School, St Andrews University and Oxford before entering the English legal profession in London.

Though the sons of the higher gentry gravitated towards an English schooling, most Highland gentlemen continued to receive a practical education in the Lowland towns and cities according to their abilities and intended careers. Or, as we shall see, they were sent into the army in their early teens and effectively denied a book-based education – or an education in anything that was useful to themselves or their family, other than being a soldier. In the

Campbell family of Barcaldine, the lawyer laird Duncan Campbell sent his eldest son Alexander to a formal university education in Edinburgh in the 1760s with the intention that he should enter the highest level of the legal profession as an advocate. The first in this family to receive a school education in England – at Harrow in the 1790s – was Alexander's son Duncan, who had no professional ambitions as such, other than to be a gentleman living on the income provided by his estate; although he did become a military officer during the Napoleonic wars. This youngest Duncan was mostly raised in Edinburgh, and his knowledge of the Highlands was slight. His life and decisions were shaped by his mother, Mary Campbell (daughter of Campbell 'of the bank'), who was also raised in Edinburgh and sent most of her six children to fashionable schools in the south of England.

Duncan Campbell the younger was a profligate consumer of luxuries and eventually bankrupted the estate. His sister and her husband, who was a Highland clergyman, lived way beyond their means. The trend towards an English education for the Highland elite was subject to much criticism among contemporaries. It undermined commitments to a practical life in farming or in some other useful career. It alienated the gentry from the culture of the ordinary people and disposed them to extravagant styles of living. As observed by Dr Johnson in 1773, talking about Sir Alexander MacDonald of Sleat with his want of commitment to clanship and mean tenancy practices, but reflecting on a broader cultural problem: 'The Highland chiefs should not be allowed to go further south than Aberdeen. A strong-minded man, like Sir James MacDonald, may be improved by an English education; but in general they will be tamed into insignificance.'[50]

EDUCATING AND SOCIALISING GIRLS

In addition to breaking their contacts with Highland society, education in England exposed the sons of lairds to a wider pool of potential marriage partners than was available at home. Sir Alexander MacDonald, brother to the scholarly James, married a Yorkshire lady of great beauty and some fortune. Others followed suit. The impact on Highland gentlewomen was lamentable, resulting in high levels of spinsterhood in families where there were large numbers of daughters. As remarked by Boswell, on visiting the family of the laird of Raasay, which included ten daughters, 'they work in every way proper for young ladies. Miss – plays on the guitar. What can disturb them? I can only say that I was disturbed by thinking how poor a chance they had to get husbands.'[51]

Marriage and motherhood was the only 'career' for the daughters of the Highland gentry. Their education was designed to fit them for this end, though what really mattered in the marriage market were family connections and the dowry. The eldest daughter, like the eldest son, had advantages over younger siblings because they carried larger dowries and were given a better education. Dowry provision was often established in the marriage settlements of parents, and the larger the number of daughters, the smaller their dowries became. The marriage contract of Donald MacDonald of Moidart and Moire MacLeod, niece to John MacLeod of Dunvegan, made in 1666, in addition to defining the nature of the bride's 'tocher' and her jointure if widowed, also defined the provision for any daughters born to the marriage. If there were two daughters there would be 12,000 merks between them, if three daughters there would be 15,000 merks – but in both cases 7,000 would go to the eldest. Payment was to be made at the age of fifteen, if their paternal grandfather had died by that time, or on marriage. The daughters were to be 'interteined and educat honestlie as beseems ther degrie and qualitie without any trubble or burden to the said portionis'; that is, without additional costs to male relatives.[52]

Differential dowries declined from the mid-eighteenth century, but elder daughters were still educated in a manner that distinguished them from their younger sisters. More was spent on refined 'accomplishments', and they were likely to travel further afield. But compared with sons, the sums expended on daughters were small, and levels of formal educational attainment, particularly in the first half of the eighteenth century, were low. As boys moved away from traditional Highland knowledge practices, girls were left behind. Yet young girls' experiences before mid-century are hard to distinguish from those of boys. They were nursed in similar ways and dressed alike. Newborn infants generated little comment beyond the usual congratulations, but in male eyes the birth of a daughter was a cause of disappointment.[53] It is likely that higher-than-average infant and child mortality prevailed among girls than among boys. There was probably poorer feeding in childhood, and medical attention was less marked. In letters between men there was frequent reference to the health and well-being of sons but little relating to daughters. Mothers may have accorded special care to their girls, but the experience of modern societies with an extreme male-preference is generally one of maternal neglect of female babies.[54] Certainly, in all of the families that have been examined for this study, in most generations up to the mid-eighteenth century, when there was a shift in affectionate relationships within families, there were more male children living to adulthood than female.

Though some young daughters in large families were farmed out to other relatives, most girls remained in the parental home for longer than boys. Fostering was uncommon other than in unusual circumstances, or where a mother was ill or had died, or the child was illegitimate and raised within her father's family. Girls of fostering age were useful in their parents' home, as Highland gentry families were usually large and households were labour-intensive. Servants were numerous. Pennant in the 1760s observed that a tacksman worth as little as fifty pounds could employ as many as twenty servants in and about the house.[55] But much of the domestic labour in gentry houses in the first half of the century was furnished by members of the family, and particularly by the girls. Girls provided valuable assistance to feed, clean and clothe the family and were simultaneously trained in some of the more refined domestic skills of the gentlewoman, such as maintaining fine linen and serving tea. Daughters were taught to read at home from the age of seven or eight, normally in conjunction with their religious instruction, allowing them sufficient skills to read the Bible and be admitted as functioning members of the religious community. Writing was a harder skill to master, requiring greater time, some equipment and a specialist, male writing master. Some girls were never taught to write, and illiteracy among the wives of lairds was commonplace into the 1730s.[56] Those girls that did receive formal instruction in writing usually did so in their mid-teens, when the skill was harder to master. Before mid-century, the handwriting and language used by gentry women in their correspondence had a childlike quality, suggesting a limited familiarity with the business of writing.

The knowledge practices of Highland women are less easily understood than those of men because so much education and training was conducted within the intimacy of the household and communicated orally from mother to daughter. Since the only life course available to a woman was marriage, housekeeping and childbearing, all education from an early age was focused on these areas. Submissiveness, godliness and industriousness, along with orderliness and frugality, were all that was required of the early eighteenth-century Highland gentleman's daughter. Teaching was restricted to spinning and sewing, cooking and dairying, child rearing and directing servants. Knowledge of Gaelic emerged naturally from daily exposure to servants and country people. Self-reflection, scholarship, the cultivation of emotions or 'taste' and independence of thought or action were not encouraged. This meant that the intellectual gap between men and women could be vast. Even as late as the 1740s, as illustrated in the family experience of Flora Macdonald, the daughter of a South Uist tacksman, a girl born into a lesser gentry family might still accompany cattle up to the summer shielings and be for all purposes illiterate. Male kin, though largely engaged in physical work on their farms, could read and compose in Latin for their own entertainment.[57] Whether being at the pastures was a source of freedom for girls, in contrast to the restrictions of the schoolroom in town – as suggested by poet Rob Donn, in his poetical conversation between two Highland sisters, daughters of a Sutherland tacksman, on the return of one of them from her school in Thurso – is hard to say.[58]

In the late seventeenth and early eighteenth centuries it was usual for girls of the higher and middle gentry to spend some time away from home in preparation for marriage, but this was rarely for more than a year and was often less. Some went to Edinburgh; others went no further than Perth or Inverness. Many entered the household of a senior clan member where an older woman, often a widow, known for good housekeeping and female accomplishments, provided a sort of 'finishing' education. All but one of the four daughters of Alexander Campbell of Barcaldine went to Edinburgh for a 'season' for their education and exposure to the marriage market. They lodged with relatives, took lessons from masters and mistresses, and their finances were managed by their brothers.[59] Isabell, the third sister, took a different path. In 1699 she was lodged in the household of the widowed Lady Susan Campbell of Kilmun in the small burgh of Kilsyth in Stirlingshire. The Campbell family of Kilmun was a high-ranking cadet of the earl of Breadalbane. Lady Kilmun was a middle-aged widow of standing and a frequent visitor to Edinburgh.[60] Patrick, Isabell's brother and the future laird of Barcaldine, was to marry Lady Kilmun's daughter Ann in 1700, as part of a marriage-related strategy to enhance the Barcaldine family fortunes. The presence of Isabell in the Kilmun household was tied to the politics of this important marriage. Isabell was taught to write and to cultivate other desirable feminine talents, such as fancy pastry-making, for which a pastry mistress was hired. Her expences included the purchase of several suits of clothing and a 'riding habit', which was the mark of the marriageable daughter on reaching adult status.[61] The clothing was probably made by a visiting tailor who travelled around a circuit of elite houses in the Highlands. Patrick monitored costs, but Lady Kilmun guided the purchase decisions.[62]

The youngest daughter of the family, Mary, received her education in Edinburgh in 1705, where she took lessons in writing and singing and spent significant sums on an accumulation of fine clothing.[63] She lodged in the household of Mrs Dundas. Her brother Patrick, now a married man with children of his own, was again responsible for his sister's expenditure. Mary lived in higher style than her older sisters, with an education that included more 'accomplishments', possibly because the family was wealthier following the Kilmun marriage or because she was a favourite child, indulged by an ageing father. But ready cash, as always, was monitored with care. Each of the girls was allowed only small sums of money to spend on her own account and none of them was required to correspond with their father on money matters – or, indeed, any other subject. All practical issues were arranged by their menfolk.

All four daughters of Alexander Campbell were married in their mid-teens to form alliances that were of strategic importance to their father and brothers. The eldest married John Campbell of Achallader, senior chamberlain on Breadalbane's Perthshire estates, and spent her adult life in elevated circles, often in Edinburgh and sometimes in London. Margaret first married Campbell of Kenloch, but was widowed in her twenties and was married again in 1711 to one of the MacDonnell family of Keppoch, a neighbour in Argyll. Isabell married Andrew Cameron, a younger member of the great Jacobite family of Lochiel, occupying lands to the north of Argyll. It was in this family that Patrick Campbell was also to find a second spouse in 1707 following the early death in childbirth of his first wife, Ann of Kilmun. The life courses of Isabell and Patrick ran in parallel. The youngest, Mary, was married in 1705 to Duncan Stewart of Innernahyle, a modest laird of another Jacobite family living immediately to the north of Barcaldine, but with powerful relatives in Perthshire on the Atholl estate, close to the Breadalbane heartland. Whether any of these connections reflected the individual personalities, physical attractiveness or personal inclinations of the girls in question is doubtful. Dowry negotiations and political alliances were all that mattered.

The rearing and informal education of the next generation of daughters in the 1720s and 1730s had much in common with that of their aunts at the turn of the century, but shifts were starting to occur in the integration of Highland gentry women into the modern world of goods and urban consumerism, and this was reflected in the lives of teenage girls.[64] For the first time, women began to assume a presence in the written family record, reflecting rising literacy levels, an expectation that they give a personal account of behaviour and expenditure and, in some families, new levels of affectionate intimacy between fathers and daughters. The Campbell family of Barcaldine, in common with many Highland gentry families, made significant changes in their manner of living at this time. A modern mansion house was built in the 1720s to replace the old and uncomfortable Barcaldine Castle, and Patrick Campbell's family entered a phase of significant spending on fashionable furnishings and household equipment.[65] Rising gentility and a new style of domestic life called for daughters of enhanced accomplishments, which required greater contacts with elite urban sociability and access to a wider spectrum of formal education.

Patrick Campbell had five grown daughters, one by his first marriage and the full sister of John of Barcaldine, and four by his second marriage, full sisters of Colin of Glenure. The Edinburgh accounts for Isobell and Jean, the younger two, in the late 1730s are particularly detailed because they were kept under the auspices of their brother Duncan, a cleaver and methodical man committed to careful record keeping.[66] He was the first member of the family to become a practising lawyer. Isobell seems to have absorbed this culture of record keeping in its feminised form, for she was the first daughter of the family to maintain a regular correspondence with her father and sent him careful notes on her expenditure, including the colour of the clothes she purchased.[67] Isobell and Jean lodged with Mrs Janet Foggo, who kept a fashionable school for the daughters of the gentry. Patrick Campbell, now an elderly widower, died at Barcaldine in February 1740, and the girls, under the guidance of Mrs Foggo, purchased full sets of mourning clothes. But the melancholy event did not interrupt their Edinburgh schooling, or the character of their lives there. Neither attended the funeral. The sisters purchased large quantities of clothing in Edinburgh and made connections with merchants and dressmakers that they would maintain in later life. Mrs Foggo managed their day-to-day cash from funds deposited by Duncan with the chief cashier at the Royal Bank of Scotland, their kinsman John Campbell 'of the bank'. The cost of Isabell's ten-month sojourn came to £63 12s. 1 ½d. This was paid through a complex series of financial arrangements based on 'cash sent in from your son Duncan, 18 Guineas, whereof two to repay the like sum advanced to himself 2nd March 1737, the rest to be laid out for your daughter Miss Tibby'; 'by a years interest on £500 [loan] due to you by Methvon'; and 'by cash sent with your son Duncan' of £10, leaving a deficit to be paid of £11 5s. 5 ½d.[68] When this carefully monitored account was closed, Isabell (Tibby) had 10s. 8d. in hand as an advance for sundries, and the sum was returned.

Both girls attended dancing classes and balls hosted by the dancing master. They paid separate accounts for dancing instruction, for the dancing master's servant and for coals for the dancing room. They took pastry-making classes at Mrs Johnston's pastry school. They took classes in reading and writing, where they also paid for paper, pens and ink, and were given instruction in sewing and knitting by Mrs Foggo, who acted as a sort of female 'governor'. The 'doctrixes' and servants at Mrs Foggo's school were given presents on 'Hansall Monday'. Their social life was busy, with balls to attend, charity dances and afternoon tea parties – called 'companie afternoons' – where they charged their father through Mrs Foggo for 'tea and shuggar' to entertain their friends. Each girl was given a Bible during her stay in Edinburgh, as well as a 'pastry book'. A couple of blank writing books were also purchased from the writing master. This was the first recorded instance in the Barcaldine family papers of any form of book ownership by women

As with the earlier generation of daughters, the aim was not to develop any particular skills to a high degree, but rather to acquire a veneer of social accomplishments prior to marriage, when the real business of life began. As remarked of one of the older sisters, Mary, during her stay in Edinburgh in 1732 when she lodged with the widow Elizabeth Campbell of Greenyards, who was Patrick's cousin: 'When she gets a little experience I sincerely believe she will make as pretty a woman as [any] in Argyllshire . . . she has improved in all the different parts of it [her education] to admiration except in her reading which is no fault in her nor her master, but in having too little time to attend it.'[69]

For most girls a marriage followed quickly after the end of formal education. Isabell (Tibby) made a particularly good match with Archibald Campbell of Melfort in the early 1740s. Her younger sister Jean remained a spinster, though, probably because of the death of their father.

Unlike the earlier generation, the experience of these young women when entering marriage and housekeeping in the early 1740s was likely to be one of greater material comfort within the home, a declining expectation of outdoor farm work, more emphasis on the management of genteel hospitality to reflect the status of their husbands, and opportunities to spend time away from their Highland estates, particularly during the harsh winter months. But they were still practical housewives who worked daily in the kitchen and dairy and took directly responsibility for childcare. Yet among the educated urban elite of the 1740s, the range of schooling and skills available to daughters was expanding. This had an impact on the daughters of the Highland gentry because so many families were entering the ranks of urban professionals.

An Essay on Female Conduct, penned by a medical man in the 1740s for the benefit of his only daughter, outlined a wider spectrum of accomplishments and learning than ever before. Margaret Monro, the twelve-year-old daughter of Alexander Monro, professor of anatomy at Edinburgh university, and Isabella, third daughter of Donald Macdonald of Sleat, was advised to acquire the skills of reading, writing, arithmetic, dancing, music, marketing, book-keeping, religion, housewifery and 'women's work' – that is, 'Sewing, Spinning, Knotting, Stockings Knitting, Washing and dressing Linens, Platting caps, shaping Frocks, Gowns &c. Pastry Cookery and all the other Parts of what is called Women's work'.[70] The father tutored the child, along with her brothers, in modern languages and Latin, as well as geography and history. But in giving her an education, he also cautioned:

> I don't propose to make you so learned that you can have any Pretensions to be a Critick in Languages, that might give you too much a Taste for Books and make you neglect the necessary female Offices; and I flatter myself that you will have good Sense enough to know that you are not to display any of this sort of Knowledge, or to make use of any uncommon words without resolving to be envied, criticised and laughed at. If I observe you exposing yourself to censure by making ill Use of any sort of Knowledge which I may give you the opportunity of acquiring, I shall soon stop short and let you remain as ignorant as I can of everything beyond what related the plainest domestick Life.[71]

Fear of the 'bluestocking' was common in eighteenth-century gentry society, but the chance of becoming one was rare indeed when most Highland gentlewomen spent only a very few months on formal learning and lived a life thereafter of practical busyness. Those that did show some inclination to book reading were mostly preoccupied with religious texts or novels, as recorded in the daily journal of Elizabeth Rose of Kilravock in the 1770s.[72] Elizabeth Rose had been taught to write at an early age, though her mother, the daughter of a military gentleman and educated in the early 1730s, was barely literate; 'no school learning was wasted on the Colonel's daughter'.[73] As an eleven-year-old in the late 1750s, Elizabeth wrote to her uncle, a medical man in London, to describe her daily routines. It is a rare insight to the life of a young girl living on the family estate. 'My work goes on in the manner I before wrote you of; sewing, writing, playing at the spinet etc etc and diversions change with the seasons. I have at present a fine little garden, in which I grow many good things.'[74]

Elizabeth's early education was partly provided by the 'governor', Mr Reid, who was employed in the Kilravock household to teach her two younger brothers along with two cousins, the Malcolm boys, who lodged with the Roses. Her uncle's responses to his niece give a nice indication of what was expected of girls.

> Reading and writing and playing on the spinet is all very well – indeed, extremely well. The two first deserve great application . . . methinks music is well as an amusement, but not as a study . . . You say you romp too much with the Malcolms. It seems your mamma chides you sometimes for this, and I take it for granted you endeavour to correct what is perhaps too much . . . Sliding on the ice you are fond of, it seems. It is a wholesome but a dangerous exercise, especially for your sex . . . Cutting paper is an innocent amusement.[75]

The message was clear enough for a young girl of more than average education and intelligence. Even in the last few decades of the eighteenth century, when the cultivation of female sensibility added a further dynamic to book reading, when the period of formal schooling away from home had been extended and rising 'gentility' had begun to undermine the practice of housewifery, most young women who lived in the Highlands gained only the rudiments of a formal education. As described by the novelist Susan Ferrier, a lawyer's daughter and frequent visitor to Argyll, the daughters of a modest farming laird at the end of the eighteenth century were mostly educated via the long-established practical home-based system.

> To attend the parish church and remember the text; . . . to knit stockings, scold servants, cement china, trim bonnets, lecture the poor . . . these acquirements, accompanied with a great deal of lecturing and fault-finding, sufficed for the first fifteen years; when the two next, passed at a provincial boarding-school, were supposed to impart every graceful accomplishment to which women could attain.[76]

For girls of this background in adult life, 'their walk lay amongst threads and pickles; their sphere extended from the garret to the pantry', much as it had always been.[77]

But there were some changes. Gentry girls were now only rarely educated in the houses of elite families in Highland Scotland, mainly because so many noble wives were English- or Lowland-born and unaccustomed to such responsibility. In criticising the want of clan feeling by Sir Alexander Macdonald and his English wife, Dr Samuel Johnson in 1773 was moved to reflect on their failure to make provisions for the female youth of their extended kin network: 'They should have had so many of the gentlemen's daughters to receive their education in the family, to learn pastry and such things from the housekeeper, and manners from my lady.'[78] Moreover, the kinds of education that had formerly been the preserve of the gentry were filtering down the social scale. As remarked by Boswell in 1773, while lodging with a tenant farmer in Glenmoriston, 'our landlord's daughter, a modest civil girl very neatly dressed . . . told us she had been a year at Inverness and learnt reading and writing, sewing, knotting, working lace and pastry. Mr Johnson made her a present of a book of arithmetic.'[79]

With longer periods of formal schooling outside the Highlands, the daughters of those Highland gentlemen who adopted professions to supplement their estates were increasingly likely to be educated in England. The eldest daughter of Duncan Campbell of Barcaldine, the lawyer, was educated for several years at a boarding school in York. And his granddaughter, the eldest daughter of Alexander Campbell of Barcaldine and Mary Campbell 'of the bank', born in the 1780s and mostly raised in Edinburgh, was sent to a smart boarding school in Clapham on the outskirts of London for most of her teenage years.[80] Well-educated professional men, from the Highlands as elsewhere, sought sophisticated educations for their daughters. Reared in households where learning was a key to income, a family culture of advanced education inevitably influenced the experience of girls.

Elizabeth Grant of Rothiemurchus, the daughter of an Inverness-shire laird and his English wife was born in Charlotte Square in Edinburgh in 1797, the eldest of five children.[81] Her father pursued a legal career, and his daughters were educated by a succession of private tutors and schools in both Edinburgh and London. Elizabeth Grant was a clever young woman with considerable literary talents, who was also able to supplement the family income in her early twenties by writing short stories with sentimental Highland themes for commercial magazines. She was not unusual, for by the later decades of the eighteenth century a distinct group of highly educated Highland gentlewomen had evolved, often the daughters of professionals, who had spent many years in the Lowland cities and even abroad. Indeed, the woman most admired by Dr Johnson in 1773 when travelling in the Highlands was a Miss MacLean, the daughter of the minister of Erray, who had lived for over thirty years in Glasgow. As Boswell observed:

> She is the most accomplished lady that I have found in the Highlands. She knows French, music, and drawing, sews neatly, makes shell-work, and can milk cows; in short, she can do everything. She talks sensibly, and is the first person whom I have found that can translate Erse poetry literally.[82]

This last skill was particularly prized in Highland gentry and professional circles at a time when direct daily engagement with Gaeldom and the knowledge practices of the ordinary people was being undermined by prolonged physical distance. On one evening during the Boswell–Johnson visit, Miss MacLean entertained the company with reciting and translating the poems of John MacLean, a famed Mull bard, recently deceased, who could neither read nor write himself. One poem was an 'elegy on Sir John MacLean's being obliged to fly his country in 1715; another a dialogue between two Roman Catholic young ladies, sisters, whether it was better to be a nun or to marry'.[83] It was women such as these, often the daughters of clergymen, who were bilingual and had scholarly habits formed in childhood, who helped their fathers or clergymen husbands to collect and preserve the songs, stories and poetry of Gaeldom.

By virtue of her education, expanding horizons and changing knowledge practices, the Highland gentleman's daughter in the early nineteenth century was a very different type of woman to what she had been a hundred years before. She was also a great deal more expensive for her family to support.

3 Gentlemanly Careers

INTRODUCTION

The younger sons of the land-owning gentry were always obliged to seek alternative ways of making a living other than that of their fathers. Only the eldest could succeed to property, and few families, even among the wealthy, had sufficient resources to support their younger boys beyond adolescence. Among the lesser gentry it was also common for elder sons to have additional sources of income. Indeed, in eighteenth-century England, most significant estate development, including the building of new country houses, was funded by extra-estate income from professional or commercial employment.[1]

Studies of Highland estates in the long eighteenth century have mostly focused on the ambitions and behaviour of landowners as though the laird was the only person who made decisions about the uses of his land. In a few cases of female ownership, the focus has fallen on professional factors as being the decision makers in estate and tenancy policy.[2] Yet even a passing acquaintance with the personal correspondence of the Highland gentry reveals that estate strategies and fortunes, and the fortunes of lairds and their families, were closely tied to the lives, career histories and values that were generated by the non-landed careers of a wide network of male kin. Parents made careful plans for the future lives of their younger sons, partly to give the son the best chance of retaining his gentry status through his own endeavours, and partly to advance the interests of the family and estate. Career diversification was the key objective and this meant that young men of gentry background became merchants or professionals, particularly lawyers, doctors, government office holders, occasionally clergymen and, increasingly, soldiers.[3] Many men who inherited Highland estates were younger sons trained from youth to other expectations. Eldest sons were rarely leisured *rentiers* and were increasingly likely to have a career beyond farming. These careers shaped attitudes to land and its uses, and they also influenced relationships with other family members. Luxury and consumption were determined by the income flows of non-landed employment and by the occupational cultures of non-landed work.

This was well understood by contemporaries. The Macdonald family of Sleat on Skye furnishes an illustration in the middle decades of the eighteenth century. The young heir, Sir James, was raised by his widowed mother to be an anglicised gentleman scholar, causing much alarm among his Highland tutors and tacksmen over the costs to the estate and the likely alienation of the laird from his people.[4] Assurances were given that James would visit Skye each year, and he did make some improvements for the benefit of the tenantry. But James died in his mid-twenties and his younger brother Alexander, a lawyer in the English system, raised to this from youth and married to an English wife, inherited the estate. His attitudes to land and its uses were founded in the mentality of the modern legal profession. He was individualistic and legalistic. He was not popular, and his ruthless tenancy policies in the early 1770s prompted bitter recriminations and mass emigration. For one clan historian, 'while one would not go so far as to agree with Dr Johnson's observation that his education had unfitted him for the position of chief, yet it must be conceded that he was wholly devoid of sympathy either with the culture, or the manner of life, of his own people'.[5] The death of Sir James Macdonald was mourned for decades.

Like the legal profession, the careers that absorbed the sons of the Highland gentry were predominantly urban and defined by institutions with complex rules and cultures. Many involved service to the British state. All required some initial investment in education or training, with greater sums spent on youths at the top of the sibling hierarchy than at the bottom. Finding employment for a son entailed a cost for the father, but it also offered benefits for the family. Individual abilities or inclinations were rarely considered. Sons or brothers who were employed in the professions or government service or trade could generate wealth and patronage. They offered privileged access to specialist knowledge and information. Gentry culture was tenacious in these men and inspired many to great efforts in order to re-enter, through land purchase or marriage, the class into which they were born. Successful relatives were a source of family prestige. Those who failed could equally generate family disgrace and even financial ruin.

The culture of the landed gentry had a major influence on which occupations were socially acceptable. The notion of a 'gentleman' evolved through time, but was only ever consistent with certain types of work and in particular with work that was linked to the landed as clients, that allowed participants to dress in gentlemanly ways and provided some capacity for genteel leisure to be undertaken in conjunction with the work. Financial reward was one consideration; respectability was another. The legal profession was always considered a respectable and potentially well-rewarded career for the sons of the gentry, in Scotland and elsewhere.[6] But only few could afford to enter the ranks of this expensive and privileged profession. Notions of a hierarchy of career respectability and status were sensitive and changing. Attitudes to direct participation in 'trade' hardened as the century progressed, causing many who were trained to this area of work to seek alternatives. In the words of Patrick Campbell, third son of Duncan Campbell of Glenure, a teenage soldier during the Seven Years War who worked for over a decade as a tenant farmer and cattle trader, to be an officer in the army was 'far more respectable and I am sure profitable . . . than being a Morvern drover or tenant'.[7]

If 'respectability' and 'profit' were important considerations, the availability of suitable connections or patronage to make a career possible was a further factor that influenced a young man's route in life. Choosing a son's career was a complex issue that usually involved wide discussion with trusted kin whilst simultaneously testing the patronage avenues that were most likely to secure an apprenticeship or post. Published career advice was available. One of the earliest and most widely circulated was directed at those who aimed to get their sons into the well-paid labour market in London, which was an important route to empire taken by many of the younger sons of the Highland gentry.[8] Robert Campbell's *The London Tradesman, being a Compendious View of all of the Trades, Professions, Arts, both Liberal and Mechanic, now Practised in the Cities of London and Westminster*, published in 1747, gave a clear indication of the cost of entering each area of work as well as its gentlemanly credentials. This kind of information was also circulated informally within networks of family and friends.

The following account of gentry careers begins by exploring the work and culture of farming lairds and their gentlemanly tacksmen, who were often brothers or sons. Some understanding of their experience helps us to appreciate how very different were the lives and culture of those later lairds who relied on non-estate incomes, or those younger brothers and sons who left the land in favour of urban employments or the army. We next consider the important pairing of the landowning gentry with the legal profession. The church and medicine were favoured careers in some families and introduced distinct work cultures to the Highland gentry. More significant, however, was employment in trade, which after farming was the primary career destination for the younger sons of the Highland gentry in the first half of the eighteenth century. Yet business apprenticeships and careers were almost entirely abandoned in the 1750s and 1760s in favour of military employment. Highland lairds were resourceful in seeking out ways of advancing the family interest through obtaining non-landed careers for their sons, but as the eighteenth century progressed the costs increased and the options narrowed. The end result, with profoundly damaging consequences, was the dominance of the army, the profession most associated with a culture of conspicuous consumption, leisure and individualism. The military profession is critical to understanding the relationship between eighteenth-century lairds and luxury, and it forms the subject of the next chapter.

THE FARMING LAIRD

The main life course that was available to the younger or illegitimate sons of lairds before mid-century was connected with farming as tacksmen or estate managers. The Highland system of land allocation and clan organisation relied on robust networks of tacksmen as senior tenants.[9] Holding land 'on tack' and sub-leasing to lesser tenants was consistent with periodic employment elsewhere, such as military service abroad, and some professionals who were permanently settled in the Highlands were also tacksmen on family estates. Family resources were invested in such men. They held high social status, were often major players on the economic scene and were valued for their capacity to render important kin services such as fosterage. Bonds of trust were cemented by frequent interactions and a common attachment to the wider interests of family and estate. In the first half of the eighteenth century the tacksmen kin of the Campbell family of Barcaldine were routinely consulted on a range of topics, and older tacksmen were empowered to proffer advice and warnings to younger lairds. In the words of Rob Donn, describing a Sutherland tacksman, 'foolish lads, lacking sense, obtained wisdom by listening to you'.[10]

Though tacksmen did not own land, their relationships with land as practical farmers were much the same as that of the farming laird. So how did men who were destined to inherit estates or be significant tacksmen develop knowledge of farming and land management? Most Highland gentlemen learned practical farming through living in the Highlands from childhood and observing the techniques that were practised by relatives and neighbours. Formal training was rare, though there were instances of young men destined for land ownership who did undertake an informal apprenticeship in practical agriculture. James Boswell described the young laird of Coll as 'a little brisk young man, [who] had been a good deal in England studying farming, and was resolved to improve his father's lands without hurting the people or losing the ancient Highland fashion'.[11] He did not say how Coll would accomplish this ambiguous agenda. John Ramsay of Octertyre, an observer of farming life in Stirlingshire and Perthshire, described the 'passion' for improvement among local landowners mid-century – but in this part of the southern Highlands it was farm servants and gentleman overseers who were sent away to learn 'English' methods.[12] Others, including the infamous Patrick Sellar, a farming lawyer and factor on the Sutherland estate in the early nineteenth century, were critical of Highland lairds for their failure to train their sons in up-to-date farming through a study of 'improved' farms. It seems a practice that was common elsewhere was not particularly common in the Highlands.[13]

The senior elements of the Campbell family of Barcaldine were in most regards full-time farmers in the first half of the eighteenth century, with little experience of any other way of life. Alexander Campbell, the late seventeenth-century patriarch, in addition to running his own estate, was chamberlain for the earl of Breadalbane, managing his patron's property and financial business in the Lorn area of Argyll. His son, Patrick, may have travelled further afield – though even Alexander took a pleasure jaunt to Bath as companion to an ailing senior kinsman[14] – but, like his father, he rarely left the Highlands, and for most of his long life he was a practical farmer and land manager. Patrick's extensive correspondence of the 1720s and 1730s is full of the daily details of the farm. He took a direct interest in cheese production, orders for barrel hoops, the grazing for horses, supplies of salmon and tree bark, disputes with labourers and neighbours, and the affairs of 'the company', one of the several trading consortia of local lairds that flourished at this time.[15] Most of Patrick's brothers, including Colin Campbell of Invernan, were similarly preoccupied with practical matters, and their homes and outbuildings reflected this. At the time of Colin's death in 1731, the house and byre were full of planks of dressed wood awaiting sale. The daily domestic routines of his wife, a laird's daughter with some claims to gentility, required her to negotiate the products of the farm in the family living spaces. The passing of this aspect of 'traditional' life among the Highland gentry, which mostly occurred with the building boom in new country houses in the middle decades of the century, caused few regrets.[16]

The next generation of this and other families, coming to manhood in the 1720s and 1730s, also lived in the Highlands as children but were less familiar with practical farming because they were absent during their years of formal education, which for many was followed by a non-farming career. Yet farming lairds with day-to-day involvement with their farms remained the norm.

Hugh Mackay of Bighouse was typical.[17] He managed the estate he inherited through his wife, negotiating the minutiae of the livestock that was transferred from his practical farming mother-in-law in the 1740s. He was a cattle drover for many decades in partnership with a Sutherland tacksman, Iain Mac Eachainn, whose death in 1757 was memorialised by Rob Donn as a symbol of the passing of an older way of life: 'Where shall we go to find / A man to replace you in your clan / In the role of gathering or spending?'[18] Hugh Mackay of Bighouse was also one of a trio of senior Mackay lairds who in the 1760s administered the vast Reay property when an idiot brother incapable of running his own affairs succeeded their senior kinsman.[19]

John Campbell of Barcaldine, son of Patrick, was of much the same age and experience as Hugh Mackay of Bighouse. His childhood was spent close to his father and with the nearby clergyman laird, Campbell of Archattan, who ran a school for the sons of the local gentry. He traveled widely in the Highland counties as a youth to carry out family commissions and observe farming practices. His father and many close relatives were farming lairds or tacksmen, and being in their company taught him much as a boy. Yet John Campbell's formal education took him in a different direction to that of his father and uncles, along a route that on the surface had little to do with farming. Like several of his younger brothers, John attended schools and masters in Perth and Stirling in his teens before moving onto Edinburgh. In 1721, aged twenty-one, he attended the 'writing chamber' of Colin Kirk, lawyer to the earl of Breadalbane.[20] In contemporary parlance he was sent to the 'lattern' or desk, a frequent choice for those of 'moderate estate' who could not afford a Dutch or German university.[21] John told his father: 'I believe [Kirk] will take all the pains imaginable to let me know some business.' He was taught basic commercial and criminal law along with accounting, French, Latin and Greek. He was also encouraged to mix in the social circle of the earl of Breadalbane, his father's patron, which included senior members of the Perthshire Campbell clan, such as Sir Duncan Campbell of Lochnell and Lord Monzie. These were kin connections who corresponded with Patrick Campbell on a variety of subjects, including agricultural improvement. Lord Monzie, for instance, remarked in a letter of 1728 that the earl was full of new improvement ideas that he had heard in the coffee houses of London, though he doubted whether these were suitable for Luing or Lismore.[22] Patrick Campbell sought advice from these men on John's future course in life. There was some debate about a career in the army, and even more debate about a suitable spouse.[23] Three years passed in this manner, and some of the Campbell elite expressed concern that John was idling away his youth doing nothing in particular beyond socialising and courting. John complained at his want of a proper income. The family agreed that the best course was to take him back to Argyll and put him to work as a farmer.

Established on a farm on his father's estate and living in Barcaldine Castle, initially with his paternal grandmother and then with a wife from 1728, John Campbell remained in the same situation for nearly sixteen years until Patrick's death in 1740. He was a practical farmer and his father's right-hand man. He corresponded almost daily with Patrick, living a few miles away at the newly built Dulfuir House, on family matters and farming affairs, and their households and farming interests operated in parallel. A hand-delivered note written from Barcaldine Castle in 1731 is typical:

> I had yours and will be at Ardchattan tomorrow if you can spare me a saddle to ride upon for both my own is away to Perthshire. I believe your hunting stock is the only saddle you have that will do for my little mare. If you come first . . . you'll wait for me at Achnaba and I'll endeavour to be there as soon as I can.[24]

His father lent him money – small sums such as the five pounds in cash that he requested in August 1739,[25] and large loans such as the 2,000 merks that was advanced to John in the mid-1720s for stocking his farm, which he was able to repay from a bond from 'young Kethick', his wife's brother, as part of the marriage settlement.[26] He even borrowed furniture from his father's house to entertain visitors in proper style.[27] Father and son shared workmen and corresponded about tenants and the sale of estate produce. Patrick sought advice from his legally trained son on fishing rights and judicial matters such as the prosecution of absconding soldiers.[28] But surviving notes and letters give only the briefest glimpse into their mutual affairs, which were mostly discussed in person.

John Campbell of Barcaldine was close to his father, but farming methods and styles of management were changing, and it was increasingly necessary for practical lairds to have skills beyond those of stock raising and tree planting. Patrick's style of management was focused on the minutiae of the farming year. John Campbell was a practical man, but his estate correspondence suggests a more distant relationship with the day-to-day affairs of the farm. More of his commercial dealings were conducted through his man of business in Inverary, John Campbell the lawyer, a relative who was also chamberlain for the dukes of Argyll. John spent more of his time indoors, sitting at a desk with books and papers, engaged in such technical and legal but essential business as that connected with his role as local commissioner of supply. He entered into complex financial arrangements with Edinburgh banks, notably Douglas Heron & Co, and spent more time away from the Highlands on city business than his father. John Campbell was active in the local militia during the Jacobite uprising, offering important support to the duke of Argyll's armies, and in the late 1740s he was one of the first crown factors to be appointed to run the forfeited Jacobite estates. This statement of loyalty, which was probably necessary in a family with strong kin connections with Jacobite lairds, was also a deliberate act of opportunism designed to supplement his income through factor's fees and access to new business opportunities. Though it gained him credit with his noble patrons, it also ensured that in middle age John Campbell was mostly absent from his own estate.[29]

John Campbell ran the extensive annexed estates of the exiled Jacobite earl of Perth for nearly twenty years on behalf of the barons of exchequer in Edinburgh. He was also a justice of the peace. His half-brother, Colin of Glenure, was a crown factor in Argyll, as was Mungo Campbell, John's illegitimate son, a qualified lawyer and Colin's assistant. These posts were in the patronage gift of Campbell noblemen, and represented considerable success for the Barcaldine family. They offered leverage for further patronage positions, particularly in the army. In order to carry out his duties, John Campbell and his wife, with their numerous younger children, established a home and farm in Crieff.[30] His older sons became soldiers. He was now close to the heartland of his principal patrons, the earl of Breadalbane and Campbell of Achallader, the earl's chamberlain. He was also within a short distance of two of his brothers in Stirling, Robert the merchant and Duncan the lawyer.

John Campbell's considerable knowledge of farming and sophisticated understanding of local psychology are revealed in his regular reports to the Edinburgh office.[31] He brought an 'improved' mindset to the problems of an under-developed estate and a tenantry lacking in 'proper industry.' He was a strong advocate for founding schools and making better religious provision to encourage industriousness and loyalty; two conditions that were always linked by improving lairds. He was keen to establish a spinning school in Crieff, and identified the wife of a local lawyer as the best candidate for running such a school. He saw scope for a tannery, using local bark, and a linen cloth manufactory, making use of the 'great quantities of linen yarn brought to market here weekly . . . which is bought up and sent in packs to Glasgow, Paisley etc'.[32] He was astute in getting the tenants to pay their rents, and he identified local farmers whose initiatives were worth encouraging. Of one he observed that although 'he is quite a common countryman . . . it is well known that a farm improved by a person of this sort does more service in a neighbourhood and creates an emulation beyond any improvement that can be made by a gentleman'.[33] In a critical assessment, Campbell of Barcaldine has been described thus: 'A west Highland gentleman of the finest type, he was also, by any contemporary standard, an outstanding factor.'[34]

John Campbell's abilities as 'an outstanding factor' were grounded in his practical skills as a farming laird, but he was also endowed with that another set of knowledge practices that increasingly defined the Highland gentleman, the law. Estate modernisation through commercial development, new types of tenancy agreements and the enforcement of property rights, property sales and purchases all required a familiarity with the law. A qualified lawyer was necessary to enter into commercial contracts or to prosecute infringements of rights. Knowing something of the technical background to such procedures helped ambitious lairds as they sought to develop their estates. Patrick Campbell acknowledged as much when he sent each of his two older land-inheriting sons into a legal office for training. The third son did, of course, become a lawyer by profession. Patrick was not alone in this move, for at the time that John was attending the 'writing chamber' of Colin Kirk in Edinburgh in the early 1720s, the son of another senior Breadalbane connection, Campbell of Carwhin, was there as well, and a few years earlier, John Campbell, later 'of the bank', had been trained in the same office.[35] Legal knowledge was useful to lairds, and of all the alternative outlets for making a living the law was considered the most acceptable for the sons of the Scottish gentry. But legal knowledge shaped a distinctive set of attitudes to Highland estates. These are hinted at in some of John Campbell's factors reports, and are clearer still in the writings and behaviour of those lawyer lairds who dominated the Highland scene in the middle and later decades of the eighteenth century.

THE LAWYER LAIRD

In much of England and Lowland Scotland for generation after generation the gentry were first and foremost lawyers who also owned land.[36] Legal practice generated an income, but land gave status and political rights. A lawyer had privileged access to the patronage and influence of the landed elite, their principal clients. The size of the legal profession in Scotland grew substantially in the eighteenth century, and most of the expansion was linked to agricultural improvement.[37] Though not a 'quick-rich' career, the law offered the chance to engage in a steady accumulation of wealth, and men were more likely to move into land ownership through their own efforts via this route than through any other career. Duncan Campbell, third son of Patrick of Barcaldine, provides an illustration. With little likelihood of inheriting land – although in the event he did succeed to an estate – Duncan was trained to be a professional lawyer. His early education in the 1730s was similar to that of his elder brothers, for, as was stressed in a contemporary career manual, a lawyer's 'education ought to be Liberal. This is not only necessary to qualify them for their profession; but to enlarge the mind and give it a bias above little pettifogging practice.'[38] He served a formal apprenticeship, partly in Glasgow and partly in Edinburgh, and practised his profession throughout his long life. In common with many Scottish lawyers, through a combination of a good income from his practice, detailed knowledge of the land market and business acumen, he was able to accumulate a significant independent landholding in Stirlingshire and was by far the most successful of Patrick Campbell's sons. In old age in the 1770s he purchased Barcaldine from his debt-ridden eldest brother, John, for the large sum of £24,000, which was only possible from the profits of law combined with his technical ability to raise significant loans.

Thomas Sellar, the father of Patrick, the Sutherland factor and sheep farmer, offers another illustration of a provincial lawyer's progress into landowning. Thomas Sellar was an Elgin lawyer and procurator fiscal in the later eighteenth century. His office was responsible for managing several big estates for absent owners and for training many young gentlemen farmers and factors. He acted on behalf of the Mackenzies of Seafield, who owned Morayshire estates, and for the Grants of Castle Grant near Huntley. He also managed lesser estates, including a property called Westfield, close to Elgin. Westfield went through several changes of ownership in the second half of the eighteenth century before being acquired in 1781 by an Edinburgh advocate, Francis Russell of Blackhall, as part of that lawyer's entry into landed status. Russell employed Thomas Sellar for his local expertise, and appointed him as factor to introduce an improvement programme of drainage, tree and hedge planting and tenancy consolidation. When Russell died, the estate was purchased by Sellar. He and his son Patrick, also a lawyer, perfected their system of farming and stock management on the Westfield estate, and it was these methods, backed by considerable expertise in the law, that led Patrick Sellar to the status of being one of the most successful Highland sheep farmers in the first half of the nineteenth century, through his tenancy of great farms on the Sutherland estate. Patrick Sellar, even as a tenant in Sutherland, retained ownership of the Westfield estate, and in later life purchased a second property in Morven in Argyll.[39]

Lawyer lairds such as Thomas Sellar of Westfield and Duncan Campbell of Glenure – or others from the families that figure in this study, including John Sinclair of Freswick, an advocate and sheriff in Caithness from the 1750s to the 1780s, or Alexander Macdonald of Sleat, who practised at the English bar – exercised a profound influence in the Highlands. They combined their legal knowledge and judicial functions with financial and technical expertise. They were hands-on farmers, and many were also successful entrepreneurs. Law and land were complementary and advanced the interests of the Highland gentleman and his family. But circumstances changed in the later decades of the eighteenth century. Those who kept an eye on practical farming affairs from a home base in one of the provincial towns, like the Sellars of Elgin, remained much the same as far as daily life was concerned. But though they made money, their social status in the eyes of an increasingly metropolitan landed elite probably declined.[40] Those who abandoned provincial Scotland in order to follow more ambitious careers in Edinburgh or even London were a different matter entirely.

Duncan Campbell of Glenure and Barcaldine raised his eldest son, Alexander, to be an advocate in Edinburgh in order to occupy one of the highest social positions in Scotland. In the absence of a court or parliament, the legal profession had become an important element in the political and cultural leadership of the country. To be a successful Edinburgh advocate was to occupy a position of prestige. But the style of living that went with such a career was expensive. Alexander Campbell married the daughter of John Campbell 'of the bank, who was a lawyer by training, though he was basically a businessman. He was a wealthy *bon viveur* and lived a life of fashionable luxury in Edinburgh. His brother-in-law was an Edinburgh advocate. Alexander was the first of the family to own a town house in Edinburgh, purchased in the 1780s, largely at the insistence of his wife, where he lived for a large part of the year while pursuing his legal interests. His relationship with Barcaldine was more detached than was his Stirlingshire lawyer father's, and most of the management of the property from the 1780s went through the hands of a non-kin factor. One of his near contemporaries was John Grant of Rothiemurchus, father of Elizabeth, the 'Highland Lady'. John Grant began his legal training in Glasgow in the early 1790s. He inherited the Rothiemurchus estate in Invernes-shire on the death of his uncle in 1796, and another uncle left him a valuable property in England. With an income assured, he could have abandoned his studies, but

> he thought a knowledge of law necessary to the usefulness of a country gentleman, he really liked the profession; and the French revolution, in the startling shake it had given to the aristocracy of all Europe while it was annihilating its own, had made it a fashion for all men to provide themselves with some means of earning a future livelihood, should the torrent of democracy reach to other lands.[41]

He completed his training in Edinburgh shortly after marrying and moved into a fashionable house in Charlotte Square. But John Grant was ambitious and, unlike Alexander Campbell of Barcaldine, who was happy to remain in Scotland, he wanted to be a 'great lawyer' in London and enter public life. With hindsight, his daughter viewed this as a mistake. London was expensive, and the cost of buying a parliamentary seat was crippling.[42]

By the 1820s, John Grant's elder son, William, was training in Edinburgh for a legal career. Every season, the family travelled en masse and at great expense between their Highland estate, where they lived in high style, and rented houses in London and Edinburgh.[43] But debts were mounting. To save money, John's wife and daughters took to living permanently in the Highlands, whilst the lawyer laird was 'to proceed as usual, London and the House in spring, and such improvements as amused him when at home'. A trust was devised to protect the estate, and William, who had no taste for his legal studies, was to 'devote himself to the management of the property. Take the forest affairs into his own hands . . . and turn farmer as well, having qualified himself by a residence of some months in East Lothian at a first rate practical farmers.'[44] With little real understanding of land management or farming, his interventions were disastrous. By the mid-1820s the family was being pursued from all directions by creditors demanding payments amounting to over £60,000. William was imprisoned for debt in Edinburgh, and when John Grant lost his seat he also lost his legal protection as a member of parliament and he fled the country. Many of the family's possessions were sold, and Grant of Rothiemurchus left Britain with his respectability barely intact.

The advocate's profession demanded an expensive style of living, but it was an increasingly crowded career when new men from urban middle-class backgrounds joined the ranks of Edinburgh lawyers. Estate ownership was an important source of prestige for lawyers, but estate wealth was now being used to supplement inadequate legal incomes. Greater professional competition meant that lawyer lairds devoted more of their time to legal employments in town, which invariably accelerated the urban orientation of their styles of living and consumer behaviour. Men of this type were likely to select their marriage partners from among the women they encountered in urban professional and business circles. These women had little knowledge of Highland life and were unable and unwilling to manage a Highland house and family life.

Just as profound as the impact on social behaviour was the impact of legal careers on ways of thinking and ways of administering Highland estates. The legal mindset, shaped by Enlightenment rationality, was focused on the hegemony of documents. Duncan Campbell of Glenure and Barcaldine, the first full-time lawyer laird of his family, was also the first of the family to systematically preserve the records of the estate and its finances, and of his own personal affairs. Duncan's vision of the world – his socially constructed sense of reality – was based on the papers and documents that lay on the desk in front of him. He was methodical and calculating, obsessed with locks and keys to preserve the security of his physical property, and overly preoccupied with his property rights.[45] This reflected his individual personality, but it was also characteristic of the successful lawyer. The legal-profession mentality and culture was not consistent with the older familial and communal values of the Highlands. The infamous clearances that occurred at the hands of Patrick Sellar of Westfield while he was working as factor for the countess of Sutherland were as much a reflection of his legal mindset as of his entrepreneurial ambitions as a commercial sheep farmer. He cleared the Sutherland tenants because he was legally entitled to do so; and his deficit in sympathy arose from the fact that when seen through the lens of enlightened rationality and legal entitlements, peasants with communal attachments and traditional practices were a dangerous anachronism.[46]

The acquisition of legal skills and legal knowledge may have had some value in the Highlands in the era that has been described as one of 'pro-active' landed entrepreneurship, when lairds lived on their land for most of the year with kin for tenants.[47] But in the second half of the century, with increased absenteeism and a shift towards 're-active' land management through paid factors and modernising tenants, the advocate laird had become a liability. His urban lifestyle was expensive, and the consequences were disastrous; particularly, as we shall see, when the impact of lawyers was paralleled and exceeded by that another career to which the Highland gentry gravitated: the army.

CHURCH AND MEDICINE AS CAREERS

Though not as important as the law, there were other scholarly professions in which the sons of the Highland gentry made their careers. Before the Reformation, there was a robust tradition in some families of service in the priesthood or monastic life.[48] But Presbyterian Protestantism dampened the gentry's interest in church careers, for, compared with the church in England, which was rich, with many profitable patronage positions, the church in Scotland was poor, offering modest stipends and, outside the universities, limited status. Yet this general observation was probably less relevant to the Highlands than elsewhere. Perhaps because of lower expectations of material reward, possibly because of a stronger sense of vocation within Gaelic society, and almost certainly because Highland ministers held greater authority within their communities than was usual in Lowland Scotland, the church continued to attract the sons of the gentry.

The social life and friendship networks of Highland ministers revolved around the lesser gentry and tacksmen. The higher gentry and nobility were the patrons who often paid for their university education. Many clergy had large parishes that required frequent long-distance journeying, with accommodation and hospitality in the homes of parishioners. They also travelled to the local towns for presbytery and synod meetings with other clergymen. They ran schools or took in pupils as boarders, which was a good source of income but one that required a suitable wife to manage the household. Much of their daily existence was spent farming a glebe. The Rev. Donald Sage of the parish of Resolis in Sutherland, who was the son and grandson of Gaelic ministers, wrote an account of parish life in the north of Scotland in the late eighteenth century that evoked the physicality and hard work that was the lot of the Highland clergyman.[49] It is hardly surprising that when Patrick Campbell of Barcaldine decided to send one of his younger sons to lodge with a local clergyman prior to university and a clerical career, the boy objected so loudly that his father relented and abandoned the plan.[50]

Clergymen were badly paid. A good Highland parish, such as Kilmore and Kilbride in Lorn, would yield an annual income of no more than seventy pounds in the mid-eighteenth century.[51] James Boswell observed this relative poverty during his travels of 1773. He and Johnson visited several ministers of the Church of Scotland, and their manner of living was always modest. On Coll they visited the Rev. Hector Maclean of the parish of Coll and Tiree.

> He was about seventy-seven, a decent old man in a full suit of black and a black wig. He was like a Dutch minister or one of the assembly of devines at Westminster. Mr. Johnson said he was a fine old man – was as well dressed and had as much dignity in his appearance as the dean of a cathedral . . . The old gentleman, we were told, has a valuable library, though he has but poor accommodation for it. He has no manse; only a small farmhouse and his books are kept in large chests.[52]

Yet clergymen were also esteemed in the Highlands, and they often married the younger daughters of local lairds, which gave them further status and sometimes resulted in their children inheriting estates.

One of the prominent figures in the kinship network of the Campbell family of Barcaldine in the early eighteenth century, and a close friend of Patrick Campbell, was the minister of Ardchattan, the Rev. Colin Campbell of Achnaba. He was a celebrated mathematician, he was noted for his traditional medical knowledge and for his Gaelic scholarship, and he ran a school for the sons of the local gentry. He was also a significant landowner through inheritance and marriage into the Campbell gentry.[53] A century later, another Ardchattan incumbent, Hugh Fraser, also of landed family background though not from Argyll, was closely connected with the Campbell family of Barcaldine through marriage. Although his suit was not favoured because they had hoped for a better connection for the laird's eldest sister,[54] the family were eventually reconciled to a marriage that produced several sons who went on to brilliant professional careers. Alexander, the eldest, was professor of logic at Edinburgh University, and Duncan was principal medical officer at the military hospital in Malta.[55] Unlike the earlier Ardchattan minister, Hugh Fraser's allegiances were more to his absent elite connections than to the ordinary people. Indeed, in 1834 he warned his brother-in-law Sir Duncan, living in Edinburgh, of the impact of a popular preacher making converts in Argyll, saying 'the Barcaldine property in this parish will soon become a hotbed of fanaticism'.[56]

With their sophisticated university education, linkages up and down the social hierarchy and fixed locations in their parishes, Highland clergymen were the natural collectors and guardians of information, knowledge and traditions. It was they who furnished statistical information, parish by parish, for Sir John Sinclair of Ulbster's national project in the *Statistical Accounts* in the 1790s. They were the pioneer antiquarians in the first endeavours to capture the Gaelic poetry and songs of oral tradition before it vanished from popular memory. They were also closely involved in schooling for the ordinary people – though the parish schoolmasters were mostly drawn from humbler stock.[57] As with clergymen everywhere in Scotland, ministers were particularly intimate with the lives and interests of pious gentlewomen, who were often their most enthusiastic patrons.[58] Through their urban education and frequent interactions with elite female parishioners, clergymen were among the pioneers of politeness in the midst of rude society. Clergymen were 'gentlemen'. The culture of politeness is important in this story, for it was linked to changing family attitudes that encouraged the aspirations of women to a material culture of gentility. The circumstances in which clergymen lived may have been modest, they may have decried the lures of luxury, but they influenced lairds into a more sympathetic and emotional relationships with their womenfolk, which in turn promoted domestic consumerism.

A career in the medical profession was similarly connected with the intimate and emotional lives and patronage of elite women. Indeed, in the early eighteenth century some ministers, like Campbell of Ardchattan, were also medical men. There were large numbers of medical men of gentry background living in the Highlands through much of the eighteenth century. In the century before, there had been certain gentry families, notably the Beatons, who were traditional Gaelic medical practitioners and widely represented in many parts of the Highlands.[59] Though traditional knowledge had gradually given way to university training, most areas of Highland Scotland had a medical presence, and most gentry families included medical doctors, usually drawn from the ranks of the younger sons. Donald, the youngest son of Patrick Campbell of Barcaldine, was apprenticed to an Edinburgh surgeon in the early 1730s, but died young. One of his uncles was Archibald Cameron, fourth son of the laird of Lochiel, who was originally educated for a legal career at Edinburgh University and in Paris in the 1720s but preferred medicine and chose to settle in Lochaber for his working life.[60] In the family of Rose of Kilravock, Elizabeth Rose's favourite maternal uncle and childhood correspondent in the 1750s was the distinguished physician Dr John Clephane, son of a Highland officer.[61] Elizabeth Rose's husband for a brief time in 1779 – he died within the year – was a cousin, Hugh Rose of Brea, a medical man who had served in the army and returned to the Highlands on inheriting a small estate.[62] Dr William Sinclair of Thurso was another medical laird.

Before he inherited the Freswick estate through a complex entail, Dr William Sinclair, who was the son of a Thurso doctor, had already begun to accumulate land through purchase.[63] When his father died in the mid-1760s he left his son £3,471, with a further £900 for his daughters, a fair fortune for a small-town doctor. The Sinclairs, father and son, enjoyed a close patronage relationship with the Mackay family of Bighouse, and Hugh Mackay in particular. William junior was trained through an apprenticeship in Aberdeen, attendance at the infirmary in that city along with 'shop practice', followed by a university degree in Edinburgh. He followed a classical curriculum alongside medicine. He also spent some time in London. Life in Thurso was frustrating for someone of his polite and gentlemanly credentials and aspirations. Doubtless to preserve his status, he avoided marriage and relied on his sisters for domestic support. He thought often of emigration or a military career. When he unexpectedly inherited the Freswick estate in middle age in 1794 his life was transformed. He built a new house in Thurso and married the daughter of a neighbouring laird. He later moved south to Edinburgh, where he raised his children and lived as a leisured gentleman. This medical laird found city life congenial but inevitably more expensive than Caithness, and like many another the estate was compromised.[64]

MERCHANTS AND TRADESMEN

The Highland gentry were closely connected to the pseudo-gentry professions of law, church and medicine, and these helped to shape the 'gathering and spending' of lairds and their families. But the main non-farming career destination for younger sons in the first half of the eighteenth century was the urban business apprenticeship. A career in trade was problematic for gentry landowners. In some European cultures it was unacceptable for trade to be the principal employment of a man of gentle status. In others, trade was possible as a secondary activity but was never practised full-time. In early modern Scotland, where access to trade was closely controlled by town institutions such as the craft and merchant houses, and entry required connections and capital, to engage in commerce as a primary career was socially acceptable for the gentleman. In Scotland as in England, the objects that were traded were often produced or consumed by the landed. A kinsman in trade was useful to families. The ease with which a trading career was maintained alongside landed activity and gentlemanly status is illustrated through the life and experience of Bailie John Steuart of Inverness.[65]

John Steuart, born in 1676, was the son of Alexander Steuart of the family of Kinchardine in Strathspey. The family property had been sold in 1661, and Alexander had become an apprentice-trained Inverness merchant in 1670. John entered the same trade in 1700, again following an apprenticeship. The Steuarts were connected by blood to the Highland families of Grant, Mackintosh, Macgregor, Cameron and Maclean. John's first wife, who died young, was the daughter of an Inverness merchant; his second was the daughter of Norman Macleod of Drynoch in Skye. Both marriages advanced his career, and in particular his second wife's connections in Skye, Harris and North Uist and in the west Highlands from Glengarry to the Appin peninsula, became a dominant feature of his extensive trade in oatmeal, fish, wine and spirits, timber and slates. John Steuart was factor for the earl of Moray on the lordship of Petty, a few miles from Inverness, and for lord Bute on the estate of Rosehaught in Ross-shire. One of his cousins, an Edinburgh lawyer, was the earl of Moray's man of business. Though part of a modern commercial community with trading connections from Scandinavia to Italy, the Steuart family was also distinctly Highland in its attachments and cultural preferences. Bailie John was Episcopalian in his religious practice and a closet Jacobite, though he was happy to trade with government army storemasters, and counted Edmund Burt among his friends. He filled his impressive Inverness house with expensive luxuries from England and abroad, but his wife purchased her butter and cheese from relatives in Skye and Glenelg, where she visited regularly.

John Steuart's children followed a range of careers consistent with those of the offspring of a Highland gentleman. One of his daughters married a Lowland landowner, Richard Hay Newton of Newton, and spent her life in Edinburgh and on her husband's East Lothian estate. Two were married to ship's captains. His sons had mixed fortunes, the elder tending to do better than the younger. John junior was a clerk on a sailing expedition to China for several years, and later settled in Carolina, where he was a trader and government agent. Alexander was a wine merchant in Leith. James was employed by the East India Company and had a successful career in Bombay. Allan was apprenticed as a surgeon in Inverness before going to Edinburgh University to study medicine with financial support from a Macleod relative. He was a surgeon with the Scottish Dutch regiment in the 1740s. The three youngest sons were poorly educated due to their father's failing fortunes in old age, but also eventually settled to a trading life in Carolina.

Though some of John Steuart's sons were successful, none was able to re-enter the ranks of Highland landownership. Commerce drew families into the urban arena and scattered them to far-flung places. Commercial kin were useful for their landowning families in developing estate strategies. But commerce also promoted individualism and caused family discord. George Sutherland of Rearquhar, an old-style military tacksman in the second half of the eighteenth century, had a close relationship with one of his businessman nephews, George Gun Munro, the son of a Highland medical man who was an insurance broker in London. Munro looked after much of his uncle's financial affairs in the army and from time to time helped him to run his farm. This was a reciprocal arrangement, because Munro inherited a small estate that George Sutherland helped to manage while Munro was in London. When George Gun Munro went bankrupt in the 1770s, he happily returned to Scotland and the life of a farming laird.[66] Another nephew was vastly more successful in business. This was Andrew Sutherland, a Jamaica planter, who had amassed a fortune of £26,000 but refused to do anything to help his indigent parents and sister. He preferred to 'live among his negroes', and in the eyes of his uncle, 'he will meet the due reward of his unnatural behaviour'.[67] In the Malcolm family of Poltalloch, another successful West Indies planter and merchant caused similar concern among relatives at his want of proper attention to family interests on a languishing Argyll estate.[68] It was hard to give that much thought to farming when deeply embedded in a business career.

The Campbell family of Barcaldine had numerous kin and connections by marriage that made their principal careers and incomes through trade. Duncan Campbell of Glenure, the lawyer laird, was married to Mary

Macpherson, the daughter of a successful Glenfine cattle drover. Several of her siblings were active in business in Glasgow in the mid-eighteenth century, including a sister who was a grocer and an elder brother, James, who served an apprenticeship as a merchant in that city and was a general trader in goods from largely Highland sources.[69] He joined the army in 1750 and rose to the rank of major but kept up his business interests in the form of a military provisioning company and uniform manufacture.[70] Three of Duncan's younger brothers were apprentice-trained for business careers as youths in the 1730s and 1740s. Two switched to military employment when they got the chance. Robert Campbell, the sixth son of Patrick Campbell of Barcaldine, born in 1724, stuck with business throughout his life and had a particularly close relationship with his older brother Duncan.

The working lives of the sons of Highland gentlemen who entered commerce were intimately connected with their families and relied on family networks for business support and success.[71] Robert was still a teenager when his father died in 1740, but his education in Inverary and apprenticeship in Edinburgh and Stirling was overseen by his elder brothers Colin of Glenure and Duncan the lawyer.[72] By the late 1740s he was trading on his own account and he also acted as farm manager and man of business for his older brother Alexander, the fourth in the family, who held family land on tack. When Alexander went into the army in 1746 and left for the Low Countries, Robert was given detailed instruction concerning his financial affairs with brother Colin, with a cattle drover called McNicol and with the 'Steelbowmen', a business consortium of Argyll tenants engaged in cattle rearing.[73] Robert paid his brother's bills in Edinburgh, sold a horse to Lord Glenorchy for ten guineas, took charge of a trunk and a 'clogbag', which were sent to Stirling for storage, and arranged various domestic matters at his brother's house.[74] Robert petitioned Colin in July 1748 to use his influence with Mr Campbell 'of the bank' to get Alexander a promotion. When Alexander was injured and returned home a year or so later, it was Robert who helped him to refurnish a house when he resumed farming. And when he died in 1751, his affairs were settled by Robert, who also took over the supervision of two illegitimate daughters who were lodged in Stirling.[75] This complex relationship was not dissimilar to that which brother number three, Allan, had with the eldest, Colin, when he was away in the army. It seems that among these Campbell brothers, their interests were loosely organised in groups of three in the 1740s and 1750s. Colin (soldier, laird, crown factor), Duncan (lawyer) and Allan (factor for Colin and later a soldier) made up the first group; and Alexander (tenant farmer, soldier), Archibald (merchant then soldier) and Robert comprised the second group.

Like most traders, Robert turned his hand to a variety of businesses. He sourced all manner of domestic wares, food and drink for his kin and others in the Highlands. He supplied chapmen who travelled the Highland counties. He had contacts with tailors, dressmakers, boot- and shoemakers and could undertake clothing commissions on behalf of customers. In 1750 he advised his brother Duncan on the proper dress for a judge following the latter's appointment as sheriff depute at Killin in Perthshire. He supplied Duncan with a pattern book detailing styles, colours and prices for legal clothing, and requested that the pattern book be returned quickly since it was constantly in use.[76] He organised stonemasons and slaters from Stirling to work on Colin's house in Argyllshire as well as Duncan's house in Stirlingshire. Robert travelled around the Highland fairs in the 1750s, buying and selling. He also managed the bleaching, stamping and sale of linen from his brother's Argyll estates. By the mid-1750s he was making frequent business trips to Edinburgh and had a large network of regular trading contacts, including his former apprentice masters. He had a partner in Bonawe near Killin, a vintner called William Park, through whom he transacted much of his west Highland business. Some of his central Highland business was mediated via Duncan Robertson in Crieff, where his half-brother John Campbell of Barcaldine was based for much of the year as crown factor on the Perth estates. Business in Glasgow was conducted through various kin connections, including brother Archibald (before he joined the army) and a Macpherson sister-in-law of brother Duncan.

Robert Campbell married Kitty Cunningham in 1754. His wife's brother was a military man, and through this connection Robert entered the lucrative business of regimental provisioning. His brother Duncan and his new brother-in-law lent him £1,000 to get the business going, but a year later Robert was complaining that Lord Sutherland still had not paid for his uniforms, and he was also in conflict with his business partner. Robert was falling into arrears with family debt repayments.[77] Ever the entrepreneur, he sought to extract himself from the problem through another business venture. In the early 1760s he entered into a partnership with William and Robert Adam, the architects and builders, who were neighbours from Stirlingshire, to supply paving stones from Scotland for new streets in London. It was a potentially lucrative trade, but it made enormous capital demands. He took out a bond of £1,200 from the Royal Bank of Scotland, with his brother Duncan and Major Cunningham standing as guarantors.[78]

With so many of their siblings dead by the 1760s, Duncan, the lawyer laird, relied on Robert to help him in his considerable estate and family affairs. Robert in his turn relied on Duncan for loans and legal advice. But relationships were under strain, mainly over money. By 1770, Robert's business affairs were in turmoil and his health was failing. He was suing a partner in Scotland, he was trying to end the paving partnership, and Duncan was threatening a court action to recover his investments. Robert spent most of his time in London, from where he wrote to Duncan in November 1773, 'your patience has been great, of which I am barely sensible, but consider for a moment [what] it is to serve a brother, who may one day or other, prove the best friend you ever had to you and your family'.[79] Duncan was not impressed by this appeal to family attachments, but he agreed to defer the court action in favour of repayment by instalments. Robert was effectively a bankrupt and he died in London in November 1776, a broken man. The news reached Duncan, who had not seen his brother for at least three years and was still owed a large amount of money, through a letter from a nephew. 'His affairs are in the greatest confusion and in the hands of Executors. Mr Galloway of Stirling is one and acts as such in Scotland. Mr William Adam of the Adelphi is the acting Executor in London.' Duncan was told, 'as matters are now situated, I would advise you immediately to apply to Mr Galloway [to] date your claim with him . . . if yours is a bond debt I don't imagine you will be a loser – if an open account I don't at present know what to say to it'.[80] In the event, Duncan lost out badly.[81]

THE DECLINE OF TRADE AS GENTLEMAN'S CAREER

Robert Campbell was the last of the sons of Barcaldine to be trained for a career in trade. His own sons and nephews chose to pursue military careers, with the promise of riches and leisured lifestyles. Several of his brothers, having embarked on business careers, shifted to the army as the army expanded in the 1750s. Trade was hard work requiring constant attention. The capital needed to enter business was rising. Bankruptcy was an ever-present threat and a particular problem in the volatile 1770s, when both Robert Campbell and George Gun Munro failed.[82] The businessmen who did best in the changing commercial environment were those whose family connections were business-based. There were few as successful as Malcolm of Poltalloch, the Atlantic merchant, or Andrew Sutherland, the Jamaica planter, and they were viewed with dismay in their Highland families. At the time of his death, the rise and fall of Robert Campbell's business career was a cautionary tale in the Campbell family network. But the problems of a career in business were manifestly not just those of financial instability and risk: they were also associated with perceptions of status. Business apprenticeship leading to a life in home trade was no longer regarded as an acceptable route for a 'gentleman', even though many families clearly benefited from such kin. Commerce abroad in connection with military or colonial administration was a different matter, because the route into an agency like the East India Company was either the military or legal profession, or accountancy training in one of the great trading houses in London.[83]

Trading careers had several status problems. The first arose from the fact that commercial wealth was rarely sufficient to convert into land.[84] The suburban villa with a few acres of garden was the best that most hoped for, and Scottish towns and cities were surrounded by such houses. The daily demands of a trading business also meant that most businessmen had to stay close to their places of work. Maintaining partnerships and trust within a business community was built on frequent and sometimes expensive social interactions, such as dining and drinking.[85] A business life resulted in certain kinds of consumerism, but the hours of work were long and demanding, leaving little scope for the leisured lifestyles offered by other careers. Wives were often involved in the business, which compromised family gentility and status.[86] There was a boom in industry in Scotland, but making 'things' was even more problematic. One member of the Campbell family of Barcaldine, Charles Campbell, the younger son of one of Duncan Campbell's daughters, did try his hand at handloom weaving in Glasgow in the 1780s, a 'golden age' when weaver's incomes were high and some became successful businessmen.[87] He may have been inspired by a kinsman by marriage, David Dale of New Lanark. But Charles Campbell quickly abandoned this route in life. The work was arduous and dull. Like so many of his kin, he joined the army on a junior commission, purchased through his grandmother after much cajoling, and died not long after.[88]

Part Two

The Luxury Trap: Officers and Gentlewomen

4   Military Men

INTRODUCTION

The British army expanded over the course of the eighteenth and early nineteenth centuries.[1] Colony building and defence of empire, frequent wars abroad and political policing at home transformed Britain into a 'fiscal–military state' with a large military establishment supported by a complex tax system.[2] The numbers of soldiers fluctuated according to war status, with 12,000–25,000 at the start of the century. The peacetime establishment was in the order of 18,000 in the 1750s, and the wartime establishment peaked at 68,000 in 1761 during the Seven Years War. There was another peak of over 90,000 in 1777 at the height of the American war. The Napoleonic wars pushed the numbers to over a quarter of a million.[3]

The officers comprised about a tenth of the army and included large numbers of Scots, possibly as many as a third of the total. A high proportion came from the Highlands, and there were similar numbers from Ireland.[4] There were many Scottish and Irish regiments, but men from these countries were also numerous in English regiments.[5] From the end of the century men of prominent birth, including peers and their sons, entered the army in growing numbers, as did the sons of the urban middle class.[6] Men of all backgrounds served part-time at home in militia and volunteer regiments. Although impossible to gauge with certainty, it seems likely that around 1815 about 40 per cent of all Scottish gentlemen and as many as 50 per cent of Highland gentlemen were connected with the military.[7] Despite the post-1815 'reduction', there was a 'half-pay' system to keep the army on standby in case of war, and officers tended to maintain their military titles and lifestyles beyond retirement.[8] The consequences for the Scottish gentry of both the numbers of military officers drawn from their class and the adoption of a military culture were profound.

Much has been written about the impact of the army on the politics and identity of eighteenth-century Scotland. The cult of 'Britishness', the rise of empire and the 'myths' of the Highlands are all linked to Scottish military participation.[9] The role of military recruiting on the economics and politics of Highland Scotland has generated research that mostly suggests there were real financial benefits for lairds from putting their sons and tenants into the army. As an estate strategy, it was 'more fruitful than the soil'.[10] Yet the negative impact of military experience on those who were the ordinary officers, and in particular the disastrous implications for their families of having so many kin involved in one career, has been sidestepped. The reason for this lies in the commonly held view that the army, with its privileged connections with the empire, was a source of gain for participants; though, as one notable commentator has remarked, the precise scale of the gain awaits further research.[11] The nineteenth-century hagiography of the Highland military that seeks to valorise these men into a state of near mythical status beyond the pedestrian concerns of families and their estates offers a further explanation.

In the early decades of the eighteenth century the opportunities offered by the military profession were few, though the relationship between the Highland gentry and military service was of long standing. In the golden age of clanship in the sixteenth and seventeenth centuries, men who were raised in a martial culture at home often found careers as mercenary soldiers in the service of European kings and princes.[12] Some worked independently, but certain clans also formed strong relationships with particular parts of Europe. The Perthshire Drummonds were linked to Russia; and the Mackays of Sutherland had military connections with the Calvinist Dutch states, which generated a distinct regimental presence in Holland into the eighteenth century.[13] There were similar cadres of mercenary elites in other parts of Europe. The city–states of Italy supported many extended gentry and noble families whose men routinely found employment as professional soldiers.[14] Though the men involved were a restless group of perpetual bachelors devoted to feats of physical prowess, much given to feuding and fighting among themselves, and difficult to control within families, symbolic importance was attached to this military life. Such men were trained from boyhood in fighting skills and horsemanship along with complex social skills such as dancing and conversation, to take advantage of the military patronage that took place at court. Success as a mercenary abroad was important for family prestige and was a source of wealth for a lucky few.

The collapse of the mercenary labour market in the mid-seventeenth century left an employment vacuum. The Italian gentry shifted their careers towards that other potentially lucrative 'bachelor profession', the Catholic

Church, particularly since demand for clergymen was on the rise with the Counter-Reformation. Fewer were attracted to this poorly paid profession in Scotland, though there were some clergymen lairds in the Highlands. Well-favoured older sons were trained for the growing legal profession, but for most of the Highland gentry the main alternatives were tenant farming or trade. But as in Italy, a military culture survived in popular memory and in some aspects of masculine behaviour long after real employment had evaporated, and it is not surprising that when military careers were again available with the expansion of the British army after 1750, Highland gentlemen flocked to enlist.

The great advantage of a military career over most elite employment was that it required no particular education or training. Formal officer training was restricted to the specialised engineering regiments, and though there were a number of private military academies in London by the 1750s, which were used as quasi-schools for teenage recruits, these were not compulsory.[15] The only skill that an officer needed was horsemanship, which the gentry learned as a matter of routine when children and which could be improved through attendance at one of the many commercial riding academies found in most provincial towns in the second half of the century. All other qualifications were social or cultural. According to one contemporary, the qualities 'valued in an officer were the qualities valued by the country gentry; courage, physical toughness, a determination to stand up for one's rights, a touchy sense of honour'.[16] It is not surprising that professional commentators regretted the want of formal training. 'How much better would our Army be supplied with officers than it is at present. Men would be officers by their ability, not from distaste to other professions, or a want of proper qualifications for them.'[17] He was right, for many of the sons of the Highland gentry who entered the military profession had no ability, were unqualified for other professional work and possessed a profound distaste for the alternative careers that their fathers had proposed.

The problem with a military career is that it required personal connections and cash to purchase a commission. Though officers were paid for their service, each office had a value attached to it that had to be paid up front on joining. These values varied from regiment to regiment according to prestige and they changed through time, but they tended to operate according to a clear hierarchy. In the 1750s, the junior offices of cornet or ensign, which were normally held by teenagers, cost up to £200. A lieutenancy, which was a common entry point for young enlistees, cost twice that sum. A captaincy, which was normally a promoted post, was between £500 and £1,000; a majority could cost well over £1,000 and so on, all the way up to a colonelcy, which could cost as much as £5,000.[18] These were very large sums for families with liquidity problems. But cash alone was not enough. Just getting the opportunity to make a purchase required links to a noble patron with military influence. It also required insider information and negotiating expertise from someone who was already involved in military life. The usual regimental managers and 'fixers' were majors, but military agents also managed patronage networks.[19] The purchase price was paid to the current occupant of the office, who was either about to leave the army or move up into a higher office, normally also through purchase. If the regiment was a new formation, the purchase price was paid to the colonel. The army was quite unlike any other area of career formation or income generation. It was viewed as corrupt by many, but it was so expensive to reform – since this would have required compensation for all officers – that it survived unchanged until the later nineteenth century. The 'purchase' was a little like a business investment, only the capital did not need careful monitoring once the investment was made. Unless you were killed or behaved badly the value of a commission remained intact. But the lifestyles of officers were more attractive than those of businessmen, which accounts for why so many Highlanders abandoned businesses for a life in the army when the opportunities presented.

PATRICK CAMPBELL'S SONS

The eagerness to move into army careers is well illustrated by the Campbell family of Barcaldine. Patrick Campbell had eight sons, who came to adulthood in the 1720s through to the 1740s. His plans for their future were extensively discussed within the kin network and were consistent with the usual gentry strategy for maximising the interests of the family as a whole. As we have seen, the elder two, John and Colin, were destined to be practical landowners and were educated as 'gentlemen', partly with private tutors and partly in a lawyer's office, where they gained a smattering of the type of legal knowledge that was useful to modernising lairds. The third son, Duncan, was trained to be a professional lawyer. The fourth son, Allan, was educated in a similar manner to the elder two, with the intention of becoming a tenant on the family estate and a 'man of business' for his elder brother. Alexander, the fifth son, was intended by his father to be a clergyman, but this plan was abandoned. In the absence of other avenues and mindful of cost, Alexander, along with the next two sons, Archibald and Robert, were each provided with merchant apprenticeships. The youngest son, Donald, was apprenticed to an Edinburgh 'cherurgeon' for three years to be trained in the practical skills of the surgeon.

None of Patrick Campbell's sons was destined for a military career, and there were few soldiers among their kin. But with military opportunities rising, it is not surprising that five of these men in adulthood turned in that direction. The youngest, Donald, was the first. He qualified as a surgeon in 1734 and set his sights on the navy, which was the largest element of the military establishment at the time. According to a contemporary career manual, this was the best way of making a good income and possibly even a fortune through practical medicine. The manner of this is worth quoting, for the basic principle of a modest salary greatly enhanced by 'perks' and prizes also applied to office-holding in the army.

> The salary of a surgeon of the Navy is but inconsiderable, that is the pay he immediately receives from the Crown is but small; but his perquisites depend upon the largeness of the ship. He has forty shillings for every clap or pox of which he cures . . . he has a chest of medicines at the government expense . . . and is allowed for slops . . . all of which put together make a surgeon's place in a sixty-gun ship to be worth near two hundred pounds per annum in time of peace, besides his share of prizes in time of war, in the division of which he is ranked as Lieutenant.[20]

But Donald's career was short and unrewarding. He died at sea in 1738, a victim of fever, aged twenty-five, unmarried and poor. His father and brothers were sorely grieved.

By the early 1740s, with war in Europe and an uprising at home, four of the sons of Campbell of Barcaldine were about to join the army, mostly to serve with the earl of Loudon's regiment. Colin, the second brother, enjoyed the privileges and status of the farming laird, but he also craved the excitement and prizes that the army seemed to offer. He served on and off for nearly ten years and rose to the rank of captain, but was injured and returned home to marriage and farming. Allan, the fourth son, abandoned farming for a long military career. He started as lieutenant and rose to major, served in North America and the Caribbean, but was also stationed for many years at Chatham Barracks and in Ireland. He was still in service when he died in the late 1770s. He never married and owned no property and little fortune.[21] Alexander, once destined for the ministry but apprenticed in Glasgow instead, had soon abandoned trade and, like Allan, spent several years as a tacksman on his brother's estate before joining the army. He was seriously injured in 1748, spent two years as a half-pay lieutenant hoping to recover, retired to resume farming in Argyll, and died in 1751. He too was single and poor. Archibald did stick with his commercial pursuits in Glasgow for a while, but he was bored by a working life of long hours and little excitement.

> I can only give my mind to forming encampments, sieges and battles, my mind is so entirely hurried in castle building that now I'm a Captain then a Colonel sometimes a General but in a few minutes coming to myself after I have moved in those high stations I find the General reduced to a fifth brother that has neither credit nor money to purchase an Ensign's staff.[22]

The money was raised and he joined the army on a junior commission. Single and poor, he died of fever in 1754,

Three of Patrick Campbell's four younger sons died prematurely and in wretched circumstances. They were unmarried and undistinguished. None of the brothers generated wealth or achieved high office from their time in the army, which was the primary personal and family motive for adopting such careers. One brother had a long and safe military service spent mostly in Britain and Ireland and made a gentleman's living. But he could not afford a wife or home because domestic postings offered fewer 'perks' and prizes than service abroad. The regiment and the barracks were his life, and when he was dying in middle age his only comfort was a paid nurse and modest lodgings in an English provincial spa town.[23] The three brothers that eschewed the army, and the one who left early, lived longer, were married and had homes and thriving families. Their personal and emotional lives were similar to those of their father's generation, when all sons could marry and support a family.

MILITARY ENTREPRENEURS

Some men who entered the army as adults in the mid-eighteenth century were successful in exploiting the opportunities that the military represented, not through war prizes or spectacular promotions, but through businesses that were connected with other members of their families. They were, in effect, military entrepreneurs. A typical case was Major James Macpherson (b. 1725), the eldest son of a Highland cattle drover and brother-in-law to Duncan Campbell the lawyer.[24] Coming from a sophisticated commercial background, it is not surprising that James was apprenticed to a Glasgow merchant in his teens with the intention of following a trading career. He was in business for several years with modest success, but in 1761, at a high point of military recruitment for the Seven Year War, James, who was a bachelor in his mid-thirties, travelled to London to seek an army commission at his own expense. By exploiting family patronage as well as his Glasgow business connections, he gained a place in the 42nd Regiment of the Royal Highlanders and spent the next two years serving in England and Ireland.

James Macpherson returned to Glasgow, the regimental headquarters, at the end of the war, and the rest of his unspectacular but lucrative career was spent in Scotland. He was a captain of Edinburgh Castle in 1775 and major in charge of Dumbarton Castle by 1778. Throughout these years he was heavily involved in recruiting for his regiment and in hunting out commissions for his younger relatives. He was also engaged in the business of military supply, which generated a personal profit sufficient to allow him to marry and purchase a small estate while still a serving officer. When he left the army in October 1778 he had a comfortable income from his property and £800 in cash from the regiment on leaving, 'a little more than the price of my commission',[25] which he invested in a high-yielding life insurance policy for the benefit of his family. But he continued to maintain a series of business interests linked to the army, building on both his kin connections and connections forged during his early commercial career in Glasgow. The most important was a venture to supply uniforms to Highland regiments, which he ran in partnership with a Glasgow textile manufacturer. When he died in 1789 whilst visiting Lochfinehead, 'for the benefit of my health', he left his wife and children with a comfortable fortune.[26]

James Macpherson was not unique. Another marriage connection of the Campbell family of Barcaldine had a similarly entrepreneurial military career in the 1750s and '60s. This was Major Cunningham (later a colonel), brother of Kitty Cunningham, who had married Robert Campbell the Stirling merchant. Cunningham provided financial support for Robert's ventures into military provisioning in the late 1750s and also helped to negotiate exclusive contracts for uniform supply for the Argyll and Sutherland regiments. He was a military entrepreneur and regimental 'fixer' in both London and Stirling. He also acted as guarantor for loans to his brother-in-law's businesses. Robert Campbell's entry into the lucrative business of military provisioning was entirely determined by the opportunities offered through the military careers of his various kin. It was also a product of the fact that he spent so much time in London negotiating military patronage and purchases through the contacts provided by Cunningham on behalf of his Campbell brothers and nephews.

Robert's first venture to England was occasioned by the death of his military brother Archie, who died of fever in Naples in late 1754. The local agents for the London–Scottish merchants William and John Main handled his affairs in Italy. As the businessman in the family, Robert was given the task of settling Archie's accounts and he visited London in the summer of 1755 to deal with the matter in person.[27] Robert was back in London in September

1757 on behalf of brother Duncan to gather information about the availability of commissions for Duncan's teenage sons, and particularly for Sandy, an illegitimate son raised within the family, whose education in Stirling was overseen by Robert. He was deputed to make contacts with the earl of Breadalbane both by letter and in person, and in mid-November he was able to write that he had seen his lordship in his London townhouse and secured an ensign's commission in General Holme's regiment, which was then stationed at Edinburgh Castle.[28] His success in this petition for patronage owed much to Major Cunningham and his London firm of military agents. Cunningham had provided background information on the state of recruiting. There were 8,000 troops about to be made into regiments of 900 strong, with a captain, two lieutenants and an ensign for each company of 100 men. Cunningham also ensured that when Sandy joined the regiment his path was smoothed by personal recommendations to the senior officers. Cunningham's presence in London, his networking in elite society and his information gathering were not entirely disinterested. He benefited financially from his brother-in-law's businesses and was himself promoted to colonel just a few months later.[29]

Robert Campbell's London ventures flourished during the Seven Years War, which saw a major expansion in military recruitment and military-based businesses, mostly operating through the patronage of key aristocrats and military agents in the capital. And through being in London so frequently, and in regular contact with other Scots, Robert Campbell soon spotted further opportunities, of which the most successful involved laying pavements on newly made streets with stone supplied from a quarry in Fife.[30] His partner in this was William Adam the builder, brother of the famous architect Robert Adam and a friend from youth. William Adam had several military concerns, and in the 1780s, years after the pavement company had ended and Robert was dead, he ran another enterprise with one of the Barcaldine family supplying bricks for building work at Chatham dockyards.[31] The founding of the pavement company in 1763 coincided with the end of the Seven Years War, and Duncan again asked Robert for help in dealing with young kinsmen who found themselves unemployed in London when their regiments were 'reduced'. Robert wrote to Duncan about his third son Patrick, who had been at a private military school at Enfield near London for about a year, 'where a number of young officers are taught the theory of war'.[32] 'Let me know what you want have done with Patrick when the regiment is broke. Do you want him home, or to remain at a military academy in London for a year' – or would Duncan rather that he tried to get the boy, still in his teens, into an old regiment? In the event, Patrick went home to his father to learn 'the country business'. But the other son, Sandy, continued in London.

Sandy Campbell had been the first of five siblings to enter the army as a teenage recruit. In 1763 he was in his early twenties, a half-pay lieutenant in Colonel Perrier's regiment, recently married to his childhood sweetheart Mally and looking for employment.[33] He was offered work by his uncle Robert as overseer in the pavement business, with a salary of £140, which was similar to his military pay. But he complained to Duncan that the pavement business did not suit because his uncle demanded too much of his time. In 1765 he urged his father to lend him £300 to go into the coal trade in London. Duncan refused. He next requested a tenancy of a farm in Argyll, but a father who well appreciated his son's lack of training in either business or farming denied this request also. Sandy considered going to America in 1766, having heard something of the opportunities there from his uncle Allan the soldier and Captain John Campbell of Melford, an Argyll neighbour, who visited Sandy and Mally in London on their way home from the West Indies. But instead of America, Sandy and his family returned to Scotland in 1767 and settled in North Queensferry on the Firth of Forth, where he would try his hand at a business he already knew. He raised a loan on his half-pay as an officer and rented a quarry and a house for the family, with a garden for a cow and vegetables. There was accommodation for quarrymen and a shop for his wife to run as a grocery for the ferry passengers. He traded in meal and quarry stone and had a contract for pavement work in Glasgow. His business affairs did not flourish, though, and in March 1774 he was bankrupt and in prison. He debts amounted to about £400 and his assets, including house furniture, to no more than £80. With this and another advance on his army pay, he was able to settle with creditors at 5s in the pound. The failure finally turned his eyes to America, and in June 1774 Sandy and Mally Campbell sailed from Greenock with their three children and almost 200 Scottish emigrants, many of them Highlanders, for the three-month passage to New York. He carried letters of introduction from various kin to British army officers and merchants. The family moved from New York to Boston in 1775, and with credit of £300 established a grocery business, dealing mainly with the army. With rebellion in full force, Sandy also joined one of the local regiments as a volunteer and fought at Bunker Hill.

By 1777 Sandy was involved in numerous activities, generating a remarkable income and supporting a grand lifestyle. His friends were impressed.

> In the first place . . . Sandy is a Captain in Mcleans, in the 2nd place he is Brigade Major to De-Lancys Corps of York Independent Companies, in the 3rd place he is wood cutter general to the army and in the 4th place he has got a Lieutenancy for his son (a boy about 3 or 4 years old)

in Mcleans regiment. In short ... his income, one way or another, cannot be less than £1000 or £1200 per annum ... He has a country house on Long Island and a town house in New York.[34]

By February 1779, Sandy was also a privateer – the captain and owner of one boat and a shareholder in another. He was wealthy, but his situation was perilous. His relatives urged him to leave the army and bring his profits home, but he ignored their advice. He was killed in action that year, and his property was confiscated. Mally Campbell, with two daughters and son, returned to Barcaldine to gather her strength and recover what was left of the family fortunes. Some feeble petitions were made for compensation for the loss of the American property, but her male relatives were not particularly interested in the plight of a widow of an illegitimate kinsman. She was finally granted a government pension of £5 for each of the girls, and with the small capital she still owned in Scotland, Mally went into business in Glasgow in 1786 as a tea retailer. Her two daughters were apprenticed to a mantua maker. She did well in Glasgow and moved back to London in the early 1790s to establish a business in Oxford Street and place the girls in a fashionable mantua-making house nearby. Through family connections, her only son, now a teenager, entered the army as an ensign. His mother paid for the purchase and doubtless had high hopes for his future; but he was dead within a couple of years.[35]

THE 'RESPECTABLE' MILITARY GENTLEMEN

These various military entrepreneurs, both in and out of the army, belonged to a generation that viewed commerce as a socially acceptable career for the sons and even the daughters of the gentry. Men like James Macpherson, Major Cunningham or even poor Sandy Campbell and his wife combined entrepreneurial flair with military opportunism and were the ones who benefited most from the army, for they could expect to generate a handsome profit, often in conjunction with non-military kin, even when they were not at war. These men were also of an age when relatively few entered the military profession. As the century progressed, however, two developments trapped the gentry in Scotland, and the Highland gentry in particular, into sending their sons at an increasingly young age and in growing numbers into military employments. The first was the changing perception of business as a respectable avenue in life consistent with gentry status.[36] The second, which was connected to the first, was the growing trend for Scottish gentry families, including those from fairly modest backgrounds, to educate their sons at

English boarding schools to give them valuable network connections and anglicised gentlemanly credentials.[37] Education of this type was expensive, as were the other still-gentlemanly careers, such as the law. For families faced with a narrowing set of expensive options for their sons, the army was an attractive alternative, providing a quasi-education and employment from an early age at relatively small initial cost, and also providing opportunities for social networking within an anglicised context. Youths, often as young as twelve, were sent into regular regimental life with little or no preliminary training. Commissions purchased for teenage entry as a coronet or ensign were cheaper than several years at a decent school followed by university and a legal or medical training. An officer earned an income and could rise through the ranks if lucky in war, or if his family paid for promotion. The son in question was out of the way and fully occupied under male supervision, which was a particular boon to widowed mothers.[38] Illegitimate sons were easily sent off to seek their fortunes elsewhere. Useless and delinquent sons were similarly dispatched.

For a younger son and for the family into which he was born, the army quickly became an attractive employment, and those who still found themselves involved in farming or commerce yearned for the military option. This is well illustrated by Patrick Campbell, the third son of the lawyer laird Duncan.[39] In 1763, at the end of the Seven Years War and having spent some months in training at an English military academy, Patrick was a compulsory 'reduced' half-pay lieutenant in his mid-teens.[40] His uncle, the businessman Robert, who was based in London at the time of Patrick's 'reduction', suggested that the boy might be found a commission in a regular regiment, which was probably what he wanted for himself – but his father though otherwise: a regular commission was expensive. Patrick was called back to the Highlands, and after much negotiation Duncan got him the tenancy of a forfeited farm in 1767, from where he subsequently operated a cattle-droving partnership. But Patrick's ambition was always to return to the army, which he managed to achieve in 1775 when, for the cost of a quota of recruits, made possible by a Highland levee, Patrick Campbell, aged about thirty, entered Colonel Simon Fraser's 71st Highland Regiment at the rank of captain. In his opinion, being a field officer was a route in life that was 'far more respectable and I am sure profitable . . . than being a Morvern drover or tenant.'[41] He later sold all of his farming interests in Scotland to purchase a majority.

As a motive for being in the army, 'respectability', with all the contemporary resonance of public regard and status, was new to this second military generation of the Highland gentry. The generation before was motivated by profit and adventure. As Patrick fully appreciated from his youthful experience in London, to be an officer in the army was to be a gentleman, in receipt of a gentleman's income. Even during peacetime, many officers were granted half-pay status to keep them in war readiness, and the half-pay of a captain was just enough to maintain the decencies of gentlemanly life for a single man. Of course, the average officer income from military duties alone – estimated as £100 per year mid-century and £200 by 1815[42] – was not enough to place him on a level with those who derived their incomes from land (assuming rents were paid), law or even modestly successful commerce. But it was a socially acceptable income, associated with a cosmopolitan, leisured and high-status lifestyle. Moreover, although membership of the military establishment did not necessarily provide an income for life, it did give a status for life, for even in retirement, officers were known by their military titles. In an age when the family basis of British status hierarchies were challenged by new occupations and new types of wealth, an officer in 'His Majesty's Army or Navy' had an easily recognised and valued position. As a well-informed commentator on gentry affairs remarked: 'The profession, either navy or army, is its own justificant. It has every thing in its favour; heroism, danger, bustle, fashion. Soldiers and sailors are always acceptable in society. No body can wonder that men are soldiers and sailors.'[43] Soldiers and sailors could, if lucky, advance their status through military service. This was probably the greatest attraction of the military career over others, though some elements of elite society viewed with disdain a profession that was 'a means of bringing persons of obscure birth into undue distinction, and raising men to honours which their fathers and grandfathers never dreamt of'.[44]

From the middle decades of the eighteenth century, Scottish gentry boys grew up with military aspirations. In some families almost every son became a soldier, and those who were deliberately kept out of the military line, normally the eldest, yearned for the army life. James Boswell (b. 1740), the eldest son of an Ayrshire lawyer laird, who pestered his father to no effect, is probably the best documented.[45] Patrick Campbell, the young man who in 1775 felt it was more 'respectable' to be an officer than a tenant and drover, was a close contemporary of James Boswell, and all of Patrick's brothers – except the eldest who, like Boswell, followed his father into the legal profession – also became soldiers in their teens. When Patrick eventually re-entered the army as a captain, he was sent to America, where he married a Quaker heiress with a family background in trade. But his health was compromised by service, and he left the army to live in New York, where he died in 1782, a wealthy man in his late thirties with a wife and son who remained abroad.[46] Over the course of his military career he not only made himself a fortune – using his profession to achieve prosperity through marriage – he also travelled widely, was sophisticated in the ways of the world and was familiar with metropolitan life. This was in striking contrast to his father and elder brother, both provincial lawyers, who never travelled beyond Britain and only rarely went further than Edinburgh. The army, more than any other employment with which the Highland gentry was associated, was characterised by extensive travel and social mixing among the national elite. Even men who had been in the army and retired to Scotland continued to travel at home and overseas; a habit once formed that was hard to break. A classic case was General Thomas Graham of Balgowan, Lord Lyndoch, a Perthshire laird and Peninsular War hero, who journeyed the length of Europe in retirement, visiting the sites of great battles, and was one of the founder members of a London gentleman's club for officers.[47] Many who left the army and retired to private life never returned to their homes, but like Patrick Campbell remained abroad, or settled in London or one of the English leisure towns

The polite sociability with which officers were characterised and that made the profession so attractive to many was partly a consequence of living in circumstances where there was little active soldiering to be done and much time available for hospitality and conviviality. Indeed hospitality in the English gentlemanly manner was an increasingly important part of the social expectations of an officer, and commonly resulted in an expenditure that many could ill afford. Social mixing was also necessary for securing patronage and promotion – the more so during peace than in war, because peace brought reduction in employment opportunities. Officers had to play the patronage game to get on in life, which partly depended on family connections but increasingly relied on face-to-face sociability within the right circles and the personal credentials of the individual seeking advance. This is revealed by the life and experience of Colin Campbell, another military son of Duncan Campbell the lawyer laird, who based his attempts to secure military advance through his private social life and sophisticated networking in London.

Colin Campbell was a career officer from his teens.[48] His entry into regimental life in the early 1760s was organised by his maternal uncle, Major James Macpherson (the soldier–entrepreneur whose history is sketched above), and he served for most of his career with the 42nd Royal Highland Regiment, rising from ensign to lieutenant and finally to captain and stationed, variously, in Scotland, India, England and Ireland. His years in India from 1781–3, when he suffered serious injury, coincided with the Second Mysore War. He arrived back home to spend two years on sick leave, attempting to recover in Bath and London, with occasional visits to his family in the north. Yet despite poor health, he enjoyed a vigorous social life, networked furiously, engaged in various status-enhancing strategies and was one of the early members of the prestigious London-based Highland Society, devoted to promoting Highland interests under the patronage of the duke of Argyll.[49] It is not surprising that at about this time, Colin Campbell, who was a second son, began to lobby his elder brother to grant him the title and tenancy of Glenure, the secondary Barcaldine estate. Having achieved the tenancy he was able to call himself Captain Colin Campbell of Glenure and in effect have two status titles, one linked to his military profession and one linked to his gentry family background. On returning to military service, which meant a return to garrison duties in Scotland and then Ireland, this ambitious man turned his attention to another device for getting on the world – marriage. Like his younger brother in America, Colin Campbell married an heiress, and by the time he died of fever – the legacy of his India days – in 1797, he had become the proprietor of an Irish estate near Cork.[50]

Patrick and Colin Campbell both died young as a consequence of their military service. This was typical of military men. But, atypically, both were successful in their personal lives, for they used their military status and gentlemanly credentials to achieve wealth through socially ambitious marriages. Men of this generation only rarely considered business as a means for getting on in life, and although they might aspire to own or tenant a Highland estate, they were also averse to practical farming. Their profession encouraged a culture of leisured politeness that was well appreciated by contemporaries and viewed with contempt by many. An illustration of this occurs in the comic novel *Marriage* by Susan Ferrier, first published in 1818 but referring to the generation before.[51] In it, she describes a Highland gentleman and his military sons. Douglas of Glenfern owns a small estate with 'young plantations' and 'dingy turnip fields' and is a practical 'improving' farmer living on his property. He is a 'good looking old man, with something the air of a gentleman, in spite of the inelegance of his dress, his rough manner and provincial accent'. His two sons were raised to the military profession. The elder, a retired major, has inherited a small estate from an uncle. The younger, a recently married captain, absent without leave from his regiment and in need of an income to support a fashionable English wife, is offered a farm comprising 'three thousand and seventy-five acres of good sheepwalk' and has a good house, offices and peat stacks – 'no finer, freer-aired situation in a' Scotland', according to the laird. 'The air's sharpish, to be sure, but fine and bracing; and you have a braw peat-moss at your back to keep you warm.' Glenfern, in the usual manner of farming lairds and their sons, is willing to advance the 'stocking and steading' to help his son, who is 'perfectly ignorant of country matters', along with practical assistance – 'I shall put ye upon a method, and provide ye wi' a grieve; an' if you are active, and your wife managing, there's nae fear o' you.' He also has 'plans and proposals for building dykes, draining mosses, etc', and from such a farm, 'wi' gude management', he expects to produce an income of just over £200 pounds per annum, which was similar to a captain's pay. Accustomed to a more comfortable way of life, Captain Douglas is appalled by the proposition. To the great disgust of his father and Highland relatives, he returns to London to a life of mindless luxury with his wife's family.

In this fictional case, as in real experience, it was the practice of placing young teenagers in commissions, which was popular from the Seven Years War until banned by government in the early nineteenth century, that was most damaging to Highland families.[52] Putting boys in the army not only robbed the Highland gentry of their kin connections in urban business or commercial farming, it removed boys at an impressionable age from the controlling influences of the family and led to an early exposure to 'English' gentlemanly status systems that put a high premium on politeness and leisure. Boys who entered the army as youngsters were not trained or educated for anything that was useful to the family, other than being in the army. This might not have been a problem if the army were no more than an expedient for getting rid of surplus men, but sending boys off into the army at an impressionable age also exposed them and their kin to the 'luxury trap'.

THE LUXURY TRAP

As shown in the real and fictional biographies sketched above, soldiers were remarkable for their cosmopolitan sociability beyong the borders of Scotland. At a time when increasing numbers of the British gentry, male and female, were travelling for leisure and consumer opportunities, the Scottish military officer was doing the same as part of his profession.[53] This was doubtless important for a developing sense of Britishness and may have had other benefits for Scotland, but it also introduced a growing element of the gentry to levels of expenditure they could ill afford, which damaged their families and gave rise to expectations born out of the 'pleasures of the imagination' that resulted in luxury, hedonism, excess and despair.

In a regimental system where men of modest background mixed with men of wealth, the expenditure norms of the latter set the tone for the former. Officers were expected to provide their own uniforms and horses, which could be very expensive. Indeed, they were often in debt before they even joined their regiments. Major Allan Campbell warned his brother Duncan of this when Duncan was preparing his son Colin for life in the army.

You'll find it necessary to set him down in London a free man provided with shirts, stockings, a suit of plain blew or brown cloaths and other little necessaries . . . I can assure you that all the pay that he is to receive since he came to the regiment will be little enough to defray the expense of two suits of regimentals, fees of commission, sword, sash, gorget, espatroon, regimental hat etc. etc.[54]

Mess costs could be high, making some regiments prohibitive to all but the very rich, and the costs of the fashionable social life into which many officers were drawn could be great. It was easy to raise a loan on the security of an officer's salary, and many young men and even teenage boys found themselves in considerable financial difficulty soon after entering military life. The cost to their fathers was often very much more than the cost of commissions, and family relationships were consequently strained. Family correspondences were full of exhortations to greater financial prudence from fathers to sons, and contemporary fiction gives many cautionary tales of improvident and un-principled officers.[55] The two youngest sons of Duncan Campbell of Glenure, James and Hugh, contracted such high debts that their father eventually abandoned them to their creditors. From the start of his military career, Hugh was vastly interested in fine clothing. In 1778 he wrote from New York:

Dear Father, I am sorry that I am under the necessity of drawing upon you for forty pounds Stirling: but I can assure you that it was consistent with nature to keep up the character of an officer and gentleman . . . I am not a gambler nor am I a man of gallantry, but after all my money goes and I don't know how rightly.[56]

Keeping up the character of an officer and gentleman not only involved costly clothing but the maintenance of horses and packs of hunting dogs in some cases.[57] There were servants and attendants, and also the furniture and paraphernalia of domestic life and hospitality, which frequently travelled with an officer even when on active duty. During the Napoleonic Wars, Colonel Mackay of Bighouse had his personal piper and a butler with him when he travelled around Europe. The butler later worked in Sutherland as the parish schoolmaster and domestic factotum for the Bighouse family.[58] Military men of the later eighteenth century were famous for the tendency to high consumption and their search after comfort in situations of hardship. This was a far cry from the austerity and restraint that was commonly recommended in the military manuals of the day.[59] James Boswell, always attracted by the glamour of military men, noted such a case in his travels through the Highlands in 1773, when he and Johnson visited Sir Allan Maclean on Mull.

Sir Allan, like all other officers, who, though by their profession obliged to endure fatigues and inconveniences, are peculiarly luxurious . . . I take it the suffering, or at least the contemplating of hardships to which officers are accustomed (for from Sir Allan's account even of the American expeditions, it appeared that though the poor common soldiers are often wretchedly off, the officers suffer little, having their commodious camp equipage, and their chocolate, and other comforts carried along in little room, and prepared by their men, who are most subservient beings), makes them fonder of all indulgences.[60]

Such conspicuous consumption when allied to gambling and 'gallantry' – that is, the pursuit of fashionable women and heiress hunting – ensured that many military men spent more than they ever earned and were locked into the pitiful business of keeping up appearances to get by in life.[61] Excitement, extravagance, an excessive preoccupation with clothing and outward image and an immoderate engagement in expensive sociability gave the military profession its fashionable image. But members of the profession could also be easily characterised as reckless, foolish and morally suspect. Many officers were libertines who brought despair to their loved ones, and many ruined their family fortunes or were a constant drain on family resources. Each of the three Barcaldine brothers – John the laird, Duncan the lawyer, Robert the merchant – encountered serious problems with their military sons. The scandal caused by David, the youngest son of Robert, though never detailed, was such that 'I fear he has ruined his fathers family if he is catched he'll surely be hanged'.[62] David was partly responsible for his father's bankruptcy and, in the eyes of relatives, drove Robert into an early grave.

The impact on family finances inevitably extended to family estates and tenancy arrangements. In its organisation and culture, the army operated to maintain a hierarchical status quo that placed a high value on links with land. Land was the basis of status and it was also, in a practical sense, an important source of military recruits in some areas at certain points in time.[63] Thus men of gentry background who were unlikely to inherit land in their own right nevertheless sought to connect land ownership to their military office as a device for improving their own status within the officer corps. Such behaviour was not unique to soldiers – it was also seen among lawyers. But it was pronounced in this profession and did have a negative impact on the use of land in many parts of Scotland and particularly in the Highlands, where increasingly debt-ridden landlords were eager to give tenancies to military relatives in return for secure rental payments from guaranteed military pay. The tenants on Peter Grant's farms at Rothiemurchus during the Napoleonic wars were mostly half-pay officers who had returned to their native Highlands in middle life or old age, having served in the army from an early age. They were active in the local volunteer regiments, which held the older elements of the clan together in the countryside, providing a focus for masculine sociability and leisure, and they were popular with the ordinary people.[64] But they rarely benefited the estate.

The problem with military tenants by the later eighteenth century was they were not good farmers. Career soldiers who entered the army in their teens were not familiar with farming practice, and given their tendency to travel, they were not resident on their farms for sufficient spans of time to allow them to develop any agricultural knowledge or skills. As Alexander Campbell of Barcaldine, the lawyer laird, wrote to his brother, Captain Colin Campbell, when the latter pleaded for the tenancy of Glenure in the 1780s, 'you are not accustomed to the country business'.[65] Because the properties that were tenanted by soldiers were small and most officers could not afford to employ an agent or factor, these farms often languished. Their purpose was prestige. So when Alexander Campbell finally and reluctantly granted his brother the property and title of Captain Colin Campbell of Glenure, his fears were realised. Colin rarely visited the estate, and most of his interest in the property was invested in building a new high-status dining room onto the house and commissioning a new suite of dining room furniture.[66] Relationships were strained, the brothers argued over an inheritance from their mother and all communication ceased for over ten years.[67] During his mature adult life in the last two decades of the eighteenth century, Alexander Campbell of Barcaldine deliberately cut all contact with three of his four younger soldier brothers, mainly over financial matters. His older 'natural' soldier brother Sandy, and his other younger soldier brother Patrick, were already dead by the early 1780s. Alexander was never to meet Patrick's wife or son, who remained in America; he never met the Irish wife and children of Colin; and he abandoned the impoverished widow and children of Sandy to their own devices.

FAMILY FORMATION

For the Campbells of Barcaldine, as with other families, the resort to military careers for younger sons became increasingly necessary for short-term financial and status gains, but it was also increasingly damaging to long-term family relationships and family finances. Fathers and elder brothers now found it nearly impossible to control the behaviour of their military kin in the interests of the family once they were launched on their military careers and motivated by self- and not family concerns. Another group who suffered were women. The purchase system made enormous demands, and raising the necessary lump sum to get a young man into office could pose financial difficulties. One way that gentry families sought to get access to capital sums for the purchase of commissions was to target those members of the family with assets but limited intrinsic economic or production value for the family as a whole; thus widows and older spinsters with annuities were frequently under pressure to help out. The elderly Mary Macpherson, estranged wife of Duncan the lawyer, was petitioned repeatedly by her grandson Charles Campbell to buy him a commission in the 1770s.[68] In the early nineteenth century, Lady Louisa Stuart, a middle-aged spinster living on a modest annuity, was asked on several occasions by her widowed and impecunious sister Lady Caroline Portarlington to give up significant sums to purchase teenage commissions for her younger sons, as neither the sisters' wealthy brother nor Lady Caroline's elder son was willing to help.[69]

Widows and older spinsters were invariably marginalised, and the rise in military careers worsened their position. The fact that the military provided the gentry with a socially acceptable avenue for disposing of surplus males – one, moreover, that put responsibility onto the son to make his own fortune – was attractive to families. Unfortunately, there were no equivalent routes in life for surplus gentlewomen: and surplus gentlewomen there were, particularly as more and more men entered the army, for rates of marriage among officers were low, many died young and those that married often did so outwith Scotland. The 'spinster problem', which was endemic in landed families, was partly a consequence of mass employment in the military profession. The cost to families of maintaining their unmarried female kin was considerable and growing, for as with sons, by the second half of the eighteenth century the earlier route of commercial apprenticeships for unmarried daughters was no longer consistent with gentry status, though many women of gentle birth were forced into such a life. The history of the children of William Sinclair, second son Sir James Sinclair of Mey in Caithness, who died in 1792 leaving many debts and little provision for five teenage daughters and as many sons, is a poignant account of desperate endeavours to cling to gentry status. The siblings were scattered in all directions. The boys looked for fortunes overseas and died young. One of the girls was a dressmaker, one a governess and another was a housekeeper. Two were married below their rank. The husband of one abandoned his wife and the other defrauded the sisters. They all looked to their eldest brother Lieutenant (later Captain) John Sinclair, of the 79th Regiment for help and support. With his military contacts with their principal family patron, the earl of Caithness, he rendered some assistance, but he died in 1815 leaving an illegitimate daughter who was taken in by the sisters to add to their burdens. Two years later they were being sued by Lord Caithness over family finances going back over twenty years, and they were still being pursued by a tailor in Glasgow with an account due by their dead military brother.[70]

In an age of rising family consumption, the Highland gentry, whether knowingly or otherwise, used the army as a useful device to limit the numbers of their sons and daughters who could marry. Most spinsters were destined for a fate of genteel, celibate, marginalised poverty, in much the same way that most of the men they might have married were destined as soldiers for a fate of genteel, unmarried – though not necessarily celibate – poverty beyond the shores of Scotland. The illegitimate children of soldiers, of whom there were many, were not supported to the same degree as the natural children of earlier generations, because they were mostly in places unconnected with the family estate. Complex inheritance disputes also arose out of the irregular marital status of the Highland gentry's military kin. In the Sinclair family of Freswick, for instance, the heir to John Sinclair, the Caithness lawyer laird, was his eldest son William, a lieutenant in the 78th Regiment in the 1770s and a cause of 'much trouble and distress from his extravagant habits'. In despair of a legitimate line of succession, and with the death of his only other child, John Sinclair executed a strict entail on his estate in 1775 to determine that it went to someone who was worthy: 'A cousin or nephew are equal with me in the scale. Whoever merits most will be preferable.' This measure resulted in a favoured distant relative, Dr William Sinclair of Thurso, eventually succeeding to the estate. The entail was a cause of great family discord.[71]

Yet the life of a military bachelor was not always one of dissolute impropriety, and some did manage to support a farming presence in the Highlands when they were useful to patrons. A well-documented case is that of George Sutherland of Rearquhar (b. 1720), who farmed a small estate that he held on tack from the earl of Sutherland from 1761 to his death in 1815[72] He was a military tacksman of the old school, the fourth son of a military tacksman. He joined the army in 1745 as a foot soldier in the ranks of the Scots Brigade in the Dutch Service, and served for twelve years before getting his first commission on merit at the start of the Seven Years War. He was in his late thirties, and it must have been galling to see teenage boys buying their way into the same office. But his was a different sort of military career to theirs. He was granted his first land on lease by his patron, the earl of Sutherland, to secure a parliamentary vote in county elections, and though he spent much of his time in the regular army he was mostly based in northern Scotland, where his principal duties were political policing and recruiting. He was a useful figure in the government management of the Highlands, and his steady rise through the ranks reflected this fact. When the earl of Sutherland purchased the Skelbo estate in 1787, Major George Sutherland was granted the tack of Rearquhar for 'all the days of his natural life' for an annual rent of just £43. The income from his sub-tenants was greater, as his noble patron well appreciated. This property, which he visited most years, was managed at a distance through the good offices of nephews, including William Taylor, the postmaster and sheriff's clerk in the nearby town of Tain, who was another of the earl of Sutherland's patronage clients. Some of his sub-tenants were 'Chelsea Men', elderly retired rank-and-file soldiers of distinguished service who held pensions from the Royal Chelsea Hospital in London. The farming arrangements and tenancies were deliberately of the older style and not intended for commercial gain. The symbolic presence in a Highland district of such a military laird and his men was more to do with political capital than profit.

Though George Sutherland was a distinguished soldier of long and loyal service, he was also a conspicuous consumer, and the records of his personal affairs in later life revealed the usual preoccupations with fine things. In 1804 his moveable property was valued at £1,250. It included rich clothing, silver buttons and buckles, plate, furniture, high quality horses and saddlery, and many valuable guns and swords. His most valued personal possession was a gold watch made by John Jardine of London, worth £31 10s. He had furnished his house with domestic goods shipped from Edinburgh back in the 1760s, when he had prizes from fighting during the Seven Years War. His nephew in London had supplied him with pictures and prints at much the same time. He also spent large sums on clothing in London in the 1760s. Even in great old age, long retired and with most of his shopping carried out through merchants in Highland towns, he still indulged in fine clothing and surrounded himself with the sorts of domestic luxuries that James Boswell, many decades before, had recognised as the common practice of the military gentleman.[73]

THE END OF BARCALDINE

The impact of military careers for such large numbers of the Highland gentry was profound. More than any other profession, military men preserved traditional values while simultaneously adapting to the new polite and urban world. Some military men like George Sutherland of Rearquahar even lived in an old-fashioned way in the Highlands as a symbolic gesture to the past in order to generate political leverage in the present. But most military men found their natural habitat in the urban context. London, along with the leisure and county towns, were full of officers on leave or half-pay, many of them Highland Scots, most of them bachelors. They were seeking to entertain themselves, sometimes recovering from illness or injury, usually spending money they could ill afford and always on the lookout for further opportunities among peers, patrons and possible heiresses.

The Campbell family of Barcaldine, along with their extensive networks of kin and many similar Highland families, reveal the astonishing popularity of military employment for the sons of the gentry from the 1750s onwards. Yet their military kin also drove this family on several occasions to states of crisis. No other career exercised such an effect on them. Duncan Campbell's son Colin was brought before the Glasgow sheriff in March 1778, when he was accused of ravishing a servant girl; Major James Macpherson was able to settle the case out of court.[74] John Campbell of Barcaldine, who supplemented his estate income through diligent employment as a crown factor for forfeited estates, was ruined in the mid-1770s and obliged to sell Barcaldine to his half-brother Duncan as a result of the costs incurred by his military sons and particularly by the recklessness of his eldest, who eventually killed himself in 1779 while serving as governor of Fort George. In the opinion of a nephew, it was 'a poor situation the honest man has brought himself to. Cheated by the one son and bullied by the other son out of his estate.'[75]

The laird who finally ruined Barcaldine with his luxury and excess was one who began his career as a teenage recruit, and through his military office and associated elite fashionable connections was drawn early into a pattern of expenditure that far exceeded his income. Duncan Campbell (1786–1842), son and grandson of lairds who had supported the estate through successful legal practice, was the first in the family to combine land ownership with a military career. He entered the army as a teenager at the start of the Napoleonic wars, swept along on the tide of 'defence patriotism' that drew unprecedented numbers of Scotsmen into the military.[76] He was encouraged to do so by his widowed mother; had his lawyer father been alive, the story may have been different. He served in Copenhagen in 1801 and fought with Wellesley in the Peninsular wars. In 1810, when painted by Henry Raeburn in military uniform – the first of the family to commission a fashionable portrait – he held 'double-rank' as lieutenant in a regiment of Foot Guards – an expensive, elite London regiment – and captain in a Scottish regiment. Even at this early stage he was getting into debt, for in 1812 Raeburn wrote to Campbell requesting that he settle forthwith his long-outstanding bill of fifty guineas.[77] His military exploits and later office as deputy lord lieutenant for

Argyll were rewarded with a baronetcy in 1831. He was passionately committed to the sort of military Highlandism that defined his age, played an important role in county politics and cut a dashing figure at the annual Highland Society ball in Oban. But he had embarked on a perilous course of reckless spending on his townhouse in Edinburgh and new building projects at Barcaldine, a cause of dismay among his own family and disgust among his business-owning in-laws in Glasgow.[78] His life of conspicuous luxury finally ended in ruin. It was a common experience among so-called 'successful' career soldiers.[79]

5　Gentlewomen

INTRODUCTION

The history of the eighteenth-century Highlands has been written as though women hardly ever lived there. This is easily understood. A focus on clanship and its martial functions, along with an overarching preoccupation with the politics of Jacobitism are the major culprits. More recent concern with the economics of Highland estates has furthered the tendency. Yet the Highland gentlewoman was transformed during the long eighteenth century. The character of this transformation not only mirrored aspects of broader change among the Scottish gentry, it was a significant factor in the changing use of estates, it shaped evolving relationships between the landowning elite and the ordinary people, and in particular it was a vital element in the consumer behaviour and luxury of lairds and their families.

It is difficult to piece together the details of women's lives in the Highlands before the 1740s.[1] Rates of literacy were lower than those of equivalent women elsewhere in Britain, and dramatically lower than those of the well-educated Highland gentleman.[2] Even when women did send the occasional letter, these were not preserved in the extensive family archives that were maintained by men. We only know that such letters did exist because they are sometimes mentioned in men's correspondence. There are no domestic account books, no diaries or recollections, no novels or other works of literature penned by such women before the later eighteenth century as there were in other places, including Lowland Scotland and England.[3] Other than the pastry books that were purchased for teenage girls in preparation for marriage, there were no women's books in household inventories before mid-century. By the time the Highland gentlewoman was 'empowered' by the art of writing to leave a record of her own existence and, of equal importance, that record was thought worthy of preservation within her family, she was living for much of the time outside the Highlands. The few exceptions were those such as Elizabeth Rose of Kilravock, heiress to a family estate, who preserved her own writings from childhood from the 1750s onwards, along with the letters of her barely literate mother from the 1730s.[4]

A sparse written record has inevitably obscured the lives of late seventeenth- and early eighteenth-century gentlewomen, including those that belonged to sophisticated families, such as Campbell of Barcaldine, where the men were part of the modernising, anglicised world of letters. We catch a glimpse of women in accounts and legal documents when they went away for a few months of education as teenagers or got married, but it really is no more than a glimpse. Indeed, of about 1,500 Campbell of Argyll documents $c.1700$, only 112 make any mention of women.[5] Much of the experience of women was still rooted in the pre-modern traditions of Gaeldom and in oral discourses, including poetry, which was more likely to be part of their daily existence than it was of their menfolk, who were increasingly away in the Lowlands. One of the finest poets of the age was Cicely McDonald of Keppoch, who was active from the later seventeenth century through to the 1720s and was connected to the Campbell family of Barcaldine. She married into the family of Lovat of Inverness-shire and is best remembered for a passionate lament on the early death of her husband. The island of Luing, also close to Barcaldine, was home to Diorbhail nic a Bhriuthainn – also known as Dorothy Brown – who wrote at the time of the Glencoe Massacre and composed searing attacks on the Campbell families of the region.[6] Margaret Campbell, Argyllshire minister's wife and daughter of Colin Campbell of Achnaba, also a minister, was a Gaelic poet of some note in the 1740s, and she composed a witty account of 'The Highland Dress' following proscription.

> The news that many fine young men
> Find most depressing
> Is that their knees will not be seen
> Or their thighs either.[7]

These were earthier observations than was usual for a gentlewoman of the day when expressing herself in English. Indeed, the role of Gaelic language as a form of expression that women found comfortable and perhaps also liberating, long after English was adopted as their first language, is evident even in the later eighteenth century. Mary MacPherson of Badenoch, the daughter and wife of Highland schoolmasters who taught English, wrote religious verse initially in English, but she switched to Gaelic at her husband's suggestion as a form of expression best suited to her intense spirituality. These were published in the 1780s with encouragement from the widowed Mrs Grant of Rothiemurchus, grandmother to the 'Highland Lady' of memoirs fame. The English poetry did not survive.[8]

Traces of the oral culture and traditional knowledge practices of Highland gentlewomen survived as memory into the early nineteenth century. Susan Ferrier, daughter of an Edinburgh lawyer, stocked her celebrated novel *Marriage* with scenes and characters that she had observed or heard about during her visits to Argyll as a girl. One of these was Lady Maclaughlan of Lochmarlie Castle, an outspoken, down-to-earth matron, wife of an ailing military man and mistress of a 'laboratory' where she brewed her herbal medicines and made her pills. She was probably modelled on an elderly relative of the duke of Argyll.[9] In pre-modern Gaeldom, among both peasants and gentry, women were the guardians of certain types of learning, conveyed from mother to daughter in the form of oral knowledge whose purpose was healing. Gentry women certainly possessed knowledge of traditional medicine. Well-settled and wealthy counties like Argyll or Perthshire had a good representation of professional surgeons to draw on, but earlier types of healer still practised and were commonly sought. These were as likely to be women as men. John Stewart of Fassnacloich was in despair in 1704 when he wrote to his cousin Alexander Campbell of Barcaldine: 'My Father is still troubled with a pain that is in his right side and can get nothing that can do him any good and being informed that there is a gentlewoman at Taymouth that has good skill in curing many . . . [I] write to you to know your opinion.'[10]

Whether she was consulted is unknown. John Campbell of Achallader, chamberlain to the earl of Breadalbane, gives another insight to the importance of female knowledge. Writing in 1734 to Patrick Campbell of Barcaldine, his brother-in-law, he mentioned that he had a female relative visiting his house in Perthshire, a Mrs Cameron of Errocht, who 'has been here this fortnight giving the history of the living and the dead from Benderloch to Lochabber since Oliver Cromwell's days'.[11] He was amused by this, but also regarded Mrs Cameron's genealogical discourses as worth describing to his kinsman.

The pre-modern social world that women occupied was complex, but much of it evades detailed observation. In order to better understand the often elusive Highland gentlewoman before she began to record her existence, it is necessary first to understand the place and role of women in the clan society that prevailed in the western and northern Highlands. Clanship was a residual form of feudalism. Feudal societies allocated status and honour on the basis of service to the feudal superior, and that service was intrinsically male. The rising status and increasing legal rights of women matched the decline of feudalism in Europe from the Middle Ages.[12] No such decline had occurred in the Highland Scotland, for though systematic Roman law and civil control from the centre had been imposed since the early seventeenth century and that traditional system of land allocation had been eroded by commerce and legal contracts since the later seventeenth century, Highland family practices, as with many other areas of social behaviour, continued to be driven by deeply entrenched, backward-looking cultural norms. The Reformation introduced a complicating factor. In Catholic families the power of women may have been increased as they assumed a role in maintaining traditional religious culture – a role that was politically dangerous for men. When harnessed to Jacobitism, this gave some women a level of political agency that went against the general trend.[13] In Protestant families, however, the power of women – already low – was eroded as it was elsewhere in Protestant society.[14] A further complicating cultural influence may have prevailed in the eastern Highlands as a consequence of longstanding influences from Scandinavia, where women had greater independence and rights to property than was usual to Gaeldom.[15] Certainly, there was a higher incidence of female inheritance here than in the west.

Regardless of religion, politics or the influence of regional traditions, the primary role of women was to get married and produce children, particularly sons, to preserve the security and fuel the expansion of their husbands' family interests. On marriage they made a legal and financial transition into the family of their husband, but the cultural contours of this residual feudal system determined that they and their new kinsmen still regarded the family of birth as the focus for a woman's emotional attachments.[16] The second role of the Highland gentlewomen was to run her husband's household, if she was lucky enough to get a husband. In gentry families, marriages were tied to political and economic considerations. A woman's chance of marriage was related to her dowry, which, like male inheritance, was determined by her place in the birth order of siblings.[17] Eldest daughters were more likely to marry than younger ones, and they usually married young. The responsibility for a husband's household was sometimes assumed at a remarkably early age if the husband was older and had a housekeeper in place. In cases where a husband and wife were both young, an older widowed kinswoman lived in the household to train the wife in practical skills. Lady Kilmun, seasoned educator of teenage girls, lived with her grandson in the 1720s (the eldest child of her eldest daughter) to help his young wife in running their home.[18] Many aspects of the role of a wife and widow living full-time in the Highlands are illustrated by the life and experience of Janet Mackay of Bighouse, who married Colin Campbell of Glenure, son of Patrick Campbell of Barcaldine, in 1749.

WIVES AND WIDOWS

Janet Mackay was the eldest daughter of Hugh Mackay of Bighouse.[19] She was born in 1732 and raised in Sutherland before being sent to Edinburgh in the autumn of 1748, aged sixteen, for a brief education in genteel accomplishments. She was introduced to adult society in Edinburgh and set on the task of finding a husband. She quickly fulfilled her family's expectations. Colin Campbell of Glenure was more than twice her age, but he was a good match, from a rising family. Colin courted Janet in Edinburgh before travelling to Sutherland with one of his brothers-in-law for support, to negotiate with her father. The Mackay family lawyer in Edinburgh enquired into the state of his property and finances. The affair moved swiftly to a successful resolution. As Hugh Mackay wrote to his lawyer in April 1749, Glenure was agreeable and

> he does not want of the Highlandman in him . . . I have no objection to the man himself in the general view, or to his family and circumstances if equal to the account I have from you . . . so if Mr Campbell is Jenny Mackay's choice for a companion in life, I approve and consent frankly as I would to any reasonable thing in my power that would make her happy – and if she loves the man it would be imprudent to reject the proposal.[20]

The fact that Glenure had offered a generous settlement on his future wife should he die merely added to the felicity of the match from the father's point of view, since he could provide only a small dowry.

Glenure and Janet were married in Edinburgh, and at the age of seventeen she went into Argyll, at a great distance from her own family, to begin married life on the remote estate of Glenure. The feelings of dislocation and loss of place and people that this typical experience on marriage evoked in gentry women was a stock subject of their poetry and song.[21] Janet was mistress of a comfortable modern house, comprising six rooms with a garret and a new kitchen wing.[22] During her short marriage she lived mostly at Glenure, making a single shopping trip to Edinburgh with her husband in 1750. She could and did ride, but extensive social visiting among neighbours was not possible from such a remote area when there was so much work to do at home and she was pregnant for much of the time – though occasional visits and ritualised riding-out among the tenantry as a device for cementing clan loyalties were probably undertaken from time to time.[23] Her husband was frequently away on business and obliged to leave his wife on her own. Although this was normal for Highland wives she was sometimes lonely, and her father made arrangements for female visitors from home, including her younger and about-to-be-married sister Mally, and Christie Munro, a cousin. The logistics of getting these girls from Sutherland to Argyll were considerable. Some women resented being left at home on their own, or with only women for company. Janet's sister-in-law, Mary MacPherson, the wife of Duncan Campbell the lawyer, who had lived for many years in Stirling before Duncan inherited Glenure, complained bitterly to her husband in the 1750s at being left alone in the Highlands.[24] Their marriage was increasingly acrimonious and eventually ended in separation.[25]

Janet Mackay had two infant daughters and was pregnant with a third when her husband was killed in 1752. The young widow gave lawyers a detailed account of the affairs of the household. Much of what she recorded related to her own labours and that of the servants in her charge. The account also gives an insight into the prosaic comings and goings that even a remote estate was capable of supporting. Janet organised the domestic cooking and was involved in cloth production for her own household use. She looked after the milk house with its extensive commercial cheese- and butter-making activities and kept a watchful eye over the meal or gunnel house. She managed ten or twelve domestic and farm servants and had daily contacts with a range of people from within the locality who made purchases of butter and cheese, as well as goats and sheep for slaughter.[26] In April 1752 she supplied three stones of butter and six of cheese to Mrs Campbell, widow of Archibald Campbell minister of Lismore, for the funeral of the latter, along with two 'southland wedders'. Donald Dow McIntyre from Balegrundle, a tenant farmer who was related to her house servant Mary McIntyre and to her 'kid and lamb herd' Duncan McIntyre, purchased one stone of cheese and a quart of butter. The wife of Duncan McIntyre, late crofter in Balnamuck, who was the mother of Janet Mackay's servants Mary and Duncan, bought half a stone of cheese. Angus McDonald, walkmilner in Achosragan, owed her for the balance of a quart of butter, deducting three shillings for 'walking a wab of cloth' that was produced at Glenure under Janet's direction. John Breck McChombrich, miller at Kentallen, also owed her for butter and cheese. In the same month, the estate supplied Captain Alexander Campbell of Barcaldine – her husband's nephew – with thirty-one wedders 'sent at his desire to the troops at the Blackmount roads'.[27] All of these people were within a radius of less than ten miles of Glenure. Janet's life was busy, even though she was lonely for company of her own status.

When Janet's pregnancy of 1752 produced a third daughter and not a son, she returned in great disappointment to her own family in Sutherland, taking nothing with her but the children and a widow's annuity. She went to stay with her sister Mally, now married into the Ballie of Rosehall family. The children were taken into Hugh Mackay's household to be looked after by their maternal grandmother. The baby was wet-nursed by the wife of Rob Donn the poet. Clanship valued rapid remarriage in cases of early widowhood. A young widow with proven childbearing capacity and housekeeping skills could secure a second useful connection for her family. Her father doubtless had plans for his eldest daughter, but she upset these by eloping within the year with Charles Baillie, son of Rosehall.[28] It was a scandal in the county. She and her husband, a military man, lived in Yorkshire for several years. Janet reconnected with her children in 1756 to help make decisions about their lodging and schooling in Tain. Duncan Campbell of Glenure was responsible for their upkeep, but his payments were constantly in arrears, generating many angry letters from Janet and her father – now reconciled with his daughter – and even a court action.[29] The girls were taught the usual array of female skills in reading and writing, some French, dancing and music. But Betty, the eldest, died in 1762, aged twelve. The youngest, named Colina after her father, never married, though she was courted by her Glenure cousin in 1772 when she and her surviving sister unexpectedly found themselves heiresses to the Bighouse estate. She refused the proposal, doubtless because of earlier resentments about the treatment of her mother.[30] Louisa, the middle daughter, married a Mackay cousin and she and her husband succeeded to the Bighouse estate.

Hugh Mackay's plans to forge links between his own family and the Campbell family of Barcaldine and Glenure evaporated with the early death of his son-in-law without a male heir. Janet's second marriage, begun in scandal and with no fixed home, was also cut short when her husband was killed in 1758 during the Seven Years War. She was twice widowed and still in her twenties. She returned to Edinburgh and was married for a third time to a local merchant, Alexander Hart, seemingly with no Highland connections, and soon faded from the family record. She died c.1768, still a young woman. The legacy of Janet Mackay's early widowhood was difficulty for her and for her daughters and a bitter rift with the family into which she had married with such hopes and promise. Young widows could at least hope to remarry; older widows faced greater difficulties.[31] A lengthy widowhood could impose a major and much resented burden on a family, even where that family had benefited from the initial income boost that the marriage had brought. Sons resented their widowed mothers, for they were a drain on a family to which they did not belong, absorbing scarce resources they would rather see given to their own children. Widows suffered in this society, though they were not averse to making their complaints known, as was suggested by John Campbell of Achallader, writing to his brother-in-law, Patrick Campbell of Barcaldine in 1732.

> This sheet I only intended to cover the gazots and not draw it out the length it has run which I believe has tired you in the reading, which I must say is a sort of relief to me at present from the chit chat of very poor Lady Marchfield by whom I am obliged to sit and have part of her doleful story of 11 children and nothing to give them, her greatest comfort is to be rid of a husband that brought her to that low state.[32]

Campbell of Achallader had also reported in another letter to his kinsman that 'the old Lady Ardownage was buried Saturday last, I may say without breach of charity, to the no small satisfaction of her son'.[33] Such remarks would have struck a chord with Patrick Campbell, for his own mother, Mary Campbell of Lochnell, outlived his father by nearly twenty years.

Mary Campbell of Lochnell was born in 1661, a younger daughter of one of the senior Argyll families.[34] Lochnell was a richer and more important family than the Campbell family of Barcaldine, and when Mary married Alexander, heir to Barcaldine, in 1676, she brought a good dowry along with important political connections. As a wife she lived in Barcaldine Castle, a small tower house, where she raised a large family and led a practical domestic existence similar to that of Janet Mackay. Periodically, as when the castle was occupied by government troops in the early 1690s, she and the children moved to a farmhouse in Auchinryre where her husband held land. She never travelled beyond the Highlands, though. Mary had four adult sons and three adult daughters, with as many infants and children that died young. Her eldest son, Patrick, was born in 1677, when she was sixteen, and her youngest surviving child was born in 1705, when she was forty-four. She saw the birth of grandchildren and great-grandchildren. While her husband was alive, she was pivotal to the affairs of the Barcaldine family.

Her husband made detailed financial provision for Mary's widowhood in 1716.[35] It was generous, befitting the standing of a matriarch of good family and the respect in which she was held. She was granted an annuity of 600 merks Scots (£60 sterling) and she was liferented the castle and all domestic movables 'excepting the hail silverwork and arms the best clock, cabinet and table.' All of the liferented property was, at her death, to become the absolute property of her eldest grandson, John. Her son Patrick, his wife and their growing family were to live in a new mansion called Dalfuir House, completed in the early 1720s. She was also granted the following stock for a farm with the intention that she would continue to run a cattle and dairying enterprise in widowhood:

- Twenty-eight 'good and sufficient cows' – milking cows between the ages of five and nine years.
- Seven 'quey stirks' (young heffers for slaughter) and seven 'quey two year olds'.
- The second-best bull belonging to her husband at the time of his decease.
- Four 'good and sufficient' mares, of her choosing, with their foals.
- Equal half of all of the plough irons possessed by her husband at his death.
- An equal division of the four plough horses at the farms of Inveregen and Condallick.
- Various quantities of oats in fields yet to be harvested.

However, her son and eldest grandson quickly set aside these provisions. Once widowed, Mary Campbell was under intense pressure to relinquish her property. A large part of her liferented land was seized for her grandson's use in the early 1720s, when he was looking for opportunities to work on his own account and complained of his lack of financial independence.[36] When John married in 1728, he and his wife set up house in Barcaldine Castle along with Lady Kilmun (John's widowed maternal grandmother, with no claim to the property, but useful household skills to help the young wife). The paternal widow, who did have a legal claim to the property, moved out with few possessions. She first went to lodge with one of her married daughters at Acha. She lived with Patrick at Dalfuir House from the late 1720s to early 1730s, just after he was widowed, doubtless to help with the housekeeping. She then moved to Glenmackrie, a farm in a remote upland cattle-raising area to the south, to lodge with another married daughter from 1734 to 1738. Her final home and place of death was with her third daughter Mary and her son-in-law Stewart of Innernahyle on their farm on the Appin peninsula. Throughout this time her annuity was in arrears and she was often unable to pay her daughters for food and board. She complained bitterly to male relatives. Relationships with her eldest son were tense, and at several times she threatened to take him to court.[37] This is how the matter was described by Donald Campbell of Balighown, writing to his nephew on 1734: 'I have lately seen your mother and she is most anxious to see you at Glinamacrie. She wrote you lately and takes it ill that you neglected to send her ane answer to her letter. I am still much out of favour and for no other reason but that I freely tell her my sincere opinion when we meet.'[38] It is worth noting that while the letter from Campbell of Balighown was preserved, the letter from Mary Campbell was not.

This harsh treatment and the repercussions for other women, including Mary Campbell's daughters, was the product of scarce resources in a cash-poor environment. Widows either voluntarily relinquished their rights in the interests of their male kin, or were pressured into doing so.[39] Patrick Campbell's mother-in-law, Susan Campbell of Kilmun, was another source of long-term financial irritation, a consequence of cash-flow problems in her family. She was a widow of high standing connected with the house of Argyll as well as Breadalbane. She lived in Kilsyth, where she ran a sort of finishing school for the daughters of the gentry, and visited Edinburgh from time to time. She became embroiled in various financial disputes and negotiations involving the marriage of her daughter into the Barcaldine family, as well as the marriage of her sister to Colin Campbell, minister of Ardchattan and uncle to Patrick. In 1700, the dowry payments for her daughter Anne were in arrears because her eldest son had not paid an annuity due to herself. John Campbell, brother of the duke of Argyll was brought in by the Barcaldine family to negotiate a settlement. 'I am doing all I can to get you some money out of Kilmun and I think you may depend on a thousand merks in a month or so,' he reported in 1701.[40] But the dispute and recriminations rumbled on for several years, embroiling a wide network of kin linked to one another through debt and financial obligations to women that they were unwilling or unable to meet.

The same sort of story was played out time and time again. Even in a comfortable professional family with a good income flow and no encumbered estate, a widow could find herself in dispute over her support. The mother of Dr William Sinclair of Thurso, who was of landed family background, discovered on being widowed in 1767 that her annuity had been reduced by her husband, without her knowledge, from £25 to £15 sterling. Thurso was a cheap place to live, but this sum, the income from about £250 invested, offered no more than an existence in poverty. She was driven to the lawyers to try to recover some capital from her husband's cash estate of £4,371 (£900 to her two daughters, the rest to William) through disinheriting one of the daughters, who, she claimed, had 'married below her rank'. Her son, still a minor, had his inheritance protected by his tutors, including Hugh Mackay of Bighouse. Relationships between mother and children were always cool and doubtless got worse; yet it was through his mother that William later inherited the Freswick estate and entered the ranks of the landed gentry.[41]

One of the major problems of rural Highland life that affected widowed gentlewomen was the shortage of housing suitable for their status, along with constant demands from lairds and their sons for access to quality land for farming. Women headed few gentry households. In rural Argyllshire in 1748, only 9 per cent of houses eligible for window tax – i.e., houses with ten windows or more – were recorded in the name of women.[42] Almost certainly these were widows with sons who were minors. Women alone tended to gravitate towards towns on the fringes of the Highlands, where domestic property was more easily available through the rental market and the cost of living was lower. In Inverness in 1753, 20 per cent of its largest houses – those eligible for window tax – were held by women, many of them run as lodging houses.[43] The other advantage of living in a town was the easier access to credit. Women had difficulty gaining credit in rural areas, unless they were acting on behalf of a husband. Credit, if it was available, was more expensive than for men, because there were fewer opportunities for reciprocal exchange. Living in town was cheaper and easier for women alone, and it certainly suited their families. Mature and responsible women acted as agents for other women still living in the Highlands. They chose clothing and textiles and carried out other commissions. They also provided lodging facilities. When Patrick Campbell of Barcaldine sent his children to Perth and Edinburgh for their teenage education in the 1720s and 1730s, they lived with female kin who provided food and lodgings and kept a watchful eye over the youngsters. When he or his grown sons travelled to Edinburgh, they did so in stages, with overnight accommodation en route with their female relatives in places like Crieff.

SINGLE WOMEN

Widows found it difficult to maintain a place in Highland gentry society and were often pushed into a poor existence on the margins of families, or else they left to live in towns. Unmarried women, of which there were large and growing numbers, found themselves with similar problems. The privileging of a kinship system based on agnatic connections and the rising costs of dowry – a feature of the early-modern gentry throughout Europe[44] – was compounded by the growing rates of absence of young men from the Highlands as they sought to make their fortunes elsewhere. There was a high and growing level of spinsterhood among gentlewomen, with possibly one third of them not able to marry. Money for their support was scarce. Such women had limited roles to play in rural society, and few devices for making their own independent living in the rural economy.

Daughters who failed to marry and had no financial provisions from their families quickly tumbled down the social hierarchy. Many became domestic 'hangers-on', servants in all but name, obliged to live in the homes of relatives and provide services of one sort or another, and their presence no more likely to be noted than that of a servant. Flora Macdonald, the Jacobite heroine, was originally destined for such a life. She was born in 1722 into a tacksman's family on South Uist. Her father died when she was an infant, her mother, a minister's daughter, soon remarried and Flora lived on the margins of her brother's family when he succeeded to the tack. She had no dowry, no education and had never travelled beyond the Highlands. Though a lesser gentleman's daughter, she spent her early womanhood hard at work at the spindle or in the byre. Her famed exploits with Prince Charles Edward Stuart made her fortune. While a prisoner in London, sympathisers raised a subscription of £1,500 for her support, a remarkable sum that far exceeded that available to most Highland gentlewomen. It allowed her to spend almost two years in Edinburgh, where in addition to being a drawing-room sensation she learned to write and acquired other genteel skills and refinements of the sort that were normally taught at the age of sixteen. The money provided a dowry and she was married in 1750, aged twenty-eight, to a kinsman of higher rank. Her husband received £700, a handsome sum, from which he purchased a stock of cattle for a good tack on Skye.[45]

Flora Macdonald's route to self-made fortune was unique. Other women who took the self-made path usually did so through exploiting the opportunities offered by urban commerce.[46] Grocery businesses were popular among women and required little capital. Duncan Campbell, who inherited the Glenure estate in 1752, married the daughter of a Glenfine cattle dealer, and one of his sisters-in-law ran such a business in Glasgow in the 1740s and 1750s.[47] His widowed daughter-in-law, the wife of his 'natural' son, Major Alexander Campbell, set herself up as a tea retailer in Glasgow in 1786.[48] Single women with good looks and some cultural attainment could make a business as a mantua maker or milliner, though this was more expensive and required a period of apprenticeship. Women of the lesser gentry in both Scotland and England were sometimes raised in the expectation that if they did not marry they should be provided with the skills to allow them to support themselves.[49] Isabella Macpherson (b. 1745), who was one of the illegitimate daughters of Colin Campbell of Glenure, provides an example.

When Colin Campbell was murdered in 1752 he left financial provision for four 'natural' daughters, to be administered by his brother and heir Duncan who, needless to say, resented the burden.[50] For a father to acknowledge and making good provision for his illegitimate children was normal in Highland gentry culture: such children were treated like younger legitimate children but had no rights of inheritance.[51] Each of Campbell's girls was gifted a capital sum of £100, to be invested in the Glenure estate at 10 per cent annual interest, to support the cost of their childhood, pay for apprenticeship fees and provide a modest dowry. Isabella Macpherson, whose mother lived in the Glenorchy area, was fostered by John Bane McIntyre, a cowherd in Calnish in Glenorchy, from 1752 to 1756 for a modest cost of £5 10s. 4d. that was consistent with the character of this household. In May 1756, aged eleven, she moved into the household of John Campbell, a miller at Kinckrakin, which was also in Glenorchy, close to the small town of Dalmally. Here she began the process of integration into adult society and was introduced to female skills and accomplishments of a higher order than those previously available to her. The cost of boarding for two years was £11 13s. 4d., and charges were also made for 'furnishing her in cloaths, linnens, shoon, reeding school dues, books, dancing school dues and every other necessary'.[52] Her older half-sister Peggy, whom she had never met before, joined her at Kinckrankin in 1757. Isabella and Peggy then moved to the town of Crieff in June 1758. They lodged in the household of Duncan Robertson, a merchant and business associate of their paternal uncle Robert Campbell, a merchant in Stirling. The cost of annual boarding was £6 for each girl, a step up from Kinckrakin. Life in Crieff offered new pleasures, and Peggy and 'Bell' engaged in conspicuous consumption of clothing and textiles for their future lives. Some clothing was made for them, and some they made themselves under the instruction of a local tailor. They continued their lessons in reading and writing, attended a sewing school and a dancing school, and learned music and arithmetic. They went to balls, began to wear stays and each had a Bible purchased for her. Regular church attendance was now possible and contributions to church collections became part of their accounts. Peggy was married in early 1761, aged seventeen, to Duncan Macdiarmid, the eldest son of John Macdiarmid, a tenant farmer, whom she had met in Crief. She remained in the area for the rest of her life, making occasional trips to Edinburgh.

Isabella was better favoured than her sister. Her writing skills were more sophisticated, she was clever and she was a kinswoman by marriage of Duncan Campbell of Glenure. She was also physically attractive. Her relatives prepared her for a life in business in a flourishing area of the women's luxury trades, one that depended on personal appearance and genteel taste as well as skills. In July 1761, aged sixteen, she was 'bound and engaged' as an apprentice in Stirling to Miss Jean Christie, a mantua maker, an arrangement made by Robert and Duncan Campbell, her uncles, in a town where both had extensive business interests. The apprentice fee was £16, paid in three portions.[53] The legal indenture specified that she was to be maintained in 'bed, board and washing in family with [Miss Christie] in a suitable manner' and that her hours of work and duties were to be defined by her mistress for the three years of the apprenticeship, 'only that during the currency of the first year of the said service [she] will have the liberty and freedom of one hour each day for attending any schools in the town of Stirling as she shall be advised for her improvement in writing or otherwise'. She served for two years before she married, and the contract was terminated. The balance due to her husband as dowry was £106 4s. 10d.[54]

Had Isabella gone on to establish herself in business, she might – depending on her skills as a dressmaker, business acumen and continued good health – have risen to be a woman of substance in her own right. It was a flourishing area of trade, and most mantua makers also traded in haberdashery and fancy textiles. Her family connections would have served her well for both customers and credit. At some point in the future, with her own household in Stirling, she might have provided lodgings for one of the rising Campbell children; a valued spinster kinswoman giving useful family service in town. She might also, of course, have failed to flourish, particularly if ill health had struck. This was the fate of Isabella Sinclair, born in Wick in 1776, one of several unmarried sisters who were left penniless by their father, William Sinclair of Mey, when he died in 1792. The sisters were forced into various expediencies to make a living in the Highlands. One became the companion and housekeeper for Ann Sinclair of Brabster, a kinswoman, and was effectively adopted into that family. Their brothers, better favoured by opportunities to travel, went abroad or joined the army, where most died young. Isabella learned mantua making in Thurso from a kinswoman, Betty Sinclair, and then moved to Edinburgh for further training. She tried to set up in business in Thurso in 1793, but her sister Jean warned her against it. 'There is upwards of twenty in that business here and half of them starving for want of work.' Back in Edinburgh as a journeywoman in 1794 she met a merchant's clerk, Mr Sutherland, and planned to marry and emigrate to the West Indies, but her health was failing, and she died soon after in Caithness.[55]

AFFECTIONATE AND SENTIMENTAL RELATIONS

The correspondence between the Sinclair sisters from the early 1790s through to the 1820s, and in particular the letters from their brother Lieutenant (later Captain) John Sinclair of the 79th Regiment, a military bachelor who fell at Waterloo in 1815, suggests great affection and a sense of common purpose among these siblings.[56] Though fortune did not smile on the family and they were scattered across the globe, they were attached by deep emotional bonds and yearned to be back together again. John, in particular, wrote frequently of his wish to see sisters Betsy, a governess, and Wilhelmina, housekeeper for Mrs Ann Sinclair of Brabster, settled in a home of their own in Thurso, to give an emotional focus for the family. Life in the army was hard, he had been badly injured in 1811 and he hoped to retire to a quieter life with his sisters. He was acutely concerned to promote the financial well-being of his womenfolk and petitioned various senior relatives to help them. His death in battle robbed these struggling gentlewomen of their only champion and protector; the prize money was little compensation for the loss of a much loved brother.[57]

This level of emotional attachment and affection relations was not unusual among the Highland gentry by the later decades of the eighteenth century. Here, for instance, is the poignant entry from the journal of Elizabeth Rose of Kilravock for 1 November 1772, when she was twenty-five years old, still single and living at home with her parents: 'At 12 forenoon, died of a fever that confined him to bed but six days, my affectionate, cheerful, harmless, healthy brother Willie, in the 31st year of his age. What an unexpected heavy blow!'[58] Women in the early eighteenth century did not write, or think, about their brothers in this way, any more than brothers in the early eighteenth century wrote, or thought, in this way about their sisters. Elizabeth Rose and her several brothers were cousins to one of the foremost Scottish architects of the cult of sensibility, the novelist Henry Mackenzie, who was born in the Highlands in 1745 and raised in Edinburgh. His father was a medical man and his mother was the sister of Elizabeth Rose's mother. Just a few years older than the Kilravock children, Henry Mackenzie, a lawyer by profession, was a regular correspondent. He guided their education and taste in music, poetry and the classics and kept up a lifelong exchange with Elizabeth about the progress of his own literary endeavours, including the vastly successful sentimental novel *The Man of Feeling*, published in 1771.[59] This was one of the best sellers of the decade, translated into many languages. The heart-rending story was designed to evoke the emotions and to cultivate empathy for the plight of others. It was an illustration in popular form, as important for male readers as for women, of a philosophy that encouraged mutual sympathy as an antidote to the harsh social relations that flowed from modern commercialism.[60]

It is not surprising that the Rose family, pioneers in the new cult of sensibility, should manifest such affections in their family relations from around the 1750s. What is remarkable is that affectionate relationships between men and women in Highland gentry society seem to have been so absent before the middle decades of the eighteenth century. Sons were unkind to their widowed mothers, often abandoning them to poverty and distress in old age. Mothers threatened to take their sons to court. Brothers hardly ever wrote to or even mentioned their sisters in family correspondence, even though letters between brothers were often intimate and loving. Fathers were less concerned with the fortunes of their daughters than the fortunes of their sons. When a young man died, it normally prompted a great outpouring of grief from the father and male siblings – as attended the death of Patrick Campbell of Barcaldine's youngest son Donald in 1731, a recently qualified surgeon who died on his first posting as ship's surgeon.[61] When daughters died – and many women died tragically young in childbirth – the communication of such news and responses among kinsmen was perfunctory. Were affections between men and women really so cool? Was intimacy so limited? Family correspondence appears to suggest this was so.

There were, of course, some exceptions. Duncan Stewart of Innernahyle, who married Mary Campbell daughter of Barcaldine in 1705, was remarkably attached to his wife and concerned for his mother-in-law. He wrote immediately, in unusually pious terms, to his father-in-law at the birth of their many children, voicing far more concern for his wife than for the babies. The following is typical, written sometime in 1713 when Mary was about twenty-eight and already a mother many times over.

> Thursday afternoon. This is to let you know that your daughter and my wife is (blessed be God) safely brought to bed of a male child and I would have spacth abroad sooner but I was still waiting a full acccompt before I would send and now (I bless God Almighty for it) I hope she is past all arduor hazards. I am afraid her mother [Mary Campbell of Lochnell] will be very much troubled about her but I hope this will satisfy her for present. Be pleased to acquaint me of any mirth you known that would be proper for my wife.[62]

The next confinement did not go well. 'Tuesday 12 hours. This is to let you know that your daughter is (blessed be God) brought to bed this morning and has ay unny daughter but she is very unwell as yet.' He was much distressed and wrote to Colin Campbell, minister at Ardchattan, who was famed for his medical knowledge, for advice.[63] Mary survived and was still alive in 1739 when, as a middle-aged woman, her childbearing years well past, she and her affectionate husband provided a home for her widowed mother in great old age. Can it be just a coincidence that the heir to this loving couple, Alexander Stewart of Invernahyle, a Jacobite who came out in the '45, in old age impressed the young Walter Scott with his kindly attentions? 'His tales were the absolute delight of my childhood.'[64]

For most men, their womenfolk were a financial burden on the family and less valued than male kin. The new commercial imperatives that were imposed on the Highland gentry from the mid-seventeenth century doubtless reinforced these sentiments. The birth of a daughter rarely generated more than basic congratulations. The birth of a son was cause for celebration. Yet a hint at change and the dawning of affectionate relationships can be seen in the correspondence between Hugh Mackay of Bighouse and Colin Campbell of Glenure. When Colin Campbell's first legitimate child, a daughter, was born in 1750, Hugh Mackay, his father-in-law, wrote:

> It is no small mercy to have a living mother and a living child and God be thanked . . . When your wife was born I was extremely out of humour that I had not then a son. However may your disappointment now prove as agreeable as to me hitherto; much joy may young Miss give you and her Mama and God grant you may be spared both.[65]

He was not being disingenuous. His three daughters were the darlings of both parents and of constant interest and concern in letters sent to Glenure and to his own male kin. Messages for Janet were always included in the frequent letters to Glenure, and she also received letters of her own from both father and mother. Hugh Mackay wrote in March 1752, just a few months before Glenure was murdered:

> Tell Jenny that I got her last epistle and that when I glean some news in Caithness, if I know will be agreeable to her, then I shall write her a long one in return. She must have been lonely in your absence and this will not agree to her natural temper. I propose a very fit agreeable companion to her, one Miss Christy Munro, a cousin of her own . . . you may both do as you please, only I would not have [her] turn matron too early.[66]

The postscript to a letter whose main subject was business and politics reads:

> What follows is for Jenny and forgive the freedom. Dear Lucky, I have the pleasure of your epistle of the 8th Febry and need not tell you that it was most agreeable as I have wrote Mr Campbell, when I glean up some nouvelles in Caithness you are sure to have a long epistle from me. Your mama is well as are all your friends here, Thank God, well may you be my dr Jenny and with my compliments to Miss Tibbie [a visting relative], Betzie & Lucie [the babies].[67]

Hugh Mackay of Bighouse, seen by some as a cold and ambitious man, who was certainly interested in his own commercial advantage, put great store by his daughters, particularly Janet, who was his eldest child.[68] His relationships with the women in his life were first and foremost based on affection and emotional intimacy. Even when Janet angered him by remarrying without his consent just a few months after being widowed and caused a scandal from Sutherland to Argyll, he soon forgave her. His written account in the early 1750s of the death of a young relative at Bighouse, communicated with delicacy, with a heart-rending description of the child's deathbed pleas to see 'Jenny and Mally', suggests a close and loving family headed by a man of sensibility.[69] His relationship with his wife appeared to be loving and indulgent. Perhaps he was unusual among Highland gentlemen in possessing such a degree of sentiment and in being willing to express his emotions in the letters that he wrote to men. What is certain is that his affectionate and sentimental disposition, and his sensitivities to women's lives, was instrumental in shaping relationships within his family, and they presaged changes to come.

THE LUXURY TRAP

As the eighteenth century advanced, women alone as spinsters or widows were increasingly likely to be pushed into the urban consumer economy. This offered short-term benefits for Highland gentry families, but it also entailed long-term negative consequences, since the women in question were exposed to styles of living and individualistic cultural expectations that were inevitably expensive and at odds with conventional female experience in the rural clan context. New ideas were raised and disseminated through female networks that included women who had little personal contact with urban life. This fuelled the demand that their lives be different – more comfortable and more genteel. Men were also absorbing modern ideas of genteel and respectful social behaviour towards women, and family relationships with women were increasingly likely to be based on sentiment and affection. James Boswell in the Highlands in 1773 was witness to some of these changes as they unfolded. He was particularly impressed by the generous hospitality and entertainment he met in the Highlands, but though Boswell praised this as part of the traditions of clanship, the large presence of women and engagement in cultivated entertainments that included dancing, music and poetry was, in reality, part of a modern manner of gentry living. The reading of highly emotional Gaelic verse was a Highland variant on the cult of sensibility, which was then the fashion in the drawing rooms of Edinburgh. The elevation of women to roles of importance and respect within gentry sociability was also a product of polite culture. The women that Boswell encountered acted as ornaments to the houses of their father or husbands. Their levels of accomplishment and gentility were constantly noted, since they seemed in striking contrast to the often modest material environment. Flora Macdonald, middle-aged and living in a primitive house, was described by Boswell as 'a little woman, of a mild and genteel appearance, mighty soft and well-bred'.[70]

Through Boswell's eyes, the variations in ways of thinking and living among the gentry were particularly reflected in the character of their women. The laird of Lochbuie on Mull was a rich man but he lived in a poor house, had a wife who dressed and behaved like the landlady of an ale house and a daughter of seventeen as 'wild as any filly in Mull' who had 'never read a play'. The wife's brother, Sir Allan Maclean, a retired military man, described the family as 'just antediluvians'.[71] The spinster daughters of the latter modern and luxurious officer were ladylike and pious, but they were raised outside the Highlands, as were a number of the women encountered in 1773. Everywhere there were spinsters, and the problems of finding marriage partners remained endemic. At Dunvegan Castle, the ancient seat of the chief of Macleod, the regular household comprised the laird and his lady, their children and the four unmarried sisters of the laird, including the eldest of the family. All of the Macleod women were 'bred in England', were genteel to a high degree and were well read in fashionable subjects. The family lived in straitened circumstances, and the inconvenience of their home was an overwhelming preoccupation for Lady Macleod, who wanted to move away from the old castle and build a new house on a farm that they owned about five miles from Dunvegan and 'to make gardens and everything fine there'.[72] Her antipathy to the castle annoyed Boswell – he was 'vexed to find the alloy of modern refinement in a lady who had so much old family spirit'. He warned, 'once you quit this rock, this centre of gravity, there is no knowing where you may settle. You move five miles first; then to St. Andrews, as the late Laird did; then to Edinburgh; and so on till you end at Hampstead.'[73] He was right, of course, for this path was followed by many families in the last thirty years of the eighteenth century, including the Campbell family of Barcaldine. They did so in many cases because the Highland gentlewoman wanted to live in town.

Alexander Campbell, eldest son of Duncan Campbell of Glenure and his wife Mary Macpherson, was an advocate by training. He married Mary Campbell, daughter of John Campbell 'of the bank', in 1785. It was an important strategic marriage for both families. But though of Highland background, Mary Campbell was a city girl, Edinburgh-bred, unaccustomed to full-time Highland life and unwilling to relinquish the comforts of Edinburgh. She had a close relationship with her own family, especially her mother and sisters, one of them married to David Dale, the wealthy Glasgow textile merchant. Mary and Alexander lived on the Barcaldine estate in their early married life, and she always referred to Barcaldine as 'home' but had problems in finding suitable, modern medical attendance for her first confinement, which frightened the young wife. Mary Campbell insisted that she spend more time in Edinburgh. Her widowed mother, a regular correspondent, supported her with sentiments such as 'I regret much you being at so great a distance from church'.[74] At many times, and particularly during and after her many confinements, Mary Campbell lived with her mother in Edinburgh while her husband and children were in the Highlands. She wrote to Alexander from St James Square on the edge of the New Town in 1789:

> I find myself very weak since ever you left this and my spirit very often depressed at times, especially at night . . . The doctors say they can give no other reason but this being the month of March. I have been out in the chaise every day except three and I am very good to myself that I may be soon home.[75]

It seems likely she was suffering from post-natal depression.

She was back in Edinburgh in the early 1790s with the older two children, again staying with her mother. The youngest children were at Barcaldine and her husband was travelling on business.

> I had a letter from home the other day and both our sweet little darlings are in good health . . . I am hopeful soon to be restored to good health and spirits. My mother has not got a house yet but we saw one yesterday that she thinks will answer . . . My mother sends you her love in which all my sisters join me.[76]

The reference to house-hunting was telling, and doubtless sounded warning bells for her husband, for it was Mary Campbell, with her strong attachment to urban life, who was responsible for the family acquiring a permanent home in the New Town of Edinburgh and for entering into the conspicuous consumption that went with such a house. By the late 1790s her husband was clearly exasperated by her spending and was demanding careful accounts. In November 1797, she and her children were living in Edinburgh while Alexander Campbell was living at Barcaldine, and she was complaining loudly of the want of money for housekeeping. In May 1798, now with the children at Barcaldine while her husband was back in Edinburgh, she sent a letter of bitter remonstrance that underlined both the growing difficulties of the marriage and her resentments at being forced to stay in the country to control the costs of family life: 'I am quite discontented at this way of life and I will not live in this *wilderness* any longer.'[77]

Alexander Campbell died in 1800 and Mary Campbell's life as a young widow with six children, the eldest boy just fourteen, was happier but more costly than her life as a wife. No one contested her generous annuity, and the bills that were set against estate income quickly mounted. She continued to spend most of her time in Edinburgh in the townhouse and travelled frequently to visit her wealthy Glasgow relatives. For most of the time the youngest children were in the country with a governess and the older children were away at school in England, but she and her eldest son and daughter also made regular summer visits to Barcaldine. Her main correspondent on country affairs when she was in Edinburgh was the fashionable governess she employed for the younger children. Miss Brandon, an Englishwoman, was hired in April 1801 to teach 'reading, writing, arithmetic, geography and music' for an annual salary of £40. Before coming to Scotland she had worked for a gentleman's family in Wales. Letters from Barcaldine make it clear that she also ran the housekeeping for her mistress. Miss Brandon left the employ of Mary Campbell in 1809 when the youngest daughter left Scotland for a boarding school in England and the boys went on to tutors in Edinburgh. She moved to the household of another Argyllshire Campbell family and was later the governess to the Mosman family living in Comley Bank just outside Edinburgh. She remained a lifelong correspondent with her former mistress.[78]

As these life histories suggest, by the early nineteenth century the Highland gentlewoman was a city resident whose experience of life in the Highlands was an increasingly transitory one, defined by summer holidays and only occasional periods of longer residence. Divorced from the reality of everyday existence for ordinary people, much of her understanding of Highland society and culture was shaped by sensibility and romanticism. Her experience was also distinct from that of her forebears in her possession of sophisticated levels of literacy and her engagement in the genteel preoccupation with sensibility and written reflection. Women with strong Highland connections wrote novels, stories, articles and diaries intended for publication, mostly for a female audience. They were also great letter writers. Foremost among these was Elizabeth Grant of Rothiemurchus, daughter of an Inverness-shire laird and his English wife.[79]

Elizabeth Grant's life was largely that of an upper middle class, city-dwelling professional-gentleman's daughter. She lived in both London and Edinburgh and for a short time also in India, where her father went to advance his fortunes and where she met her husband, an Anglo-Irish landowner. She was deeply imbued with a form of Highland identity that flowed from her family and clan. But this knowledge and culture was urban-romantic in its foundations, not generated through sustained contact with Highland living in her formative years. The characters that peopled the novels of Walter Scott were cultural touchstones as concrete to her as any actual people. Indeed, she described the wife of one of the Sobiesky Steuarts, who were visitors with Fraser of Lovat in the Beauly Firth, as performing on the harp for the visiting crowds in the manner of Flora MacIvor in the novel *Waverley*.[80]

Educated women of Highland background were increasingly prominent figures in the romantic reinvention of traditional Highland culture in the early nineteenth century. The most famous and commercially successful in her own lifetime was Mrs Grant of Laggan (1755–1838), born Anne MacVicar, who was married to the minister of Laggan in Inverness-shire and wrote *Letters from the Mountains* (1806) and *Essays on the Superstitions of the Highland* (1811), both to high critical acclaim. Anne Grant was born in Glasgow to Highland-born parents. Her mother was of the family of Stewart of Invernahyle, and she was distantly related to the Barcaldine Campbells. She spent part of her childhood in North America, where her father was an army officer. The family returned to Scotland when her father took up the post of barrack-master at Fort Augustus. She was a teenager, living for the first time in the Highlands and learning to speak Gaelic. She married James Grant, a former army chaplain, when she was twenty-four years old and settled to her married life in the parish of Laggan. Early widowhood in 1801 forced her to move south, first to Stirling and later to Edinburgh.[81] Her wide experience of travel, exposure to a variety of cultures, Lowland education and lively early correspondence with distant friends provided Anne with the means to develop her skills as a social observer and writer. A large family, small widow's pension and opportunities to generate an income through writing on a subject of increasing popular interest – the traditional culture of the Highlands – were the stimulus to a successful literary career. Like several other literary Highland ladies she attracted the patronage and friendship of Walter Scott, and was an important figure on the Edinburgh social scene.

Mrs Anne Grant, like many of her contemporaries, moved to town, where she entered the ranks of urban consumers whilst simultaneously reinventing the character and traditions of the Highland world with which she had little regular contact. It was an important combination of circumstances that help to explain the evolving fortunes of Highland gentry families, and the means by which they fell into the luxury trap.

Part Three
Consumer Behaviour, Houses and Sociability

6 Consumer Behaviour and the World of Goods

INTRODUCTION

One of the central criticisms that was levelled at the Highland gentry in the eighteenth century, and by historians ever since, was the accusation of conspicuous consumption beyond their means. It was modern luxury that drove the wedge between the gentry and the culture of the country people who lived on their estates and caused financial ruin – or so the argument runs. There can be no doubt that one distinct and growing group of Highland gentlemen, the military men, were famous for their love of material luxury. There can be no doubt also that Highland gentlewomen were inexorably drawn into the world of urban leisured consumption, with serious consequences for family finances. But consumer behaviour and the 'world of goods' were more complex than is suggested in the conventional accusation, or in the lives and ambitions of soldiers and gentlewomen. Consumer behaviour was a cultural practice that evolved with the changing character of estates and a mental horizon that extended beyond the Highlands as a result of changing employments among the gentry as a class. The 'world of goods' was used to articulate political aspirations and sympathies. The 'world of goods' was also central to understanding familial attachments and private emotional connections.[1] The material culture of houses and furniture, clothing and personal adornment, food and hospitality in eighteenth-century Highland Scotland was socially constructed by forces outside the Highlands, is culturally explained and was probably inevitable for most of the gentry.[2]

Of course, criticism of the consumption habits of the Highland elite was not new to the eighteenth century, but in pre-modern Scotland it was linked to another kind of accusation, that of lawlessness. Consumer behaviour in Highland areas in the seventeenth century was typical of many parts of pre-modern Europe. With little cash in circulation and a limited exchange economy, consuming habits were limited to the basic produce of the locality, particularly food and textiles, and a few imported luxuries for the rich. There was a strong cultural preference for leisure over work, as is usual in non-market societies, and much of that leisure was spent in securing and maintaining bonds of personal attachment within extended kinship and regional networks.[3] Conspicuous consumption, where it existed, was mainly of food and drink and mostly occurred to mark significant events in the life cycle – births, marriages and funerals – or it was seasonal, to mark the harvest or mid-winter, or it took the form of elaborate hospitality for important guests. A heavy drinking culture was particularly significant, and the alcohol consumed was either locally produced spirits, making use of precious grain, or expensive imported wines and brandy. The hosting of large celebrations, with drinking and feasting, dancing, music and sporting entertainments, was a mark of status among the Highland elite, among their peers and in the eyes of the peasantry. But such celebrations were notoriously riotous and were seen by outsiders, including the state, as a cause of poverty and lawlessness.

Concern over Highland disorder gave rise to various devices for bringing the Highland gentry under crown control, in the hope that the elite would operate as a good example to the rest of the population. Paradoxically, some of these devices added new and expensive consumption habits to an existing inclination for luxury. One of the innovations was the imposition from the later sixteenth century of what might be termed 'heraldic consumerism', whereby the king sought to gain control over warring and disorderly clan elites through the imposition of a carefully recorded heraldic order and a legal requirement for frequent processing under the watchful eye of the office of the King's Lion. Attendance at regular parliaments in Edinburgh, riding in formal processions in the capital and bearing the arms of the family on official occasions were devices for ensuring proper respect for a centrally controlled hierarchy of noblemen and crown, but they were also costly in clothing, accommodation and horses. The funerals of notables, which had long attracted mass attendance, were also brought under the control of the King's Lion at Arms to secure lawful inheritance of estates. They became public events requiring new mourning clothes, livery for horses, painted shields and hangings for houses and churches, along with food and drink for the mourners who took part in the vast processions that wound their way through the countryside and in and out of neighbouring towns. Even in the second half of the eighteenth century, notable funerals were sometimes attended in the old style, as noted with amusement by Dr William Sinclair of Thurso in 1769 at the funeral of his kinsman, Sinclair of Freswick.

Langwell was in town at our market, or, as he designs himself, Captain Robert Sutherland of Langwell and Brabster, Esq. I shall give you an account of his procession at Freswick's burial. First comes himself, mounted on a gray nag . . . low-sized crape hat-band, and a streamer from each cock at the back part, red coat and vest, white breeches, mounted with black, lappels and cuffs to the coat of that colour; on the right and left about a yard behind him, and as much to the right and left of the line in which he rode, two gilly-wet-feet, each with a leashed greyhound; then following three old-looking footmen in abreast of the line . . . he had his horse covered with a net made of white, red and green silk.[4]

The consumerist tendency implicit in heraldic discipline was paralleled from the early seventeenth century by the legal requirements that the sons of the gentry be educated in the Lowlands to break their cultural attachments to the Highlands and to introduce them to more civilised forms of behaviour. As a consequence, young men became familiar with urban consumption habits and adopted Lowland styles of clothing. But though their cultural attachments were weakened, they certainly were not lost. Men who were familiar with life beyond the Highlands engaged in the practices of culture shifting from one material environment to the other. This was less true of women, who rarely ventured outside the Highlands and whose clothing, though mostly following the Lowland norm, was less likely to be as modern and luxurious as that of men.[5] And it was not yet widely reflected in housing or domestic material culture.

Seventeenth-century Highland housing, though not without comfort, was often unsuited to the types of furnishing that defined the modern interior of the day. The tendency for ordinary people and even some of the lesser elite to live in temporary dwellings and turf houses meant that wood or textiles for wall decoration were soon damaged by damp. Defensible tower houses or castles – the usual abode of the laird and his family – were also damp, and with their narrow stairs, small rooms and small windows could not accommodate large pieces of modern furniture. Houses of this type were made comfortable and sophisticated with portable textiles and tapestries, often manufactured in Europe, and also with elaborately gilded coats of arms, which were carried from place to place. But the furniture was rustic, and larger items such as tables were built in situ.[6] Modern objects, when these were acquired, were usually easily transported small status-items such as silverware or clocks. In 1704, 'furniture, mirrors and clocks' were the third most important category of goods, by value, imported into Scotland.[7]

By the later seventeenth century, even the ordinary people were becoming aware of the world of consumption that lay beyond the Highlands, for as reported by Martin Martin, tutor to a gentleman's family on Skye, it was not unusual for Atlantic trading ships to drop anchor along the north west coast when taking refuge from severe weather. Ships such as the *Dromedary* of London, of 600 tons burden, with a rich cargo of goods from the Indies, also carried passengers, with fashionable clothing and modern manners to match.[8] What is more, an array of modern goods was available locally through itinerant salesmen with 'packs' of little luxuries for sale. Again as noted by Martin Martin, 'there are some peddlers from the shire of Moray, and other parts, who of late have fixed their residence in the isle of Skye, and travel through the remotest isles without any molestation; though some of these peddlers speak no Irish'.[9] Peddlers or packmen carried the same types of products that were seen elsewhere in rural Britain: small metal items such as buckles or buttons, textiles and ribbons, and modest quantities of tea, sugar and tobacco. Tobacco was reputedly their best-selling stock.[10] They travelled around the markets and fairs, which were frequent occurrences in Highland districts following the legislation of 1660,[11] and remained the usual source of modern goods for ordinary people throughout the eighteenth century. But they also carried scarce cash away from the region.

By the 1690s, consumer spending among those who could afford it tended to go in a few well-established directions, such as on Lowland clothing decorated with jewellery, decorative arms for men, imported drinks such as wine and brandy, tobacco and snuff, and exotic foodstuffs like sugar. Lowland clothing was a mark of social status. Exotic food and drink were integral to the culture of conspicuous hospitality that prevailed in the region, despite legislative interventions. It still placed a burden on the fragile economy[12] and was still a cause, or so it seemed to outsiders, of idleness and violence.[13] All of these consuming 'traditions' continued into the eighteenth century, but there was also growing evidence of new types of consumer spending from the later seventeenth century. A nobleman such as Lord Glenorchy, soon to be elevated to an earldom, spent part of the year in London and also visited Bath, but while living on his estate in Perthshire was regularly supplied with the latest books, new glassware and all the other paraphernalia of metropolitan luxury, mostly sent from England via a merchant in the nearby town of Perth.[14] Lord Glenorchy, who not that long before had led a military raid in Caithness, spent considerable sums on the development of his principal country house, Balloch Castle, later known as Taymouth,[15] and it is not surprising that new house building lower down the social hierarchy was also a stimulus to new patterns of consuming.

THE WORLD OF GOODS

The early eighteenth century saw a surge of modern house building in the Highlands. Houses of stone and slate in a simple neo-classical style, which replaced the older fortified towers and turf dwellings, created opportunities for comfortable domestic life, and it is not surprising that the move to a new house was often an occasion for purchasing new commodities and adopting more fashionable modes of living, even when the participants were beyond a fashionable age. Patrick Campbell of Barcaldine and his wife, Lucy Cameron, both in their fifties, moved in 1724 from Barcaldine Castle, their modest tower overlooking the coast, to a newly completed mansion, Dalfuir, a few miles inland. They left most of the older furnishings in the castle with the laird's elderly mother, who had been liferented the property on the death of her husband in 1716, 'excepting the hail silverwork and arms, the best clock, cabinet and table'.[16] Much of the now old-fashioned and well-worn household plenishings at Barcaldine Castle had been acquired by the old lady from her generous dowry at the time of her own marriage in the 1670s. They would not have suited the new house, which was filled with new things, including tea china and other objects of modern tableware, along with suitable mahogany furniture, all purchased through A. Galbraith and Co. of Edinburgh.[17] Though Lucy Cameron was in poor health when she moved, and died a few years later, this last stage in her life was spent with levels of comfort and consumer luxury that were previously unknown in the family.[18]

So how did Highland gentry families set about the business of acquiring modern domestic goods in the early eighteenth century? Sometimes these were purchased in bulk in one of the Scottish cities and carried overland or by sea at great expense. This was how Major George Sutherland of Rearquhar chose to furnish his house near Inverness in 1763, using prize money from war.[19] But it was also possible to buy fashionable furniture and other domestic luxuries from local craftsmen, normally made to order, which saved on the cost and trouble of long-distance transportation. Through demand from the rural gentry and 'middling sort', small towns like Inverary were able to support a wide array of craftsmen, mostly apprentice-trained in the Lowlands, who were capable of making good-quality fashionable objects. The furniture makers were 'joiners', not the more refined 'cabinet makers' of Edinburgh or Glasgow. But though their products were what we would today call 'country-made' and usually constructed out of local hardwoods, they were nonetheless sophisticated.[20] Individual craftsmen could have a long-term and profitable relationship with individual families. James Whyte, a joiner in Inverary, was contracted in 1739 to make a dozen chairs in fir and ash – a dining-room set – for Patrick Campbell of Barcaldine, now an elderly widower, for his house Dalfuir.[21] Whyte had also undertaken considerable joinery work in the house itself at about the same time, suggesting a phase of interior restructuring consistent with the creation or extension of a room suitable for use as a dining room. The following year he made a 'good and sufficient chest of drawers' for Colin Campbell, Patrick's son, to go into the newly built Glenure House.[22]

Another Inverary joiner enjoyed commissions from the same family, and reveals the complexity that could attend such orders. Lieutenant Alexander Campbell, fourth son of Patrick Campbell of Barcaldine – who followed a military career and in his short life was much attached to luxury and comfort – requested his cousin, John Campbell of Kintraw, to enquire in Inverary in 1743 about ordering an escritoire, commonly called a 'scrutoir', or writing desk, which was a desirable piece of portable furniture for a young man of fashion and particularly favoured by those with no settled home, such as serving officers or young men living in lodgings.[23] Kintraw replied:

> I spoke with Alex MacIntyre, joiner, and you have the prices of the different kinds of scrutoir as follow viz to a scrutoir entirely of mahoganie, five guineas; to one of mahoganie and the boxes of 'wensiol' [local wood for lining] four pounds ten shillings sufficiently mounted. To one of Virginie walnut tree four pounds fifteen shillings but he says to have the very best of mountings will stand more money than the above prices of the scrutoirs as for one of elm he says it will not answer the purpose.[24]

This awareness of what will 'answer the purpose' and reference to the 'very best of mountings' suggests that an Inverary-based craftsman, who may have travelled regularly to Glasgow, was fully acquainted with what was required in an item of furniture with high-fashion associations, which the owner would take with him on his travels beyond the Highlands. That such furniture was of symbolic importance to men is indicated in the divorce proceedings of Ann Sinclair of Brabster against her husband Robert Sutherland of Langwell, for when the latter removed his possessions from the Brabster household in 1771, the list was headed by a 'mahoganie scrutoir'.[25]

In the absence of pattern books, which were not produced in Scotland before the late eighteenth century[26] the principal way in which local craftsmen had the knowledge to make an item like a 'scrutoir' was through copying a piece that was made elsewhere, and doing so at a fraction of the price that might be charged in a major city. As late as 1789, James Morrison, a joiner and furniture maker in Lismore – a small settlement in northern Argyll –

requested the loan of a parlour chair from Alexander Campbell of Barcaldine, to make copies for Alexander's brother Captain Colin Campbell, the then tenant of Glenure House.[27] With such an original as his pattern he could doubtless have made similar chairs for other customers as well. Alexander Campbell – the lawyer laird who had married the daughter of Campbell 'of the bank' – was mostly resident in Edinburgh at this time, and the 'parlour chair' was probably Edinburgh-made. Indeed, it may have been an Edinburgh-made copy of a London-made chair from one of the major cabinet makers such as Chippendale.[28] This practice of regional copying meant that an item of furniture, in the style though not necessarily the quality or detail of a Chippendale, could be found in the Highlands within a short time of the initial design and manufacture in the metropolis. Gentry families and the local craftsmen who served them would be highly sensitive to such associations.

The making of modern consumer items in the Highlands was normally undertaken by craftsmen who were based in the small burghs that fringed the region, either along the coast or on the Lowland border. Inverness, Thurso, Crieff, Callander and Perth in the east along with Fort William, and Oban and Inverary in the west all supported a modest but significant commercial infrastructure. Most these towns expanded from the 1720s, having begun as little more than market sites. They had modern building schemes with new street layouts for fashionable housing and the construction of new institutions such as public meeting rooms. In Thurso there were twenty houses that paid window tax on ten or more windows in 1748, and thirty-five by 1768.[29] Dr William Sinclair the elder and his son, Dr William Sinclair of Freswick, lived in one of these houses. Such towns accommodated the rising class of merchants, craftsmen and shopkeepers, dancing masters and mantua makers, a handful of professionals, particularly lawyers, and small but flourishing gentry communities comprising single women, teenage children receiving an education, army officers on half-pay and a scattering of landowners. The latter group included John Campbell of Barcaldine, who in middle age and long after he had abandoned Barcaldine Castle, was a crown factor for the forfeited Perthshire estates and kept a house in Crieff for nearly twenty years from the early 1750s. Another gentleman official was David Brodie of Pitgaviny, a modest laird who was employed in the lucrative post of controller of customs in Inverness and was living in the town when he died in 1738. He had many fashionable possessions, including such modern specialist tableware as 'coffy breakfast cups' and breakfast knives. He owned a set of chairs in Russian leather, numerous pieces of fine mahogany furniture, silverware and pictures, including prints of the duke of Marlborough and eleven apostles.[30]

The material culture of Inverness, which was a garrison town as well as a trading centre, was carefully observed by Edmund Burt in the 1720s. Though he commented on the poverty and run-down appearance of this and other Scottish burghs, he also noted that there was a modern coffee house with newspapers available.[31]

> The gentlemen, magistrates, merchants, and shopkeepers, are dressed after the English manner, and make a good appearance enough, according to their several ranks, and the working tradesmen are not very ill clothed; and now and then . . . you see some of their women of fashion . . . when they appear, they are generally well dressed in the English mode.[32]

Burt was critical of the attitudes of the local working tradesmen and accused them of indolence, but he also remarked on the workmanship of a young wright, 'which was more like the work of one of your cabinet-makers in London than that of an Inverness carpenter'. Most ambitious and talented young men left the town for better opportunities elsewhere, as they did in most provincial places.[33] But Inverness, Crieff or Inverary were small nodes of modern consumer fashion of a type that could be seen throughout the British Isles.[34]

Businessmen in these Highland towns supplied a wide array of modern goods, including furniture and clothing, silverware, wigs and shoes. In all probability, they also maintained displays of goods for sale.[35] People who lived in the Highland towns owned remarkably modern household possessions, and it is striking how many goods that were manufactured elsewhere were available for sale 'off the shelf' from what were recognisable as shops. Colin Campbell of Glenure, who travelled widely in the Highlands, made 'off the shelf' purchases of consumer movables from several local towns when fitting up his new house prior to marriage. He bought a 'tea equipage' in Crieff in 1738, a white carved teapot in Inverary in 1739 and a number of items, including a punch bowl and a milk pot, in Oban later in the same year.[36] By the later decades of the eighteenth century it was even possible to find shops on some of the remoter islands, as described by James Boswell in 1773 while visiting the Isle of Coll. 'There is a man goes every year with a boat to Greenock and brings home a quantity of hardware, ribbons, and other small things: and keeps a little shop at the small village.'[37]

The relationship between a member of the gentry and shopkeepers in nearby towns could be long-term and complex and based on reciprocal arrangements of various types. In 1748, the Lady Dowager Mackay of Bighouse, who was the grandmother-in-law of Colin Campbell of Glenure, purchased a 'chagreen case with 8 fine white glass bottles', costing 12s., from a local trader called Alexander Sutherland. Sutherland rented his 'house, shop, cellar and kaile yard' from Lady Dowager Bighouse, and he was her regular supplier for many years of sugar, tea, tobacco and rum, domestic ironware, glass for windows and sundry building materials for the upkeep of her house.[38] The relationship with urban traders was also often kin-based, as in the Barcaldine family where Robert Campbell, the Stirling merchant, younger brother of John and Colin Campbell, was a regular middleman for consumer purchases for the family from the 1740s through to the 1770s.[39] Female family members, with their grocery or millinery shops, also supplied their female relations. Bailie John Steuart of Inverness, whose letter books provide a rich insight into the dealings, contracts and connections of a Highland man of business, was another merchant with strong supply relationships within a network of kin that ranged from Skye to Harris and North Uist, and on the mainland from Glengarry to the Appin peninsula. Luxuries including fancy textiles, books, prints, ready-made clothes, hats and handmade wallpaper, along with modern manufactured items of a more utilitarian character such as kitchenware, were ordered from as far afield as London, Rotterdam and the Mediterranean, and dispatched throughout the Highlands via Steuart in Inverness.[40]

As we have seen when looking at trading careers, financial disasters and bankruptcy were common among merchants and usually gave rise to a sale of household effects. The death of a property owner was also commonly followed by a sale. Through the second-hand market, which operated at all levels of society and throughout Britain, modern domestic goods that had come into a remote town such as Inverness were quickly diffused to the hinterland. When Alex Bailie, merchant and town clerk of Inverness, died in 1733 a wide range of household items were sold by auction to local buyers. Though much of what he possessed was everyday and prosaic, with a distinctly 'Highland' flavour, he owned quantities of china, which would have been imported, as well as several large mirrors, an expensive luxury. He owned a barometer and a number of framed maps, which were typical room decorations for a wealthy merchant at this time. He also owned two sets of framed prints, one entitled the *Trial of King Charles 1st* and the second the *Harlot's Progress* by William Hogarth, the latter in his possession within a very short time of its first production in London.[41] His rooms were decorated with tapestry wall hangings and had a heavily upholstered quality that was more reminiscent of Europe than of Scotland, but was typical of merchants in east-coast ports with their strong connections with the Netherlands and the Baltic. He enjoyed a high level of domestic comfort and luxury.[42]

The 'public roup' in 1763 of the possessions of John Clerk, another

Inverness merchant, provided details of the purchasers who acquired each item. The sale was attended by a broad spectrum of local society – several dozen people in all made purchases – and included other merchants as well as craftsmen like William McConchy, a shoemaker, who bought a tent bed with yellow curtains. The local schoolmaster was there, buying many items of ordinary kitchenware along with a tent bed with red curtains; from the purchases he made, he seems to have been setting up a new household. An army captain made purchases, as did the local lawyer, who bought five pieces of printed wallpaper. There were several women at the sale, including Mrs Fraser of Castlewynd in Inverness, who kept one of the largest houses in the town, probably a lodging house or an inn. Women were also often involved in pricing second-hand goods, particularly textiles. There were local farmers and lairds with a particular interest in the farming equipment and animals but also bidding for linen and domestic objects. The dead man's servant, James Clerk, was there too, and acquired a variety of modest items from the kitchen.[43] This sort of sale, which normally took place in the house of the bankrupt or deceased, was a communal occasion, providing opportunities to buy things as well as to see them in situ in the homes of the relatively rich. Those who could not afford to participate in the modern 'world of goods' could nevertheless see it at close quarters, even in the Highlands.

Roups or auctions were a frequent occurrence in the Highlands of Scotland, as they were elsewhere, embracing all manner of goods. Attendance at auctions was a normal occurrence, and several members of the Campbell family of Barcaldine furnished their houses in this way.[44] The indignity of having household property 'poinded' and auctioned to pay off debts was not unknown in the genteel families that feature in this study, as Ann Sinclair of Brabster and her cousin Dr William Sinclair of Freswick could both attest.[45] Edmund Burt, in Inverness, remarked in the early 1730s: 'We had the other day, in our coffee-room, an auction of books.' Among the collection – which he scornfully described as 'trash' – was a copy of Martin's *Descriptions of the Western Islands of Scotland*[46] published in 1703 and the most famous book about the Highlands at that time. But though they mostly took place in towns, country auctions were also a common event and could result in the penetration of luxury goods into very remote areas. In the house of Coirechatachan on Skye in 1773, James Boswell noted a number of framed prints, including a 'mezzotinto of Mrs Brooks (by some strange chance in Skye)'.[47] It later emerged that Mackinnon of Coirechatachan had bought this image of a fashionable London actress at the sale of another Skye family who were leaving for North America. Since many Skye emigrants were tenants and tacksmen with military experience, the original owner may well have spent some time in

England and acquired the print of the London actress in the capital. Of course, such participation in the visual print culture of London was not new. As noted above, prints by Hogarth on distinctly metropolitan moral topics, such as the *Harlot's Progress*, could be found in the Highlands or in other remote parts of Britain such as Ireland within a very short time of being published in London.[48]

CONSUMING THROUGH INTERMEDIARIES

Though the Highland gentry had local access to modern consumer goods, or to craftsmen who could custom-make such goods within the region, much of their consuming was inevitably done at a distance through intermediaries. This was certainly the experience of women in the first half of the century, who were largely resident on their family estates and rarely, if ever, visited the towns or cities. Husbands, brothers and sons were often commissioned to buy articles of dress and even shoes for women, young and old, and given licence to make decisions about colour and cut. In the early part of the century, when Highland gentlewomen were barely literate, their commissions were also communicated through literate intermediaries. In the 1710s and 1720s, Patrick Campbell of Barcaldine gave frequent instructions to his sons on behalf of their mother. From their teenage years, John and Colin Campbell, like all boys of similar status, had regular contacts with life beyond the Highlands and were commissioned to make purchases of various kinds in the local towns or in Edinburgh.[49] There is little account of how favourably these commissions were received, though in writing to their father the boys did occasionally enquire how their mother had liked some item or other. In remote areas, opportunities for returning unsuitable goods were few, but things that were not liked could be sold to local traders. As Baillie John Steuart of Inverness wrote to one of his business connections in London in 1733,

> This comes to advise that the 24 yards of silk stuff bought for my Daughter Margreat came safe to hand . . . but I am sorry to tell you it does not please the Women, being judged too dear of its kind. Besides, it seems the figure of it is not so agreeable to them; so that its still on hand waiting a Chap[man] will buy it.[50]

The chapman or peddlar who did eventually purchase the fabric would in all probability have cut it into smaller pieces for onward sale to country ladies in the rural Highlands.

In the early decades of the eighteenth century Highland gentlewomen had little, if any, contact with Lowlands, but from about the 1720s they were commonly sent away in their mid-teens for a few months of formal schooling – and part of the purpose of an educational sojourn in Perth or Edinburgh was to introduce them to the world of goods and give them contacts that they could exploit at a distance once married and settled to family life in the Highlands.[51] Young women acquired their knowledge of textiles and clothing through being trained to make their own costumes while at school and by placing commissions with tailors, stay makers or mantua makers. This practical training allowed them to understand better the technical process of luxury clothing production, which was useful knowledge when it came to placing orders at a distance and making judgements on costs. Young women at this stage of life purchased household textiles for their future married life and were introduced to the social rituals and ceremonies that defined 'polite' society and were built around modern consumerism. Tea parties, dancing classes and music lessons trained young women into particular forms of fashionable social behaviour that they could practise back at home – and all required an appropriate and properly schooled relationship with clothing and domestic objects from furniture and tableware to musical instruments. They also attended 'pastry' classes with a pastry master, with the aim of learning the art of refined pastry and sweetmeat making of the type that made use of luxury imported foodstuffs such as sugar and lemons. Fashionable puddings made by the lady of the house, and still preserved in surviving manuscript recipe books, required fashionable tableware, such as the syllabub glasses that were ubiquitous in Scottish gentry and middle-rank houses from the 1730s in the Highlands as elsewhere.[52]

Married women living in the Highlands and without the opportunity to go shopping in person could place personal orders through intermediaries, because they had experienced, however briefly, the fashionable urban world of goods. The use of intermediaries in consumer goods transactions was also widespread among men, including many individuals who made regular visits to Lowland cities. Sometimes these intermediaries were business associates, as when Patrick Campbell – in stocking his new house of Dalfuir in 1724 – made use of the main customer for the Barcaldine estate timber sales, A. Galbraith and Co., to buy him tea and tableware in Edinburgh, presumably with extended credit given. Intermediaries were often a personal or family connection – someone whose taste and judgement could be trusted – though in Highland society, business life and family and personal life were so intimately connected that it was hard to separate the two. The relationship between George Sutherland of Rearquhar, a military man, and his nephew

George Gun Munro, a London insurance broker, had this character. In the 1760s, George Munro made many London purchases for his uncle, including a sporting gun and 'some prints and pictures suitable as to taste and price'.[53] In return for this and many other services, Sutherland kept an eye on Munro's small property of Pontzfield near Tain. Hugh Mackay of Bighouse, who visited Edinburgh frequently for health reasons in later life, made special purchases for his friends at home, which included a pair of buckskin breeches for young William Sinclair, the trainee doctor.[54] Many years before, Hugh Mackay had made a number of purchases in Edinburgh in 1751 on behalf of his son-in-law, Colin Campbell of Glenure, all destined for Glenure House in Argyll. Though a frequent direct purchaser in Edinburgh and elsewhere, Colin Campbell also had a long-term commercial relationship with William Danskin, a merchant in Edinburgh, who was connected with the firm of Danskin and Campbell in Stirling, the trading partnership that included his brother Robert. Through William Danskin, acting on remote instruction as an intermediary, he acquired a vast array of personal and household goods over many years, such as textiles (including tartan), tea, napkins, writing paper, wax, gloves and books. Danskin, in yet another illustration of the intimate relationships between modern consumerism and other reciprocal obligations, also managed some of Glenure's private affairs in Edinburgh, including the maintenance and education of Tibbie Campbell, one of Colin's illegitimate daughters.[55] Indeed, commercial kin, including Robert Campbell, the Stirling merchant, often took responsibility for the natural offspring of lairds, partly because such children were destined for urban commercial careers in later life.

CLOTHING CULTURES

One area of consumerism that was often undertaken through intermediaries was the purchase of clothing. Women in particular gave instruction to their menfolk in town to buy clothing, and kinswomen based in towns – which often included women who had been trained as garment makers – supplied their sisters and cousins in the country. Men would also order clothing at a distance. Duncan Campbell the lawyer laird, on first being appointed a sheriff for Killin in 1750, invested in a grand ensemble of clothing befitting his new status, which was ordered from a catalogue supplied by his brother Robert in Stirling.[56] Fabric was sometimes ordered in the opposite direction, particularly in the early eighteenth century. Lord Glenorchy, writing from Perth, made the following request of Alexander Campbell of Barcaldine: 'My wife desires me to recommend to you the getting her from some good lady in your shire a good Highland plead with light colours in it for her winter gown.'[57]

Studies of Scottish clothing are dominated by the preoccupation with plaids, tartan and the kilt as the iconic representation of Highland and Gaelic culture at a time of change.[58] In the wake of the '45 rebellion, some elements of Highland clothing were proscribed by law, or reinvented as the uniform of the new Highland regiments.[59] Gaelic poetry was written about clothing, including a poem by a cousin of the Campbell family of Barcaldine, a minister's wife, on the loss of 'the Highland dress' following proscription.[60] Yet in the day-to-day experience of the Highland gentry these issues were rarely aired, and lairds who were charged with policing the legislation on clothing proscription were not always sure when an item of clothing (or fabric) was, in fact, a statement of clannish attachment, or merely an old checked blanket. Certainly they were liberal in their interpretations of what was acceptable, for having been told in November 1748 that the act prohibiting the use of plaid and philibeg had to be intimated at church doors in Gaelic, Duncan Campbell (later of Glenure), the sheriff-substitute for Perthshire at Killin, was also advised:

> You can take all the opportunities you can of letting it be known that tartan may still be worn in cloaks westcoats breeches or trews, but that if they use loose plaids they may [be] tartan but either all of one colour, or strip'd with other colours than those formerly used, and if they have a mind to use their old plaids, I don't see but they may make them into the shape of a cloak and so wear them in that way, which tho' buttoned or tied about the neck, if long enough, may be taken up at one side and throwne over the other shoulder by which it will answere most of the purposes of the loose plaid.[61]

Changes in the clothing of the Highland gentry were subtle and reveal a capacity for local cultural practices to operate alongside modern Lowland fashions. As the quotation above suggests, a striking feature of traditional clothing in the Highlands was the uncut garment made out of a single piece of cloth, draped or wrapped about the body in various ways according to gender or status, and held in place with ornamental pins, broaches, buckles or belts. The value and significance of this type of clothing, which was also found in different body arrangements in the borders of Scotland and northern England, was located in the quality and colours of the fabric, and in its interpretation and use by the wearer.[62] In Highland Scotland this garment was known as the 'arisaid' when worn by women, or the belted plaid when worn by men. According to Burt in the 1720s:

The plaid is the undress of the ladies; and to a genteel woman who adjusts it with a good air, is a becoming veil . . . It is made of silk or fine worsted, chequered with various lively colours, two breadths wide, and three yards in length; it is brought over the head, and may hide or discover the face according to the wearer's fancy or occasion; it reaches to the waist behind; one corner falls as low as the ankle on one side; and the other part, in folds, hangs down from the opposite arm.[63]

The arisaid, which was practical and adaptable, was used to articulate complex social signals, such as modesty and decorum, flirtatiousness or a rejection of sexual advances (much in the manner of a modern Indian sari) and, as noted by Burt, could even indicate political allegiance or religious devotion. Highland gentlewomen wore it in the Highlands, and also elsewhere in Britain. Increasingly, however, it came to be associated with outdoor activity and the working lives of labouring women and went out of fashion among the Highland elite. Indeed, an early eighteenth-century Scottish conduct book gave the following advice to ladies: 'It is indecent to enter the room of their superiors in a scarf, or with a plaid, or with their gowns tucked up, or in any careless dress.'[64] Yet the arisaid was still being illustrated in London-produced political print satires of the 1760s to indicate Scottish gentlewomen at court, suggesting a style of clothing with sufficient contemporary currency to be recognised as distinct.[65]

As already noted, since the seventeenth century elite men and those of the 'middling sort' in the Highlands, including commercial men, were largely dressed in the English style. This meant a typical ensemble of shirt, waistcoat, jacket or coat, breeches and stockings, shoes, hat and wig. Colin Campbell of Glenure in the 1740s owned a 'light pale bob wig' and a 'neck buckled wig'.[66] However, there was also a similarly complex and nuanced use of the plaid among men in the first half of the eighteenth century as that seen among gentlewomen. The plaid, belted or draped, was worn on top of whatever was the standard 'English' type of clothing of the day, to act as a robust outdoor garment with strong associations of locality and masculinity. For poor men, and the rural peasantry in particular, it was usually the only garment they wore over a shirt or shift, giving rise to shocked comments by some contemporaries at the nakedness of Highlanders.[67] In some circumstances, even gentlemen would be dressed in just a plaid and shirt, particularly when walking over wet ground or sitting indoors at home, for while they may have owned breeches and stockings, they chose not to wear them.[68]

A practical farming laird of the early to mid-eighteenth century who was accustomed to moving back and forth between the Highlands and Lowlands, such as Colin Campbell of Glenure, owned different types of clothing for the different parts of Scotland. Wearing the plaid when living in the Highlands was a part of his Highland persona.[69] His clothing was a statement of belonging to place and people, as important for his image and reputation among the ordinary folk as it was to his own identity. But as Edmund Burt observed in the 1720s, with considerable insight to the subtleties of local culture, this was not always true.

> Upon one of my peregrinations, accompanied by a Highland gentleman, who was one of the clan through which I was passing, I observed the women to be in great anger with him about something that I did not understand; at length, I asked wherein he had offended them? Upon this question he laughed, and told me his greatcoat was the cause of their wrath; and that their reproach was, that he could not be contended with the garb of his ancestors, but was degenerated into a Lowlander, and condescended to follow their unmanly fashions.[70]

It seems the anger of the local peasant women was at the absence of the plaid as an outer garment, with all the cultural and also economic associations that went with local manufacture by women such as themselves. In their judgement, he had abandoned a style of clothing that evoked masculinity. The anger was not because Burt's gentleman, in common with most of the others he encountered, was wearing Lowland clothing beneath the great coat, or modern shoes or a wig, the latter an important indicator of metropolitan politeness. But that he had abandoned a key outward symbol of his native cultural attachments, and his response to Burt's question suggests that he knew this full well, and whilst mildly embarrassed, did not really care.

Of course this Highland gentleman, who was not named, whilst not choosing to wear a plaid in everyday life, may have adopted some more distinctly Highland form of clothing for special occasions. Painted portraits of the period that were intended for public display – like the clan portraits commissioned by the laird of Grant and hung at Huntley Castle – show men dressed in a wide variety of clothing according to the permutations of contemporary fashion, all either constructed out of quasi-tartan fabric or topped in one way or another with a plaid-like garment to secure a local statement of symbolic attachments and identity.[71] These public statements could be extremely complex both long before and long after the '45 rebellion, as is particularly revealed in the tartan portrait of John Campbell 'of the bank'. Yet the reality of experience throughout the eighteenth century was that Highland gentlemen were dressed most of the time in styles of clothing that defined the British gentleman more generally in Britain, and they adopted symbols of their Highland connections only as occasion required.

As British gentlemen, men of this class were preoccupied with the usual clothing concerns that evoked their status and wealth. Wigs, decorative swords and fine sporting guns defined a gentlemanly status, wherever that gentleman happened to be living.[72] An accumulation of fine white linen undergarments – shirts, stocks and hose – spoke of wealth and the employment of servants to maintain such clothing in pristine condition.[73] These were constants, though young men by the end of the eighteenth century had abandoned wig-wearing for their own fashionably dressed hair. Even those Highland gentlemen who flocked into the army during the Napoleonic years were not always depicted in Highland attire in their portraits. Duncan Campbell of Barcaldine, painted by Raeburn in the early nineteenth century, wore the dress uniform of an elite English regiment, with nothing beyond his name to suggest the Highland connections that he was rapidly leaving behind.[74] Yet one late eighteenth-century commentator, John Ramsay of Ochtertyre, believed that the Highland gentleman possessed a higher level of luxury in his clothing than was usual elsewhere, and this was the legacy of seventeenth-century habits.

> The dress of our gentry resembled in some particulars their domestic economy. It was in general plain and frugal, but upon great occasions they scrupled no expense. Even within the last fifty years . . . it was the etiquette, not only when they married, but also upon paying their addresses, to get laced clothes and laced saddle furniture – an expense which neither suited their ordinary appearance nor their estate. No people formerly went deeper into that folly than the Highland gentry when they came to the low country . . . David Home Stewart of Argarty told me that, being in Morven before 1745 buying cattle, he spied early in the morning a person coming up laced from top to toe. 'Who is that?' said he to his host. 'It is our laird' said the other.[75]

Certainly the clothing purchases of Colin Campbell of Glenure in the 1740s seem to confirm these observations. In 1743 he purchased silver lace and silver cloth for making into clothing. The previous year he had bought a 'suite of archers cloathes with bonnet and sash', and in 1744 he spent over £60 on clothing in Edinburgh prior to joining the army, including a 'scarlet hussar and vest'.[76]

Women's clothing, like those of men, was mostly dictated by elite British norms, with only the arisaid remaining distinct, and by the second half of the century this was all but abandoned in favour of silken plaid shawls, which in turn evolved into the special-occasion fine tartan sash worn over one shoulder and fastened at the waist to embellish a ball gown.[77] By 1800, tartan was a fashion fabric, and tartan-military styles of women's costume had been adopted throughout Europe. Long gone were the days when the Highland gentlewoman made her own clothes from homespun fabrics, or relied on the travelling tailor. Also long gone were the days when a Highland gentlewoman carried her shoes and stockings – or had a servant carry them for her[78] – when walking out of doors, for by the end of the century genteel women rarely walked over rough ground, and many wives of Highland lairds only rarely ventured into the Highlands. One of the biggest changes in elite clothing culture among women was the shift away from wearing an apron and carrying keys to signal the identity of the practical housewife – the woman who managed her kitchen and dairy, made cheeses and fancy pastries, and who trained her daughters in similar skills and supervised the servants. But this change in clothing and social behaviour was not unique to the Highlands.

Women like men were preoccupied with luxury and fashion in their clothing. They had similar accumulations of white garments in the form of shifts, petticoats, handkerchiefs and stockings to mark their status. Linenware of this type, along with domestic linen for the bed and table, was necessary for the new codes of cleanliness and personal hygiene that defined the polite elite.[79] Women wore elaborate powdered wigs, delicate pale kid gloves and fashionable jewellery.[80] They aspired to clothing made in one of the big cities, or even in London. But they normally made do with the local mantua maker in a nearby town, who doubtless had word of the latest styles from her contacts in the cities, as did the local tailors who clothed the men.[81] Women, regardless of status or fashion, continued to have a more intimate relationship with their clothing than was usual among men.[82] Women's clothing was more likely to be made into other garments for other members of the family to signal emotional connections and rites of passage. The skirt of the fine woollen riding habit, for instance, which was the usual garment worn by a gentlewoman as a travelling dress and was often acquired newly made for her wedding trip, was symbolically made into the first trousers of her first son, a practice seen throughout Scotland and the north of England.[83] Women at all levels of genteel society spent time and creative energy organising their clothing and trimming their headgear. Clothing was passed to daughters, and often preserved for sentimental reasons. Clothing was also given to female servants as a common form of reward for good service. But Highland gentlewomen, like their menfolk, were caught in the 'luxury trap' when it came to clothing, as with other objects of consumption. An increasing expenditure on fashionable dress was necessary to maintain status and prestige, whether in Edinburgh or Argyll.

CONSUMER BEHAVIOUR IN THE LATE EIGHTEENTH CENTURY

By the second half of the eighteenth century the consumer infrastructure of Highland Scotland had evolved beyond all early recognition, and the Highland towns, though still relatively small, had become remarkably sophisticated places, with new street layouts and significant developments in new domestic and institutional building. Inverary, for instance, in the early 1790s, accommodated just over 1,000 people, including six merchants, five shopkeepers, fifteen tailors, three barbers and two milliners as well as a range of other types of craftsmen. There were several lawyers and other professionals, along with many genteel female households. The town owned one vessel employed in foreign trade and had a further half-dozen smaller boats involved in importing meal, coal, porter and 'merchants goods' from ports in the south.[84] The town of Crieff was almost twice the size of Inverary in the 1790s and provided more fashionable service trades such as clockmakers, of whom there were four, along with eleven mantua makers. There were forty-nine merchants or shopkeepers in the town, and nineteen of these sold tea.[85] The fishing industry was flourishing in Thurso and the number of professional men was rising; there were three doctors. Two young lady artists of the town, celebrated for their miniature-painting, had recently left to set up business in Edinburgh, and new assembly rooms attached to one of the two local inns were under construction, the first to be built north of Inverness.[86] Each of these towns catered to the local population, and also for the growing numbers of tourists who now visited the Highlands and were accommodated in modern inns, normally – as was the case with much of the modern burgh infrastructure – developed by local landowners such as the duke of Argyll at Inverary or Sir John Sinclair of Ulbster at Thurso. By the end of the century, road transport was greatly improved, movement in and out of the region was increasingly common, and most gentry families, including women, spent some if not all of the year living in Lowland cities, and particularly in Edinburgh. Except among the poorest of peasants, access to the modern world of goods was widespread in Highland society by the end of the eighteenth century, and a growing middle class of businessmen and businesswomen competed for customers.[87]

Local craftsmen continued to flourish in the Highland counties, and still worked on house building and furniture making to meet local demand. But increasingly the consuming activity of the Highland gentry tended to bypass the local suppliers in favour of those in Edinburgh, Glasgow or even London. The Malcolm family of Poltalloch, a small estate in southern Argyllshire, provides a good illustration of these new consumption habits, happily supported by a substantial non-estate income. Obliged to enter business to supplement the limited returns on the estate, by the later eighteenth century the head of the family, Neil Malcolm, was largely resident in London, from where he operated a considerable and lucrative trading interest with Jamaica in sugar, rum and slaves. He owned Jamaican estates and had married a Jamaica heiress. For most of the year, he and his family lived in London at a fashionable address in Upper Seymour Street. Between 1786 and 1791 he spent £775 on furnishing the house with fine furniture, gilded mirrors, goldsmiths' work and modern stoves for the kitchen. Malcolm paid tax on a private four-wheeled carriage, kept five horses for use by himself and his son, and employed five male domestic servants and three female, all subject to assessed taxes. In the 1790s, Poltalloch House in Scotland was a very modest and old-fashioned place tenanted by Neil's younger brother, who ran the day-to-day affairs of the estate and routinely urged his brother to visit more often and live among his people. Less than £40 was spent on furniture and fittings for Poltalloch House at this time, for mahogany furniture, two mirrors, some glassware and kitchenware, some of this sent from London and some sourced locally. This, and a small expenditure on maintaining the property, was minor indeed compared to the London spending.[88]

The family of Campbell of Barcaldine, with near full-time residence in Edinburgh by the end of the century, purchased furniture from Trotter (the elite maker of neo-classical house fittings, with showrooms in Princes Street), china from Wedgwood, ordered a piano and furniture from London, and the head of the family was painted by Sir Henry Raeburn, the premier portraitist in Scotland.[89] Yet Highland gentry consumerism in the modern manner, with a seemingly inevitable progression towards comfortable excess, was accompanied throughout the eighteenth century by a buoyant demand for goods of Highland origin and Highland cultural association, which generated a complex and distinct material culture. Material objects with antique or emotional family connections were always valued. Genteel women signalled the history of their families through their dress in ways that went beyond the later eighteenth century adoption of clan tartans. Antique lace was refashioned for modern head-dresses and trimming, old silver plaid broaches were worn with pride on modern costumes, and at the end of the eighteenth century there was a vogue for 'Scotch pebbles' (such as agates), which meant that old family jewels with local associations were worn in fashionable places.[90]

In addition to antique clothing items, the recycling of local antique materials into fashionable consumer goods went on in the Highlands, and signalled subtle local associations. James Boswell described at the house of Coirechatachan on Skye, tenanted by Mr Lachlan Mackinnon, how they had 'tea in good order, a treay [tray], silver tea-pot, silver sugar-dish and tongs, silver tea-spoons enough. Our landlord's father had found a treasure of old silver coins, and of these he had made his plate.'[91] The manufacture of the silver tea service had occurred many decades before the visit by Boswell and Johnson, but the lineage of the silver was remembered and told. Whether the tea service was made in the Highlands is not recorded, but it is possible that a silversmith from a nearby town such as Inverness or Perth was involved.[92]

An interest in the ownership and display of antique objects with family associations was also shaped in the later eighteenth century by the new culture of sensibility and romanticism.[93] A poignant illustration is furnished by Louisa Mackay, daughter of Colin Campbell of Glenure, who for many years in her own middle age, living in Caithness, was preoccupied with trying to gain possession of objects connected with her long-dead father. In July 1785 she wrote to her cousin Alexander Campbell of Barcaldine requesting that he give her a pair of silver cups from Glenure House.

> I must introduce once more an old acquaintance to you whom I dare say you have almost forgot. I am sorry there is so little chance of being known to you but by pen and ink, be appraised she is one of your friends in every respect . . . I was rather unwilling my first letter should be asking favours which I hope you will excuse I will not press you to grant my request [unless] its perfectly agreeable and convenient for you. I formerly made the same request to my Uncle, your father . . . no doubt he had good reasons for refusing, but still my anxiety to possess anything [that] was my fathers is too great that I cannot be easy till I attain that happiness. I am told there is a pair of small silver mugs was once his still in the family. If you have no particular fancy to them, it would be doing me the greatest favour to give them to me. Its impossible for me to give you a return equal to the value I put on them, but anything in my power I shall be happy to make any return most agreeable to you. If there is anything else in your house you [would] rather part with than the mugs it will be equally welcome to me, Tho I must say I would prefer them to anything else being a thing I could have my children of [to] teach them to value what had been held and handled by a parent whose memory I respect and love more than I can or will say.'[94]

The mugs in question, which were eventually given to Louisa Mackay, had been purchased in 1749 along with other silver items such as buckles, spurs, seals and cutlery, from Ker and Dempster, silversmiths in Edinburgh, and were engraved with the Glenure coat of arms.[95] They may have been used in Colin and Janet's marriage ceremony, since the purchases at this time also included a 'rose-set diamond ring', almost certainly for the bride. In the Glenure household inventory that was taken following Colin's murder in 1752, when Louisa was just a babe in arms, '2 silver drinking jugs' were listed in a locked closet beneath the stairs, on a shelf with other items of silverware.[96] Though moderately valuable and therefore worth keeping under lock and key, the importance they later acquired in the eyes of the daughter was entirely a product of their history and associations, with a unique Highland dimension. As we shall see in the next chapter, a subtle evocation of antiquity and local attachments was one of the characteristics of modern Highland houses and Highland interiors that paralleled fashionable luxury. These silver mugs in 1752, and even more so in 1785, formed part of a distinctly Highland domestic material culture.

7   Houses

INTRODUCTION

In 1803, Dorothy and William Wordsworth, on their famed tour of the Highlands, spent a night at Glengyle House in Perthshire, the home of Mr Macfarlane, a substantial sheep farmer. The house had been built in 1704 for a minor laird or tacksman and its internal appearance was striking.

> [Mr Macfarlane] showed us into a room upstairs, begged we would sit at our ease, walk out, or do just as we pleased. It was a large square deal wainscoted room, the wainscot black with age, yet had never been painted; it did not look like an English room, yet I do not know in what it differed, except that in England it is not common to see so large and well-built a room so ill-furnished; there were two or three large tables, and a few old chairs of different sorts, as if they had been picked up one did not know how, at sales, or had belonged to different rooms of the house ever since it was built . . . I observed what a contrast there was between the mistress and her kitchen; she did not differ in appearance from an English country lady; but her kitchen, roof, walls and floor of mud, was all black alike; yet now, with the light of a bright fire upon so many happy countenances, the whole room made a pretty sight.[1]

Dorothy Wordsworth was a careful observer of the social and material landscape of Scotland. She frequently remarked on the houses and inns that she and her brother visited and on the manner in which they were furnished. She also noted the appearance of the people, including their clothing. In common with other visitors, she saw how the Highlands offered great variation in the character of domestic accommodation. She encountered clean, comfortable and modern houses, yet on other occasions, among people of similar rank living nearby, she found a want of basic amenities and astonishing levels of domestic filth. The Macfarlane house was home to a prosperous, modern commercial family engaged in farming. The householder and his wife were dressed well, in the modern style. Yet the house, though large and comfortable enough, was primitive even when it was built a century before – the earth floor was a major impediment to cleanliness, and the furniture seemed strange.

Buildings and their contents provide a privileged insight to cultural identity and aspirations. The form and function of buildings as revealed in the layout of rooms, room names and room uses are all indicative of the societies that created them. The house was the focus of a country estate and was of great importance to the eighteenth-century landowner. Like property ownership itself, the country house and the social life that went on there was mainly a masculine preserve.[2] Houses and land gave men political rights. Women sometimes owned country estates and houses in their own right, but they were unable to take direct legal advantage of the privileges that such ownership conveyed, which could cause problems for their properties, families and tenants. In earlier times, Highland houses or castles were fortified structures designed to protect property and articulate the military might of the owner. But by the later seventeenth century, country houses, large and small, were built and furnished in styles that spoke of the wealth, taste and learning of the men that owned them.[3] Though still connected with power and status, they were sites for display of a different type to the fortified castle or tower house. But changes to houses and their contents were also driven by more complex cultural agendas.

From the early eighteenth century two ideas assumed a common currency in commentaries and debates about the material world of houses and domestic possessions. The concept of 'convenience' referred to the usefulness of a thing or place for a clearly defined and socially acceptable purpose. 'Convenience' was a concrete descriptor with moral authority. It was an agent in the sphere of consumer culture, providing a psychological rationale for consumption decisions that separated the process from the vice of luxury. Also significant for developing consumerism and particularly connected with the character and furnishing of houses was the concept of 'comfort'. At a basic level 'comfort' referred to physical comfort in heat, light or upholstery, along with the absence of dirt, smells, smoke, noise, bugs, dampness and draughts. But there was also a growing preoccupation, particularly among women, with a state of psychological comfort relative to the home and the people in the home, be they servants, family members or visitors.[4] These ideas had an impact on elite housing throughout Great Britain, including the houses of the Highland gentry.

The long eighteenth century was a period of significant country-house building in Britain and Ireland, with major investment in houses and gardens. In England in the last thirty years of the century, more capital went into building country houses than was invested in the cotton-spinning industry, the leading sector of the industrial revolution.[5] Scotland was probably much the same. The cost of constructing a new house could vary enormously. At one end of the spectrum were the great aristocratic showplaces, costing many tens of thousands. But the majority of English country houses cost less than £5,000 to build, and many cost as little as £2,500, including the interior fittings.[6] There were similar variations in Highland Scotland. Inverary and Taymouth castles, the principal seats of great aristocrats, were at one extreme. In the middle range were places like Lochnell House, a few miles north of Oban, the home of the Campbells of Lochnell, first built in the 1730s for about £5,000 and considerably rebuilt and embellished between 1818 and 1820 by the Edinburgh architect Archibald Elliot, at a cost of £15,000.[7] But this kind of expenditure was also unusual, for most of the houses of the Highland gentry were very modest by British standards and were built to a standard design by tradesmen, without an input from architects. A typical example was Balliveolan, a minor laird's house built in 1768 by John Menelaws, a mason from Greenock, for a projected cost of £290. A similar structure to Glenure House, which is described in detail below, it was a classic 'laird's box' of the type that could be seen throughout the Highlands, symmetrical in design, with two storeys and an attic, a central front doorway with a window on either side, a square hall, two main rooms on each floor and smaller rooms to the rear.[8]

Most country houses were built over several years, and as in England it was rare for the cost of new or remodelled country houses to be met out of estate income or mortgages on land. Sudden cash windfalls from inheritance, dowry or military prize money were most commonly used to fund such a venture, or extra-estate sources of income from government office holding, professional practice or trade.[9] In Scotland, as in England, prudent landowners funded their house construction from non-estate capital flows. It was usual to buy the materials for building a country house in the first year of a project. In the second year, the case of the house was constructed and it was roofed to protect the interior during the winter months when little work took place. The internal fittings – doors, windows, panelling, plasterwork and chimneypieces – were installed in the third year, and in the fourth year expenditure was dominated by the decoration and furnishings, which could cost as much as a quarter of the whole undertaking.[10] Another way to spread the cost was to build in stages over a longer period: a small house first, with wings or extensions added later.

Building materials for new houses normally came from nearby sources. Local quarries were exploited for stone and slate and the site of a new house was often determined by the proximity of building materials or water for easy transport. Indeed, the lochside location of so many new houses in the Highlands was not simply for the picturesque effect. Another source of building materials was redundant structures nearby, such as old tower houses or ruined religious buildings.

Scottish houses prior to the eighteenth century had a distinctly Scottish appearance consistent with the evolution of local styles of architecture, but newly built country houses in the eighteenth century were of an increasingly uniform design and purpose. Status and prestige, along with comfort and convenience, were the primary aims of gentry householders from the early eighteenth century. Throughout Great Britain, and in relatively poor Scotland in particular, gentlemen and women looked at their old houses and found them wanting. In 1719, the agricultural improver Sir Archibald Grant of Monymusk viewed his ancestral home with dismay – '[it has] battlements and six different roofs of various heights and directions, confusedly and inconveniently combined and all rotten, with . . . granaries, stables and houses for all cattle and of the vermine attending them, close by'.[11] He wanted a house of regular design in the neo-classical style, surrounded by formal gardens and a wall, with animals and farm buildings well out of sight, to mark a distinct division between his family and their social life on the one hand, and the source of their wealth on the other.

As in the Monymusk case, the remodelling of a house in the modern neo-classical style, or the building of a new house on a new site, along with the laying-out of formal gardens or a landscaped park, almost always went hand in hand with plans for estate modernisation. It was the land closest to the main house that was usually modernised first; the process of improvement had an important aesthetic dimension.[12] House investment in Scotland, as elsewhere, was not simply a product of fashion or the hedonistic desire to indulge in luxury, though these were, of course, in evidence. It was part of a rational and commercial agenda, with significant patriotic overtones, to bring order, control and prosperity to an estate in the interests of the nation.[13] This agenda required modernisation in all spheres and in particular embraced the behaviour of the people that lived on the estate. It involved the landowner and his family, now located in a style of house that facilitated 'politeness' and the pursuit of a genteel manner of living. It also embraced the tenants and labourers, who were expected to observe modern contractual relationships with the owner, engage in new, market-oriented forms of land use and also, in some places, live in new types of housing.[14] When it replaced some older form of dwelling on an estate, the modern country house, with the garden or designed landscape around it, always changed the relationship between the landowning family and their servants or tenants to one of greater social distance than had formerly prevailed. Rural relationships, in the Highlands as elsewhere, were critically shaped by the material culture of gentry-owned country houses.

A striking feature of the Highland region that shaped many aspects of eighteenth-century house building was the slow pace of new development in the previous century, which meant that most elite families were still living in fortified structures devoted to a fast-vanishing military agenda. Many of these buildings were small and uncomfortable and were sited with strategic aims in mind, so they were not deemed suitable for upgrading. There was an exodus from castles and towers in the first few decades of the eighteenth century in favour of new mansion houses on more convenient sites. Yet a tension over the uses of these older properties, with their older functions, was evident. Lord Glenorchy, eldest son of the earl of Breadalbane, was instructed by his father in the 1690s to move with his wife and family to Kilchurn Castle, sited on a peninsula on Loch Awe, to maintain a political presence on that part of their estates. Glenorchy's response to his father typified the attitudes of the rising generation.

> [While] my wife is willing to comply in doing anything for the good of the family, I do think the castle is a good summer place but fear it is both inconvenient and moist and unwholesome in winter. I wish we had a little mainland house. Women will not like to see all water and ice round them . . . [and] I must have milk cows got to it.[15]

Kilchurn Castle was a five-storey tower of fifteenth-century construction, and though enlarged in the 1690s with barrack accommodation, it was abandoned as a domestic residence in the early eighteenth century and soon became a ruin, only used for occasional military purposes.[16] Unlike Kilchurn, Balloch Castle on Loch Tay in Perthshire, later renamed Taymouth, which was another ancient defensive structure, became the principal home of the Breadalbane family. It was extensively remodelled by architect William Adam in the 1730s because it was well sited for modernisation and, being close to Perth and to Edinburgh, was suitable for the new types of social and political life expected of a Highland nobleman.[17] Other towers, such as Barcaldine Castle, ceased being the main family residence but remained in domestic use by lesser members of the family and later by tenants. With little or no maintenance and a tendency to remove stonework to build other structures nearby, many castles and towers fell into decay. Few lamented their passing as family homes, though, by the later eighteenth century, the ruined castle had acquired a new function in the romantically aestheticised Highland landscape, affording a different sort of prestige to landowners.[18]

With many existing houses not deemed suitable for continued domestic use, there was a significant building of new houses in the eighteenth century Highlands – a product, in many ways, of pent-up demand. There were several features of the Highland economy and terrain that dictated the scale and pace of building a new house when compared with other parts of Britain. As in all aspects of Highland gentry life, one of the most important factors was the availability within families of liquid cash to undertake such works. The Highland gentry were poorer than similar groups in other parts of Britain, yet building a house in such a remote and often inhospitable part of the country was more expensive than elsewhere. Building materials, slates, wood and glass often had to come from great distances, and the cost of transportation was inevitably high. Architects and skilled workers were also imported from outside the region and charged a premium for their efforts. The building season was short because of the northerly climate, and buildings in progress were often damaged in the winter months. Yet gentlemen across the social spectrum and throughout the long eighteenth century built houses in large numbers. This is illustrated in a case study of Argyll.

A SIGN OF THE TIMES: HOUSE BUILDING IN ARGYLL

The extensive western county of Argyllshire was relatively accessible and more prosperous in the eighteenth century than many areas of the remote Highlands. The county had several small towns and supported a more diverse middle layer of society than was found in other parts of the north-west, with a long surviving class of tacksmen, who did not vanish from the social scene as swiftly as some have suggested, and many lesser landowners, who remained in large numbers, notwithstanding the process of gradual estate consolidation.[19] There were also many professional men. But though the scale of modern house building in Argyll was perhaps greater than elsewhere, the chronology of construction and the form and function of the houses that were built were broadly representative of the Highlands as a whole.

TABLE 7.1 HOUSE-BUILDING IN ARGYLLSHIRE, C.1700–1840

House Builder	All	1700 to 1740	1740 to 1770	1770 to 1800	1800 to 1820	1820 to 1840
Aristocratic/ Noble	16	1	1	6	1	7
Large Laird	14	5	6	2	1	0
Small Laird	18	6	6	6	0	0
Gentleman (no land)	13	0	0	2	4	7
Tacksman	8	3	2	3	0	0
Minister	11	0	0	1	3	7
Totals	80	15	15	20	9	21

Table 7.1 shows a chronological and typological breakdown of house building in mainland Argyll and the adjacent islands between c.1700 and 1840 and is based on an analysis of detailed descriptions and plans for eighty houses.[20] The table, which incorporates the various houses of the Campbell family of Barcaldine and Glenure along with their local kin connections, uses fairly broad categories of house builder and has some inevitable overlap, particularly between the small and larger laird. The date of building is set at the time of first construction of a house, but in many cases original small houses were later augmented by remodelling and extensions as part of a building process that could continue over decades and might result in the near obliteration of the first modest structure. The table does not include investment in rebuilding or remodelling that was undertaken on surviving castles and tower houses, of which there were many instances in this part of the Highlands, particularly in the first few decades of the eighteenth century, and again in the 1820s and 1830s. The table is indicative rather than fully comprehensive of all building activity, but it does reveal a robust and evolving pattern of house building, with a steady flow of construction, particularly among traditional resident groups such as tacksmen and smaller lairds. There was a surge in house construction in the last three decades of the eighteenth century, a pattern that was also seen in England.[21] This was followed by a lull during the first two decades of the nineteenth century, which was a time of war and uncertainty. After 1820 there was a new phase of house building, with the construction of a series of Church of Scotland manses for a professional group with a marked presence

in the Highlands, major investments in noblemen's houses and also in country villas set in garden grounds for non-landowning gentlemen.

Aristocratic and Noble Houses

At the top of the hierarchy of residential buildings, and the associated display of status and aspirations, were the houses of the great aristocracy, dominated in this part of the Highlands by Inverary Castle, the principal seat of the dukes of Argyll, who also owned a major London residence. Based on an original sixteenth-century tower house, Inverary was rebuilt from the 1740s in a quasi-classical early-romantic castellated style that sought to suggest progressiveness while simultaneously asserting the lineage, traditions and authority of Clan Campbell in an area that was still politically turbulent. In the process of rebuilding, the grounds were beautified, the estate was improved and a run-down village that interrupted the view of Loch Fyne was demolished, to be replaced a short distance away with the elegant, small planned burgh of Inverary, which – with its courthouse, resident professionals and tradesmen selling luxury goods – was intended by the duke to be a model of modernity.[22] With a design input from both William and Robert Adam and also from the London-based Scottish architect Robert Mylne, Inverary Castle was a pioneering and iconic statement of Highland noble identity and was copied by other aristocratic and gentleman house builders, including the earl of Breadalbane at Taymouth Castle in 1806.[23] Numerous neo-baronial mansion houses, big and small, were built in the Highlands from the 1820s onwards, their castellated designs an echo of Inverary.

The principal house of the earl of Breadalbane in Argyll, which was mainly used as the residence of his senior chamberlain in the county, was Ardmaddy Castle, at the head of Ardmaddy Bay close to Kilninver.[24] The origins of this house was in a late-medieval tower built by the family of MacDougall of Rarey, which had been seized by the earl of Argyll in the later seventeenth century and was sold along with the estate of Nether Lorn to the first earl of Breadalbane in 1692 for £20,000 Scots. Expensive restoration work was done on the tower in the early eighteenth century, but in 1728 it was reported that 'the house of Ardmaddie is quit ruinous . . . it is not more lodgable than a barn'. Ten years later, Colin Campbell of Carwhin – the Breadalbane chamberlain and a family connection, whose son eventually succeeded to the earldom – decided to invest in a new house, incorporating the old tower into a fashionable Palladian style of classical building. Extensive additional work was undertaken in 1790 to develop some of the offices into large public rooms and to add a new kitchen wing. There were plans for further developments in 1837 from the Edinburgh architect James Gillespie Graham, who also worked on Taymouth Castle and was famed for his neo-baronial designs, but these were not put into effect.

The extensive redesign of Ardmaddy in the eighteenth century was typical, if on a larger scale, of the type of building work that was undertaken on many defensive tower houses and is worth describing in detail. The original tower, comprising a vaulted ground floor with rear cellars, a great chamber above and garret bedrooms, had been extended in 1737 through the addition of two fine sandstone wings, a remodelled entrance and stair, new internal fittings including wood panelling, marble fireplaces, modern six-panel doors and sash windows, and a slate roof with attics. Each floor had four main rooms. The offices were on the ground floor and in the cellars, while the first floor was dominated by a large dining room and the main bedchambers. The extension of 1790 added a new wing that included a modern drawing room. At the same time there was a remodelling of the dining room entrance and internal fittings to include a dado, plastered walls to replace the now old-fashioned wood panelling and a grander fireplace for this most important of public rooms. Ardmaddy Castle was decorated on the exterior with the elaborate coat of arms of the earl of Breadalbane, carved in 1737. It overlooked an extensive landscaped park and walled gardens, which were embellished with architectural features, including a large ornamental bridge of mid-eighteenth century construction. Beyond the gardens there were jetties and a boathouse on Ardmaddy Bay. Though a relatively small property and never more than a secondary residence for the Perthshire-based earl, the house was designed to represent the status of a major nobleman in an important part of his estate and provided a venue for his social and political life when visiting Argyll.[25]

The Houses of Larger Lairds

The houses of the larger lairds in Argyll were not dissimilar to Ardmaddy Castle, though the gardens and designed landscapes were generally on a more modest scale. Some had architectural features and follies, such as Lady Margaret's Tower in the grounds of Lochnell House, the home of the Campbell family of Lochnell at the head of Ardmucknish Bay, which was built in 1737.[26] But most lairds could only afford a small decorative garden surrounding the house. Gatehouses were often added to these properties at the end of the eighteenth century, and a wall surrounding the main body of the estate was a major investment and a symbol of status and privacy. Larger lairds were a substantial group in Argyll, comprising about fourteen families, closely intermarried. Most of their house building took place in the first two thirds of the eighteenth century, though alterations, extensions and major embellishments were undertaken throughout the century and beyond.

Patrick Campbell of Barcaldine built Barcaldine House, which was initially styled Dalfuir, in the early 1720s to replace the inconvenient small coastal tower that the family had occupied since the seventeenth century. The new house better reflected the rising status of the family and was on a pleasant greenfield site, further inland than the tower and adjacent to the main road dissecting the Appin peninsula from the Ballachulish ferry in the north to the Connel ferry in the south. Built and designed by James Duff, a local mason who worked on several Argyllshire houses and who also added the new kitchen wing in 1733, the original house was a symmetrical three-storey, three-bay mansion of a type that was seen throughout the western Highlands.[27] When the laird and his lady first moved to Dalfuir they embarked on an unprecedented phase of spending on domestic goods of a type that could now be employed to proper social effect in a modern setting. In particular, they purchased tea and dinnerware, with furniture to match.[28] The house was more accessible than their previous home, and the rooms were larger and more convenient for entertaining. Extensive additional construction took place in the later 1750s, when Barcaldine was owned by John Campbell, who mostly lived in a rented house in Crieff where he was a crown factor on the forfeited estates of the duke of Perth; and again in 1815, under the ownership of the profligate soldier Duncan Campbell, when a large drawing room was executed by a local mason from Oban and internal restructuring and refitting took place, including extensive Adamesque plasterwork in the public rooms. Plans for a castellated extension were prepared in 1815 by the fashionable but expensive architect James Gillespie Graham, but these were not put into effect other than in a new court of offices. However, a large, two-storey library wing – an important status symbol for the gentleman of the day, regardless of whether or not he read his books – was built in the Jacobean style in the 1830s.[29]

It was usual for the houses of significant lairds like Campbell of Barcaldine to have sunk basements for the kitchens and substantial garrets for servants' bed and workrooms, along with office wings for food processing and storage. Servants and service functions were kept entirely separate from the family and were normally out of sight on the main approach to the property.[30] These houses were predominantly classical and symmetrical in design, with several bays on either side of a central door, and they often had a rising external staircase with a heavily carved and embellished portico. Interiors were wood-panelled to protect the furnishings and inhabitants from the damp, and elaborate plaster ceilings were usual from mid-century. Like the houses of smaller lairds, many of these mansions were extended over the course of the century to allow more specialised room use. Establishing a modern formal dining room – essentially a male room – was the primary objective in the first half of the century, and a large, fashionably furnished drawing room – a female room – was the main priority in the later eighteenth century. By the early nineteenth century, as Duncan Campbell of Barcaldine demonstrated, a formal library, with its costly contents of books, pictures and antiquities, was the main aspiration of the status-conscious gentleman.[31] Correspondence between men of this type commonly included details of their architectural ambitions and newly created or remodelled rooms. In the 1830s, Robert Downie, who owned Appin House, a few miles from Barcaldine and of a similar size and age, wrote to his neighbour Duncan Campbell about his fashionable Gothic extension with its new dining and drawing rooms, urging Campbell to make use of his workmen in Campbell's own building plans for Barcaldine.[32] Downie, a rich Bengal planter from Fife who became MP for the Dunfermline burghs in the 1820s, had purchased the Appin estate in 1816 as part of his personal strategy for social advancement. The property had been fragmented and had passed through several hands in the eighteenth century following the financial failure of the original Jacobite owners, the Stewarts of Appin.[33] It was businessmen like Downie, with their vast incomes and limited dependence on the local economy, who drew weaker and poorer men like Duncan Campbell, with a longstanding family status to defend, into a pattern of competitive and conspicuous expenditure on high-status additions to their houses that eventually led to ruin.

Of course the relationship between major lairds and their houses changed as the period progressed and absenteeism became more commonplace. Duncan Campbell may have invested a great deal of money that he could ill afford, and a great deal of his personal identity and family status, in embellishing Barcaldine House, but for much of the time he lived in Edinburgh. Absenteeism often caused tension within families as to how a Highland house should be developed. Poltalloch House on the east shore of Loch Craignish was the ancestral home of the Malcolms of Poltalloch, and in the later eighteenth century the head of the family, Neil Malcolm, lived in London, from where he directed his considerable business in Atlantic trade and Jamaican plantations. Younger brother George, who acted as estate factor and was much preoccupied with the poor relationship between the family and the workers, leased the house. Anxious to have a property befitting the status of the Malcolm family of Poltalloch, George embarked on a programme of rebuilding and refurbishments in 1798, so that the house might comprise 'a regular set of farm buildings on a small scale, with a cart and coach house, a small, neat mansion house and two out office houses at the extremity of the back square, as well as a garden wall of proper height'. In doing this, he met much resistance from his brother, who had little interest in funding such an enterprise at such an inconvenient distance from his own daily affairs. George sought to explain his purpose in a lengthy memorandum of 1790 about Poltalloch and Strone,

> where I spent the greatest part of my youthful days, and the place of my greatest attachment, the improvement of which engage a good deal of my thoughts by day and night. It would give me great uneasiness were I to imagine my plans were not to be executed. It is the place of my ancestors and very difficult to improve, but such is my fondness for it, although no property of mine, that I would willingly bestow £3500 upon it, to make it look reputable, for it was here the head of the family for centuries resided and they were men of credit and respectability in the community, and we cannot perpetuate their memory so well as by any means as by improving the original seat, so as to attract the attention of all sorts of people who will be anxious to know who originally lived there.[34]

George went on to detail the improvements he wanted to make and the impact, economic and cultural, that he believed this would have. 'The house [is] to have two fronts, the south front and west end to be faced with free stone, and the doors and windows of the north front and the east end to be faced with freestone.' With proper attention to roads, this was all intended to make it easier and safer for Neil Malcolm to make more frequent visits to his estate, to see the tenants and 'at all seasons to direct their operations, assist them with his advice and reason with them on their obstinacy and attachments to old bad habits and customs'. He hoped such visits and attentions in the landlord to the interests of his tenants would soon induce them to abolish the old ways and reconcile them to the new.[35]

George Malcolm had a long-term programme for the house and estate and retained a strong attachment to the interests of his forefathers that he hoped he could also promote in his brother through encouraging him to visit his home. Neil, in London, had rather different ideas. He was committed to retaining a property in the area for status reasons, but not the old house on the old estate. At the same time that the above memorandum was written, Neil Malcolm entered into negotiations to buy the nearby Dultroon Castle and estate on the shores of Loch Crinan, a dramatic and very visible site, overlooking the entrance to the Crinan canal, in which he had been a significant investor. Dultroon Castle was a fifteenth-century tower house built on earlier fortifications, with extensive eighteenth-century additions, and was owned by a heavily indebted member of the Campbell clan. It was a much grander residence than Poltalloch House and more easily accessed by sea. The estate purchase was completed in December 1792 for £6,200 and the castle followed in 1796. Neil Malcolm set about making major improvements with the very best of supplies and craftsmen shipped in from the south. The modest house in which George had invested so much hope fell into decay and was a ruin within a few decades. George died in Jamaica in the early nineteenth century. In the mid-nineteenth century the castle was also abandoned in favour of a massive new mansion house built a few miles north of Dultroon by Neil Malcolm's heir. Called New Poltalloch House, it was designed in the grand Jacobean style by the London offices of the fashionable architect William Burn.[36]

The Houses of Small Lairds, Tacksmen and Gentlemen

Small-scale landowners were the largest group of house builders in Argyll, and this category of laird constructed new houses throughout the eighteenth century. These were people that in the seventeenth century had occupied primitive tower houses and early defensible structures and in some cases lived in semi-permanent turf huts indistinguishable, other than in size, from those of the peasantry. Indeed, even in the early eighteenth century, the main residence of the MacGregors of Glenstrae in Lorn was a clay and wicker building resting on a stone foundation and surrounded by a moat.[37] With rising wealth and aspirations to gentility, it is not surprising that many lairds decided to build afresh on sites that were chosen for accessibility and beauty, or enclosed their existing little houses within new, more modern structures.

The lesser gentry looked for comfort, economy and just a little classical elegance in their new or rebuilt houses. In the words of one Stirlingshire landowner, John Drummond, writing in 1734 on the proposed rebuilding of his house, Quarrell, 'I . . . desire no more vaults nor any grates to the windows'. The house was to be transformed from 'echoes of ruines' into 'a convenient little habitation . . . done frugally and effectively'.[38] Usually no more than a rectangular two-storey block with a central staircase and two main rooms on each floor, the 'convenient little habitations' that were built throughout the north of Scotland signalled a revolution in comfortable living for the Highland gentry, with opportunities to develop a 'polite' domestic sociability that was not possible in older houses. These new buildings were made of stone, were harled and painted, and had slate roofs. The windows, though small, were fully glazed, and each room had a modern hearth and chimney. The interiors were wood-panelled, a fashion that remained strong throughout the century, when plastered walls above the dado had become usual elsewhere, probably for practical reasons given the problems of damp in the Highlands and the expense of plasterwork. The central stair and hall gave privacy to each of the rooms, and the kitchens were usually in a separate wing or block. They were furnished in the modern manner, with tables and chests of drawers rather than the chests and cists of the previous century. Pictures and mirrors were hung on the walls, and there were carpets on the floor.

Tacksmen, the middlemen in the system of land tenure and military mobilisation that prevailed under clanship, survived as an identifiable group in Argyll throughout the eighteenth century, though their functions in Highland society and economy were changing. Some became army officers for the crown, others were professionals such as lawyers or doctors, but all continued to lease land, farming it on their own account or sub-leasing to lesser tenants. As in times past, such men were usually family connections of the major lairds. Eight new tacksmens' houses were built in Argyll in the eighteenth century, two of them associated with the Campbell family of Barcaldine and the earl of Breadalbane. John Campbell, who was the younger brother of Patrick Campbell, the laird of Barcaldine, built Rarey House in the 1730s. On land that had originally belonged to the MacDougalls of Rarey, it had been acquired by the earl of Breadalbane in the late seventeenth century and then leased to John Campbell as tacksman. The house was a small, plain one-storey structure with an attic, made of harled rubble. It was extended from a single rectangular block to an L-shape in the later eighteenth century. The door was in the centre of the main house, with a simple staircase behind. With a roof of slate, glazed windows and modern fireplaces, it afforded basic comforts.[39]

A larger house, something akin to the 'laird's box' of smaller Highland landowners, was built by a second Breadalbane tacksman in the latter part of the century. Captain Neil Campbell was the younger son of Archibald Campbell of Melfort. His mother was Annabell, daughter of Patrick Campbell of Barcaldine. After military service, he retired to take up farming in his home county, renting land on tack from the Breadalbane estate, where he built a two-storey harled rubble house in 1789. The house, called Dregnish, had a conventional central hall and stair, with three rooms on each floor, including a first-floor parlour.[40] Also in the 1780s an Inverary lawyer, Duncan Campbell, gained the tack of the township of Stronmagachan in Glen Aray to farm, but only on the condition that he built a house and lived on the property. Originally of one storey but later raised to two floors, it was a small U-plan dwelling costing £93 to construct and was soon being described as the owner's 'country villa', contrasting with his principal townhouse in Inverary.[41]

By the later eighteenth century, much of the new house building or house extending in Argyll was the work of absentee lairds such as Campbell of Barcaldine, or of gentlemen of Highland background who purchased or leased small estates for their retirement, having made their fortunes elsewhere through trade, or professional or military service. Grand gentlemen's houses were usually built in the pure classical style of Lowland Scotland or, after the turn of the century, in the elaborate neo-baronial or Jacobean style that was adopted for great houses throughout the Highlands. Typical was the house of Robert Campbell, a lawyer and sheriff-depute for Argyll, who built a three-storey mansion, Asknish House, on Loch Gair in 1785. It was a substantial dwelling, designed in the fashionable Palladian manner in a landscaped garden, with the main rooms on the first floor and a large ground-floor dining room.[42] Or there was Barbreck House, near Loch Craignish, built in 1793 by the successful career soldier General John Campbell, whose family had lost land through forfeiture many decades before. This was a highly decorated house of three storeys and attic with flanking two-storey pavilions, elaborate pediments and other external stonework, set in a designed landscape but with no estate attached.[43]

There were about a dozen gentleman's houses of various sizes built in Argyll between c.1780 and 1840. The larger houses were rural, normally on sites overlooking water, but the early nineteenth century also witnessed a spate of construction of smaller villas with gardens on the outskirts of towns such as Oban or Campbeltown for local tradesmen and professionals, or increasingly for use as summer homes by wealthy Glasgow families. These householders often had connection with lairds but were not themselves the owners of land. For instance, James Ewing, MP and lord provost of Glasgow, built Castle House at Dunoon in 1822 on land that was feued from the Milton estate. It was in the castellated Gothic style, the architect was David Hamilton of Glasgow and it was described at the time as a 'handsome marine villa'.[44] A number of manses were also built in the early decades of the nineteenth century following government initiatives to regularise the presence of the clergy in Highland districts. Alongside a series of new churches, these houses, which were built to a standard design by Thomas Telford, were modest but comfortable and served the dual functions of domestic accommodation for a family and office facilities for the minister and his parish. They had five rooms on two levels and were in much the same style as middle-class suburban housing in the Lowlands.[45]

GLENURE HOUSE AND THE 'SOCIAL LIFE OF THINGS'

Glenure House, on a remote site at the junction of Glen Creran and Glen Ure, was built by Colin Campbell of Glenure, the second son of Patrick Campbell of Barcaldine, and was typical of the houses of smaller lairds or significant tacksmen from the 1720s onwards.[46] It is one of the best examples of Highland gentlemen's houses to survive little changed to the present, and because of the peculiar circumstances of the Appin murder and subsequent inheritance, it was the subject of several detailed inventories which give insights to the rooms in the house and the 'social life of things' in the mid-eighteenth century.[47]

The first phase of construction at Glenure began in 1740, just two years after Colin Campbell was gifted the estate by his father to create a cadet branch of the family, and was probably based on an earlier farm building. The house comprised a rectangular two-storey structure with garret, with a separate, lower, two-storey kitchen block and dairy at right angles to the main building, connected by a one-storey corridor. The external masonry was harled and whitewashed. There was a plain central front door leading into a hall of about ten feet square with a curved central stair to the rear, and two main rooms leading from either side of the hall, each measuring about twenty feet square. There was another small room behind the staircase. The upper storey had more apartments, some connected with one another in the older fashion of room layout. On the ground floor the room closest to the kitchen was described mid-century as a dining room and the other was described as the 'laich' or lower bedroom. The dining room was originally panelled and had an alcove niche for displaying china, a common feature of the period. Colin Campbell employed several craftsmen to build his house. His accounts list a joiner from Inverary, a mason from Beath in Fife and a wright from Edinburgh, where he also purchased fireplaces and Dutch tiles for the fire surrounds and an array of modern furniture and prints, particularly for the dining room.[48] The kitchen, which had an internal slop-sink and large brick-lined oven, was constructed in 1751 by a mason from Stirling, a contact of brother Robert the merchant.[49]

Glenure was built over several years to match the owner's flow of funds and changing family needs following his marriage in 1749. The dining room was undergoing refurbishment when Glenure was murdered, for there was hair for plaster stored in the garret alongside a set of ten matching black-and-white framed prints that would have been destined for such a room once the older pine panelling was removed and the new, more fashionable, plastered walls were finished. There were also numerous new locks in the garret, waiting to be fitted to room and closet doors as part of the process of upgrading the house, along with new handles, bells and bell-pulls, and cords and brass fittings for sash windows. One can speculate on what Colin Campbell might have done next with his house had he not been killed. He may have converted one of the upper rooms into a formal drawing room for his wife, or he may have extended the house to accommodate a growing family since in 1752 he and Janet had two children with another on the way and, with their servants for house and dairy, Glenure was certainly full. Had he lived to old age and prospered, it is possible that he might have aspired to a library – though it is equally possible that he and his family would have left this small remote house for somewhere more convenient. Because the house was only rarely occupied following Colin's death and the departure of Janet Mackay and her daughters, few changes were made in the second half of the century. Colin's brother and heir, Duncan, who had a home elsewhere and was often absent, made few changes. His son, Captain Colin Campbell – a mostly absent military bachelor – was the tenant of Glenure in the 1780s and made some alterations and additions using local tradesmen. He upgraded the dining room and created a new small room behind it on the ground floor, which in the later eighteenth century was described as a 'drawing room'. He also remodelled the interior of the kitchen and upgraded the windows and fireplaces.[50]

An inventory of household possessions taken by Colin Campbell's executors in 1752 suggests that most of the main rooms at Glenure were given over to the dual purpose of sitting and sleeping, but there were significant differences between the room occupied by the laird on the ground floor, to the left of the front door, which was a comfortable sitting room and bedroom as well as a secure store for valuable things, and the more feminine rooms on the upper floors. In the usual pre-modern manner, most of the rooms were defined in the inventory according to the colour or type of their textile furnishings and their location in the house. The exception was the dining room, which was described specifically with reference to function and was furnished with objects that were associated with the exclusive male culture of dining and drinking.[51] This room more than any other in the house highlights the processes of modernisation in consumption and social behaviour that were taking place in the Highlands by the 1740s, and underlines the masculine agenda of the typical country house.

The dining room contained twelve chairs, one of them a 'carver', and a variety of small tables, but not one of the large and expensive mahogany dining tables that was then becoming fashionable in towns. There was also a writing desk with a locked cupboard above, suggesting that the dining room was used as the laird's main place for indoor business transactions and record keeping. In effect, it was an office and study as well as a room for dining and entertaining. The inventory of 1752 suggests that the laird dominated the ground floor, and not surprisingly it was here that most objects of value were also located. The laird's room, immediately across the hall from the dining room – which was described in the inventory as 'yellow bedroom in the ground flatt and east end of said house' – contained bed and bedding, a 'large easy chair with blue and white chequer slip', a large chest of drawers, a looking glass and a table, along with an old armchair and four ordinary chairs. There was a 'new large grate with brasses' and a 'standing press containing white iron and copper work and puther with locks and keys', which also housed much of the valuable china dinnerware.

The upper rooms were more sparsely furnished, though the two main bedrooms on the first floor were comfortable, bright and stylish, and these seem to have been the realm of Colin Campbell's wife, along with her children and female indoor servants. Janet Mackay's room, immediately above the laird's bedroom, was called the 'chince room'. It was the only one in the house with window hangings, a fashionable luxury, made of material that matched the bed curtains and the slipcover on an armchair. The chintz was multi-coloured and the bed quilt was white. The room had a carpet, a pair of carved candle branches – more elaborate than elsewhere in the house – and four fashionable coloured Indian prints in frames, which were purchased as part of a set of eight in Edinburgh in 1750.[52] There was a looking glass, a small veneered chest of drawers and a chest for clothing. There were four chairs and another two in a closet, but no table, suggesting that female entertaining or domestic needlework took place elsewhere, possibly in the second upper-storey bedroom, the 'green room'. This second room contained a new 'green' bed with a flowered bed quilt, four more of the 'fine Indian prints in frames', a new large grate with brasses, a carpet, a chest of drawers, four chairs and a square table – all rendering it suitable for sociable tea drinking or work with textiles. There was a third, small bedroom on the first floor with brown bed hangings, which also contained a concealed press in the pine panelling, with all of the bed linen and napery under lock and key. The presence here of six chairs and a small round table suggests that female servants used this as a workroom, and it was probably also a servant's bedroom. There was more lighting equipment upstairs than downstairs, consistent with women's domestic work such as sewing, which was undertaken indoors and at night. Colin Campbell was not a great reader and probably had little need downstairs for bright light in the evenings. Indeed, the few books that he owned, and that had been recorded in a personal inventory of 1740, were stored in a trunk in the garret when he died.[53]

As well as being a place of storage, the garret floor had a small bedroom for the two young children of the house and also accommodated the indoor servants in makeshift arrangements for spinning and sleeping. The house contained a lot of equipment for processing woollen yarn, including a new checkreel, two spinning wheels and several sets of combs and cards, and these were kept in the garret. Whether or not Janet Mackay was active in this branch of domestic economy is unclear. Spinning was considered a respectable housewife's skill among Highland gentlewomen in the first half of the eighteenth century, but Janet may have been one of the new generation of women who regarded such things as servants' work.

In the division of the house, the upper female rooms mirrored the lower male ones. Sleeping and intimate family life took place in the rooms on the side of the house that was furthest away from the kitchen block. Work and hospitality were conducted on the side of the house that was closest to the kitchen. The storage of hard objects, mostly manufactured outside the house, and in particular those associated with dining and drinking, was downstairs in the male domain. Textile items associated with sleeping and comfort, much of it made by the women of the house, were upstairs in the female domain. There were considerable quantities of fine linen in Glenure House, including damask tablecloths and napery along with sheets and pillowcases for family and servants. All of the china, delft, silver, pewter and cutlery was kept in a locked closet beneath the stairs on the ground floor or was locked in the press in the laird's bedroom. The quantity was vast, the quality was high and much of it was new, having been purchased at the time of the couple's marriage. Silver tableware purchased in Edinburgh from jewellers Ker and Dempster was engraved with the family crest.[54]

The ground-floor stair closet also housed a good stock of dried fruit, bottled fruit, anchovies, sugared almonds, spices, sugar and tea. A variety of wines and spirits, some in great quantities, were here or in the garret, including claret, port, rum, whisky, brandy, strong ale, cider and vinegar. Alcohol played a major role in the hospitality that attended Colin Campbell's funeral, if the empty bottles recorded in the inventory are any indication. In addition to the thirty-nine empty 'chopin', or half-pint, bottles at Glenure, stored in one of the outbuildings, there were also twelve dozen that had been lent to Lady Barcaldine, Janet's sister-in-law at Dalfuir House, and a further five dozen bottles were at Ardchattan Priory, the house adjoining the Campbell burial ground. Some few dozen with liquor (probably whisky) had also been sent to Captain Newton at Strath Appin, one of the officers charged with finding Colin's murderer. Other foodstuffs stored in the kitchen or outhouses included dozens of cheeses and quantities of butter and salt lying in the 'milk house', much of this produced by Janet Mackay and her servants and available for sale. And there were several large gunnels containing meal or grain in the 'meal house'.

In common with all Highland houses, though rarely revealed in such detail, the several floors and spaces of Glenure House allowed for different forms of status to be displayed to varying audiences and for a gendered identity and sociability to be constructed by the householder and his wife.[55] The contents of this small but modern gentleman's dwelling spoke eloquently of comfortable domesticity and modern aspirations. It was a way of living that marked a growing gulf between the lifestyle of a relatively wealthy man attached to a powerful family and that of poorer tenants or the peasantry. The material culture of the house also revealed the growing sense of threat that went hand in hand with a more luxurious style of living. There was a new preoccupation with security in the form of many new locks and keys. This may have been a product of Colin Campbell's appointment to the office of crown factor for forfeited estates in an area with a strong Jacobite presence, but it also reflected an awareness of the gulf between rich and poor that was developing in the Highlands, since the concern with domestic security was also apparent in other less politically sensitive households. David Nevag, a merchant in Edinburgh, had supplied Dalfuir House, the home of Colin's father, with a large stock of new locks, handles and hinges in 1733.[56] The Dowager Lady Mackay of Bighouse, grandmother to Colin Campbell's wife, was similarly preoccupied in the early 1740s with ordering new locks for her house in Sutherland.[57] Duncan Campbell, the Stirling lawyer who inherited Glenure from his brother in 1752, was obsessed with locks and keys and security to an unusual degree. An inventory of Glenure House in 1759 at the time of Duncan's ownership records that in addition to new locks on all rooms and cupboards (replacing those fitted just a decade before) there were new locks on the meal house, stable, milk house, hen house, peat store and on a fish house at Loch Etive. Duncan made frequent detailed inventories of all of his possessions in the guardianship of named servants, suggesting a deep wariness when it came to entrusting his property to estate workers.[58] This might have reflected an anxious personality or a particularly legalistic mindset, but such anxiety was clearly not unusual among the Highland gentry by the mid-eighteenth century.

BOSWELL'S HIGHLAND HOUSES

The progressive transformation of houses in Argyll gave rise to changing forms of domestic behaviour, new patterns of sociability and a growing gulf between the lives and cultures of the rich and the poor. Other, more remote, parts of the Highlands were not so quickly modernised as Argyll, but they too were changing. James Boswell, with his keen eye for social details and craving for personal domestic comforts, provides a telling account of diversity in the houses of the middle and upper layers of Highland society and the differently nuanced lifestyles he observed in the remoter Highlands and islands when journeying there with Samuel Johnson in the autumn of 1773.

Travelling up the east coast to Inverness, and from there to the west, one of the first Highland houses described in detail by Boswell was the military governor's house at Fort Augustus at the head of Loch Ness. Boswell and Johnson were entertained by Deputy Governor Trapaud, a veteran of Culloden, of an Irish-Huguenot military family, and his wife Ann, who was the daughter of John Campbell of Barcaldine and niece of Colin Campbell of Glenure. The Trapaud family home was a 'well-built little square, a neat, well-furnished house with prints, etc., in short, with all the conveniences of civilised life in the midst of rude mountains'.[59] This, of course, was exactly the right sort of place for a senior army officer whose role in life was to bring order and control to the 'barbarous' north. The structure of the house was a metaphor in stone for the governor's professional objectives, and the governor's wife was a Highland gentlewoman well trained by her upbringing in Argyll and Crieff to the business of managing a 'polite' Highland household.

Politeness was in evidence at the next house that Boswell and Johnson visited at Glenmoriston, though the building itself was unpromising. A local man who was also a tenant farmer had constructed the house, which operated as an inn.[60] It was a primitive structure, three connected rooms in length with a little room projecting and entirely made of turfs and heath, with an interior wainscoting of plaited hazel wands. Yet the owner was a gentleman, well-educated, familiar with Latin, and a poet, and his well-dressed daughter, who waited on the travellers with their tea, had been educated at a boarding school in Inverness and could read and write. Other gentlemen and households were less impressive. At Armadale on the Isle of Skye, Boswell and Johnson visited Sir Alexander Macdonald, chief of his clan, who was English-educated and had an English wife, but his house 'seemed very poor for a chief', though it did have a fine garden. It was in Boswell's eyes 'a good tenant's house, having two storeys and garrets'. Sir Alexander had little of the chief about him, kept a limited table and gave shabby hospitality. Boswell was 'quite hurt with the meanness and unsuitable appearance of everything.'[61] Another Skye host, Mackinnon of Coirechatachan, also had a two-storey house, 'with a low parlour, with a carpet on the floor, which we had not seen at Armadale'.[62]

Here there was an upstairs bedroom for Johnson and Boswell shared a similar room with four other visiting men. The house of the laird of Rasaay, their next stop on the journey, was a recent construction of eleven 'fine' rooms, the former house having been burned down by government troops in 1745 not long after it was built. Many of the rooms at Rasaay contained several beds, which allowed the family to entertain a large company.[63]

Dunvegan Castle, the seat of clan Macleod, 'partly old and partly new, upon a rock on the sea' was the greatest house that Boswell and Johnson visited on Skye. It had many fine old rooms and a modern drawing room in what had formerly been the laird's bedchamber. But 'every room in the house smoked but the drawing-room',[64] a great inconvenience during a wet and windy autumn. The lady, who was 'English-bred', was desperate to move away from the castle to a 'pretty farm, rich grounds, fine garden' – a lament with many echoes of Lord Glenorchy when he was forced by his father to live in Kilchurn Castle in the 1690s. But for Boswell the house had the 'veneration acquired by the . . . lapse of time during which the family has lived here, [and] many circumstances of natural grandeur suited to the seat of a Highland chief'.[65] He urged Lady Macleod to forget her ideas of modern comfort and convenience in favour of family traditions and status.

On the Isle of Coll, the travellers spent time at the house of Captain Lauchlan Maclean, who had made money in the East Indies and rented land as tacksman from his kinsman the laird. His was a 'poor temporary house, or rather hut, just a little larger than the common country house' comprising three rooms or 'divisions', built of stone without mortar and with no plaster or internal finishing. 'It was as cold as a stable', but they were well entertained by the captain's wife, who was a daughter of the local minister.[66] The houses on Coll were mostly primitive, but at Grishipoll there was an 'excellent slated house of two storeys' which had been built by the young laird while his elder brother was alive and was now rented to another tacksman – a Mr McSweyn – who had also been the laird's foster father.[67] The main house was a modern dwelling on Breachacha Bay, two 'gun-shots' away from the old castle that had been home to the family of Maclean of Coll until the 1750s. The new building, just a few decades old, was a 'neat gentleman's house with four rooms on a floor, three storeys and garrets. The dining room and the other three rooms on that floor [the first] were well wainscoted with good fir, and were very snug in dry weather.' But many windows, including those in the dining room where the visitors spent most of their time, let in water during the frequent storms that beset the island. One of the ground-floor rooms was a secure charter room, and the house also had a formal garden, 'a piece of ground enclosed with a stone dike'. 'There [were] two neat wings or pavilions to the house . . . we felt ourselves very comfortable . . . Mr Johnson relished it much at first, but soon remarked there was nothing becoming a chief about it. It was quite a tradesman's box.'[68] The house was sparsely furnished because the young bachelor laird was rarely there and there were no regular servants. The guests were looked after by temporary help in the form of a serving lass from Glasgow, who was visiting her family on the island at the time.

The laird's house on Coll was a modern mansion built to a standard pattern with a fashionable dining room much of the same character as those in Argyll. It may have looked like a tradesman's 'box' to Johnson, but it was certainly on a grander scale than most of the houses of the Highland gentry. Other dwellings described by Boswell were eccentric and unexpected. On Erray, he and Johnson visited the rented house of the elderly Dr Hector Maclean, a former medical professor at Glasgow University.

> We arrived at a strange confused house built by Mackinnon the proprietor about sixty years ago . . . we were conducted through a large unfinished cold kitchen to a narrow timber stair, and then along a passage to a large bedroom with a coach roof, ornamented with some bad portraits, prints of several eminent physicians and a piece of shell-work made by Miss Maclean . . . Mr Johnson was taken with the appearance of the room . . . [It] is the prettiest room we have seen since we came to the Highlands.[69]

On the island of Inchkenneth, they stayed with Sir Allan Maclean, chief of the clan, who lived with his two grown daughters. 'Military men acquire excellent habits of having all conveniences about them. Sir Allan Maclean, who had been long in the Army, and had now a lease of this island [from the duke of Argyll] had formed a commodious habitation, though it consisted but of a few small buildings, only one storey high.' He was, of course, a conspicuous consumer and 'had, in his little apartments, more things than I could enumerate in a page or two'.[70]

The minister's house on the Ross of Mull, as with most of the ministers' houses that Boswell and Johnson visited, was not a manse as such. It was a 'good farm-house of one storey, dry and well furnished' but so small that the guests had to sleep in the room in which they had supped.[71] In these remote parts of the Highlands and islands, many middle-status families lived in primitive or inadequate houses. This was especially true of ministers and was one of the reasons for the government investment in standardised manse building in the 1820s. Major tacksmen and tenants like Sir Allan Maclean or Captain Lauchlan Maclean on Coll lived in temporary housing which they made comfortable with their modern furniture and possessions but which they hoped to replace with finer, purpose-built dwellings when their finances allowed. Some houses, such as that of Lochbuie on Mull, were modern but unfinished, probably for reasons of cost. The Lochbuie mansion had interior walls prepared for plastering, but plaster had not been applied. Other modern houses, such as that of the laird of Coll, were not able to withstand the ferocious weather in their exposed locations. The difficulty of building and maintaining good houses in the remote Highlands and islands was obvious to the visitors. Indeed, it was only when the travellers returned to the mainland and began travelling south through Argyll that they found consistently comfortable inns and consistently fine modern housing. The inn at Inverary was described as being as good as any in England. Inverary Castle was praised for its magnificence and the duke of Argyll for his great hospitality. Rossdhu, the 'beautiful seat of Sir James Cameron' and Cameron House, the home to the Smollett family – both on the banks of Loch Lomond, in prosperous farming areas close to the Lowlands – were lauded for their elegance and comfort. But these were unusual. For the mass of the eighteenth-century Highland gentry, houses were smaller and simpler than gentleman's houses elsewhere, and their aspirations to politeness and gentility were almost always greater than the actual domestic settings would allow. This is why Dorothy Wordsworth in 1803 was so struck by the contrast between the primitive character of Glengyle House in Perthshire and the modern appearance and manners of the Macfarlane family. It is also why so many families opted to move beyond the Highlands to a social life elsewhere.

8 Sociability and Hospitality

INTRODUCTION

New houses with their modern contents were important for individual householders in the Highland counties. They signalled identity and aspirations, along with the wealth and status. These houses were advocates for improvement and civilisation in 'backward' areas. They became venues for enlightened forms of order to prevail, between servants and masters, or between tenants and their lairds. They offered unprecedented levels of convenience and comfort and also secured a new sense of psychological propriety. Houses with their modern contents shaped the mental world of the people that lived there. They were also the stage on which elaborate forms of sociability and hospitality could be performed.

Of course, sociability and hospitality in the Highlands were not new to the newly built houses. Edmund Burt in the 1720s described many elaborate social occasions when he was entertained in traditional style in the primitive houses and towers of lairds and noblemen. On one occasion he and some fellow English officers were invited to dinner at the castle of a clan chief in the county of Ross. This was probably Castle Downie, the home of Simon Fraser, Lord Lovat. They found the 'castle' with some difficulty, for through Burt's critical eye it seemed 'only a house fit for one of our farmers of fifty pounds a year, and in the courtyard a parcel of low outhouses, all built with turf'.[1] They were met in state by the chief and his attendants, and 'conducted into a parlour pretty well furnished'. Music was played throughout the meal and they were served 'a great number of dishes, at a long table, all brought in under cover' and mostly 'disguised after the French manner' – that is, covered with sauces or vegetables. They drank good wine, but the conversation was poor and mostly revolved around the chief, who dominated the male company entirely. Burt later remarked, 'I make little doubt but, after our noble host had gratified his ostentation and vanity, he cursed us in his heart for the expense, and that his family must starve for a month to retrieve the profusion.' The comment was ungenerous, but in reality such a style of living as that supported by Lord Lovat, with his 'public' tables and retinue of supporters, was costly. Indeed, Lovat moved to Inverness in 1738 to save money by not holding 'court' at the castle.[2]

Ritualised hospitality on occasions that marked the cycle of births, marriages and deaths was a notable feature of the pre-modern Highlands, and retinues of servants and supporters always attended lairds. Burt described the typical visiting party of eight to fourteen men, including the 'hanchman' – a personal assistant – a bard, several gillies or servants to carry goods and lead horses and hunting dogs, and a piper who, being a gentleman, also had his own servant to carry the pipes.[3] Highland noblemen might have a retinue of many dozens of men, including lesser lairds with their own servants and gentlemen. Funerals were a major focus for hospitality and sociability among men. Formal invitations were dispatched to large numbers, and to not attend without a written and plausible excuse was to risk giving insult. The wake on the day before the funeral was a sombre and silent affair until the whisky started to flow. The day of the burial began with a large company gathered at the deceased's house. They were served by the 'nearest relations and friends' from long tables with 'several pyramids of plum cake, sweetmeats, and several dishes, with pipes and tobacco' and wine in profusion. Though gentlewomen conventionally did not attend funerals, it was the women of the family who made the elaborate displays of food, and the womenfolk of the visiting men's families did participate, albeit at a distance, for 'in the conclusion, some of the sweetmeats are put into your hat or thrust into your pocket, which enables you to make a great compliment to the women of your acquaintance'.[4]

The extent of a funeral retinue was often noted in letters. John Campbell of Barcaldine wrote to his father Patrick in August 1724 to describe the funeral of Campbell of Funab. There were 'twelve Campbells in mourning', by which he meant twelve Campbell lairds dressed and mounted in mourning clothes, with their own kin retinues.[5] Since he was there to represent his father, John had to be appropriately dressed for this ritual of pomp and display and had borrowed mourning attire from his cousin, Campbell of Ardchattan. It was costly to attend funerals, and the expense for the deceased's family was enormous. But the status implications were also important for hosts and guests alike. The funeral in 1731 of Colin Campbell of Invernan, tacksman and younger brother of Patrick Campbell of Barcaldine, who died in his early thirties, leaving a widow and young family, provides a good illustration. The cost of the funeral was £210 (Scots). This was paid from the sale of Invernan's moveable property (cattle, horses, farm stock and house furnishings) that had raised £1,552. Campbell of Invernan was not a rich man. His house was small and primitive and his possessions were shabby and few. But as the brother of a laird and kinsman to the earl of Breadalbane, the status and respectability of the family demanded a great funeral. The cost of sending printed letters of invitation to the principal guests was £2 8s. The guests were provided with £25 worth of cheeses, and mutton to the value of £6. There were eight and a half gallons of 'acquavit' costing £62 and six dozen bottles of claret from a merchant in Inverary, who also supplied a dozen fine wine glasses for the principal gentlemen mourners, along with wax candles, materials for the coffin and the mourning draperies for the house, funeral carriage and horses, at a total cost of £95. The funeral started at the house of Invernan, with the burial procession, comprising many dozens of men, crossing Loch Etive by ferry for the interment at Ardchattan Priory. Both the ferryman and the coffin maker were paid £4 for their services. The clergyman, Donald Taylor, was paid £3.[6]

Conspicuous hospitality based on celebratory feasting was a mostly male affair, but it did involve women in some circumstances. In Susan Ferrier's early nineteenth-century novel *Marriage*, an elderly Highland lady, living in Edinburgh but reflecting on the social life of her own girlhood, recounts the cycle of events that were celebrated by women. The wedding was one great occasion, but more important was the birth of a child.

> The day after the bairn was born, the leddy sat up i'her bed, wi'her fan intill her hand; an' aw her freends cam' an' stud roond her, an' drank her health an' the bairn's. Than at the leddy's recovery there was a graund gien that they caw'd the *cummerfealls*, an' there was a great pyramid o'hens at the tap o' the table, an' anither pyramid o' ducks at the fit, an' a muckle stoup fu' o' posset i' the middle, an' aw kinds o' sweeties doon the sides; an' as sune as ilk ane had eatin their fill they aw flew till the sweeties, an' fought, an' strave, an' wrastled for them, leddies an' gentleman an' aw; for the brag was wha could pocket maist.[7]

Doubtless, as with funeral celebrations, those treats and sweets that were 'pocketed' and taken away were given to family and friends at home.

This kind of hospitality and sociability made little reference to the character or furnishings of domestic spaces. Indeed, much of it took place out of doors. The personal behaviour of the host was not indicative of his status, but rather his status was contained in the numbers of people involved and in the quantities of food and drink provided. The behaviour of both men and women was physical and rowdy. Drunkenness was normal and expected. All of this was soon to change.

POLITENESS AND THE 'IMPROVEMENT' IN MANNERS

New forms of sociability and hospitality put a greater emphasis than before on the interior spaces of houses, on the personal behaviour of the hosts and guests, and on the proper conduct of the physical self relative to furniture, domestic objects and food and drink. Social behaviour of the type that came to be called 'polite' was shaped by changes in the hierarchy of wealth and status in Britain that arose with new commerce, new structures of government and the new professions.[8] It was urban in its formulation, was particularly associated with the social life of elites in London, and was taught to the sons of the Highland nobility and gentry from the early eighteenth century. Teenage boys spent time in Edinburgh for their formal education and so that they could benefit informally from the company and example of men of high status and ability. The young heir to the earl of Breadalbane was in Edinburgh in 1708 to attend classes at the university, and was also taken to coffee house assemblies with his elders to learn a 'public and easy air'.[9] John Campbell of Barcaldine, as a youth in the early 1720s undergoing a legal education in the Edinburgh office of Colin Kirk the writer, also mixed daily in the company of distinguished men, including Lord Glenorchy, the earl of Mar, the duke of Argyll and close kinsmen such as Sir James Campbell of Auchinbreck.[10] From men like these, who were all familiar with life in London, he acquired the habits of politeness that defined the gentleman of the day. His education in 'improved' manners and behaviour may also have been advanced through reading Adam Petrie's popular conduct manual, *Rules of Good Deportment, or of Good Breeding for the Use of Youth*, which was published in Edinburgh in 1720.

Petrie had been the private tutor to a Highland gentry family, the Sinclairs of Stevenson, and was later a parish schoolmaster in East Lothian, under the patronage of the widowed countess of Haddington.[11] His little book was aimed mainly at young men in the middle stations of life and was a best seller. It advocated a quiet, sober and decorous manner, free from excessive preoccupation with titles or family connections, as the ideal for all men and a greater mark of the gentleman than mere wealth and ostentation. In particular, his notions of proper physical manners and of deportment and good breeding were best displayed through genteel social relationships with women of equal rank, including wives, and through well-regulated conversations with social superiors.[12] He gave guidance on uses of the body and ways of walking, on how to enter a room where there were ladies or men of higher standing, on salutations, travelling and visiting, letter writing, on clothing and on eating and drinking. His rules included the appropriate use of napkins and eating utensils and, in a reference to one of common practices of unrefined sociability, such dictats as 'it is rude to put up fruits or sweet-meats in your pocket, except, you are pressed to do it'.[13] Petrie gave advice on the differentiation of outdoor clothing from that worn indoors. 'It is rude and impudent to enter the house or chamber of a great person wrap'd up in a cloak or big coat, or with boots or whip, or with dirty feet, or without your gloves on your hand.' 'As for ladies, it is indecent to enter the room of their superiors in a scarf, or with a plaid, or with their gown tucked up, or in any careless dress.'[14] Though some of the details were particular to Scotland, and the tone was pious, in broad terms none of this was new, since similar guidance had been current in London journals, famously the *Spectator*, from the early years of the century.[15] But such rules of politeness were newly packaged and available to a Scottish reading public, which included young Highland gentlemen in Edinburgh for their education.

Manners in Scotland were changing in parallel with changes in the material environment of the gentleman's house. Many contemporaries attributed this to the impact of union. To quote William Macintosh of Borlum, an advocate of improved agriculture, whose 1729 treaties on farming methods included many references to the growing luxury of the Scottish gentry, with their 'modish and well-bred' styles of living,

> In every month we hear 'The country is mightily improved since the Union.' And if you ask wherein, you are told, 'If I don't see how much more handsomely the gentry live now than before the Union in dress, table and house furniture? . . .' This epidemick, this increase of spending – but to be modish and well-bred, I ought to have said this new improvement – has in these 20 years strangely over-run the nation in the very remotest corners.[16]

Macintosh was struck by changes in 'housekeeping' and the impact on styles of hospitality and on food and drink.

> Where I saw the table served in Scots clean fine linen, I see now Flemish and Dutch diaper and damask. And where with two or three substantial dishes of beef, mutton and fowl, garnished with their own wholesome gravy, I see now served up several services of little expensive ashets, with English pickles, yea Indian mangoes, and catch-up [ketchup] or anchovy sauces.[17]

He was particularly critical of the shift towards tea drinking and French wines – 'the expense of liquor is as much increased as that of eating'[18] – and lamented the evidence of all of this in the houses he visited.

> In very little houses, and as little estates to supply them, when you come in to one of them, you shall see on a table a heap of empty tea cannisters, and under it pil'd up full of empty flasks or bottles; where, before, a very few for holding the dram of waters [whisky] was all there was use for there.[19]

His main criticism was of the insupportable cost of such luxury for Scotland as a whole, but he also mourned the passing of older styles of domestic sociability and the implied feminisation of the gentleman's house with the food, drink and domestic paraphernalia of women.

> When I came to my friend's house of a morning I used to be asked if I had my morning draught yet? I am now asked if I have had my tea? And in lieu of the big quaigh with strong ale and toast, and after a dram of good, wholesome Scots spirits, there is now the tea-kettle put to the fire, the tea-table and silver and china equipage brought in, and marmalade and cream.[20]

Whilst some others of similar rank shared these opinions in the 1720s and '30s – Duncan Forbes of Culloden, a major figure on the British political scene, was a famous critic of tea drinking – Macintosh of Borlum knew full well that his views were out of step with the times. 'I doubt not I shall be call'd a strange unmodish fellow, a very Goth, to cry out against handsome living.'[21] The times were changing, partly because of the availability in Scotland of conduct books and written advice on new styles of behaviour. And with most of the Scottish nobility spending long periods in London or Bath, where conspicuous 'politeness' was essential for social and political acceptance, and in Edinburgh, where they influenced young men like John Campbell of Barcaldine, it is not surprising that 'improved' manners and new forms of hospitality and sociability were quickly adopted.[22] With the aristocracy also resident on their estates at certain points in the year, the 'demonstration effect' of social improvement was even conveyed to those of the lesser gentry who rarely ventured beyond the Highlands.

SOCIABILITY AND HOSPITALITY AT INVERARY CASTLE

Correspondence from Taymouth Castle to Campbell lairds from the 1720s onwards hints at the character of improved sociability in the household of the earl of Breadalbane.[23] But a better indication of the 'demonstration effect' of the new politeness in aristocratic houses is given by two well-informed observers of social life at Inverary Castle, the Rev. Alexander Carlyle and James Boswell.

In the 1750s, the third duke of Argyll was mostly based in London, but each year he travelled to Inverary to spend a month or so on his estate, where he would host a series of major social events, inviting many family members and friends from beyond Argyll as well as a constant flow of lesser kin and gentlemen from the locality. The elderly Archibald Campbell was unmarried, and the wife and daughters of his principal political agent in Scotland, Fletcher of Saltoun, known as Lord Milton, managed the hospitality at Inverary.[24] Some visitors were accommodated in the castle, but the house was being remodelled and had few bedrooms, so most found lodgings in the burgh nearby and spent their days and evenings in the company of the duke at the castle or on the estate. One of the guests in the autumn of 1758 was Alexander Carlyle, minister of Inveresk near Edinburgh and friend of Lady Milton and her daughters, who had been invited to Inverary in the hope that he might impress the duke and gain his patronage for a university post in Glasgow.[25]

It was a difficult journey on horseback for a Lowlander, but having found a good room at the local inn, Carlyle went up to the castle.

> His Grace told me immediately that Miss Fletcher had made him expect my visit, and that he was sorry he could not offer me lodging, but that he would hope to see me every day to breakfast, dinner, and supper . . . We sat down every day fifteen or sixteen to dinner; for besides his two cousins and the Fletcher family, there were always seven or eight Argyllshire gentlemen, or factors on the estate, at dinner. The duke had the talent of conversing with his guests so as to distinguish men of knowledge and talents without neglecting those who valued themselves more on their birth and their rent-rolls than on personal merit.[26]

The hospitality was informal but distinctly masculine, like much conspicuous hospitality in the Highlands, even of a 'polite' variety. The duke 'waived ceremony very much, and took no trouble at table, and would not let himself be waited for, and came in when he pleased, and sat down on the chair that was left, which was neither at the head nor foot of the table'. In short, Carlyle was impressed with the duke's modest demeanour, his social skills in negotiating the different characters of the gentlemen present, his focus on the comfort and 'ease' of his visitors, his conversational abilities, and his deliberate avoidance of overt statements of his own high rank. These were all indicative of 'good breeding'.

Carlyle went on to observe – with the sort of approval one might expect from an Enlightenment clergyman – the duke's sobriety and personal inclination for the company of the ladies. But, mindful of his guests and the preferences of most Highland gentleman for male company and heavy drinking, these were permitted, with a 'toast-master' presiding, while the duke remained in the room but did not partake.

> After the ladies were withdrawn and he had drunk his bottle of claret, he retired to an easy-chair set hard by the fireplace: drawing a black silk night-cap over his eyes, he slept, or seemed to sleep, for an hour and a half. In the mean time . . . [the] toast-master pushed about the bottle, and a more noisy or regardless company could hardly be.[27]

The 'dinner' and 'toasting', which began at two o'clock and ended at six, when most of the local gentlemen visitors departed for the journey home, was followed by tea with the ladies, when the duke 'played two rubbers at sixpenny whist, as he did in London'. Supper followed at nine. The next day there was a visit to the castle from Jack Campbell of Stonefield, recently married to one of the duke's nieces, along with a new set of local gentlemen invited to dinner in much the same manner as the day before. At each meal, 'the provisions for the table were at least equal to the conversation; for we had sea and river fish in perfection, the best beef and mutton and fowls and wild game and venison of both kinds in abundance . . . the wines, too, were excellent'. On his final day at Inverary, which was a Sunday, Alexander Carlyle preached at the burgh kirk for a congregation that included the duke and his houseguests. He stopped for a night at Levenside, the house of Campbell of Stonefield, on his return journey to the Lowlands, thus furthering his connections with the great man's family.[28] But the death of Archibald, third duke of Argyll a few years later ended the minister's ambitions for a university post in Glasgow.

The local gentry were regularly invited to social occasions in the grand houses of noblemen. The brother of the fourth duke of Argyll, Lord Frederick Campbell, along with his wife, invited the now elderly Duncan Campbell of Glenure and his wife to a dinner and ball at Inverary in July 1778.[29] James Boswell in October 1773 observed the round of sociability and hospitality that was offered at Inverary Castle, and also noted the growing emphasis on female participation, consistent with evolving notions of domestic politeness among the elite. Boswell, with Johnson, was not in the area by the duke's invitation: the inn at Inverary burgh was simply a stop on their Highland tour. But on presenting himself at the castle after dinner (when the ladies were absent) Boswell found the 'amiable' duke 'sitting at the head of his table, with Campbell of Airds and several more gentlemen'.[30] He was 'graciously received' as befitted an old London acquaintance, and invited to tea with the duchess and other ladies. The following morning the travellers were shown over the house and grounds and remained at the castle for dinner. There were several 'gentlemen' present, and Boswell's own self-conscious 'politeness' was put on display at dinner since, from being placed mid-way down the table, 'it was my duty to give about the soup, which I did with all imaginable ease'. Alcohol consumption seems to have been lower than formerly and 'it was not the rule here to drink to anybody' – that is, the practice of 'toasting', which was a mortifying experience for shy or inarticulate men and also encouraged drunkenness, had been abandoned at the duke's table.[31]

After dinner, when the ladies had withdrawn, Boswell was particularly struck by a 'Colonel Livingstone . . . the member for the County of Argyll', whose behaviour exhibited a particular aspect of masculine politeness.

> The duke wanted to show a specimen of marble. He sent the Colonel for it, who brought a wrong piece; upon which he had to go back again to the other room, where it lay. He was conscious of an appearance of servility, but could not rebel. As he walked away, he whistled, to show his independency. Mr. Johnson thought this a nice trait of character.[32]

But later, back at the inn, Johnson was witness to behaviour that was less than dignified or polite when John Macaulay, an old friend of Boswell, passed an evening with the travellers and a dispute ensued. ' "Mr Macaulay, Mr Macaulay! Don't you know it is very rude to cry eh! eh! when one is talking?" Poor Macaulay had nothing to say for himself. But the truth is, it was a sin of ignorance, or mere rusticity.'[33]

THE 'IMPROVED' SOCIAL LIFE OF THE HIGHLAND GENTRY

Ignorance of 'good breeding' and evidence of 'mere rusticity' clearly still existed among some elements of the Highland gentry, even in the later decades of the eighteenth century. Among most, however, from about the 1720s onwards, there was a painful awareness of the need to present an outward show of polite hospitality and sociability, even in the most simple of material circumstances. Lesser families than those of the duke of Argyll could not expect to support the types of hospitality routinely seen in the houses of the great. But when important visitors were expected, they made elaborate preparations to support the norms of politeness. In the early 1730s, John Campbell of Barcaldine, living in the old-fashioned Barcaldine Castle, wrote to his father in the new and newly furnished Dalfuir House, a few miles away, with a request to borrow half a dozen chairs for a few days in anticipation of a passing visit from a distinguished relation by marriage, Cameron of Lochiel –

'for if Lochiel call here I don't think we'll have a chair to the piece of his company'.[34] There was nothing to suggest that the visitors were coming for dinner or overnight accommodation – the Lochiel estate was just a few hours ride away – and there is no record of whether the visit actually took place. But John Campbell was clearly anxious to create the right impression, and the ladies of the household, which included his mother-in-law 'Lady Kethick', the widow of Campbell of Kethick, were doubtless well able to show the family to advantage as they presented tea and refreshments to their 'well bred' guests, sitting on fashionable new chairs rather than the rustic benches that had long formed the principal seating arrangements at Barcaldine Castle.

It is easy to see why the Highland gentry in the first half of the eighteenth century were inclined to adopt the concepts of 'politeness' or 'good deportment' and translate these into their own personal behaviour and social life. The Highland gentleman, living in a poor part of the country, was doubtless familiar with the frequent charge of unruliness and want of civilisation, and the formula for 'improved' society, as advanced by Adam Petrie and others, stressed manners rather than material circumstances as the mark of gentility. But at its core the politeness agenda was ambiguous, for the manners that defined 'good deportment' could only be demonstrated through social interactions that imposed expectations of certain types of clothing, housing and domestic possessions, such as the chairs requested by John Campbell of Barcaldine from his father. Politeness was sociable and performative, it involved the Highland gentry in the giving and receiving of hospitality on an unprecedented scale in the Highlands and beyond, and it was inevitably costly.

The social life of the 'improved' Highland house was complex and built around a number of defined activities within the day and over the course of the year, several of them of a highly ritualised character. Visitors carefully scrutinised the conduct of hospitality and noted the room used for entertaining, its contents and the behaviour of participants.[35] The dining room was an important part of the male prestige agenda, but in small houses it was generally used for multiple purposes, including as a sitting room and place of business and sometimes as an occasional bedroom. But if the 'eating room' was used as a bedroom it certainly signalled a loss of status and polite credentials.[36] Seen through male eyes, the most important social occasions over the course of the day were breakfast, dinner and supper, punctuated by the lesser and more feminised activity of tea taking. Rules of hospitality were precise for visitors who arrived between the set mealtimes.[37] Male visitors were also offered hospitality in the form of outdoor excursions, which included hunting and fishing. Most social visitors to Highland gentry households, as elsewhere in rural situations, were adult men. Women and children only rarely visited because of the complex travel arrangements that this would entail, though many women were temporarily living in the households of their kin, particularly widows with their married daughters, or single women with their married sisters.[38] From the female standpoint, domestic sociability revolved around tea taking, dinner and supper, and women commonly used the best bedroom to entertain their female guests.

Breakfast was a particularly important occasion for male social interaction in small groups in both town and country. It was held in the domestic dining room or in a public place, such as a country inn or urban coffee house, at any time between eight and ten. It could be a preliminary to a shooting party or some other outdoor excursion, an occasion for a business meeting with a factor, lawyer or neighbouring land owner, or a purely social occasion. It could, of course, be a combination of all of these. Men mostly wore their formal outdoor day clothes and wigs when taking breakfast. In the early eighteenth century the breakfast drink was strong ale and whisky, with oatmeal or barley cakes and meat to eat. But changes were afoot with the introduction of tea and of sugar-based foods. The breakfasts enjoyed by Boswell and Johnson in 1773 included tea and oatcakes with marmalade or current jelly and cream, along with eggs, meat and bread, and ale and spirits.[39] The breakfasts that were on offer at the end of the century in some of the better Highland inns could be very lavish.[40] For women at home, breakfast was an intimate and informal occasion focused on the bedroom and commonly involving the children of the house. It was a preliminary to the female domestic affairs of the day, it included giving instructions to servants, and it could be undertaken in a bed gown or in a type of fashionable indoor clothing that was termed 'undress'. The occasional female visitor on an early morning visit also participated in the bedroom breakfast. Such a practice was new to Scotland in the 1720s and not entirely approved of by such anti-luxury commentators as William Macintosh of Borlum, who found, on calling on a friend: 'The lady was not dress'd to appear with the Laird and his gentleman at the morning tea, she her visitants, masters and misses [children] have it in their bedchamber.'[41]

Dinner was another significant focus for male sociability and performative hospitality, and like breakfast it was sometimes a non-domestic occasion at an inn or chophouse in town. Women were present at formal dinners in rural gentry houses, though this was not always true in the houses of the business or professional classes in eighteenth-century Scottish towns.[42] But the women usually 'withdrew' to a bedroom, parlour or drawing room (depending on the size and configuration of the house) for their own conversation and indoor female work such as sewing once the meal had been consumed and before the serious and lengthy business of masculine drinking began. The timing of dinner shifted gradually over the course of the eighteenth century from about midday at the start of the century to close to seven o'clock in fashionable urban circles by the early nineteenth century. In the Highlands in the 1770s when encountered by Boswell and Johnson, dinner was served in the middle of the afternoon. The change was part of a complex agenda of work and leisure among the fashionable male elite. It gave men scope for a sociable but mostly sober breakfast, then several daylight hours for work, outdoor leisure or travel, followed by a dinner that was usually marked by high alcohol consumption and much conversation, taking many hours and precluding any possibility of further work in the evening. The shift in the dinner hour was partly designed to distance the genteel from the labouring population, including household servants, who had their main meal in the middle of the day. It was driven by politeness, but it caused problems for those elements of the gentry who were not so leisured that they could afford to give up so much of the afternoon to sociability. The eventual settling on an evening hour for dinner in fashionable urban circles was mostly influenced by the needs of elite businessmen and professionals.[43]

Like the hour at which it was served, the food and alcohol presented at Highland dinners was sensitive to changes in fashion. Edmund Burt in Inverness in the 1720s described being offered salmon and trout, hens and eggs, game birds and hares, and they had plenty of roots and greens. Elite cuisine was in the French style, with lots of sauces. Lemon and sugar were always available for puddings, and butter was the main fat used in all cooking. But for much of the year he and his fellow officers hankered after beef, veal and lamb.[44] By the second half of the century there was more meat routinely available in gentry houses and a wider variety of sweet things, the latter nicely indicated in the inventory of stored and bottled foods at Glenure House in 1752.[45] Boswell was particularly impressed by a meal he was served at Coirechatachan, the home of an elderly tacksman on Skye.

> We had for supper a large dish of minced beef collops, a large dish of fricassee of fowl, I believe a dish called fried chicken, . . . a dish of ham or tongue, some excellent haddocks, some herrings, a large bowl of rich milk, frothed, as good a bread-pudding as I ever tasted, full of raisins and lemon or orange peel, and sillabubs made with port wine and in sillabub glasses. There was a good table-cloth with napkins; china, silver spoons, porter if we chose it, and a large bowl of very good punch.[46]

A formal dinner could be a lengthy affair. It was an opportunity to engage in various forms of performative hospitality and entertainment in the most luxuriously furnished room in the house and to present highly elaborate meals prepared by specialised servants, often hired for the occasion.[47] The puddings were the most expensive and elaborate part of the meal, and it was not uncommon in the first half of the eighteenth century for these to be made by the ladies of the house, since gentlewomen were taught the skills of pastry making as part of their education. Such direct engagement in the domestic economy of the household was no longer considered genteel in the second half of the century, but there were other forms of female display that succeeded pastry making, notably the playing of musical instruments to entertain the company after dinner. In most Highland gentry households, female music making replaced entirely the convention of a male piper, which had been an earlier indicator of status. This new arena of female display was an increasingly important device for signalling the wealth and polite taste of the family. Instruments were costly, as were music lessons, and musical ability was linked to sensibility and feminine emotions. Some people were astonished at the talent of Highland ladies. In 1764 Miss MacLeod, the sixteen-year-old daughter of the laird of MacLeod, sang Scottish and Italian songs for her parents' guests and drove one of the audience 'into a silly amazement, how a young lady from the barbarous coast of the Isle of Skye could possibly be such a mistress of the Italian music and Italian tongue'.[48]

Performance on musical instruments was one aspect of eighteenth-century genteel hospitality that made demands on women.[49] Another was performance at the tea table. The formally ordered tea party was the most important female-directed occasions for sociability and hospitality in the eighteenth-century genteel household.[50] Highland girls resident in Edinburgh or Perth for their schooling were taught how to act as hostesses at tea parties, how to mix the tea and present the cups in an elegant manner, and the proper way to behave and talk when invited as a guest. The tea party allowed for small-scale and flexible hospitality with an emphasis on politeness. It was an occasion to display valuable household objects such as tea china, fine wood canisters and furniture. Light food, particularly sweet pastries and puddings, might accompany the tea. Young women who were anxious to demonstrate their physical attractions and graceful movements sometimes wore special clothing to show the wrists and lower arms to advantage (in much the same manner as a musical performance on the harp or piano). Some tea china, particularly Wedgwood's basalt-ware, was deliberately designed and coloured to highlight the whiteness of a gentlewoman's hands.[51] Poets, including Alan Ramsay in the 1720s, wrote poetry for reading and discussion over tea.[52] Tea drinking could take place at any time of the day and in various rooms or spaces, including the garden, according to the season and who was involved. Tea in the evening was often the preliminary to card playing and supper. Tea was served at assembly rooms and balls. Tea was sober and rational. To join the ladies for tea and teatime conversation soon after dinner – though not too soon – was the mark of good sense and sensibility in a gentleman. Propriety demanded that a man who was drunk should not present himself at the tea table – and though many men did, it generated censure.[53] Though a formal invitation might be given in advance, it was the form of hospitality most likely to be offered to unexpected visitors. Women entertained men of equal status with tea. If the local clergyman or lawyer called to see the lady of the house, he was offered tea. Gentlewomen also offered such hospitality to visiting females of lesser status than themselves (though not lesser males), such as their dressmaker, the wives of tenant farmers, or retired and trusted servants. In these circumstances, the tea, and the social rituals it demanded, smoothed and feminised a conversation that might have business content. Tea drinking was controversial in Scotland when first introduced at the start of the century, but it was soon established as a necessary device for female sociability and hospitality.

Much of the formal social life of the eighteenth-century country house was conducted around the entertainment of visitors. Some visitors, particularly men, were present for just a few hours; others were there for longer. Providing indoor entertainment for long-stay visitors could be hard work and unrewarding, particularly for women who had few opportunities for movement beyond the confines of the house. As one noble spinster remarked in 1778 in a letter to her married sister,

> For my part I am sufficiently accustomed to dumb people, for here are brothers Frederick and William, who speak about six words a day and instead of being any company, only serve to give me the vapours by walking up and down the room without ceasing . . . I have brought down my work and sat with these two gentlemen to try if any acquaintance could be made with them, and I tell you I am entertained with their eternally walking backwards and forwards, and now flinging themselves upon the couch, yawning and asking such questions as 'When do we go to London?'[54]

Her sister, in turn, living in a country house in provincial Ireland, found the business of entertaining a stream of visiting men a major imposition on her 'comfort and convenience'.[55] Short-term visitors in rural areas were unlikely to be women because of the expense of carriage transport, which included the cost of horses and specialist male servants. Changing views on the propriety of horse riding were also having an impact on female mobility. Adam Petrie in his conduct book of 1720 gave warning to men and women of the dire consequences that women might suffer if they sat for long periods on a horse.[56] And by the later years of the century, riding for pleasure was also thought to be the cause of rough behaviour and coarse appearance in a woman.[57] Yet to be within 'polite' walking distance of a range of social acquaintances was a social advantage that few gentlewomen enjoyed while living in the Highland counties. Indeed, easy movement from one gentleman's house to another was not always possible for men, as the journey made by Boswell and Johnson in 1773 confirms. It was only in the more accessible southerly Highlands, or in the summer when roads were dry and travel by pony cart without recourse to male servants could be used (as described by Elizabeth Grant of Rothiemurchus in the early nineteenth century) that women could engage in the elaborate and frequent social rituals of visiting and entertaining among nearby families and friends. This sort of social life was promoted as a female ideal in contemporary conduct literature and in fiction, but it was unavailable in most Highland areas. So despite the investment in new country housing, it is not surprising that many of the Highland gentry, and gentlewomen in particular, came to the view that 'politeness' and an aspiration to improved sociability and hospitality were not entirely compatible with full-time living in the Highlands.

SOCIABILITY AND HOSPITALITY BEYOND THE HIGHLANDS

The new country houses that were built by the Highland gentry were designed to facilitate improved and fashionable leisure. But by the second half of the eighteenth century, Highland gentry families, in common with gentry families elsewhere in Britain, were choosing to spend more of their time living in towns.[58] In some cases this was a nearby county town. Peter Grant, father of Elizabeth Grant, the 'Highland lady', as a child in the 1770s–80s spent the summer at Inverdruie, a small house on the Rothiemurchus estate, and the winter months in nearby Elgin, where his parents kept a house while he attended the local school.[59] But increasingly the Highland gentry gravitated towards Edinburgh. In the first half of the century, many gentlemen spent part of the year in the capital for reasons of work or family business, but they tended to live in temporary lodgings, hired by the week or season, and their sociability was built on male networking and tavern life.[60] Young women spent a few months in town for 'improvement' and education prior to marriage, but they mostly lodged with their schoolmistresses or with female kin and socialised under strict supervision with other teenage girls. Only the very wealthy or those with full-time professional or business interests kept a family home in town. Even men who had this level of urban commitment commonly preferred to leave their wives in the country for the sake of economy and to watch over the estate.

Most married women did not like being left alone on their husbands' estates. Aristocratic women complained most bitterly, because they had few if any practical roles when living in the country. According to one, it was like 'pensioning in a convent'.[61] Ordinary Highland gentlewomen in the first half of the eighteenth century were involved in the practical affairs of estates and households. Since most were of Highland upbringing and spoke Gaelic, the environment was familiar even when they were settled at a distance from their own families. Most husbands were only away for short periods and sent their sons on errands to town when the sons were old enough, so most women enjoyed the company of their menfolk much of the time. Even if they did yearn for town, the logistics of family travel in the first half of the century were often insuperable. According to one contemporary observer, there were no gentleman's carriages north of the Tay before the later 1720s, and when the first was driven into Inverness in 1725 the locals stood in the streets and marvelled at the event.[62] Even in the 1740s, and despite the building of a network of military roads, the road journey from Inverness to Edinburgh could be perilous. Simon, Lord Lovat, travelling with his two grown daughters, described a journey by private coach that took eleven days, with four serious vehicle breakdowns involved and his daughters obliged on several occasions to either walk long distances or to sit behind the coachman on a horse.[63] Most Highland gentlemen simply did not bother to have a coach, or when they did make the investment were regularly troubled by disasters on treacherous roads, as in 1782 when Duncan Campbell of Barcaldine and Glenure's carriage was overturned and destroyed at Tyndrum. There were several people injured in this accident, including 'Mrs MacDougall's black boy', a young black servant.[64]

With a shift towards town living for Highland families and a growing emphasis on indoor life, some women rarely if ever visited the family seat. Sir John Sinclair of Ulbster, of *Statistical Accounts* fame, whose estate was in the far north-east, established a permanent family home in Edinburgh in the late 1780s, with a townhouse in Charlotte Square from the mid-1790s, following his second marriage to Lady Diana Macdonald of Sleat. His mother and his first wife had been near-permanent residents in Caithness, living at Ulbster while he travelled back and forth to Edinburgh and London and lived in lodgings when in town. Once settled in a townhouse,

Sir John and his teenage sons made regular summer visits to see the estate and visit their neighbours, always journeying on horseback. But his wife and daughters remained in the city and were only able to visit Ulbster when the road across the Ord north of Tain, which was built by the countess of Sutherland in the second decade of the nineteenth century allowed, for the first time, safe carriage travel.[65]

Sir John Sinclair's acquisition of a townhouse was at a time when many of the wealthier elements of the Highland gentry were establishing their permanent family residence in Edinburgh. For some this was seen as necessary for career status among gentlemen who were obliged to work full-time in one of the professions, notably the law, to supplement an estate income. This seems to have been the reasoning of Sir Peter Grant of Rothiemurchus when he established his family in a townhouse in Charlotte Square in the 1790s.[66] In some families, including the Grants, it was a necessary corollary of a wealthy Lowland or English wife. But for many it was a contentious move, resulting in conflict between husband and wife or between estate owner and his kin, mainly over issues of cost. There were several financial considerations to be taken into account when moving the family into a townhouse. The first was the cost of the house itself, though renting out the country property could offset this. The arguments for and against such a move in a debt-laden family are well articulated by Jane Austen in her 1818 novel *Persuasion*. But as the foolish, spendthrift Sir Walter Elliot discovers, a move to a smaller house in the town, in this case to Bath, while it might result in some savings on servants and carriages, could also expose the family to new opportunities for spending. Finding a tenant for a Highland country house was, needless to say, difficult, so for most Highland gentry families, a townhouse was an additional cost that could not be offset. Yet it was the cost of conspicuous consumption in town that most sensible men feared. Grant of Rothiemurchus was not a sensible man, and his family were eventually bankrupted by a costly lifestyle. Alexander Campbell of Barcaldine was sensible, and though he could not withstand the constant demands from his wife to be allowed to live full-time in Edinburgh, he did manage to keep expenditure under control. It was his son, Duncan, raised in the city and a soldier by profession, who eventually ruined the family.

Although 'redundant' single women had long gravitated towards urban living in the smaller provincial towns, a permanent family home in the principal city was a different matter. A townhouse in Edinburgh was expensive. At the end of the eighteenth century there were about 2,000 households in the New Town. Some of these were flats occupied by business families. Noblemen and the landed gentry mostly occupied the townhouses, and the most prestigious address was Charlotte Square.[67] A house in Charlotte Square built by a speculative builder and fully fitted, cost between £3,000 and £4,000. Renting a similar house could cost more than £500 a year.[68] The furniture was an additional cost that could run into thousands of pounds. There were, though, ways of saving money on the fittings and furniture. Pine, painted to look like finer woods, was often used for doors and shutters, and furniture could be hired by the season from a fashionable furniture emporium such as Trotters of Princes Street – or even by the day for special occasions. But the basic cost of acquiring a townhouse and then maintaining it in a manner appropriate to the status of the family, with the associated costs of sociability and hospitality, was considerable.

When the family of Campbell of Barcaldine first settled full-time in Edinburgh in the later eighteenth century they chose an address in the cheaper east end of the New Town, at 3 Picardy Place. The Grant family of Rothiemurchus also moved to this street in 1816 when their finances came under strain.[69] A newspaper advertisement of 1827 for a property across the road from the Campbells gives some idea of what the house might have looked like, and how it was organised.

> It consists on the ground floor [basement] of a servant's hall, butler's and housekeeper's rooms, laundry, with bath and washing tubs, fitted with pipes for cold and hot water, two wine cellars, one spirit cellar, and in the back court kitchen, scullery, various larders, pantries etc. In the front court there are five cellars etc. In the other floors, there are dining room, parlour, a suit of four drawing rooms and ten rooms besides dressing rooms, sleeping places and innumerable accommodations of every kind. The house is completely fitted up for gas.[70]

This house on the north side of the street, which was described as 'most elegantly and commodiously fitted up', also had a stable for five horses and a double coach house. The Campbell property did not include a coach house, though they did keep a carriage and horses housed nearby. Picardy Place was increasingly commercial by the 1820s, and Duncan Campbell of Barcaldine moved to a much grander townhouse in Moray Place in the new West End. He had difficulty raising the necessary purchase price of £3,700 – the sum did not include the internal fittings – and his lawyer (and cousin) John Archibald Campbell WS recommended that the family rent instead, suggesting a smaller and less fashionable house in the still respectable Queen Street, at forty guineas per month. Needless to say, this advice was ignored.[71]

The importance of the townhouse for female culture and sociability clearly shaped the design and internal layout of the house as well as the furnishings, just as male culture and status defined the design and furnishing priorities of the country house.[72] Drawing rooms, which normally dominated the first floor, were elaborately furnished in a style to accommodate women's social lives, with musical instruments, light-coloured upholstery and many mirrors and feminine pictures. The drawing room was the most important, status-loaded and costly room in the late-eighteenth-century Edinburgh townhouse.[73] On the ground floor, closest to the outside world, was the dining room, a bedroom for visiting men, and a family parlour used as an everyday sitting and eating room. The upper floors were given over to family and servant bedrooms, with a schoolroom and nursery for the children. Basements were for servant uses, which in town almost invariably meant female servants. The female agenda – of wives and mothers, daughters and serving women – along with the needs of children, were at the heart of the daily life of the gentry townhouse.[74] When a woman was widowed it was normal, where family finances allowed, for the widow to be willed the life-interest, or even the outright ownership, of the townhouse. But when men were widowed and their daughters were grown and gone to homes of their own, the townhouse was commonly given up or sold in favour of the country residence and the use of lodgings when visiting the city. The single gentleman did not need a townhouse for either his status or comfort, but the married gentlewoman did. The ascendance of the townhouse at the end of the eighteenth century spoke eloquently of changes in the gender politics of gentry families throughout Great Britain. It was also, of course, a major factor in the growing expenditure of the Highland gentry.

The arguments used by Mary Campbell of Barcaldine in the 1780s to persuade her husband Alexander to allow her to live in town full-time are worth describing in detail. Mary was a city girl by upbringing, the daughter of John Campbell 'of the bank', who, as chief cashier to the Royal Bank of Scotland from the 1740s to his death in the 1770s, lived most of the time in Edinburgh. Mary's widowed mother, a Lowland gentlewoman, also lived in Edinburgh. When Mary first married in 1785 she moved to Argyll to live at Barcaldine House, but her first pregnancy raised questions over the availability of a doctor to attend the birth. Childbirth in times past had always taken place at the husband's country house, and for status reasons it was important that an heir be born on the estate. Married women of gentry background were increasingly unwilling to face their confinements without proper medical attendance by a qualified physician, but physicians were unwilling to leave their lucrative urban practices to attend to patients in the country, however wealthy and distinguished. Alexander Campbell of Barcaldine searched high and low for a proper medical attendant for his wife's confinement. None could be found that was willing to spend weeks in rural Argyll awaiting the birth, and Mary Campbell, though safely delivered by a local midwife, was reluctant thereafter to have her babies in the country.[75]

Issues concerning children were one of the reasons for choosing to live in town. John Campbell of Barcaldine (Mary's uncle), when he was crown factor on the forfeited Perthshire estates in the 1750s and 1760s, had quickly established a family home in the town of Crieff, where there was a good array of private tutors for his large family. Perth and Stirling, with their well-known grammar schools for the older boys, were not that far away. Mary Campbell's complaints about living in the Highlands were certainly focused on her own interests, but the children and their education were also a concern. She wrote to her husband in Edinburgh from Barcaldine House in May 1798.

> I am quite miserable and unhappy when I sit down and reflect on the uncomfortable way I pass my time, to be so neglected by you. I think myself neglected when the newspapers come so seldom that I do not know in this *critical* period no more of what is going on in the world . . . I am quite discontented at this way of life and I will not live in this *wilderness* any longer . . . there is another and greater cause for vexing me just now and that is seeing my children [the eldest was twelve years old] spending their time so idly and so neglected in their education which is a very great sin upon both your head and mine.[76]

Letters from his mother-in-law about her wish to see the children,[77] or concerns that her daughter and grandchildren were so far from a church when living in the Highlands,[78] merely fuelled the 'pester-power' that Mary Campbell was able to exert on Alexander, and eventually she got her way. She settled in Edinburgh to a life of extensive sociability within a network of female family and friends, as is well described in her letters. If this new attitude to Highland living was typical of women like Mary, who had a Highland family, then wives of non-Highland background, which was a growing trend, were even less likely to want to live there full-time.

Mary Campbell, though not a practical housewife, did take an interest in the estate when she lived there. She wrote to her husband in Edinburgh about the progress of the harvest and the state of the weather.[79] But when she lived in Edinburgh, her main correspondent at Barcaldine was an English governess, hired to teach the children when they were young, who ran the house in Mary's absence, watching over the jam and cheese making and reporting on the servants.[80] When the children went away to school, it was to a boarding school in Clapham for Maria, the eldest daughter, and to Harrow for Duncan, the heir. Wealthy Highland families often followed their children to England

and to live in townhouses in London.[81] Ambitious men who were eager to shine in a London professional or political career, like Peter Grant, also moved their family southwards. This was a step too far for the Campbells of Barcaldine, though the family, including Mary, had begun a pattern of regular leisure travel beyond Scotland that included visits to London and Bath.

In addition to enhanced opportunities for domestic sociability and hospitality, much of the attraction for women of living in Edinburgh was in the commercial leisure facilities that the city provided. Shopping, the theatre and concerts, clubs and assemblies, parks and promenades – the walk to St Bernards Well, a mineral spring on the Water of Leith, was established in 1789 – were all available to women without the necessary presence of men. The sociability attached to fashionable churches was also available. Social visiting, supper parties and musical evenings, in and out of the home, were the bedrock of gentry leisure in Edinburgh by the later decades of the eighteenth century, and it was possible for women of this class to enjoy an independent social life, irrespective of marital status or age. Even spinsters living alone could host elaborate parties that included male guests, whilst gentlemen, single or married, could enjoy a parallel masculine social life in their numerous societies and clubs.[82]

Leisure travel beyond the city was also made possible by a base in Edinburgh, with its network of good roads and coach services. Alexander Carlyle, the minister at Inveresk, made regular leisure jaunts to Dumfries, Moffat and Duns in the Scottish borders, which were all spa towns, and further afield to Harrogate. At Harrogate in the summer of 1764 he noted the presence of a large company of Scots, including the laird of McLeod and family en route via the spa to see the racing in the nearby Yorkshire town of Wetherby.[83] The health-related leisure concerns of the British elite were absorbed en masse by the Highland gentry, and in the second half of the century every leisure town and resort had its complement of Highland Scots.[84] Ewan Cameron of Fassfern, a brother-in-law of Alexander Campbell of Barcaldine, was at 'Strath Piffer Wells', a spa resort near Inverness, for his health in 1796.[85] Numerous others of the Barcaldine family and friends visited Bath, normally travelling via Edinburgh, to take the waters for their health and pleasure, including in particular the military men, who were also seeking patronage. Colonel Alexander Campbell, son of Barcaldine, was there for his health in 1779, and true to military form he was causing a scandal. As reported by a cousin in Argyll, Patrick Campbell of Ardchattan, who had heard it through a friend, Alexander was in need of money and his altercations with his wife, Helen Sinclair of Ulbster, made him 'the talk of the town'.[86] Another visitor at about the same time was the now elderly Hugh Mackay of Bighouse, who died in Bath in the hot summer of 1780 and caused a great deal of trouble and cost to his family when they had to repatriate his body in a lead coffin for the burial in Scotland.[87] In death, as in life, this Highland gentleman was distinguished by an inclination to conspicuous consumption.

Conclusion: From Luxury to Loss in Five Generations

Over the five generations that spanned the long eighteenth century, the Campbell family of Barcaldine experienced a complete revolution in their fortunes and styles of living. They began in the later seventeenth century as small-scale landowners who were also chamberlains to the earl of Breadalbane, living in a remote tower house. They acquired more land, advanced the family fortunes and built a new country house, established a cadet family, purchased a townhouse in Edinburgh, were granted a baronetcy – and then they lost the estate in the early 1840s to end up more-or-less back where they had begun as paid property managers for the earl of Breadalbane. Of course they were not in any real sense back to where they had begun in the seventeenth century. The first of the mid-nineteenth-century landless Barcaldine lairds spent his retirement years in Wimbledon near London.[1] Many of his siblings had gone abroad, particularly to India, and his eldest son emigrated to Australia. Relationships with women, with kin and with the Highland country people were entirely different to what they had been before. Hugh Fraser, minister at Ardchattan, was right when he warned Sir Duncan Campbell, the first baronet, in 1834 of the changing religious habits of the local peasantry on the Barcaldine estate.[2] A spirit of gloomy religious 'fanaticism', to use the term applied by David Stewart of Garth in 1822, had gripped a despondent peasantry who no longer had either respect for or attachments to their chiefs and landlords.[3] And it is fair to say that the lack of interest and regard flowed equally in the other direction.

The Campbell family of Barcaldine was not unusual. There were many families like them and some have featured in this study, though their detailed histories are less well served by consistent records. But not all estates passed so easily from father to son down the generations, as was evident at Barcaldine, for they were a fertile and hardy family, with an excellent rate of survival of children to adulthood. Indeed, it is the very large numbers of surviving children that makes this family so very revealing of a broader Highland gentry experience. In each generation a succession of fathers made plans and provisions for their sons and daughters that highlight, sometimes poignantly when hopeful youngsters died, the changing expectations and ambitions of their class as a whole. Other families, though motivated by similar ambitions, were less lucky in the fate of their offspring. Many sons died young, and estates passed via complex entails or other inheritance provisions to women or to distant relatives who were not raised to the life and responsibilities of landowning. Hugh Mackay of Bighouse lost all of his sons in youth, his family estate passed several times through female ownership, which imposed massive financial burdens on the property, and his eldest brother, the lord of Reay, was succeeded by a man who was mentally deficient. In times past an unsuitable male heir, with physical or mental health problems, or a female heir would have been replaced in the interests of the clan. But in the modern age of law, the tenets of private property legislation and ownership rights prevailed. Yet regardless of varying patterns of inheritance, most estates and the families that owned them were encountering financial crises by the early nineteenth century that in many cases ended with the sale of property that had been in family hands for many hundreds of years.

There can be no doubt that the Highland gentry lost their estates because their expenditure on houses and sociability and other forms of consumption was greater than their income. Few had the accumulation of wealth behind them that was seen in the Malcolm family of Poltalloch, who through sugar plantations in Jamaica and a cattle station in South America possessed such riches that the mid-nineteenth-century laird could indulge his interest in Old Master paintings to become one of the leading art collectors of the day.[4] Even on the eve of disaster, Sir Duncan Campbell of Barcaldine in the 1830s built a vast extension to Barcaldine House, designed by a fashionable London architect, to house a library for books that he hardly ever read.[5] He simply could not afford this ultimate statement of gentlemanly status, and he knew it; but he lived as though he could. Elizabeth Grant of Rothiemurchus recorded a similar experience in her family, with a father who furnished a great library with books and antiquities and paintings at their house of Doune in 1813. Elizabeth wrote the catalogue for the books. 'It was bound in blue morocco, with gilt leaves, and lay always for reference on the large oval table.' She even knew who purchased the catalogue when the whole lot had to be sold to pay off family debts. It caused her pain to think about their loss, as it did in other families.[6] Peter Grant and Duncan Campbell were certainly not fools, but they did fall into the luxury trap, and the consequences for them and many like them was bankruptcy and voluntary exile to far-flung places in the hope of rebuilding their fortunes.[7]

Yet two generations before, the story had been very different. Those men and women of the Highland gentry who came to adulthood during the mid-eighteenth century were blessed with a mostly comfortable co-existence in the modern world of urban consumerism and politeness in parallel with the material simplicity of a practical Highland farming life and the culture of Gaeldom. Colin Campbell of Glenure and his wife Janet, her father Hugh Mackay of Bighouse and their kinsman John Campbell 'of the bank' may have been witness to the turbulence of the Jacobite Rebellion of 1745 and victims to some of its immediate consequences such as the Appin Murder, but they managed a complex process of culture shifting between the modern and the traditional. They loved owning fine new things in the fashionable manner; they dressed in the high metropolitan style of the day and spent a great deal of time and effort in getting their purchases just right. But they were also the last generation of the Highland gentry to live a day-to-day existence that was fully embedded in the social, cultural and material life of the Highlands. Of course, even in this generation there were changes in behaviour and values that alarmed some local observers, though such alarm was not occasioned by fears of bankruptcy, but rather that the love of wealth and its trappings was causing the gentry to regard their estates as no more than a source of income, and not as a focus for their cultural attachments and obligations. Rob Donn Mackay, the great Sutherland poet, who subjected Hugh Mackay of Bighouse to a level of critical scrutiny unparalleled in Gaeldom, was correct in his assessment that the rising generation of gentlemen had a very different approach to their 'gathering and spending' than the old.

Attitudes to Highland estates were changing among lairds, as they came to see their property as a commercial asset to be exploited for the best return regardless of traditional uses or the interests of their tenants. Charting these changes in practice has been the work of numerous scholars of recent times and was a major preoccupation among contemporary analysts, from Boswell and Johnson in the 1770s through to David Stewart of Garth, the military laird, in the 1820s. But attitudes and behaviour in the broader compass of social and cultural experience were just as important for understanding the changing fortunes of the Highland gentry in the long eighteenth century. Indeed, some contemporaries such as David Stewart or John Ramsay of Ochtertyre, or even the early eighteenth-century agricultural improver William Mackintosh of Borlum, did identify a 'change in manners' as critical to the shaping of the Highland gentry. This study has highlighted two crucial areas in which the 'change in manners' had a powerful impact on the tendency towards conspicuous consumption. The first relates to the position of women in gentry families, and the second emerged with the mass military employment of gently raised youths.

Up to the middle years of the eighteenth century the Highland gentry tended to operate a family management system that involved a low dependency on family financial support among women. This changed to one of high dependency from about the 1760s onwards. In the first half of the century, gentlewomen worked for the benefit of the family, whether they were living in or out of the Highlands. They were active participants in the commerce of estates, and those who were pushed into the urban economy because they were widows or unmarried were expected to work to support themselves and provide services for kin. Women brought in dowries, which were linked to annuities when a husband died. But it was easy for men to squeeze an annuity, or not pay it at all, and this was commonplace in the families of lairds. When women did 'go to town' to engage in consumption, their expenditure was tightly controlled by men. Indeed, part of the training in family management that young men received with their education was through the supervision of their sisters when the latter were sent from home for a brief spell of education and consumption prior to marriage. It is fair to say that the Highland gentry, with their tight resources and primitive masculine culture, did not treat their womenfolk well. But this changed with the adoption of a culture of politeness and the move into non-landed employments that took lairds and their ladies into the towns. In the second half of the century, Highland gentlewomen did not work and were supported within families as leisured wives and daughters. They were consumers, not producers, and their patterns of consumption were a central feature of family status as well as a major expense.

A second aspect of changing dependency ratios in Highland gentry families was seen in the shifting pattern of employment of non-inheriting sons, and increasingly even of inheriting sons, that went with a massive rise in military participation. Just as women were entering the ranks of consumers, families were losing a raft of male kin traditionally employed in business and practical farming who had provided useful services to their families and were able to support themselves and sometimes make fortunes. New notions of respectability and status killed these avenues for employment among the gentry because they were inconsistent with a leisured, gentlemanly ideal. Young men, often just teenagers, flocked to join the army from the late 1750s, and in doing so exposed a large element of the Highland gentry to the most luxurious, individualistic, fashionable and reckless profession of the age. Some soldiers made a fortune, but most did not, and they cost their families dear in money and in a fracturing of the social bonds that had secured the Highland gentry on their Highland estates.

Both of these trends in real experience were underpinned by a change in manners that might be termed 'politeness', which in turn was born out of exposure to the attitudes and values of modern metropolitan culture.

The gravitation towards the army or towards leisured dependency among women was fuelled by changes in class and status hierarchies in Britain that the Highland gentry could not have resisted, even if they had tried. David Stewart of Garth in 1822 endeavoured to suggest an alternative way for impoverished and unhappy lairds to live their lives on their estates with their tenants, as of old.

> If unable to vie with their Southern neighbours in luxury and splendour, might not gentlemen have possessed in their mountains a more honourable distinction – that of commanding respect without the aid of wealth, by making a grateful people happy, and thus uniting true dignity with humanity?[8]

But this was an unrealistic expectation. In generations past, the younger sons of lairds had filtered down to an economic situation in the Highlands that reflected their position in the family hierarchy and their father's wealth, or the want of it, but they still retained their links with kin and their status as gentlemen. This was remarked on by commentators like Edmund Burt in the early eighteenth century, who noted how a great lord would dismount from his horse to embrace a cousin with marked affection because he was of his family, even though the man was poor and dressed in rags.[9] Family and land had been the main sources of identity and status in the pre-modern Highlands, and although these factors retained a disproportionate role within the Highland psyche, in the modern metropolitan context it was individual wealth and possessions, education, employment and personal behaviour that were more important for identity and social regard. That was why a son in the lower levels of a family hierarchy could so easily lose his 'respectability', to use the term employed by contemporaries, if he tried his luck in trade or tenant farming, where status was low and the work was physical and arduous. Hence the great popularity of the army as a device for disposing of young family members in a gentlemanly manner and sending them off on their own to a mostly leisured lifestyle where, if they were lucky, they might make a fortune. It meant that the army was full of young men on the bottom rungs of both the landed and professional status hierarchy, desperately clinging to their gentlemanly credentials, building their identity not through real day-to-day economic and social connections with their family and estate, but through behaviour and appearance, and a romantic fantasy of military Highlandism.

By the later eighteenth century the seeds of pending failure had been sown. Longstanding cultural modes of behaviour that predisposed the Highland gentry to conspicuous consumption in clothing, food and drink were accelerated by the new lifestyles of Highland gentlewomen and by the changing employments of many Highland gentlemen. Social relationships and economic activities that tethered the gentry to a daily life in the Highlands were increasingly fractured by an inability to sustain a presence on estates that was compatible with the new imperatives of work and sociability, and by the new culture of consumer-driven politeness. Yet the whole flimsy edifice was still held together by a fantasy of romantic Highlandism made real in the 'world of goods' and materiality, which was embraced collectively not just by men and women of Highland family background, but by the fashionable elite elsewhere in Britain. Romantic consumerism was not unique to the Highlands, of course, but it did assume a particular manifestation among the Highland gentry in their expensive reinventions of Highland 'traditions' in housing, clothing or hospitality.[10] What is more, the underlying dynamic of romantic consumerism, the appeal to the individual emotions and to a hedonistic indulgence in a tragic sense of loss mirrored in untamed nature, chimed well with the times when so many Highland lairds faced bankruptcy.[11]

The man best known for his celebration of traditional culture and styles of living of Highland Scotland was Walter Scott, writing in the first three decades of the nineteenth century. Scott was a lawyer of Borders gentry background. He was Edinburgh-bred, like many Highland lairds in the later eighteenth century, and his real encounters with actual people engaged in authentic traditional practices in the northernmost parts of Scotland often left him bemused. In 1814 Scott accompanied a friend on a tour of the Scottish lighthouses. He witnessed many things that were hard to understand or were viewed with disapproval. A preference among the peasantry for leisure over work was one; another was revealed in popular attitudes to land ownership and boundaries. So the man who put a wall around a field and called it his own was avaricious in the eyes of the local people, rather than a good businessman protecting his property. And the idle youth who fell to his death while climbing cliffs in search of inedible seagull eggs was a hero, not a fool.[12] It is hardly surprising that Walter Scott found it hard to enter the mindset of the people he observed, for their social construction of reality was so very different to his own. Highland gentlemen, with their similar mindsets to Scott, were also bemused. It was so much easier to believe in a Highlands of the past, where lairds were warriors and gentlemen and the peasantry was simple and loyal, and to reinvent this in the present through baronial houses, military parades, Highland balls and grand tartan processions, like the one that Walter Scott and others, including David Stewart of Garth, organised for King George IV's great royal visit to Edinburgh in 1822.[13] This event was described at the time as a 'collective hallucination', and the same could be said of a great deal more of the behaviour of the Highland gentry.

Walter Scott cultivated an array of so-called 'traditional' Highland personalities in Edinburgh in the 1820s in whom he invested this romantic sense of the past. They were celebrities in their day, regarded by some as great men and by others are mere eccentrics. The most famous was probably Alastair Ranald Macdonnell of Glengarry, who had inherited a small north-western estate from his uncle while still a minor, been schooled at Eton and Oxford, and taken an expensive Grand Tour in the 1790s, but who had abandoned his authentic modern persona in favour of an invented life of a laird. Glengarry was much fêted in the early nineteenth century as the last of the ancient clan leaders. He maintained the 'traditions' of chiefs in his dress, and pipers, and re-created Highland games. He built a Highland summer house using the ancient system of bent willow and turf, and founded a 'Society of True Highlanders' in Inverness in 1815, where the business was entirely conducted in Gaelic. He was a soldier in various local regiments, garbed in increasingly extravagant uniforms, and was constantly getting into scrapes and fights, some serious, over matters of clanship and honour. He was prosecuted, and acquitted, for murder in 1798 following a duel that led to the death of Lieutenant Norman Macleod, grandson of Flora Macdonald. The fight had erupted over a disputed Highland dance at an Inverness ball. Dressed in a fanciful tartan costume, with a retinue in attendance, he was one of those who processed at George IV's visit to Edinburgh in 1822, and marked the occasion with uproar and alarm because of his insistence that he be allowed to carry arms at the official reception. Macdonell of Glengarry, needless to say, brought financial ruin to his family estate. He made a powerful impact on Walter Scott and others, though, and inspired that most celebrated of literary evocations of the Highland gentleman at the time of the '45, Fergus MacIvor in Scott's novel *Waverley*.[14]

This is how Walter Scott described Macdonnell of Glengarry in 1826, just a few years before the eccentric 'traditional' Highlander died in a very modern steamship accident.

> This gentleman is a kind of Quixote in our age, having retained, in their fullest extent, the whole feelings of clanship and chieftainship, elsewhere so long abandoned. He seems to have lived a century too late . . . to me he is a treasure, as being full of information as to the history of his own clan and the manners and customs of the highlands in general. Strong, active, muscular, he follows the chase of the deer for days and nights together, sleeping in his plaid when darkness overtakes him. The number of his singular exploits would fill a volume . . .[15]

The world of Glengarry, built on a fantasy of fragmented and re-created cultural attachments and expensively grandiose behaviour, was more extreme than usual among Highland gentlemen in the early nineteenth century. But in their great baronial building projects, Highland societies, military balls and elaborate tartan costumes, those less remarkable lairds and ladies that have peopled this study were similarly engaged in a world of fantasy, the product of tragically fragmented and re-created cultural attachments, mostly conducted in Edinburgh or abroad, and made real through consumption.

Elizabeth Grant of Rothiemurchus, a modern laird's daughter raised in Edinburgh, probably best captured the reality of life on Highland estates in her recollections written in the mid-nineteenth century. Although her life was one of relative detachment from the Highlands, the world she described was concrete enough and the account she gave of the house and estate that her father owned but only rarely visited was typical of many properties by the early nineteenth-century. It was striking for a tendency towards domination by the middle-aged and elderly; the younger gentry, male and female, now lived elsewhere. The younger country people were nowhere to be seen: many had gone away to find work, and those who remained in the Highlands were culturally invisible. Only a few elderly Gaels were still connected on a daily basis. Many of the household servants were English. The tenants on her father's farms were mostly half-pay officers – usually younger sons, cousins or the natural offspring of lairds – who had returned to their native Highlands in middle life having mostly served abroad in the army. The combination of government pension and small farm income allowed them to sustain a modestly genteel life. The family house, Doune, was a sort of family asylum for elderly relatives and dependents, whilst the laird and his family mostly lived in town. Doune's permanent residents in 1803 comprised:

> My great Uncle Sandy the Parson with his English wife, her sister and all their carpet work, two of the five sons, an old Donald, a faithful servant of my grandfather's . . . and old Christy who had gone from Strathspey to wait on my father and my Aunt Lissy, and their Bonne Mrs Sophy Williams . . . she had her pension and her attick and so had Mr Dallas, one of the line of tutors, when he chose to come to it.[16]

This was a world away from the Highlands of romance, or the estates and houses of fifty or a hundred years before, when lairds and their ladies and their many sons and daughters, living full-time on their farms, first embarked on a life of luxury through modern consumerism that was eventually concluded with so much loss.

Notes

PRELUDE

1. NAS GD170/972/25, Letter from Hugh Mackay to Colin Campbell, 15 January 1752.
2. For the meaning of such pictures, see S. Nenadic, 'Print collecting and popular culture in eighteenth century Scotland' *History* 82 (1997), 203–22.
3. NAS GD170/345/3, Bill for accommodation and washing, 20 February 1752.
4. NAS GD170/391-8:b, Children's expenses.
5. NAS GD170/310-314, Bills and household expenses.
6. See H. Cheape, *Tartan: The Highland Habit* (Edinburgh, 2006), 26–7. J. Holloway, *Patrons and Painters: Art in Scotland, 1650–1760* (Edinburgh, 1989), 111.
7. I. Grimble, *The World of Rob Donn* (Edinburgh, 1979), 53–4.
8. A. Macleod, ed., *Songs of Duncan Ban Macintyre* (Edinburgh, 1952) 49.
9. *Ibid*, 69.
10. S. Carney, *The Appin Murder: The Killing of the Red Fox* (London, 1994).
11. NAS GD170/972/2/2, Letter from Hugh Mackay to his lawyer Mr Crawfurd, April 1749.

INTRODUCTION

1. T. C. Smout, *A History of the Scottish People, 1560–1830* (London, 1969), 327.
2. T. M. Devine, *The Scottish Nation 1700–2000* (London, 2000), 185.
3. C. Whatley, *Scottish Society, 1707–1830: Beyond Jacobitism, Towards Industrialisation* (Manchester, 2000), 252–3.
4. W. Macintosh, *Essay on Ways and Means of Inclosing, Fallowing, Planting etc* (Edinburgh, 1729), 234.
5. See, for instance, Boswell on the aspirations of Lady MacLeod. J. Boswell, *Journal of a Tour to the Hebrides with Samuel Johnson*, ed. by F.A. Pottle and C. H. Bennett (London, 1936), 184.

6. Grimble, *Rob Donn*, 90, verse 3.
7. *Ibid.*, 97.
8. R. Black, ed., *An Lasair: Anthology of Eighteenth Century Scottish Gaelic Verse* (Edinburgh, 2001), 309–11, 503.
9. This assumption is central to the 'Highland myths' that were first invented with the so-called discovery of Ossian in the 1760s and elaborated by antiquarians and novelists. See P. Womack, *Improvement and Romance: Constructing the Myth of the Highlands* (London, 1988). M. G. H. Pittock, *The Invention of Scotland: The Stuart Myth and Scottish Identity, 1638 to the Present* (London, 1991).
10. R. A. Dodgshon, 'Pretense of blude and place of thair dwelling: The nature of Highland clans, 1500–1745', in R. Houston and I. Whyte, eds, *Scottish Society, 1500-1800* (London, 1997).
11. See D. Watt, 'The laberinth of thir difficulties': The influence of debt on the Highland elite 1550–1700', *Scottish Historical Review* 85 (2006), 28–51.
12. R. A. Dodgshon, *From Chiefs to Landlords: Social and Economic Change in the Western Highlands and Islands, c.1493–1820* (Edinburgh, 1998).
13. E. Richards, *Leviathon of Wealth* (London, 1973). E. Richards, *History of the Highland Clearances Vol 1: Agrarian Transformation and the Evictions, 1746–1886* (London, 1982).
14. A. Macinnes, *Clanship, Commerce and the House of Stuart, 1603–1788* (East Linton, 1996).
15. H. Williamson, 'Scots, Indians and empire: The Scottish politics of civilisation, 1519–1609', *Past and Present* 150 (1996), 46–83.
16. J. Goodare, *State and Society in Early Modern Scotland* (Oxford, 1999), ch. 8.
17. K. M. Brown, *Noble Society in Scotland: Wealth, Family and Culture from Reformation to Revolution* (Edinburgh, 2000).
18. G. Donaldson, *Scottish Historical Documents* (Edinburgh, 1970), 171–5.
19. J. Goodare, 'The Statutes of Iona in context', *Scottish Historical Review* 77 (1998), 31–57.
20. A. Nicholson, *History of Skye: A Record of the Families, the Social Conditions and the Literature of the island* (Skye, 1995), 73.
21. I. D. Whyte, *Scotland before the Industrial Revolution* (London, 1995), 180–1.
22. D. Armitage, 'Making the Empire British: Scotland in the Atlantic world, 1542–1717' *Past and Present* 155 (1997), 34–63.
23. Nicholson, *Skye*, 67–89.
24. Dodgeson, *Chiefs to Landlords*, 113.
25. V. Wills, ed., *Reports on the Annexed Estates from the Records of the Forfeited Estates Preserved in the Scottish Record Office* (Edinburgh, 1973). A. Smith, 'The administration of the Forfeited Annexed Estates, 1752–1784', in G. Barrow, ed., *The Scottish Tradition* (Edinburgh, 1974).
26. A.J. Durie, 'Lairds, improvement, banking and industry in eighteenth century Scotland: Capital and development in a backward economy. A case study', in T. M. Devine, ed., *Lairds and Improvement in the Scotland of the Enlightenment* (Glasgow, 1979).

27. J. Sinclair, *An Account of the Highland Society of London from its Establishment in May 1778 to 1813, Drawn up at the Desire of the Society with an Appendix Containing a List of Members, Rules etc* (London, 1813).
28. R. J. Adam, ed., *Papers on Sutherland Estate Management, 1802–16*, 2 vols (Edinburgh 1972).
29. Donaldson, *Scottish Historical Documents*, 169.
30. S. Murdoch, *Britain, Denmark, Norway and the House of Stuart, 1603–1660* (East Linton, 2000), 208–13.
31. Grimble, *Chief of Mackay*, 181–3.
32. Mcinnes, *Clanship, Commerce*.
33. Williamson, 'Scots, Indians and empire'.
34. The case is summarised in R. Mackay, *History of the House and Clan of Mackay* (Edinburgh, 1829), 373–9.
35. G. Hanlon, 'The decline of a provincial military aristocracy: Siena, 1560–1740', *Past and Present* 155 (1997), 64–108.
36. B. Lenman, *The Jacobite Clans of the Great Glen, 1650–1784* (London, 1984). T. M. Devine, *Scotland's Empire, 1600–1815* (London, 2003).
37. A. Mackillop, *More Fruitful than the Soil: Army, Empire and the Scottish Highlands, 1715–1815* (East Linton, 2000).
38. J. E. Cookson, 'The Napoleonic Wars, military Scotland and Tory Highlandism in the early nineteenth century', *Scottish Historical Review* (1999), 60–75.
39. Donaldson, *Scottish Historical Documents*, 178.
40. R. G. Asch, *Nobilities in Transition: Courtiers and Rebels in Britain and Europe* (London, 2003).
41. P. J. Corfield, *Power and the Professions in Britain, 1700–1850* (London, 1995). G. S. Holmes, *Augustan England: Professions, State and Society, 1680–1730* (London, 1982).
42. P. R. Coss, 'The formation of the English gentry', *Past and Present* 147 (1995), 38–64.
43. Described in Armitage, 'Making the empire British'.
44. Brown, *Noble Society*, Introduction. Goodare, *State and Society*.
45. Nicholson, *Skye*, 73. M. Glendinning, *The Architecture of Scottish Government From Kingship to Parliamentary Democracy* (Dundee, 2004), 85–91.
46. W. McMillan, *Scottish Symbols, Royal, National and Ecclesiastical: Their History and Heraldic Significance* (Paisley, 1916).
47. A. Du Toit, 'Balfour, Sir James of Denmiln and Kinnaird, first baronet (1603/4–1657)', in *Oxford Dictionary of National Biography* (Oxford, 2004)
48. The costs are detailed in *Ancient, Heraldic and Antiquarian Tracts by Sir James Balfour* (Edinburgh, 1837).
49. The unattributed portrait is in the Scottish National Portrait Gallery Edinburgh.
50. M. Martin, *A Description of the Western Islands of Scotland ca. 1695* (Edinburgh, 1999), ch. XV: 'A brief account of the advantages the Isles offer by sea and land, and particularly for a fishing trade'. For biographical details see 'Introduction' by C. W. J. Withers. D. U. Stiubhart, 'Martin, Martin (d. 1718)', *Oxford Dictionary of National Biography*, (Oxford, 2004).

51. Martin, *Western Isles*, 204.
52. For the theoretical discourse in Scotland, see I. Hont and M. Ignatieff, 'Needs and justice in the Wealth of Nations: An introductory Essay', in I. Hont and M. Ignatieff, ed., *Wealth and Virtue* (Cambridge, 1983). On 'mechanical arts' and the world of goods, see M. Berg, *Luxury and Pleasure in Eighteenth Century Britain* (Oxford, 2005).
53. R. Saville, *Bank of Scotland: A History, 1695–1995* (Edinburgh, 1996), ch. 4.
54. S. Schama, *The Embarrassment of Riches: An Interpretation of Dutch Culture in the Golden Age* (London, 1988).
55. N. McKendrick, J. Brewer and J. H. Plumb, *The Birth of a Consumer Society: The Commercialisation of Eighteenth-Century England* (London, 1982), 14–18.
56. J. Mason, 'The Edinburgh School of Design', in *Book of the Old Edinburgh Club*, 27 (1949), 67–97.
57. A. J. Youngson, *The Making of Classical Edinburgh, 1750–1840* (Edinburgh, 1966).
58. Wills, *Reports*.
59. M. Pittock, *The Myth of the Jacobite Clans* (London, 1995).
60. NAS GD170, Campbell Family of Barcaldine Papers.

CHAPTER 1: FAMILIES AND ESTATES

1. *Scotsman* 14 August 1839, 1.
2. See W. Orr, *Deer Forests, Landlords and Crofters* (Edinburgh, 1982).
3. A. Macinnes 'Who owned Argyll in the eighteenth century?', in *Power, Property and Privilege: The Landed Elite in Scotland from c.1440 to 1914* (St Andrews, 1989).
4. NAS GD170, Printed catalogue notes.
5. For an account of this relationship with land, see Dodgeson, *Chiefs to Landlords*, ch. 2.
6. NAS GD170/243/11, Account of the funeral expenses and possessions of Colin Campbell of Invernan, 1731.
7. On this complex issue see Dodgeson, *Chiefs to Landlords*; E. Creegan, 'Tacksmen and their successors: A study of tenurial reorganisations in Mull, Morvern and Tiree in the early eighteenth century', *Scottish Studies* 13 (1969), 93–144.
8. For an example, see R. C. Macleod, *The Book of Dunvegan: Being Documents from the Muniment Room of the Macleods of Macleods at Dunvegan Castle, Isle of Skye*, vol. 1 (Aberdeen, 1933), 138.
9. See NAS GD170/797, Letters from John Campbell of Achallader to his cousin Patrick Campbell.
10. Black, *An Lasair*, 219, 475–77.
11. The details of this and subsequent marriage and family connections are pieced together from family correspondence in NAS GD170, Campbell of Barcaldine Papers.
12. Macinnes, 'Who owned Argyll?'

13. E. Richards and M. Clough, *Cromartie: Highland Life, 1650–1914* (Aberdeen, 1989).
14. The actions taken by John Campbell 'of the bank' during the Jacobite occupation of Edinburgh highlights the ambiguous political allegiances of the family. A. Turton, ed., *The Diary of John Campbell: A Scottish Banker and the Forty-Five* (London, 1995).
15. NAS GD87/25, Letter from Lord Glenorchy to his kinsman John Campbell of Barcaldine, 3 March 1747.
16. R. Turner, 'Archibald Cameron', in *Oxford Dictionary of National Biography* (Oxford, 2004).
17. NAS GD170/722, Letters from Donald Cameron to his uncle, Patrick Campbell of Barcaldine, 1720–1739.
18. Grimble, *Rob Donn*, 63.
19. *Ibid*, 82–3.
20. This convoluted family history is detailed in R. Mackay, *History of the House and Clan of Mackay; Containing Accounts of Many Other Scottish Families, a Variety of Historical Notices, More Particularly of those Relating the Northern Division of Scotland During the Most Critical and Interesting Periods with a Genealogical Table of the Clan* (Edinburgh, 1829). D. Sage, *Memorabilia Domestica: or Parish Life in the North of Scotland* (Wick and Edinburgh, 1889). Grimble, *Rob Donn*, ch. 11.
21. See chapter 4.
22. Detailed in chapter 5.
23. Mackay, *Clan of Mackay*, 515–6.
24. Colonel Alexander Campbell to his father John Campbell of Barcaldine. Quoted in Grimble, *Rob Donn*, 188.
25. NAS GD170/1626, Letters from Colina Campbell to her cousin Alexander Campbell of Barcaldine.
26. J. Henderson, *Caithness Family History* (Edinburgh, 1884), 93–6.
27. NAS GD139/238/1-25, Papers relative to the decree of divorce (21 December 1774) obtained by Mrs Ann Sinclair, 4th of Brabster, against Robert Sutherland of Langwell.
28. *A Genealogical Deduction of the Family of Kilravock, Written in 1683–4 by Mr Hew Rose, Minister of Nairne, Continued by the Reverend Lachlan Shaw Minister of Elgin in 1753. With Illustrative Documents from the Family Charter Room, and Notes* (Edinburgh, 1858).
29. E. Richards, 'Gower, Elizabeth Levenson, duchess of Sutherland and suo jure countess of Sutherland (1765–1839)', in *Oxford Dictionary of National Biography* (Oxford, 2007).
30. B. Sawyer, *Property and Inheritance in Viking Scandinavia: The Runic Evidence* (Alingsas, 1988).
31. See, for instance, the fate of the Cromartie estate under successive absent female owners. Richards and Clough, *Cromartie*, chs 11, 12.
32. This relationship is detailed in NAS GD139/369/1-26, Letters from Lieutenant John Sinclair (to his sisters), 1792–1815; and NAS GD139/394/1-36, Letters

from Robert Sinclair Sutherland, eldest son of George Sutherland Sinclair of Brabster, 1807–62.
33. NAS GD347, Papers of the Sutherland Family of Rearquhar, including GD347/73/1-64, Letters from George Gun Munro to his uncle George Sutherland of Rearquhar, 1767–96. E. R. Mackay, *George Sutherland of Riarchar: The Last of the Tacksmen* (Dornoch, 1971).
34. A more detailed discussion of George Sutherland of Rearquhar occurs in chapter 3.
35. George Gun Munro did marry in old age, to a lady of independent means who was beyond her childbearing years. See NAS GD347/73/58, 64, Letters from George Gun Munro to George Sutherland of Rearquhar, 7 August 1787, 4 February 1796.
36. NAS GD136, Papers of the Sinclair Family of Freswick, Caithness.
37. NAS GD136/425, Letters to William Sinclair from his sister Mrs Jane Robertson, 1778–94.
38. NAS GD136/1276, Observations by William Sinclair of Freswick on William Sinclair, a bastard son born in 1784, written *c.*1830. On 'little Jean', see GD136/435/159-60, Letters from Katharine McGregor to Dr William Sinclair.
39. NAS GD136/465, Letter from Arthur St Clair, major general in the service of the United States to Dr William Sinclair, 14 August 1793.
40. Henderson, *Caithness Family History*, 51–9.
41. Macleod, *Duncan Macintyre*, Introduction.
42. *Ibid*, 53, 440.
43. *Ibid*, xii, xxxi. Three collections were published in Gaelic during his lifetime, the first in 1768. He also competed successfully in Highland Society competitions.
44. NAS GD170/801, Letter from John Campbell of Danna to his uncle Patrick Campbell, 14 July 1729.
45. NAS GD170/391/8, Accounts for Colin Campbell's daughter Isabel.
46. Macleod, *Songs of Macintyre*, 125–7.
47. Black, *An Lasair*, 495–8.
48. NAS GD170/1901, Letter from Donald Mcintyre to Alexander Campbell of Barcaldine, 19 March 1783.
49. NAS GD170/2570, Letter from Duncan Macintyre, minister of Kilmalie to Sir Duncan Campbell of Barcaldine, 18 April 1827. GD170/2582, Letter from John Macintyre, minister of Kilmonigeaig, to Sir Duncan Campbell of Barcaldine, 31 August 1831.
50. NAS GD136/409-10, Letters from Dr William Sinclair to his son William, 1767. These includes personal news about Hugh Mackay and his health problems.
51. NAS GD170/412, Papers relating to the children of deceased Alexander McPherson, drover in Glenfine, 1735–61.
52. Grimble, *Rob Donn*, 82–3.
53. Black, *An Lasair*, Introduction, describes the context.
54. H. Scott, *Fasti Ecclesiae Scotticanae* (Edinburgh, 1923), vols iv, vii.
55. NAS GD170/611, Letters of Colin Campbell of Achnaba, miniser of Ardchattan, to his nephew, Alexander Campbell of Barcaldine, 1692–1719.

56. Scott, *Fasti*, vol. iv, 81. J. Henry, 'Colin Campbell of Achnaba (1644–1726)', in *Oxford Dictionary of National Biography* (Oxford, 2004).
57. Scott, *Fasti*, vol. iv, 87. See, for example, the case of Joseph Macintyre, minister of Kenmore from 1765, who in the same year married Christian McVean, daugher of the previous incumbent.
58. Sage, *Memorabilia Domestica*, 33, 105–7.
59. Scott, *Fasti*, vol. iv, 82–3. NAS GD170, Campbell of Barcaldine papers.
60. Sage, *Memorabilia Domestica*, 38–9.
61. Studies by Dodgeson, *Chiefs to Landlords*; Macinnes, *Clanship, Commerce*; Mackillop, *More Fruitful*, are mostly gender blind.
62. An honourable exception is in the work of E. Richards on the aristocratic Sutherland and Cromartie estates. Richards, *Leviathon*; Richards and Clough, *Cromartie*.
63. NAS GD170/1176/8, Letter from Patrick Campbell to his father Duncan Campbell of Glenure, 24 December 1774.
64. E. Richards, *History of the Highland Clearances. Agrarian Transformation and the Evictions, 1746–1886* (London, 1982), ch. 18.
65. Henderson, *Caithness*, 93–6.
66. Richards, *Leviathon*; Richards, *Cromartie*.
67. L. Timperlay, 'The pattern of landholding in eighteenth century Scotland', in M. L. Parry and T. R. Slater, eds., *The Making of the Scottish Countryside* (London, 1980).
68. NAS GD136/1272, Observations by William Sinclair of Freswick on his debts.
69. The circumstances are detailed in chapter 8.
70. This history is pieced together from the family correspondence at NAS GD136/524; 549; 557; 572.
71. NAS GD139/394/1-36, Letters from Robert Sinclair Sutherland, eldest son of George Sutherland Sinclair, 5th of Brabster, 1807–62.

CHAPTER 2: CHILDREN

1. NAS GD170/629, Letters from Sir John Campbell of Glenorchy to Barcaldine, his chamberlain, 1683–1712, Letter of 2 April 1683.
2. Martin, *Western Isles*, 139–40.
3. *Ibid.*, 9.
4. Stiubhart, 'Martin, Martin'.
5. T. Pennant, *A Tour in Scotland in 1769* (Warrington, 1769) 179. Mackay, *House of Mackay*, 547.
6. On ministers as antiquarians, see C. Kidd, 'Subscription, the Scottish Enlightenment and the moderate interpretation of history', *Journal of Ecclesiastical History* 55 (2004).
7. Sage, *Memorabilia Domestica*, 28–9.

8. M. C. W. Hunter, *The Occult Laboratory: Magic, Science and Second Sight in Seventeenth Century Scotland* (Woodbridge, 2001). F. Valletta, *Witchcraft, Magic and Superstition in England, 1640–1670* (Aldershot, 2000).
9. F. J. P. Poole, 'Socialization, enculturation and the development of personal identity', T. Ingold, ed., *Companion Encyclopedia of Anthropology* (London, 1994), 831.
10. Quoted in Nicholson, *History of Skye*, 81–2.
11. C. W. J. Withers, *Gaelic Scotland: The Transformation of a Culture Region* (London, 1988).
12. The Russian nobility offers a parallel. S. M. Dixon, *The Modernisation of Russia, 1676–1825* (Cambridge, 1999).
13. NAS GD170/329, Inventory, 4 September 1740.
14. See the 'The Highland Dress' a poem of the early 1750s by Margaret Campbell. She was the wife of the minister of Ardchattan and probably the daughter of Rev. Colin Campbell of Achnaba and therefore related to Colin Campbell of Glenure. Black, *An Lasair*, 187–91.
15. P. McNeill and G. Riello, 'The art and science of walking; gender, space and the fashionable body in the long eighteenth century', *Fashion Theory: The Journal of Dress, Body and Culture* 9 (2005), 175–204.
16. See J. E. Bowman, *The Highlands and Islands: A Nineteenth-Century Tour* (Gloucester, 1986), 71.
17. Boswell, *Journal*, 132, 153.
18. Jolly, *Flora Macdonald*.
19. Burt, *Letters*, 238.
20. V. Fildes, *Wet Nursing: A History, from Antiquity to the Present* (Oxford, 1988).
21. The wife of poet Rob Donn was wetnurse for Colina, posthumous child of Colin Campbell of Glenure in 1753. NAS GD170/1129, Letters from Janet Mackay to Duncan Campbell of Glenure, her brother-in-law, 1753–56.
22. See chapter 5 and the case of Mary Campbell of Barcaldine.
23. See P. Aries, *Centuries of Childhood, a Social History of Family Life* (Harmonsworth, 1973). C. Heywood, *A History of Childhood: Children and Childhood in the West from Medieval to Modern Times* (Cambridge, 2001).
24. NAS GD170/2109/3, Letter from Anna Campbell to her daughter Mary, wife of Barcaldine, 1 September 1786.
25. Burt, *Letters*, 238.
26. *Ibid.*, 219.
27. Macinnes, *Clanship*, 13, gives a full description of the practice.
28. Boswell, *Journal*, 222.
29. Nicholson, *History of Skye*, 195.
30. Macleod, *Book of Dunvegan*, vol. 2, 42–4.
31. For similar education among the nobility, see Brown, *Noble Society*, ch.8.
32. Nicholson, *History of Skye*, 85.
33. Macleod, *Book of Dunvegan*, vol. 1, 120–1.
34. Martin, *Western Isles*, Introduction.
35. Nicholson, *History of Skye*, 102.

36. J. Bannerman, *The Beatons: A Medical Kindred in the Classical Gaelic Tradition* (Edinburgh, 1986).
37. W. C. Dickinson, *Two Students at St Andrews, 1711–1716. Edited from the Delvine Papers* (Edinburgh, 1951).
38. NAS GD170/205/2, Account of money given to Barcaldine's son to buying necessaries to himself and sister, 1693.
39. NAS GD170/205/4, Account of the funeral expenses of Colin Campbell, son of Barcaldine, 5 January 1694.
40. NAS GD170/609, Letters from Archibald Campbell, writer in Inverary, to Alexander Campbell of Barcaldine, 1708.
41. NAS GD170/243, Patrick Campbell of Barcaldine, family expenses, 1717–40.
42. Macleod, *Book of Dunvegan*, vol. 1, 197–8.
43. NAS GD170/756/1, Letter from Colin Campbell to his father Patrick of Barcaldine, 1 December 1727.
44. NAS GD170/793, Letters from John Campbell to his father Patrick of Barcaldine, 1721–28.
45. NAS GD170/756/2, Letter from Colin Campbell to his father Patrick of Barcaldine, November 1731.
46. Macleod, *Book of Dunvegan*, vol. 2, 170.
47. Boswell, *Journal*, 172.
48. K. Glover, 'Elite women and the change of manners in mid-eighteenth century Scotland', PhD Thesis, University of Edinburgh, 2007. Ch. 2 provides further details of this case.
49. 'Educating a Scots laird – a document', edited by B. Bonnyman, University of Glasgow, Adam Smith Business Records Centre: UGD 37/2/1.
50. Boswell, *Journal*, 255.
51. Boswell, *Journal*, 153. As it turned out, all found husbands. Flora married the heir to the earl of Loudon, a brilliant match, but died giving birth to her first child, a daughter.
52. Macleod, *Book of Dunvegan*, vol 2, 58.
53. See Hugh Mackay of Bighouse comments on this topic in chapter 5.
54. E. Croll, *Endangered Daughters: Discrimination and Development in Asia* (London, 2000).
55. Pennant, 'Tour', in A. J. Youngson, ed., *Beyond the Highland Line* (London, 1974), 187.
56. The two wives of Patrick Campbell of Barcaldine, both born in the 1680s, seem to have been illiterate. His mother, the redoubtable Mary Campbell of Lochnell, wrote with a childlike hand.
57. Jolly, *Flora Macdonald*, ch. 1.
58. Grimble, *Rob Donn*, 11–12.
59. NAS GD170/205/2, Account of money given to Barcaldine's son to buying necessaries to himself and sister, 1693.
60. The life of Susan Campbell of Kilmun is detailed in chapter 5.
61. Nenadic, 'Middle rank consumers'.

62. NAS GD170/205/6, Account sent by Patrick Campbell to his father, Alexander of Barcaldine, 9 November 1699.
63. NAS GD170/205/5, Bills and Accounts for Mary Campbell, daughter of Alexander Campbell of Barcaldine.
64. NAS GD170/243/6-9, Patrick Campbell's family expenses.
65. See chapter 7.
66. NAS GD170/243/6;8, Accounts for Isobel Campbell, 1737–8; Accounts for Jean Campbell, 1739–40.
67. NAS GD170/243/6, Account of 17 November 1737 from Isobel Campbell to her father.
68. *Ibid.*, Account of 28 November 1738 from Duncan Campbell to his father.
69. NAS GD170/779, Letter from Elizabeth Campbell to Patrick Campbell of Barcaldine, 31 October 1732.
70. Alexander Munro (Primus) 'The professor's daughter; an essay on female conduct', transcribed, with introduction and notes by P. A. G. Monro, *Proceedings of the Royal College of Physicians of Edinburgh* 26 (1996), Supplement No. 2, 12.
71. *Ibid.*, 17.
72. NAS GD1/726/1, Journal of Elizabeth Rose of Kilravock.
73. *Genealogical Deduction*, 412.
74. *Ibid.*, 431.
75. *Ibid.*, 461.
76. S. Ferrier, *Marriage: A Novel* (Edinburgh, 1818), 211.
77. *Ibid.*, 231.
78. Boswell, *Journal*, 241.
79. *Ibid.*, 104.
80. NAS GD170/2139, Letters from Maria Helen Campbell to her mother Mary, 1808–11.
81. Grant, *Highland Lady*.
82. Boswell, *Journal*, 308.
83. *Ibid.*, 305.

CHAPTER 3: GENTLEMANLY CAREERS

1. R. Wilson and A. Mackey, *Creating Paradise: The Building of the English Country House, 1660–1880* (London, 2000).
2. See Richards, *Leviathon*.
3. Holmes, *Augustan England*.
4. See chapter 2.
5. Nicholson, *Skye*, 197–8.
6. Holmes, *Augustan England*. V. Larminie, *Wealth, Kinship and Culture: The Seventeenth-Century Newdigates of Arbury and their World* (London, 1995).

7. NAS GD170/1176/12/2, Letter from Patrick Campbell to his father Duncan, 2 March 1778.
8. T. M. Devine, 'Scottish Elites and the Indian Empire', in T. C. Smout, ed., *Anglo-Scottish Relations from 1603–1900. Proceedings of the British Academy*, 127 (Oxford, 2005). S. Nenadic, 'Military men, businessmen and the "business" of patronage in 18th century London', in S. Nenadic, ed., *Scots in London in the Eighteenth Century: Patronage, Culture and Identity* (forthcoming).
9. Dodgeshon, *Chiefs to Landlords*.
10. Grimble, *Rob Donn*, 91.
11. Boswell, *Journal*, 213.
12. J. Ramsay, *Scotland and Scotsmen in the Eighteenth Century*, vol. 2. (Edinburgh, 1938), 229–31.
13. E. Richards, *Patrick Sellar and the Highland Clearances: Homicide, Eviction and the Price of Progress* (Edinburgh, 1999).
14. NAS GD170/667, Letter from Colin Kirk to Alexander Campbell of Barcaldine, 31 January 1717.
15. NAS GD170/241, Estate correspondence, 1708–39. Macinnes, *Clanship*.
16. Grimble, *Rob Donn*, ch. 3.
17. NAS GD 87/2/7, Papers of the Mackay Family of Bighouse.
18. Grimble, *Rob Donn*, 89.
19. Mackay, *Clan Mackay*.
20. NAS GD170/791/1, Letter from John Campbell to his father Patrick of Barcaldine, 10 January 1721.
21. Ramsay, *Scotland and Scotsmen*, 63–4.
22. NAS GD170/817, Letter from Patrick Campbell Lord Monzie to Patrick Campbell of Barcaldine, 22 November 1728.
23. NAS GD170/816, Letters from Patrick Campbell WS to his cousin, Patrick Campbell of Barcaldine, 1721–2.
24. NAS GD170/793/12, Letter from John Campbell to his father Patrick of Barcaldine, 19 September 1731.
25. NAS GD170/793/30, Letter from John Campbell to his father Patrick of Barcaldine, 15 August 1739.
26. NAS GD170/793/20, Letter from John Campbell to his father Patrick of Barcaldine, October 1735.
27. NAS GD170/793/31, Letter from John Campbell to his father Patrick of Barcaldine, 'Tuesday morning' c.1735.
28. NAS GD170/793, Letters from John Campbell to his father Patrick of Barcaldine. 1721–39.
29. For a detailed account of estate development with a focus on management, see B. D. Bonnyman, 'Agricultural improvement in the Scottish Enlightenment: The third duke of Buccleuch, William Keir and the Buccleuch estates, 1751–1812', PhD Thesis, University of Edinburgh, 2004.
30. Wills, *Reports*, vol. 1, 25.
31. *Ibid.*, 19–25.
32. *Ibid.*, 22.

33. *Ibid*, 19–20.
34. *Ibid*, ix.
35. J. S. Gibson, 'Campbell, John (*c*.1703–1777)', in *Oxford Dictionary of National Biography* (Oxford, 2004).
36. Smout, *Scottish People*. N. Phillipson, 'Lawyers, landowners and the civic leadership of post-Union Scotland', *Juridical Review* 120 (1976), 97–120.
37. T. C. Smout, 'Scottish landowners and economic growth, 1650–1850', *Scottish Journal of Political Economy* 11 (1964), 218–34.
38. Campbell, *London Tradesman*, 71.
39. Richards, *Patrick Sellar*, 22–3.
40. Changing attitudes can be charted through R. J. Adam, ed., *Papers on Sutherland Estate Management, 1802–16*, 2 vols (Edinburgh, 1972), and are indicated in Bonnyman, 'Agricultural Improvement'.
41. Grant, *Highland Lady*, vol. 1, 6.
42. *Ibid.*, vol. 2, 66.
43. Youngson, *Beyond the Highland Line*, 227.
44. Grant, *Highland Lady*, vol. 2, 155.
45. See chapter 7.
46. Richards, *Patrick Sellar*.
47. The terms 'pro-active' and 're-active' are used by Macinnes, *Clanship*.
48. K. M. Brown, 'From Scottish lords to British officers: State building, elite integration and the army in the seventeenth century', in N. Macdougall, ed., *Scotland and War AD 79–1918* (Edinburgh, 1991).
49. Sage, *Memorabilia Domestica*.
50. NAS GD170/733, Letters from Alexander Campbell minister of Glenary to Patrick Campbell of Barcaldine, 1733–7.
51. *Fasti*, vol. iv, 95.
52. Boswell, *Journal*, 255–6.
53. *Fasti*, vol. iv, 81.
54. NAS GD170/2443, Letters from Hugh Fraser, minister of Ardchattan, to Sir Duncan Campbell of Barcaldine, his brother-in-law, 1817–34. NAS GD170/2444, Letters from Maria Helen Campbell to Sir Duncan of Barcaldine, her brother, 1815–33.
55. *Fasti*, vol. iv, 82–3.
56. NAS GD170/2443, Letter from Hugh Fraser, minister of Ardchattan, to Sir Duncan Campbell of Barcaldine, his brother-in-law, 25 January 1834.
57. Boswell, *Tour*, 283 describes the son of a Coll tenant educated at the laird's expense to be the parish schoolmaster.
58. *Diary of George Ridpath, Minister of Stitchel, 1755–61*, edited by J. B. Paul (Edinburgh, 1922).
59. Bannerman, *The Beatons*.
60. R. Turner, 'Cameron, Archibald (1707–1753)', in *Oxford Dictionary of National Biography* (Oxford, 2004).
61. *Genealogical Deductions*, 431.
62. *Ibid.*, 503–4.

63. NAS GD136/304-11; GD136/425; GD136/468, Correspondence of Dr William Sinclair of Langwell (later of Freswick).
64. NAS GD136/1272, Observations relating to debts by Dr William Sinclair of Freswick, 1819.
65. W. Mackay, ed., *Letter Book of Bailie John Steuart of Inverness* (Edinburgh, 1915).
66. NAS GD347/73, Letters from George Gun Munro to his uncle George Sutherland of Rearquhar, 1761–1806.
67. NAS GD347/12, Journal of George Sutherland of Rearquhar, 1745–1812, 118–19.
68. Argyll and Bute District Archives: Malcolm of Poltalloch Papers. See chapter 7.
69. NAS GD170/412, Papers relating to Gilbert, James, Hugh, Mary and Katharine McPherson, children of deceased Alexander McPherson, drover in Glenfine, 1735–1761. Patrick Campbell of Barcaldine was one of the 'curators' for the children on the death of their father.
70. This career is further detailed in chapter 4.
71. D. Graham-Campbell, 'The younger generation in Argyll at the beginning of the eighteenth century', *Scottish Studies* 18 (1974).
72. NAS GD170/1491/1-13, Letters from Robert Campbell to his brother Alexander, 1740–51. NAS GD170/952, Letters from Robert Campbell to his brother Colin of Glenure, 1745–52. NAS GD170/243, Accounts following the death of Patrick Campbell of Barcaldine concerning his son Robert.
73. Mcinnes, *Clanship*, 142–51 details such commercial arrangements.
74. NAS GD170/1464a/2, Letter from Alexander Campbell to his brother Robert, 4 June 1747.
75. NAS GD170/14641/9,10,11, Letters from Alexander Campbell to his brother Robert, 1747–50.
76. NAS GD170/1180/15/1, Letter from Robert Campbell to his brother Duncan, May 1750.
77. NAS GD170/1186/81–84, Letters from Robert Campbell to his brother Duncan, September 1759 to December 1760.
78. NAS GD170/1186/90, Letter from Robert Campbell to his brother Duncan, February 1763.
79. NAS GD170/1186/102/1, Letter from Robert Campbell to his brother Duncan, 6 November 1773.
80. GD170/1179/2, Letter from Patrick Campbell to his uncle Duncan, 9 November 1776.
81. NAS GD170/1220, Letter from Henry Galloway, merchant in Stirling to Duncan Campbell of Glenure, 31 January 1777.
82. J. Hoppit, *Risk and Failure in English Business, 1700–1800* (Cambridge, 1987).
83. Nenadic, 'Military men'. Devine, 'Scottish elites'.
84. Foreign trade was the exception as shown by the Malcolm family of Poltalloch whose estate purchasing is detailed in chapter 7.
85. Nenadic, 'Middle rank consumers'.
86. L. Davidoff and C. Hall, *Family Fortunes: Men and Women of the English Middle Class, 1780–1850* (London, 1987).

87. N. Murray, *The Scottish Handloom Weavers, 1790–1850: A Social History* (Edinburgh, 1978).
88. NAS GD170/1454, Letters from Charles Campbell to Mary McPherson, Lady Glenure, 1786–7.

CHAPTER 4: MILITARY MEN

1. For a recent survey, see S. D. M. Carpenter, 'The British Army' in H. Dickinson, ed., *A Companion to Eighteenth-Century Britain* (Oxford, 2002), 473–80.
2. J. Brewer, *The Sinews of Power: War, Money and the English State, 1688–1783* (London, 1989).
3. C. Cook and J. Stevenson, eds., *The Longman Handbook of Modern British History, 1714–1980* (London, 1983), 220.
4. J. E. Cookson, *The British Armed Nation, 1793–1815* (Oxford, 1997), chs 5, 6.
5. P.E. Razzell, 'Social Origins of Officers in the Indian and British Home Army, 1758–1962', *British Journal of Sociology* 14 (1963), 248–60. A. K. Murray, *History of the Scottish Regiments in the British Army* (Glasgow, 1862).
6. L. Colley, *Britons: Forging the Nation, 1707–1837* (London, 1992), 184.
7. Estimate based on P. Mathias, 'The social structure in the eighteenth century: a calculation by Joseph Massie', *Economic History Review* 10 (1957), 30–45, and P. Colquhoun, *Treaties on the Wealth, Power and Resources of the British Empire* (London, 1815). The calculation is detailed in S. Nenadic, 'The impact of the military profession on Highland gentry families, *c.*1730–1830', *Scottish Historical Review* 85 (2006), 75–99.
8. Scottish fiction provides good illustrations. See Ferrier, *Marriage*, and S. Ferrier, *The Inheritance* (Edinburgh, 1824).
9. Colley, *Britons*; M. Pittock, *Inventing and Resisting Britain* (London, 2001).
10. MacKillop, *More Fruitful*. MacInnes, *Clanship*.
11. Devine, *Scotland's Empire*, 334.
12. S. Murdoch, *Britain, Denmark, Norway and the House of Stuart, 1603–1660* (East Linton, 2000), 208–13.
13. I. Grimble, *Chief of Mackay* (London, 1965), ch. 5.
14. G. Hanlon, 'The decline of a provincial military aristocracy: Sienna, 1560–1740', *Past and Present* 155 (1997), 64–108.
15. Carpenter, 'British Army', 478.
16. P. C. Bruce, *The Purchase System in the British Army, 1660–1871* (London, 1980).
17. S. Bever, *The Cadet: a Military Treaties, by an Officer* (London, 1762), 114.
18. Bruce, *Purchase System*.
19. S. Nenadic, 'Military men'.
20. Campbell, *London Tradesman*, 56–7.

21. Allan's career can be pieced together from letters to his brother Duncan. NAS, GD170/1067.
22. NAS GD170/1074, Letter from Archibald Campbell to his brother Duncan, n.d., c.1751.
23. NAS GD170/1067/12, Letter from Allan Campbell to his brother Duncan, 10 July 1781.
24. NAS GD170/1354/1-72, Letters from Major James Macpherson to his brother-in-law Duncan Campbell of Glenure, 1744–83.
25. NAS GD170/1354/51. Letter from James Macpherson to his brother-in-law Duncan Campbell, November 1778.
26. NAS GD170/1354/72, Letter from James Macpherson to his brother-in-law Duncan Campbell, 11 September 1789.
27. NAS GD170/1186/56, Letter from Robert Campbell to Duncan Campbell, 11 March 1755.
28. NAS GD170/1186/63, Letter from Robert Campbell to Duncan Campbell, 8 October 1757.
29. NAS GD170/1186/67/2, Letter from Captain George Grant to Duncan Campbell, 12 December 1757.
30. NAS GD170/1186/89-91. Letters from Robert Campbell to Duncan Campbell, February to December 1763.
31. National Register of Archives for Scotland, 63: Blair Adam: Boxes 1, 2, 3 William Adam Papers.
32. NAS GD170/1186/90, Letter from Robert Campbell to his brother Duncan, 8 February 1763.
33. The following life history is pieced together from NAS GD170/1063-9, Letters from Alexander Campbell to his father Duncan, 1763–5.
34. NAS GD170/1065/3/1, Letter from Alexander Campbell to his cousin Duncan Campbell, 1 March 1777.
35. NAS GD170/1705, Letters from Mary Campbell, relict of Major Alexander Campbell, 1768–93.
36. Explored in chapter 3.
37. Explored in chapter 2.
38. See the letters of Anne McVicar Grant, a Highland widow, for a poignant account. J. P. Grant, *Memoir and Correspondence of Mrs Grant of Laggan*, 3 vols (London, 1845).
39. NAS GD170/1176/1-15, Letters of Major Patrick (Peter) Campbell to his father Duncan Campbell of Glenure. NAS GD170/391, Accounts and Papers of Major Patrick Campbell with his father Duncan Campbell of Glenure.
40. Patrick's early experience in London is mentioned in letters sent from there by his Uncle Robert: NAS GD170/1186/1-102.
41. NAS GD170/1176/12/2, Letter from Patrick Campbell to his father Duncan, 2 March 1778.
42. Colquhoun, *Treatises*. Mathias, 'Social structure'.
43. J. Austen, *Mansfield Park* (London, 1966), 136. First published in 1814.

44. The words are from Sir Walter Elliot, the status-conscious and foolish baronet in J. Austen, *Persuasion* (London, 1965), 49. First published in 1818.
45. P. Martin, *A Life of James Boswell* (Yale, 1999).
46. NAS GD170/1176/1-15, Letters of Major Patrick (Peter) Campbell to his father Duncan. NAS GD170/391, Accounts and Papers of Major Patrick Campbell with his father Duncan Campbell of Glenure.
47. A. Brett-James, *General Graham, Lord Lynedoch* (London, 1959), ch. 26.
48. NAS GD170/1628/1-50, Letters from Captain Colin Campbell of Glenure to his brother Alexander Campbell of Barcaldine. GD170/1090/1-43, Letters from Captain Colin Campbell of Glenure to his father Duncan Campbell of Glenure.
49. J. Sinclair, *An Account of the Highland Society of London from its Establishment in May 1778 to 1813, Drawn up at the Deisre of the Society with an Appendix Containing a List of Members, Rules etc* (London, 1813).
50. NAS GD170/1628/50, Letter from Captain Colin Campbell of Glenure to his brother Alexander Campbell of Barcaldine, Cork 1797.
51. Ferrier, *Marriage*, 10–11, 16, 79–90.
52. Carpenter, 'British Army'.
53. J. Brewer, *The Pleasures of the Imagination: English Culture in the Eighteenth Century* (London, 1997), ch. 16.
54. NAS GD170/1067/6/1, Letter from Allan Campbell to his brother Duncan, 12 January 1775.
55. The most famous example is the devious seducer Captain Wickham in Jane Austen's *Pride and Prejudice*.
56. NAS GD170/1118/8/1, Letter from Hugh Campbell to his father Duncan, 22 July 1778.
57. Brett-James, *Lord Lyndoch*.
58. See *Autobiographical Journal of John Macdonald Schoolmaster and Soldier, 1770–1830* (Edinburgh, 1906).
59. As in Bever, *The Cadet*, ch. 13: 'Concerning the education, study, application and behaviour of officers in private life'.
60. Boswell, *Journal*, 327.
61. See examples quoted in Hayes, 'Scottish officers'.
62. NAS GD170/1067/5, Letter from Allan Campbell to his brother Duncan, 2 March 1774.
63. See Mackillop, *More Fruitful*.
64. Grant, *Highland Lady*.
65. NAS GD170/1628/30, Letter from Captain Colin Campbell of Glenure to his brother Alexander Campbell of Barcaldine, May 1786.
66. NAS GD170/1628/41-43, Letters from Captain Colin Campbell of Glenure to his brother Alexander Campbell of Barcaldine, 1788.
67. NAS GD170/1628/50, Letter from Colin Campbell, Cork 1797, which re-established communication with his brother Alexander and provides an account of what he'd been doing during ten years of silence.
68. NAS GD170/1454, Letters from Charles Campbell to Mary McPherson, Lady Glenure, his grandmother, 1786–7.

69. C. Clark, ed., *Gleanings from an Old Portfolio, Containing Some Correspondence between Lady Louisa Stuart and her Sister Caroline, Countess of Portarlington, and Other Friends and Relations*, vol. 2 (Edinburgh, 1896).
70. This history is pieced together from the following correspondence: NAS GD139/327, Letters from Barbara Eliza Sinclair; GD139/369, Letters from Jean Sinclair; GD139/369, Letters from Lieutenant John Sinclair.
71. Henderson, *Caithness*, 51–9.
72. Mackay, *George Sutherland*.
73. NAS GD347/63, Personal and Household Accounts of George Sutherland, 1763–1804.
74. NAS GD70/1354/46, Letter from Major James MacPherson to his brother-in-law Duncan Campbell, 4 March 1778.
75. NAS GD170/1176/8, Letter from Patrick Campbell to his father Duncan, 24 December 1774.
76. J.E. Cookson, 'The Napoleonic wars, military Scotland and Tory Highlandism in the early nineteenth century', *Scottish Historical Review* 78 (1999), 60–75.
77. D. Thomson, *Raeburn* (Edinburgh, 1997), 140–1.
78. NAS GD170/2350, Letters from John Archibald Campbell, W.S. to Sir Duncan Campbell of Barcaldine, 1815–34.
79. See Brett-James, *Lord Lyndoch*.

CHAPTER 5: GENTLEWOMEN

1. The equivalent gentlewoman in England is more easily understood. See A. Vickery, *The Gentleman's Daughter: Women's Lives in Georgian England* (New Haven and London, 1998).
2. D. U. Stiubhart, 'Women and gender in the early modern western Gaidhealtachd', in Ewan and Meikle, eds., *Women in Scotland*, 241.
3. On European literacy rates and gentry women's writing, see O. Hufton, *The Prospect Before Her: A History of Women in Western Europe, 1500–1800* (London, 1995), ch.11. On Scotland see R.A. Houston, 'Women in the economy and society of Scotland, 1500–1800', in R.A. Houston and I. D. Whyte, eds., *Scottish Society 1500–1800* (Cambridge,1989).
4. NAS GD1/726, Papers of the Rose Family of Kilravock, 1731–1886.
5. R. Reddington-Wilde, 'A woman's place: Birth order, gender and social status in Highland houses', in Ewan and Meikle, eds., *Women in Scotland*.
6. J. S. Blackie, *The Language and Literature of the Scottish Highlands* (Edinburgh 1876), 116–7; Anne C. Frater, 'Women of the Gaidhealtachd and their songs to 1750', in Ewan and Meikle, eds., *Women in Scotland*.
7. Black, *An Lasa*ir, 189, verse 7.
8. *Ibid.*, 503.
9. Ferrier, *Marriage*, Introduction.

10. NAS GD170/689, Letter from John Stewart to Alexander Campbell of Barcaldine, 13 October 1704.
11. NAS GD170/797/173, Letter from John Campbell of Achallader to Patrick Campbell of Barcaldine, 6 July 1734.
12. For a broad discussion, see M. E. Wiesner, *Women and Gender in Early Modern Europe* (Cambridge, 1993), 30–1.
13. M. Craig, *Damn' Rebel Bitches: The Women of the '45* (Edinburgh, 2000).
14. Wiesner, *Women and Gender*, ch. 6.
15. Sawyer, *Property and Inheritance*.
16. Reddington-Wilde, 'A woman's place', 207.
17. On birth order and inheritance for both men and women, see R. Reddington-Wilde, 'The power of place: Spatial analysis and social organization of the Campbells in early modern Argyll, Scotland' (PhD Thesis, Harvard University, 1995), ch. 5.
18. NAS GD170/793/31, Letter from John Campbell to his father Patrick of Barcaldine, 'Tuesday morning', *c.*1735.
19. The details of Janet Mackay's life are gleaned from Campbell of Barcaldine Papers, NAS GD170 and the Mackay of Bighouse Papers, NAS GD87.
20. NAS GD170/972/2/2, Letter from Hugh Mackay of Bighouse to his solicitor, Mr Crawford, April 1749.
21. Frater, 'Women and their songs'; Stiubhart, 'Women and gender'.
22. Described in detail in chapter 7.
23. This practice is described in Boswell, *Journal*, 224.
24. NAS GD170/1355, Letters from Mary Macpherson to her husband, Duncan Campbell of Glenure, 1753–80.
25. For background, L. Leneman, *Alienated Affections: the Scottish Experience of Divorce and Separation, 1684–1830* (Edinburgh,1998).
26. NAS GD170/391/7, Family accounts: Janet Mackay.
27. NAS GD170/391/7a, Documents pertaining to the maintenance of Janet Mackay and her children from the Glenure Estate, 1752.
28. NAS GD170/391/7, Duncan Campbell of Glenure Papers concerning the financial affairs of Janet and her daughters. Also NAS GD170/1313, Letters from Hugh Mackay of Bighouse.
29. A court action raised in Edinburgh in 1757 was eventually settled in favour of Janet and her father in 1760. NAS GD170/391/7a.
30. NAS GD170/1626, Letter from Colina Campbell to her cousin Alexander Campbell of Barcaldine, 9 August 1772.
31. On the broad implications of widowhood see Hufton, *Prospect Before Her*, ch. 6.
32. NAS GD170/797/21, Letter from John Campbell of Achallader to Patrick Campbell of Barcaldine, 4 February 1732.
33. NAS GD170/797/9, Letter from John Campbell of Achallader to Patrick Campbell of Barcaldine, 28 December 1727.
34. Macinnes, 'Who owned Argyll'.

35. NAS GD170/243/10, Family expenses for Mary Campbell of Lochnell.
36. NAS GD170/793/6, Letter from John Campbell to his father Patrick Campbell of Barcaldine, 26 February 1724.
37. NAS GD170/768/1-3, Letters from Donald Campbell of Balighown to his nephew Patrick Campbell of Barcaldine, 1734–38.
38. NAS GD170/768/3, Letter from Donald Campbell of Balighown to his nephew, Patrick Campbell of Barcaldine, 9 August 1734.
39. A similar case from the Campbell family of Kilberry c.1716, which also involved spinster daughters giving up their financial rights, is detailed in Reddington-Wilde, 'Power of place', 201–8. On the financial pressures on widows, see B. Hill, *Women, Work and Sexual Politics in Eighteenth-Century England* (Oxford, 1989), ch.13.
40. NAS GD170/632/5, Letter from John Campbell to Alexander Campbell of Barcaldine, 8 November 1701.
41. NAS GD136/408, Letters from Mrs Barbara Sinclair to Samuel Mitchelson, lawyer, 1767.
42. NAS E326/1/7, Argyllshire Window Tax.
43. NAS E326/154, Inverness-shire Window Tax.
44. Detailed in L. Stone and J. C. Fawtier Stone, *Open Elite? England 1540–1800* (Oxford,1984). L. Stone, *Family and Fortune: Studies in Aristocratic Finance in the Sixteenth and Seventeenth Centuries* (Oxford, 1973).
45. W. Jolly, *Flora Macdonald in Uist: A Study of the Heroine in her Native Surroundings* (Perth, 1886).
46. E. Sanderson, *Women and Work in Eighteenth-Century Edinburgh* (London, 1996).
47. NAS GD170/1356, Letters from Mary Macpherson to Duncan Campbell of Glenure, 1758–63.
48. See chapter 4.
49. Hill, *Women, Work*, ch. 6: 'Female apprenticeship' gives examples.
50. NAS GD170/391/8, Accounts for the maintenance of Isabella Macpherson.
51. Frater, 'Women of the Gaidhealtachd'.
52. NAS GD170/391/8, Accounts for the maintenance of Isabella Macpherson.
53. A large sum for the period. See Hill, *Women, Work*, 92, 95.
54. NAS GD170/391/8, Accounts for the maintenance of Isabella Macpherson.
55. NAS GD139/372, Letters from Barbara Eliza Sinclair to her sisters, 1793–1818. GD139/366, Letters from Jean Sinclair to her sisters, 1792–1824.
56. NAS GD139/369, Letters from Captain John Sinclair to his sisters, 1792–1815.
57. NAS GD139/372/14, Letter from Barbara to Wilhelmina, 9 February 1818 mentions the Waterloo prize money.
58. *Genealogical Deduction*, 486.
59. *Ibid.*, 421–84.
60. J. Dwyer, *Virtuous Discourse: Sensibility and Community in Eighteenth Century Scotland* (Edinburgh,1987).
61. See chapter 3.

62. NAS GD170/688/2, Duncan Stewart of Innerhyle to Alexander Campbell of Barcaldine, n.d., c. 1713.
63. NAS GD170/688/3, Duncan Stewart of Innerhyle to Alexander Campbell of Barcaldine, n.d.
64. J. S. Gibson, 'Stewart, Alexander of Invernahyle (1707/8–1795)', in *Oxford Dictionary of National Biography* (Oxford, 2004).
65. NAS GD170/792/14, Letter from Hugh Mackay of Bighouse to Colin Campbell of Glenure, 30 April 1750.
66. NAS GD170/792/26, Letter from Hugh Mackay of Bighouse to Colin Campbell of Glenure, 2 March 1752.
67. *Ibid.*
68. See Grimble, *Rob Donn*.
69. GD170/972, Letters from Hugh Mackay of Bighouse to Colin Campbell of Glenure, 1749–52.
70. Boswell, *Journal*, 159.
71. *Ibid.*, 343.
72. *Ibid.*, 183.
73. *Ibid.*, 184.
74. NAS GD170/2109/3, Letter from Anna Campbell to Mary Campbell of Barcaldine, 1 September 1786.
75. NAS GD170/1704/1, Letter from Mary Campbell to Alexander Campbell of Barcaldine, 11 March 1789.
76. NAS GD170/1704/2, Letter from Mary Campbell to Alexander Campbell of Barcaldine, n.d., c.1792.
77. NAS GD170/1704/7, Letter from Mary Campbell to Alexander Campbell of Barcaldine, 8 May 1798. This letter is quoted in full in chapter 8.
78. NAS GD170/2103, Letters from Miss F. Brandon to Mary Campbell of Barcaldine, 1801–14.
79. Grant, *Highland Lady*.
80. Grant, *Highland Lady*, vol. 2, 187.
81. Gifford and McMillan, *Scottish Women's Writing*, 130–1.

CHAPTER 6: CONSUMER BEHAVIOUR AND THE WORLD OF GOODS

1. The theoretical approach used here is informed by A. Appadurai, *The Social Life of Things: Commodities in Cultural Perspective* (Cambridge, 1986). M. Douglas and B. Isherwood, *The World of Goods. Towards an Anthropology of Consumption* (London, 1979).
2. For a broad approach, see L. Weatherill, *Consumer Behaviour and Material Culture in Britain, 1660–1760* (London, 1988).
3. Dodgshon, 'Pretense of blude'.
4. Quoted in Henderson, *Caithness Family History*, 170.

5. Burt, *Letters*, hints at the dowdier appearance of women.
6. C. Mckean, *The Scottish Chateau: The Country House in Renaissance Scotland* (Straud, 2001), 61, gives an account of the practice of moving furniture and textiles from house to house, and the damage it caused.
7. Saville, *Bank of Scotland*, 60.
8. Martin, *Western Isles*, 357.
9. *Ibid.*
10. Boswell, *Journal*, 173.
11. McNeill and MacQueen, *Atlas of Scottish History*, 295.
12. On Scotland's balance-of-trade problems on the eve of union, see Saville, *Bank of Scotland*, 60.
13. Pennant, *Tour in Scotland*, 193–4.
14. NAS GD112/35/20, Breadalbane Muniments, Accounts of Special Interest, 1703–4. GD112/3/78/8-16, Household accounts while Breadalbane was at Bath, 1693.
15. Mckean, *The Scottish Chateau*, 105–6.
16. NAS GD170/243/10, Family expenses, 1717–40.
17. NAS GD170/238, China account, 1723–4
18. NAS GD170/243/10, Family expenses, 1717–40.
19. NAS GD347/63, Personal and household accounts of George Sutherland of Rearquhar, 1763–1804.
20. D. Jones, *Looking at Scottish Furniture: A Documented Anthology, 1570–1900* (St Andrews, 1987).
21. NAS GD170/247, Furniture and wright work, 1733–40.
22. NAS GD170/322, Furniture, 1740–51.
23. For an account of the female version of the writing desk, see D. Goodman, 'Furnishing discourses: Readings of a writing desk in eighteenth-century France', in M. Berg and E. Eger, eds, *Luxury in the Eighteenth Century: Debates, Desires and Delectable Goods* (Basingstoke, 2003).
24. NAS GD170/1487, Letter from John Campbell of Kintraw to his cousin Alexander Campbell, son of Barcaldine, 31 January 1743.
25. NAS GD139/238/12, Divorce of Ann Sinclair of Brabster.
26. D. Jones, 'Scottish Cabinet Makers Price Books, 1805–1825', *Regional Furniture* 3 (1989), 27–39; F. Bamford, *A Dictionary of Edinburgh Wrights and Furniture Makers, 1660–1840* (London, 1983).
27. NAS GD170/1993, Letter from James Morison to Alexander Campbell of Barcaldine, 1 May 1789.
28. Bamford, *Dictionary*.
29. NAS E326/1/25, Window Tax.
30. NAS CC11/1/5, Inventories for Inverness 1739–1759.
31. Burt, *Letters*, 273. B. Cowan, *The Social Life of Coffee: The Emergence of the British Coffeehouse* (New Haven, 2005).
32. Burt, *Letters*, 48.
33. *Ibid.*, 59–60.
34. H. Berry, 'Polite consumption: shopping in eighteenth century England', *Royal Historical Society Transactions* 12 (2002), 375–94.

234   *Lairds and Luxury*

35. See J. Stobart, A. Hann and V. Morgan, *Spaces of Consumption: Geographies of Shopping and Leisure in the English Town, 1680–1830* (London, 2007).
36. NAS GD170/313, China and glass, 1741–50.
37. Boswell, *Journey*, 282.
38. MacKay family papers in private hands, copied to the author. NAS GD87/2/15, Papers relating to the executry of Katherine Ross, Dowager Lady Bighouse, 1757–9. GD136/75, Inventory of cattle and household furniture of Katharine Ross, Dowager Lady Bighouse. See also W. A. Mackay, 'The lesser elites of northern Scotland' (MSc Thesis, University of Edinburgh, 1994).
39. NAS GD170/1186, Letters from Robert Campbell to his brother Duncan of Barcaldine, 1747–72.
40. Mackay, *Letter Book*.
41. Nenadic, 'Print collecting'.
42. NAS CC11/1/4, Inverness Inventories.
43. NAS CC11/1/6, Inverness Inventories.
44. NAS GD170/1464A/9, Letter from Alexander Campbell to his brother Robert, 3 May 1750, describes attendance at several 'roups' to furnish a house on taking up a tack in Achnaba.
45. NAS GD139/362, Letters from James Horne WS to Mrs Ann Sinclair of Brabster, 1783–88, mentions the poinding at Skibo. NAS GD136/1147, Roup of household goods at Barrock, September 1820. This was the family home of William Sinclair's wife.
46. Burt, *Letters*, 273.
47. Boswell, *Journey*, 121.
48. T. Barnard, *Making the Grand Figure. Lives and Possessions in Ireland, 1641–1770* (New Haven, 2004), ch. 5.
49. For an example, see NAS GD170/756/4, Letter from Colin Campbell to his father Patrick of Barcaldine, 8 February, no year (*c*.1732), which mentions sending his father a pair of shoes from Edinburgh.
50. Mackay, *Letter Book*, 374.
51. Nenadic, 'Highland gentlewoman'.
52. Nenadic, 'Middle rank consumers'.
53. NAS GD347/73, Letter from George Gun Munro to George Sutherland of Rearquhar, 15 April 1767.
54. NAS GD136/409, Advice from Dr William Sinclair of Thurso to his son William, 1767.
55. NAS GD170/314, Clothes, tailoring, materials, 1734–52.
56. NAS GD170/1186/15/1, Letter from Robert Campbell to his brother Duncan, May 1750.
57. NAS GD170/630/16, Letters from Lord Glenorchy to Alexander Campbell of Barcaldine, 1691–1716.
58. H. Cheape, *Tartan: The Highland Habit* (Edinburgh, 2006).
59. See Pittock, *The Invention of Scotland*.
60. Black, *An Lasair*, 188–91.

61. NAS GD1701213, Letter from James Erskine to Duncan Campbell (later of Glenure), his sheriff-substitute of Perthshire in Killin, 22 November 1748.
62. Cheape, *Tartan*.
63. Burt, *Letters*, 48.
64. Petrie, *Rules of Good Deportment*.
65. For examples see the anti-Bute prints of the 1760s in the collection of the Lewis Walpole Library, available online.
66. NAS GD170/326, Colin Campbell's wig accounts.
67. Burt, *Letters*, 232.
68. *Ibid.*, 193.
69. NAS GD170/329, Inventory of clothes, 4 September 1740.
70. Burt, *Letters*, 235.
71. For Highland portraits, see J. Holloway, *Patrons and Painters: Art in Scotland, 1650–1760* (Edinburgh, 1989).
72. M. Finn, 'Men's things: Masculine possessions in the consumer revolution', *Social History* 25 (2000), 1–35.
73. For a general survey, see D. Roche, *The Culture of Clothing: Dress and Fashion in the Ancien Regime* (Cambridge, 1994). A. Ribeiro, *Dress in Eighteenth Century Europe* (Yale, 2002). For an example, see GD87/31/1, Inventory of Colonel Alexander Campbell's clothes and linen, 1765.
74. Thomson, *Raeburn*, 140–1.
75. Ramsay, *Scotland and Scotsmen*, vol. 2, 82–3.
76. NAS GD170/314, Colin Campbell's accounts for clothing and tailoring.
77. Cheape, *Tartan*.
78. Burt, *Letters*, 235.
79. Roche, *Culture of Clothing*. G. Vigarello, *Concepts of Cleanliness. Changing Attitudes in France Since the Middle Ages* (Cambridge, 1988).
80. M. Pointon, 'Jewellery in eighteenth century England', in M. Berg and H. Clifford, eds, *Consumers and Luxury: Consumer Culture in Europe, 1650–1850* (Manchester, 1999). For an example, see NAS GD87/20/8, Inventory of lace gowns etc. of Helen Sinclair in 1765 prior to her marriage.
81. See NAS GD139/366, Letters from Miss Jean Sinclair, 1792–1824, for conversations among sisters concerning their clothing, the latest fashions and prices.
82. This was true of all female-owned goods. See A. Vickery, 'Women and the world of goods: A Lancashire consumer and her possessions, 1751–81', in J. Brewer and R. Porter, eds, *Consumption and the World of Goods* (London, 1994).
83. Nenadic, 'Middle rank consumers'.
84. J. Sinclair, ed., *The Statistical Account of Scotland: Drawn up from the Communications of the Ministers of Different Parishes*, 21 vols (Edinburgh, 1791–99), vol. 5, 287, 'Account for Inverary'.
85. *Ibid.*, vol. 9, 583, 'Account for Crieff'.
86. *Ibid.*, vol. 20, 493, 'Account for Thurso'.
87. The competition could be brutal. Jean Sinclair warned her sister Bell against setting up in business as a mantua maker in Thurso in 1793. NAS GD139/366, Letter from Jean Sinclair to her sister Isabell, 3 November 1793.

236   *Lairds and Luxury*

88. Argyll and Bute District Archives, Malcolm of Poltalloch Collection, Neil Malcolm's London accounts.
89. NAS GD170/537, Furniture and other accounts, 1800–34. GD170/2661, Letter from Oakley & Evans of London on furniture sent to Barcaldine House, 1815.
90. Ferrier, *Marriage*, 498–9 gives an account of this fashion.
91. Boswell, *Journey*, 120.
92. G. P. Moss, *Highland Gold and Silversmiths* (Edinburgh, 1999).
93. S. Nenadic, 'Romanticism and the urge to consume in the early nineteenth century', in M. Berg and H. Clifford, eds, *Consumers and Luxury. Consumer Culture in Europe, 1650–1850* (Manchester, 1999).
94. NAS GD170/1922, Letters from Louisa Mackay of Bighouse to her cousin Alexander Campbell of Barcaldine, July 1785.
95. NAS GD170/340, Colin Campbell, bills and accounts. Over £30 was spent at Ker and Dempster on silverware and jewellery in 1749–50.
96. NAS GD170/329, Inventory of household furniture at Glenure, 1752.

CHAPTER 7: HOUSES

1. D. Wordsworth, *Recollections of a Tour Made in Scotland AD 1803* (New Haven, 1997), 97–8.
2. M. Girouard, *Life in the English Country House: Social and Architectural History* (London, 1980). C. Christie, *The British Country House in the Eighteenth Century* (Manchester, 2000). I. Gow and A. Rowan, eds, *Scottish Country Houses* (Edinburgh, 1995).
3. Mckean, *Scottish Chateau*.
4. J. Crowley, *The Invention of Comfort: Sensibilities and Design in Early Modern Britain and Early America* (New York, 2001).
5. Wilson and Mackley, *Creating Paradise*, 293–4.
6. *Ibid.*, ch. 7.
7. *Argyll: An Inventory of the Ancient Monuments, vol. 2: Lorn* (Edinburgh, 1975), 266.
8. *Ibid.*, 253.
9. Wilson and Mackley, *Creating Paradise*.
10. *Ibid.*, ch. 1.
11. M. Glendinning, R. MacInnes and A. MacKechnie, *A History of Scottish Architecture from the Renaissance to the Present Day* (Edinburgh, 1996), 113.
12. I. D. Whyte, 'Agriculture in Aberdeenshire in the seventeenth and early eighteenth centuries: Continuity and change', in D. Stevenson, ed., *From Lairds to Louns: Country and Burgh Life in Aberdeen, 1600–1800* (Aberdeen, 1986).
13. T. A. Markus, ed., *Order in Space and Society* (London, 1982).
14. T. C. Smout, 'The landowner and the planned village in Scotland, 1730–1830', in N. T. Phillipson and R. Mitchison, eds, *Scotland in the Age of Improvement* (Edinburgh, 1970).

15. NAS GD170/630, Letters from Lord Glenorchy to Alexander Campbell of Barcaldine, 1691–1716.
16. J. Keay and J. Keay, *Collins Encyclopaedia of Scotland* (London, 1994), 571.
17. National Monument Record of Scotland [NMRS] 931.
18. J. D. Hunt, *Gardens and the Picturesque. Studies in the History of Landscape Architecture* (London, 1992).
19. E. Cregeen, 'The changing role of the house of Argyll in the Scottish Highlands', in N. T. Phillipson and R. Mitchison, eds, *Scotland in the Age of Improvement*. Timperlay, 'Pattern of landholding'.
20. The houses are listed in *Argyll: An Inventory of the Ancient Monuments*, vols 1–7 (London, 1971; 1975; 1980; 1982; 1984; 1988; 1992).
21. Wilson and Mackley, *Creating Paradise*, ch. 1.
22. Glendinning, MacInnes and MacKechnie, *History of Scottish Architecture*, 130.
23. NMRS, NN7 4 NE 14.00. Also, NAS GD112/21/80,77–79, Personal accounts of the earl of Breadalbane, including building work to Taymouth Castle.
24. *Argyll: An Inventory, vol. 2: Lorn*, 248–52.
25. *Ibid.*
26. *Ibid.*, 265.
27. *Ibid.*, 253–56.
28. NAS GD170/238, Patrick Campbell of Barcaldine, China and furniture accounts.
29. NAS GD170/514/5, Barcaldine house accounts, 1801–38.
30. B. Hill, *Servants: English Domestics in the Eighteenth Century* (Oxford, 1996).
31. For a general survey, see I. Gow, *The Scottish Interior* (Edinburgh, 1992).
32. NAS GD170/2417/2, GD170/2417/3/1, Letters from Robert Downie to Duncan Campbell of Barcaldine.
33. *Argyll: An Inventory, vol. 2: Lorn*, 245–7.
34. Argyll and Bute Archives, Poltalloch Collection DR/2/9, Observation of George Malcolm esq. on the estates of Neill Malcolm esq. in Argyllshire, 14 March 1798, 14–18. *Argyll: An Inventory, vol. 7: Mid Argyll and Cowal*, 349–54.
35. *Ibid.*
36. *Argyll: An Inventory, vol. 7: Mid Argyll and Cowal*, 349–54.
37. *Argyll: An Inventory, vol. 2: Lorn*, 267–8.
38. Glendinning, MacInnes and MacKechnie, *History of Scottish Architecture*, 114.
39. *Argyll: An Inventory, vol. 2: Lorn*, 267.
40. *Ibid.*, 254.
41. *Ibid.*, vol. 7, 365–6.
42. *Ibid.*, 317–20.
43. *Ibid.*, 320–5.
44. *Ibid.*, 326–7.
45. A detailed description of a similar house in Sutherland is given in Sage, *Memorabilia Domestica*, 74–5.
46. *Argyll: An Inventory, vol. 2: Lorn*, 456–8.
47. NAS GD170/329, Inventory of household furniture, 1752. GD170/404/4, Inventory of household furniture, 1759. GD170/381/8, Building papers, 1779.

48. NAS GD170/310, Building, house repairs and unspecified accounts, 1740–51. The tiles were purchased 1750 from 'William Mercer at the Crown, opposite the Tron Church' and cost £2 14s. 6d. They are still in the house today.
49. NAS GD170/952, Letter from Robert Campbell to his brother Colin of Glenure, 9 May 1750. GD170/310, Contract with Duncan Campbell, mason in Stirling, for kitchen extension, 15 May 1751.
50. NAS GD170/444/5, Accounts for building work at Glenure House, 1788.
51. Nenadic, 'Middle rank consumers'.
52. NAS GD170/310, Building and house accounts: Receipt from Andrew Good, wright in Edinburgh, 1750 for eight black frames with gilt edges.
53. NAS GD170/329, Inventory of books, 4 September 1740.
54. NAS GD170/340, Colin Campbell's silver accounts, 1738–51.
55. See M. Hellman, 'Furniture, sociability and the work of leisure in eighteenth century France', *Eighteenth-Century Studies* 32 (1999), 415–45.
56. NAS GD170/247, Furniture and wright work, 1733–40.
57. Family papers in private hands, copied to the author.
58. NAS GD170/404/4, Inventory of kitchen, garden and loft items at Glenure in 1752 under the care of the gardener. An inventory of 1759 gives a separate list of keys to all rooms and cupboards.
59. Boswell, *Journal*, 101.
60. *Ibid.*, 102.
61. *Ibid.*, 115. The original family seat at Sleat had been destroyed by fire.
62. *Ibid.*, 120.
63. *Ibid.*, 134.
64. *Ibid.*, 175.
65. *Ibid.*, 185.
66. *Ibid.*, 253.
67. *Ibid.*, 259.
68. *Ibid.*, 264.
69. *Ibid.*, 302.
70. *Ibid.*, 313.
71. *Ibid.*, 339.

CHAPTER 8: SOCIABILITY AND HOSPITALITY

1. Burt, *Letters*, 84–6.
2. E. M. Furgol, 'Simon Fraser, Lord Lovat', in *Oxford Dictionary of National Biography* (Oxford, 2004).
3. Burt, *Letters*, 220.
4. *Ibid.*, 119.
5. NAS GD170/793/7, Letter from John Campbell to his father, Patrick of Barcaldine, 18 August 1724.

6. NAS GD170/243/11. Account of the funeral expenses of Colin Campbell of Invernan, February 1731.
7. Ferrier, *Marriage*, 286–7.
8. P. Langford, 'The uses of eighteenth-century politeness', *Transactions of the Royal Historical Society* 12 (2002), 311–3.
9. NAS GD112/39/223/8. Letter from Andrew Fraser to the earl of Breadalbane, 22 December 1708.
10. NAS GD170/793/3, Letter from John Campbell to his father Patrick of Barcaldine, 26 June 1721.
11. R. Chambers, *Domestic Annals of Scotland Vol 3: Reign of George* (Edinburgh, 1874), 456.
12. A. Petrie, *Rules of Good Deportment, or of Good Breeding for the Use of Youth* (Edinburgh, 1720).
13. *Ibid.*, 93.
14. *Ibid.*, 15–16.
15. R. Sweet, 'Topographies of politeness', *Transactions of the Royal Historical Society*, 12 (2002), 355–74.
16. Mackintosh, *An Essay*, quoted in H. G. Graham, *The Social Life of Scotland in the Eighteenth Century* (London, 1900), vol. 1, 19.
17. Macintosh, *An Essay*, 229.
18. *Ibid.*, 229.
19. *Ibid.*, 234.
20. *Ibid.*, 231.
21. *Ibid.*, 236.
22. For the context, see J. Brewer, *The Pleasures of the Imagination: English Culture in the Eighteenth Century* (London, 1997).
23. NAS GD170/631, Letters of John Campbell of Achallader to Barcaldine, his cousin, 1707–20.
24. See Glover, 'Elite women', ch. 5.
25. A. Carlyle, *Autobiography of the Rev. Alexander Carlyle Minister of Inveresk Containing Memorials of the Men and Events of His Time* (Edinburgh, 1860).
26. *Ibid.*, 381.
27. *Ibid.*
28. *Ibid.*, 383.
29. NAS GD170/1116/2/1, Invitation to dinner and a ball, Inverary, 19 June 1778.
30. Boswell, *Journal*, 352.
31. Elaborate toasting and male sociability were still the norm among the urban business elite well into the nineteenth century. See J. G. Lockhart, *Peter's Letters to his Kinsfolk* (London, 1919).
32. Boswell, *Journal*, 355.
33. Boswell, *Journal*, 357.
34. NAS GD170/793/31, Letter from John Campbell to his father Patrick of Barcaldine, n.d., *c.*1731.
35. Fiction gives the best perspective on this. See Ferrier, *Marriage*.
36. Boswell, *Journal*, 254.

37. See Petrie, *Rules*, ch. 7.
38. NAS GD170/972, Letter from Hugh Mackay of Bighouse to Colin Campbell of Glenure, 1 November 1749, gives an account of the arrangements made for sending his daughter Mally from Sutherland to visit her sister, newly married to Glenure, in Argyll.
39. Boswell, *Journal*.
40. Youngson, *Beyond the Highland Line*, 220.
41. Macintosh, *An Essay*, 231.
42. Nenadic, 'Middle rank consumers'.
43. B. G. Carson, *Ambitious Appetites: Dining, Behaviour and Patterns of Consumption in Federal Washington* (Washington, 1990).
44. Burt, *Letters*, 65.
45. NAS GD170/329, Inventory of household furniture, 1752.
46. Boswell, *Journal*, 120.
47. Burt, *Letters*, 84–6. One of Boswell's criticisms of Sir Alexander Macdonald at Armadale is that he did not have an Edinburgh cook. Boswell, *Journal*, 114.
48. Carlyle, *Autobiography*, 455.
49. R. D. Leppert, *Music and Image: Domesticity, Ideology and Socio-Cultural Formation in Eighteenth-Eentury England* (Cambridge, 1988).
50. E. Kowaleski-Wallace, *Consuming Subjects: Women, Shopping and Business in the Eighteenth Century* (Columbia, 1997), 19–36.
51. H. Young, *The Genius of Wedgwood* (London, 1995), 50. A. Forty, *Objects of Desire: Design and Society, 1750–1980* (London, 1986).
52. A. Ramsay, *The Tea-Table Miscellany: or, a Collection of Choice Songs, Scots and English* (Glasgow, 1753).
53. See Vickery, *Gentleman's Daughter*.
54. Clark, *Gleanings from an Old Portfolio*, vol. 1, 17.
55. *Ibid.*, 184–5.
56. Petrie, *Rules*, ch. 4.
57. Ferrier, *Marriage*, 65.
58. P. Borsay, *The English Urban Renaissance: Culture and Society in the Provincial Town* (London, 1989).
59. Grant, *Highland Lady*, 5.
60. Graham, *Social Life*, vol. 1, 102.
61. M. W. Montagu, *Complete Letters* (Oxford, 1965), vol. 1, 217.
62. Graham, *Social Life*, vol. 1, 40–1.
63. *Ibid.*
64. NAS GD170/1121/4, Letter from Isabell Campbell of Achallader to her brother Duncan of Barcaldine, 16 October 1782.
65. R. Mitchison, *Agricultural Sir John. The Life of Sir John Sinclair of Ulbster 1754–1835* (London, 1962).
66. Grant, *Highland Lady*, ch. 1.
67. Youngson, *Making of Classical Edinburgh*.
68. *Ibid.*, p. 224

69. Grant, *Highland Lady*, 63.
70. *Scotsman*, 10 March 1827, 4.
71. NAS GD170/2350, Letter from John Archibald Campbell WS to Duncan Campbell of Barcaldine, 8 December 1825.
72. R. Stewart, *The Classic English Town House* (London, 2006).
73. R. Reid, *The Georgian House and Its Details* (Bath, 1989).
74. See I. G. Brown, *Elegance and Entertainment in the New Town of Edinburgh: the Harden Drawings* (Edinburgh, 1995).
75. NAS GD170/1627, Letter from Collector Colin Campbell to Alexander Campbell of Barcaldine, 29 June 1786. GD170/1802, Letter from William Hamilton, surgeon in Glasgow unable to attend the lying in, 12 June 1786. GD170/1942, Letter from Barcaldine to Dr Donald Maclean surgeon in Oban requesting that he attends the lying in, 10 June 1786.
76. NAS GD170/1104/7, Letter from Mary Campbell to her husband Alexander of Barcaldine, 8 May 1798.
77. NAS GD170/2109/4, Letter from Anna Campbell to her daughter Mary Campbell of Barcaldine, 28 May 1791.
78. NAS GD170/2109/3, Letter from Anna Campbell to her daughter Mary Campbell of Barcaldine, 1 September 1786.
79. NAS GD 170/1704/2, Letter from Mary Campbell to her husband Alexander of Barcaldine, n.d., *c.*1790.
80. NAS GD170/2103, Letters from G. Brandon, governess, to her mistress Mary Campbell of Barcaldine, 1801–14.
81. Glover, 'Elite Women', ch. 2.
82. Brown, *Elegance and Entertainment*. Grant, *Highland Lady*.
83. Carlyle, *Autobiography*, 455.
84. R. Porter, *Disease, Medicine and Society in England, 1550–1860* (Basingstoke, 1993).
85. NAS GD170/1585, Letter from Ewan Cameron of Fassfern to his brother-in-law Alexander Campbell of Barcaldine, 13 October 1796.
86. GD/170/1177, Letter from Patrick Campbell of Ardchattan to his uncle Duncan Campbell of Glenure, 27 February 1779.
87. NAS GD87/1/101, Letter from Alexander Campbell to his father John of Barcaldine, 3 November 1770. Grimble, *Rob Donn*, 187.

CONCLUSION: FROM LUXURY TO LOSS IN FIVE GENERATIONS

1. NAS GD170/2975-2986, Correspondence of Sir Alexander Campbell of Barcaldine, 1833–58.
2. NAS GD170/2443, Letter from Hugh Fraser to his brother-in-law Duncan Campbell of Barcaldine, 25 January 1834.
3. Stewart, *Sketches*, part 2, section 1: 'Change of Manners'.

4. S. Coppel, 'John Malcolm of Poltalloch (1805–1893)', in *Oxford Dictionary of National Biography* (2004).
5. NAS GD170/514, Barcaldine House, 1801–38, Building and repair costs.
6. Grant, *Highland Lady*, 302–3.
7. Remarkably, in later generations, many families, including the Campbell family of Barcaldine, achieved this ambition and managed to repurchase some elements of the family property.
8. Stewart, *Sketches*, 153.
9. Burt, *Letters*, 39.
10. Nenadic, 'Romanticism'.
11. C. Campbell, *The Romantic Ethic and the Spirit of Modern Consumerism* (Oxford, 1987).
12. W. Scott, *Northern Lights or a Voyage in the Lighthouse Yacht to Nova Zembla and Lord Knows Where in the Summer of 1814* (Hawick, 1982).
13. Pittock, *Invention of Scotland*, 88–90.
14. Thomson, *Raeburn*, 152–4.
15. W. Scott, *The Journal of Sir Walter Scott, 1825–32. From the Original Manuscript at Abbotsford* (Edinburgh, 1891) 120–1.
16. Grant, *Highland Lady*, 28–9.

Bibliography

MANUSCRIPT SOURCES

National Archives of Scotland

CC86. Commissary Court Productions.
E326/1/7. Argyllshire Window Tax.
E326/1/54. Inverness-shire Window Tax.
GD1/726. Papers of the Rose Family of Kilravock, Inverness-shire.
GD13. Papers of the Campbell Family of Ballieveolan, Argyllshire.
GD87. Papers of the Mackay Family of Bighouse, Sutherland.
GD112. Breadalbane Muniments.
GD136. Papers of the Sinclair Family of Freswick, Caithness.
GD139. Papers of the Sutherland Family of Forse, Sutherland.
GD170. Papers of the Campbell Family of Barcaldine, Argyllshire.
GD347. Papers of the Sutherland Family of Rearquhar, Inverness-shire.

Argyll and Bute District Archives

Malcolm of Poltalloch Collection

University of Glasgow

Adam Smith Business Records Centre: UGD 37/2/1.
'Educating a Scots Laird – A Document', edited by B. Bonnyman.

PRINTED SOURCES

Adam, R. J., ed., *Papers on Sutherland Estate Management, 1802–16*, 2 vols (Edinburgh, 1972)

Ancient, Heraldic and Antiquarian Tracts by Sir James Balfour (Edinburgh, 1837)
Autobiographical Journal of John Macdonald Schoolmaster and Soldier, 1770–1830 (Edinburgh, 1906)
Bever, S., *The Cadet: A Military Treaties: By an Officer* (London, 1762)
Blackie, J. S., *The Language and Literature of the Scottish Highlands* (Edinburgh, 1876)
Boswell, J. *Journal of a Tour to the Hebrides with Samuel Johnson.* Preface and Notes by Pottle, F. A. and Bennett, C. H. (London, 1936)
Bowman, J. E., *The Highlands and Islands: A Nineteenth-Century Tour* (Gloucester, 1986)
Burt, E., *Letters from the North of Scotland.* Introduction by Withers, C. W. J. (Edinburgh, 1998)
Campbell, R., *The London Tradesman, being a Compendious View of all the Trades, Professions, Arts, both Liberal and Mechanic, now Practiced in the Cities of London and Westminster* (London, 1747)
Carlyle, A., *Autobiography of the Rev. Alexander Carlyle Minister of Inveresk Containing Memorials of the Men and Events of His Time* (Edinburgh, 1860)
Chambers, R., *Domestic Annals of Scotland* (Edinburgh, 1874)
Clark, G., ed., *Gleanings from an Old Portfolio, Containing Some Correspondence between Lady Louisa Stuart and her Sister Caroline, Countess of Portarlington, and Other Friends and Relations*, 3 vols (Edinburgh, 1896)
Colquhoun, P., *Treaties on the Wealth, Power and Resources of the British Empire* (London, 1815)
Dickinson, W. C., *Two Students at St Andrews, 1711–1716 Edited from the Delvine Papers* (Edinburgh, 1951)
Ferrier, S., *Marriage: A Novel* (Edinburgh, 1818)
Ferrier, S., *The Inheritance* (Edinburgh, 1824)
A Genealogical Deduction of the Family of Kilravock, Written in 1683–4 by Mr Hew Rose, Minister of Nairne, Continued by the Reverend Lachlan Shaw Minister of Elgin in 1753. With Illustrative Documents from the Family Charter Room, and Notes (Edinburgh, 1858).
Grant, J. P., *Memoir and Correspondence of Mrs Grant of Laggan*, 3 vols (London, 1845)
Grant, E., *Memoirs of a Highland Lady* (Edinburgh, 1992)
Henderson, J., *Caithness Family History* (Edinburgh, 1884)
Jolly, W., *Flora Macdonald in Uist: A Study of the Heroine in her Native Surroundings* (Perth, 1886)
Lockhart, J. G., *Peter's Letters to his Kinsfolk* (London, 1819)
Mackay, R., *History of the House and Clan of Mackay; Containing Accounts of Many Other Scottish Families, a Variety of Historical Notices, More Particularly of those Relating the Northern Division of Scotland During the Most Critical and Interesting Periods with a Genealogical Table of the Clan* (Edinburgh, 1829)
Macintosh, W., *Essay on Ways and Means of Inclosing, Fallowing, Planting etc* (Edinburgh, 1729)
Mackay, W., ed., *Letter Book of Bailie John Steuart of Inverness* (Edinburgh, 1915)
Macleod, A., ed., *Songs of Duncan Ban Macintyre* (Edinburgh, 1952)

Macleod, R. C., *The Book of Dunvegan: Being Documents from the Muniment Room of the Macleods of Macleods at Dunvegan Castle, Isle of Skye*, 2 vols (Aberdeen, 1933)
Martin, M., *A Description of the Western Islands of Scotland* ca. *1695* (Edinburgh, 1999)
Montagu, M. W., *Complete Letters* (Oxford, 1965)
Munro, A., 'The professor's daughter; an essay on female conduct', transcribed, with introduction and notes by Monro, P. A. G., *Proceedings of the Royal College of Physicians of Edinburgh* January 1996, vol. 26:1, Supplement No. 2.
Murray, K., *History of the Scottish Regiments in the British Army* (Glasgow, 1862)
Petrie, A., *Rules of Good Deportment or of Good Breeding for the Use of Youth* (Edinburgh, 1720)
Pennant, T., *A Tour in Scotland in 1769* (Warrington, 1769)
Paul, J. B., *Diary of George Ridpath, Minister of Stitchel, 1755–61* (Edinburgh, 1922)
Ramsay, A., *The Tea-Table Miscellany: Or, a Collection of Choice Songs, Scots and English* (Glasgow, 1753)
Ramsay, J., *Scotland and Scotsmen in the Eighteenth Century*, 2 vols (Edinburgh, 1938)
Records of Clan Campbell in the Military Service of the Honourable East India Company, 1600–1858. Compiled by Major Sir D. Campbell of Barcaldine (London, 1925)
Wills, V., *Reports on the Annexed Estates from the Records of the Forfeited Estates Preserved in the Scottish Record Office* (Edinburgh, 1973)
Sage, D., *Memorabilia Domestica: Or Parish Life in the North of Scotland* (Wick and Edinburgh, 1889)
Scott, W., *The Journal of Sir Walter Scott, 1825–32 from the Original Manuscript at Abbotsford* (Edinburgh, 1891)
Scott, W., *Northern Lights or a Voyage in the Lighthouse Yacht to Nova Zembla and Lord Knows Where in the Summer of 1814* (Hawick, 1982)
Sinclair, J., *An Account of the Highland Society of London from its Establishment in May 1778 to 1813, Drawn up at the Deisre of the Society with an Appendix Containing a List of Members, Rules etc* (London, 1813)
Sinclair, J., ed., *The Statistical Account of Scotland: Drawn up from the Communications of the Ministers of Different Parishes*, 21 vols (Edinburgh, 1791–9)
Stewart, D., *Sketches of the Character, Institutions and Customs of the Highlanders of Scotland* (Edinburgh, 1822)
Turton, A., ed., *The Diary of John Campbell: A Scottish Banker and the Forty-Five* (London, 1995)
Wordsworth, D., *Recollections of a Tour Made in Scotland* (New Haven, 1997)

RECENT BOOKS

Appadurai, I., *The Social Life of Things: Commodities in Cultural Perspective* (Cambridge, 1986)
Argyll: An Inventory of the Ancient Monuments, 7 vols (London, 1971; 1975; 1980; 1982; 1984; 1988; 1992)

Aries, P., *Centuries of Childhood, a Social History of Family Life* (Harmonsworth, 1973)
Asch, R. G., *Nobilities in Transition: Courtiers and Rebels in Britain and Europe* (London, 2003)
Bamford, F., *A Dictionary of Edinburgh Wrights and Furniture Makers, 1660–1840* (London, 1983)
Bannerman, J., *The Beatons: A Medical Kindred in the Classical Gaelic Tradition* (Edinburgh, 1988)
Barnard, T., *Making the Grand Figure. Lives and Possessions in Ireland, 1641–1770* (New Haven, 2004)
Baumgarten, L., *What Clothes Reveal: The Language of Clothing in Colonial and Federal America* (Yale, 2002)
Berg, M., *Luxury and Pleasure in Eighteenth Century Britain* (Oxford, 2005)
Berg, M. and Clifford, C., eds, *Consumers and Luxury: Consumer Culture in Europe, 1650–1850* (Manchester, 1999)
Berg, M. and Eger, E., eds, *Luxury in the Eighteenth Century: Debates, Desires and Delectable Goods* (Basingstoke, 2003)
Berger, P. and Luckman, T., *The Social Construction of Reality: Everything that Passes for Knowledge in Society* (New York, 1967)
Berry, C. J., *The Idea of Luxury: A Conceptual and Historical Investigation* (London, 1994)
Black, R., ed., *An Lasair: Anthology of Eighteenth Century Scottish Gaelic Verse* (Edinburgh, 2001)
Blackie, J. S., *The Language and Literature of the Scottish Highlands* (Edinburgh, 1876)
Borsay, P., *The English Urban Renaissance: Culture and Society in the Provincial Town* (London, 1989)
Brett-James, A., *General Graham, Lord Lynedoch* (London, 1959)
Brewer, J., *The Pleasures of the Imagination: English Culture in the Eighteenth Century* (London, 1997)
Brewer, J., *The Sinews of Power: War, Money and the English State, 1688–1783* (London, 1989)
Brewer, J. and Porter, R., eds, *Consumption and the World of Goods* (London, 1994)
Brown, I. G., *Elegance and Entertainment in the New Town of Edinburgh: The Harden Drawings* (Edinburgh, 1995)
Brown, K. M., *Noble Society in Scotland: Wealth, Family and Culture from Reformation to Revolution* (Edinburgh, 2000)
Bruce, P. C., *The Purchase System in the British Army, 1660–1871* (London, 1980)
Campbell, C., *The Romantic Ethic and the Spirit of Modern Consumerism* (Oxford, 1987)
Carney, S., *The Appin Murder: The Killing of the Red Fox* (Edinburgh, 1994)
Carson, B. G., *Ambitious Appetites: Dining, Behaviour and Patterns of Consumption in Federal Washington* (Washington, 1990)
Cheape, H., *Tartan: The Highland Habit* (Edinburgh, 2006)
Christie, C. *The British Country House in the Eighteenth Century* (Manchester, 2000)
Colley, L., *Britons: Forging the Nation, 1707–1837* (New Haven and London, 1992)
Cookson, J. E., *The British Armed Nation, 1793–1815* (Oxford, 1997)

Corfield, P. J., *Power and the Professions in Britain, 1700–1850* (London, 1995)
Cowan, B., *The Social Life of Coffee: The Emergence of the British Coffeehouse* (New Haven and London, 2005)
Craig, M., *Damn' Rebel Bitches: The Women of the '45* (Edinburgh, 2000).
Croll, E., *Endangered Daughters: Discrimination and Development in Asia* (London, 2000)
Crowley, J., *The Invention of Comfort: Sensibilities and Design in Early Modern Britain and Early America* (New York, 2001)
Cruikshank, E. and Corp, E., eds, *The Stuart Court in Exile and the Jacobites* (London, 1995)
Davidoff, L. and Hall, C., *Family Fortunes: Men and Women of the English Middle Class, 1780–1850* (London, 1987)
Devine, T. M., *Scotland's Empire, 1600–1815* (London, 2003)
Devine, T. M., *The Scottish Nation, 1700–2000* (London, 2000)
Devine, T. M., ed., *Lairds and Improvement in the Scotland of the Enlightenment* (Edinburgh, 1979)
Devine, T. M., ed., *Scottish Elites* (Edinburgh, 1994)
Dickinson, H., ed., *A Companion to Eighteenth-Century Britain* (Oxford, 2002)
Dixon, S. M., *The Modernisation of Russia, 1676–1825* (Cambridge, 1999)
Dodgshon, R. A., *From Chiefs to Landlords: Social and Economic Change in the Western Highlands and Islands, c.1493–1820* (Edinburgh, 1998)
Donaldson, G., *Scottish Historical Documents* (Edinburgh, 1970)
Douglas, M. and Isherwood, B., *The World of Goods. Towards an Anthropology of Consumption* (London, 1979)
Dwyer, J., *Virtuous Discourse: Sensibility and Community in Eighteenth Century Scotland* (Edinburgh, 1987)
Ewan, E. and Meikle, M. M., eds, *Women in Scotland, c.1100–1750* (East Linton, 1999)
Fildes, V., *Wet Nursing: A History from Antiquity to the Present* (Oxford, 1988)
Forty, A., *Objects of Desire: Design and Society, 1750–1980* (London, 1986)
Gifford, D. and McMillan, D., eds, *A History of Scottish Women's Writing* (Edinburgh, 1997)
Girouard, M., *Life in the English Country House: Social and Architectural History* (London, 1980)
Glendinning, M., *The Architecture of Scottish Government From Kingship to Parliamentary Democracy* (Dundee, 2004)
Glendinning, M., MacInnes, R. and MacKechnie, A., *A History of Scottish Architecture from the Renaissance to the Present Day* (Edinburgh, 1996)
Goodare, J., *State and Society in Early Modern Scotland* (Oxford, 1999)
Gow, I., *The Scottish Interior* (Edinburgh, 1992)
Gow, I. and Rowan, A., eds, *Scottish Country Houses* (Edinburgh, 1995)
Graham, H. G., *The Social Life of Scotland in the Eighteenth Century* (London, 1900)
Grant, I. F., ed., *Everyday Life on an Old Highland Farm, 1769–1782* (London, 1924)
Grimble, I., *Chief of Mackay* (London, 1965)
Grimble, I., *The World of Rob Donn* (Edinburgh, 1979)

Heywood, C., *A History of Childhood: Children and Childhood in the West from Medieval to Modern Times* (Cambridge, 2001)
Hill, B., *Servants: English Domestics in the Eighteenth Century* (Oxford, 1996)
Hill, B., *Women, Work and Sexual Politics in Eighteenth-Century England* (Oxford, 1989)
Holloway, J., *Patrons and Painters: Art in Scotland, 1650–1760* (Edinburgh, 1989)
Holmes, G. S., *Augustan England: Professions, State and Society, 1680–1730* (1982)
Hont, I. and Ignatieff, M., eds, *Wealth and Virtue* (Cambridge, 1983)
Hoppit, J., *Risk and Failure in English Business, 1700–1800* (Cambridge, 1987)
Houston, R. A. and Whyte, I. D., eds, *Scottish Society 1500–1800* (Cambridge, 1989)
Hufton, O., *The Prospect Before Her: A History of Women in Western Europe, 1500–1800* (London, 1995)
Hunt, J. D., *Gardens and the Picturesque. Studies in the History of Landscape Architecture* (London, 1992)
Hunter, M. C. W., *The Occult Laboratory: Magic, Science and Second Sight in Seventeenth Century Scotland* (Woodbridge, 2001)
Jones, D., *Looking at Scottish Furniture: A Documented Anthology, 1570–1900* (St Andrews, 1987)
Keay, J. and Keay, J., *Collins Encyclopaedia of Scotland* (London, 1994)
Kowaleski-Wallace, E., *Consuming Subjects: Women, Shopping and Business in the Eighteenth Century* (Columbia, 1997)
Larminie, V., *Wealth, Kinship and Culture: The Seventeenth-Century Newdigates of Arbury and their World* (London, 1995)
Leneman, L., *Alienated Affections: The Scottish Experience of Divorce and Separation, 1684–1830* (Edinburgh, 1998)
Lenman, B., *Integration and Enlightenment: Scotland 1746–1832* (Edinburgh, 1992)
Lenman, B., *The Jacobite Clans of the Great Glen, 1650–1784* (London, 1984)
Leppert, R. D., *Music and Image: Domesticity, Ideology and Socio-Cultural Formation in Eighteenth-Century England* (Cambridge, 1988)
MacInnes, A., *Clanship, Commerce and the House of Stuart, 1603–1788* (East Linton, 1996)
Mackay, E. R., *George Sutherland of Riarchar: The Last of the Tacksmen* (Dornoch, 1971)
Mckean, C., *The Scottish Chateau: The Country House in Renaissance Scotland* (Straud, 2001)
McKendrick, N., Brewer, J. and Plumb, J. H., *The Birth of a Consumer Society: the Commercialization of Eighteenth-Century England* (London, 1982)
MacKillop, A., *More Fruitful than the Soil: Army, Empire and the Scottish Highlands, 1715–1815* (East Linton, 2000)
McNeill, P. G. B. and MacQueen, H., *Atlas of Scottish History to 1707* (Edinburgh, 1996)
Markus, T. A., ed., *Order in Space and Society* (London, 1982)
Martin, P., *A Life of James Boswell* (Yale, 1999)
Moss, G. P., *Highland Gold and Silversmiths* (Edinburgh, 1999)
Murdoch, S., *Britain, Denmark, Norway and the House of Stuart, 1603–1660* (East Linton, 2000).

Mitchison, R., *Agricultural Sir John. The Life of Sir John Sinclair of Ulbster 1754–1835* (London, 1962)
Murray, N., *The Scottish Handloom Weavers, 1790–1850: A Social History* (Edinburgh 1978)
Nenadic, S., ed., *Scots in London in the Eighteenth Century: Patronage, Culture and Identity* (forthcoming)
Nicholson, A., *History of Skye: A Record of the Families, the Social Conditions and the Literature of the Island* (Skye, 1995)
Orr, W., *Deer Forests, Landlords and Crofters* (Edinburgh, 1982)
Oxford Dictionary of National Biography (Oxford, 2004–7)
Phillipson, N. T. and Mitchison, R., eds, *Scotland in the Age of Improvement* (Edinburgh, 1970)
Pittock, M. G. H., *The Invention of Scotland: The Stuart Myth and Scotish Identity, 1638 to the Present* (London, 1991)
Pittock, M. G. H., *The Myth of the Jacobite Clans* (London, 1995)
Porter, R., *Disease, Medicine and Society in England, 1550–1860* (Basingstoke, 1993)
Reid, R., *The Georgian House and Its Details* (Bath, 1989)
Ribeiro, A., *Dress in Eighteenth Century Europe* (Yale, 2002)
Richards, E., *History of the Highland Clearances Vol 1: Agrarian Transformation and the Evictions, 1746–1886* (London, 1982)
Richards, E., *Leviathon of Wealth* (London, 1973)
Richards, E., *Patrick Sellar and the Highland Clearances: Homicide, Eviction and the Price of Progress* (Edinburgh, 1999)
Richards, E. and Clough, M., *Cromartie: Highland Life, 1650–1914* (Aberdeen, 1989)
Roche, D., *The Culture of Clothing: Dress and Fashion in the Ancien Regime* (Cambridge, 1994)
Sanderson, E., *Women and Work in Eighteenth-Century Edinburgh* (London, 1996)
Saville, R., *Bank of Scotland: A History, 1695–1995* (Edinburgh, 1996)
Sawyer, B., *Property and Inheritance in Viking Scandinavia: The Runic Evidence* (Alingsas, 1988)
Schama, S., *The Embarrassment of Riches: An Interpretation of Dutch Culture in the Golden Age* (London, 1988)
Scott, H., *Fasti Ecclesiae Scotticanae* (Edinburgh, 1923)
Sharpe, J. A., *Early Modern England: A Social History, 1550–1760* (London, 1987)
Smout, T. C., *A History of the Scottish People, 1560–1830* (London, 1969)
Smout, T. C., ed., *Anglo-Scottish Relations from 1603–1900. Proceedings of the British Academy*, 127 (Oxford, 2005)
Stewart, R., *The Classic English Town House* (London, 2006)
Stobart, J., Hann, A. and Morgan, V., *Spaces of Consumption: Geographies of Shopping and Leisure in the English Town, 1680–1830* (London, 2007)
Stone, L., *Family and Fortune: Studies in Aristocratic Finance in the Sixteenth and Seventeenth Centuries* (Oxford, 1973)
Stone, L. and Fawtier-Stone, J. C., *Open Elite? England 1540–1800* (Oxford, 1984)
Thomson, D., *Raeburn* (Edinburgh, 1997)

Valletta, F., *Witchcraft, Magic and Superstition in England, 1640–1670* (Aldershot, 2000)
Vickery, A., *The Gentleman's Daughter: Women's Lives in Georgian England* (New Haven, 1998)
Vigarello, G., *Concepts of Cleanliness. Changing Attitudes in France Since the Middle Ages* (Cambridge, 1988)
Weatherill, L., *Consumer Behaviour and Material Culture in Britain, 1660–1760* (London, 1988)
Whatley, C. A., *Scottish Society, 1707–1830: Beyond Jacobitism, Towards Industrialization* (Manchester, 2000)
Whyte, I. D., *Scotland before the Industrial Revolution* (London, 1995)
Wiesner, M. E., *Women and Gender in Early Modern Europe* (Cambridge, 1993)
Wilson, R. and Mackley, A., *Creating Paradise: The Building of the English Country House, 1660–1880* (London, 2000)
Withers, C. W. J., *Gaelic Scotland: The Transformation of a Culture Region* (London, 1988)
Womack, P., *Improvement and Romance: Constructing the Myth of the Highlands* (London, 1988)
Young, H., *The Genius of Wedgwood* (London, 1995)
Youngson, A. J., ed., *Beyond the Highland Line. Three Journals of Travel in Eighteenth Century Scotland* (London, 1974)
Youngson, A. J., *The Making of Classical Edinburgh, 1750–1840* (Edinburgh, 1966)

ARTICLES AND ESSAYS

Armitage, D., 'Making the Empire British: Scotland in the Atlantic world, 1542–1717', *Past and Present* 155 (1997), 34–63
Berry, H., 'Polite consumption: Shopping in eighteenth century England', *Royal Historical Society Transactions* 12 (2002), 375–94
Brown, K. M., 'From Scottish lords to British officers: State building, elite integration and the army in the seventeenth century', in Macdougall, N., ed., *Scotland and War AD 79–1918* (Edinburgh, 1991)
Brown, K. M., 'The Scottish aristocracy, anglicization and the court, 1603–38', *Historical Journal* 36:3 (1993), 543–76
Campbell, D. G., 'The younger generation in Argyll at the beginning of the eighteenth century', *Scottish Studies* 18 (1974)
Carpenter, S. D. M., 'The British army', in Dickenson, H., ed., *A Companion to Eighteenth-Century Britain* (Oxford, 2002)
Cookson, J. E., 'The Napoleonic Wars, military Scotland and Tory Highlandism in the early nineteenth century', *Scottish Historical Review* 78 (1999), 60–75
Coss, P. R., 'The formation of the English gentry', *Past and Present* 147 (1995), 38–64
Cregeen, E., 'Tacksmen and their successors: A study of tenurial reorganisations in Mull, Morvern and Tiree in the early eighteenth century', *Scottish Studies* 13 (1969), 93–144

Cregeen, E., 'The changing role of the house of Argyll in the Scottish Highlands', in Phillipson, N. T. and Mitchison, R., eds, *Scotland in the Age of Improvement* (Edinburgh, 1970)

Devine, T. M., 'Scottish elites and the Indian Empire', in Smout, T. C., ed., *Anglo-Scottish Relations from 1603–1900. Proceedings of the British Academy*, 127 (Oxford, 2005)

Dodgshon, R. A., 'Pretense of blude and place of thair dwelling: The nature of highland clans, 1500–1745', in Houston, R. A. and Whyte, I. D., eds, *Scottish Society, 1500–1800* (London, 1997)

Durie, A. J., 'Lairds, improvement, banking and industry in eighteenth century Scotland: Capital and development in a backward economy. A case study', in Devine, T. M., ed., *Lairds and Improvement in the Scotland of the Enlightenment* (London, 1979)

Finn, M., 'Men's things: Masculine possessions in the consumer revolution', *Social History* 25 (2000), 1–35

Frater, A. C., 'Women of the Gaidhealtachd and their songs to 1750', in Ewan, E. and Meikle, M. M., eds, *Women in Scotland, c.1100–1750* (East Linton, 1999)

Goodare, J., 'The Statutes of Iona in context', *Scottish Historical Review* 77 (1998), 31–57

Goodman, D., 'Furnishing discourses: Readings of a writing desk in eighteenth-century France', in Berg, M. and Eger, E., eds, *Luxury in the Eighteenth Century: Debates, Desires and Delectable Goods* (Basingstoke, 2003)

Hanlon, G., 'The decline of a provincial military aristocracy: Siena, 1560–1740', *Past and Present* 155 (1997), 64–108

Hann, A. and Stobart, J., 'Sites of consumption: The display of goods in provincial shops in eighteenth century England', *Cultural and Social History* 2 (2005), 165–88

Hellman, M., 'Furniture, sociability and the work of leisure in eighteenth century France', *Eighteenth-Century Studies* 32 (1999), 415–45

Hont, I. and Ignatieff, M., 'Needs and justice in the Wealth of Nations: An introductory Essay', in Hont, I. and Ignatieff, M., eds, *Wealth and Virtue* (Cambridge, 1983)

Houston, R. A., 'Women in the economy and society of Scotland, 1500–1800', in Houston, R. A. and Whyte, I. D., eds, *Scottish Society 1500–1800* (Cambridge, 1989)

Jones, D., 'Scottish cabinet makers' price books, 1805–1825', *Regional Furniture* 3 (1989), 27–39

Kidd, C., 'Subscription, the Scottish Enlightenment and the moderate interpretation of history', *Journal of Ecclesiastical History* 55 (2004)

Langford, P., 'The uses of eighteenth-century politeness', *Transactions of the Royal Historical Society* 12 (2002), 311–3

MacInnes, A., 'Who owned Argyll in the eighteenth century?', in Association of Scottish Historical Studies Symposium, University of St Andrews, *Power, Property and Privilege: The Landed Elite in Scotland from c.1440 to 1914* (St Andrews, 1989)

MacInnes, A. I., 'Landownership, land use and elite enterprise in Scottish Gaeldom: From clanship to clearance in Argyllshire, 1688–1858', in Devine, T. M., ed., *Scottish Elites* (Edinburgh, 1994)

McNeill, P. and Riello, G., 'The art and science of walking; gender, space and the fashionable body in the long eighteenth century', *Fashion Theory: the Journal of Dress, Body and Culture* 9 (2005), 175–204

Mason, J., 'The Edinburgh School of Design', *Book of the Old Edinburgh Club*, 27 (1949), 67–97

Mathias, P., 'The social structure in the eighteenth century: A calculation by Joseph Massie', *Economic History Review* 10 (1957), 30–45

Nenadic, S., 'Consuming at a distance: The Highlands of Scotland in the first half of the eighteenth century', *British Journal for Eighteenth Century Studies* 28 (2005), 215–28

Nenadic, S., 'Experience and expectations in the transformation of the Highland gentlewoman c.1680–1830', *Scottish Historical Review* 80 (2001), 201–20

Nenadic, S., 'The impact of the military profession on Highland gentry families, c.1730–1830', *Scottish Historical Review* 85 (2006), 75–99

Nenadic, S., 'Middle rank consumers and domestic culture in Edinburgh and Glasgow, 1720–1840', *Past and Present* 145 (1994), 122–56

Nenadic, S., 'Military men, businessmen and the "business" of patronage in eighteenth century London', in Nenadic, S., ed., *Scots in London in the Eighteenth Century: Patronage, Culture and Identity* (forthcoming)

Nenadic, S., 'Print collecting and popular culture in eighteenth century Scotland', *History* 82 (1997), 203–22

Nenadic, S., 'Romanticism and the urge to consume in the early nineteenth century', in Berg, M. and Clifford, H., eds, *Consumers and Luxury. Consumer Culture in Europe, 1650–1850* (Manchester, 1999)

Pennell, S., 'Consumption and consumerism in early modern England', *Historical Journal* 42 (1999), 549–64

Phillipson, N., 'Lawyers, landowners and the civic leadership of post-Union Scotland', *Juridical Review* 120 (1976), 97–120

Pointon, M., 'Jewellery in eighteenth century England', in Berg, M. and Clifford, H., eds, *Consumers and Luxury: Consumer Culture in Europe, 1650–1850* (Manchester, 1999)

Poole, F. J. P., 'Socialization, enculturation and the development of personal identity', in Ingold, T., ed., *Companion Encyclopedia of Anthropology* (London, 1994)

Razzell, P. E., 'Social origins of officers in the Indian and British home army, 1758–1962', *British Journal of Sociology* 14 (1963), 248–60.

Reddington-Wilde, R., 'A woman's place: Birth order, gender and social status in Highland houses', in Ewan, E. and Meikle, M. M., eds, *Women in Scotland, c.1100–1750* (East Linton, 1999)

Smith, A., 'The administration of the Forfeited Annexed Estates, 1752–1784', in Barrow, G., ed., *The Scottish Tradition* (London, 1974)

Smout, T. C., 'The landowner and the planned village in Scotland, 1730–1830', in Phillipson, N. T. and Mitchison, R., eds, *Scotland in the Age of Improvement* (Edinburgh, 1970)

Smout, T. C., 'Scottish landowners and economic growth, 1650–1850', *Scottish Journal of Political Economy* 11 (1964), 218–34

Stiubhart, D. U., 'Women and gender in the early modern western Gaidhealtachd', in Ewan, E. and Meikle, M. M., eds, *Women in Scotland, c.1100–1750* (East Linton, 1999)

Sweet, R., 'Topographies of politeness', *Transactions of the Royal Historical Society* 12 (2002), 355–74

Timperlay, L., 'The pattern of landholding in eighteenth century Scotland', in Parry, M. L. and Slater, T. R., eds, *The Making of the Scottish Countryside* (London, 1980)

Vickery, A., 'Women and the world of goods: A Lancashire consumer and her possessions, 1751–81', in Brewer, J. and Porter, R., eds, *Consumption and the World of Goods* (London, 1994)

Wall, C., 'The English auction: Narratives of dismantlings', *Eighteenth Century Studies* 31 (1997), 1–25

Watt, D., ' "The laberinth of thir difficulties": The influence of debt on the Highland elite *c.*1500–1700', *Scottish Historical Review* 85 (2006) 28–51

Weatherill, L., 'A possession of one's own: Women and consumer behaviour in England, 1660–1760', *Journal of British Studies* 25 (1986), 131–56

Whyte, I. D., 'Agriculture in Aberdeenshire in the seventeenth and early eighteenth centuries: Continuity and change', Stevenson, D., ed., *From Lairds to Louns: Country and Burgh Life in Aberdeen, 1600–1800* (Aberdeen, 1986)

Williamson, A. H., 'Scots, Indians and empire: The Scottish politics of civilization, 1519–1609', *Past and Present* 150 (1996), 46–83

UNPUBLISHED THESES

Bonnyman, B. D., 'Agricultural Improvement in the Scottish Enlightenment: The Third Duke of Buccleuch, William Keir and the Buccleuch Estates, 1751–1812', University of Edinburgh, PhD Thesis, 2004.

Glover, K., 'Elite Women and the Change of Manners in Mid-Eighteenth Century Scotland', University of Edinburgh, PhD Thesis, 2007.

Lodge, M. M., 'The Militia Issue: The Case of the Buccleuch Fencibles, 1778–1783', University of Edinburgh, MLitt Thesis, 1985.

Mackay, W. A., 'The Lesser Elites of Northern Scotland', University of Edinburgh, MSc Thesis, 1994.

Reddington-Wilde, R., 'The Power of Place: Spatial Analysis and Social Organization of the Campbells in Early Modern Argyll, Scotland', Harvard University, PhD Thesis, 1995.

OTHER SOURCES

Barcaldine Castle Guide (*c.*2000).

Index

Aberdeen 54
Adam, Robert 166
Adam, William 163
Adam, William 'of the Adelphi' 84–5, 96
America 97–8, 100, 102, 104, 146
American War of Independence 97–8, 105
An Essay on Female Conduct by Alexander Monro 60
annuities 22, 24–5, 55, 116–17, 119–21, 132, 141, 208
antiquarians 41
antiques 156–8
Appin Murder xiii, 26, 117, 123, 158, 174, 177
apprentices 52, 68, 74, 80, 81, 83, 93, 107, 124–5, 141
Ardchattan Priory xiii, 22, 35, 48, 70, 71, 79, 177, 185
Argyll, dukes of 6, 71, 72, 103, 113, 121, 155, 166, 181, 182
  Argyll, 3rd duke of 188–90
  Argyll, 4th duke of 190–1
  see also Inverary Castle
Argyllshire landowners 21
auctions 145–7
Austen, Jane 199

babies 44, 55, 127, 128, 185
  see also childbirth, children

bachelors 30–1, 90, 108–9
Baillie family of Rosehall 26, 28, 118
Balfour, Sir James of Denmilne and Kinnaird 10–11
bankruptcy 2, 19–20, 36, 38, 54, 76, 82, 85, 97, 104, 105, 137, 146, 169
Barcaldine Castle 58, 71, 119–20, 141, 143, 163–4, 168, 191–2, 202
Barcaldine estate 19–20, 38, 71–2, 74, 75, 79, 102, 109–11, 119, 130–2, 148, 205
Barcaldine House 20, 71, 111, 119–20, 131,141–2, 148, 168–9, 177, 178, 191, 201–2, 205
Bath 69, 101, 140, 188, 203–4
Beaton family 47–8, 80
  see also medical profession
'beneficial luxury' 11–13
  see also luxury, consumerism
Board of Trustees for Fisheries and Manufactures 13
Boswell, James 2, 43, 52, 54, 62, 63, 68, 78, 100, 109, 144, 146, 156–7, 197
  on food and drink 193, 194
  on hospitality 190–1, 193, 194
  on houses 178–82
  on manners 104–5, 129–30, 191
Breadalbane, earls of 21, 26, 51, 57, 58,

69, 72, 96, 163, 166–7, 172, 185, 188
  see also Glenorchy, lord, Taymouth Castle
Brodie, David of Pitgaviny 143
Burt, Edmund 44. 45, 144, 146, 150–1, 152, 183–4, 194, 209

Caithness, earls of 25, 38, 107–8
Callander 143
Cameron family of Lochiel 25–6, 58, 191–2
Cameron, Dr Archibald 26, 80
Cameron, John of Lochiel 25, 26
Cameron, Lucy 25, 141
Campbell, clan 7, 51, 70
Campbell family of Barcaldine and Glenure 15, 19–20, 21, 22, 25–7, 30, 32, 35, 68, 82, 106, 110, 113, 146, 156, 172, 205
  landholdings of 21, 110
  see also Barcaldine Castle, Barcaldine estate, Barcaldine House, Glenure House
Campbell, Alexander of Barcaldine (b. 1647) 22, 49, 57–8, 69, 149–50
  daughters, 57–8
  see also Campbell, Mary (of Lochnell) (b. 1652) [wife], Campbell, Patrick of Barcaldine [son], Campbell, Colin of Invernan [son] Campbell, Isabel [daughter], Campbell, Mary (b.c.1690) [daughter]
Campbell, Alexander of Barcaldine and Glenure (b. 1745) 33, 36, 54, 63, 75–6, 106, 131–3, 143, 157, 199, 200–2
  see also Campbell, Duncan of Barcaldine and Glenure [father], MacPherson, Mary [mother], Campbell, Mary 'of the bank' [wife], Campbell, Sir Duncan of Barcaldine and Glenure [son],

Campbell, Helen Maria [daughter]
Campbell, Col. Alexander 25, 110, 117, 203–4
  see also Campbell, John of Barcaldine [father], Sinclair, Helen [wife]
Campbell, Lieut. Alexander 51, 83, 92–6, 142
  see also Campbell, Patrick of Barcaldine [father], Cameron, Lucy (of Lochiel) [mother]
Campbell, Lieut. Alexander (Sandy) 96–98, 106, 123
  see also Campbell, Duncan of Barcaldine and Glenure [father], Campbell, Mally [wife]
Campbell, Maj. Allan 83, 92–6, 97, 103–4
  see also Campbell, Patrick of Barcaldine [father], Cameron, Lucy (of Lochiel) [mother]
Campbell, Maj. Archibald 52, 83, 92–6
  see also Campbell, Patrick of Barcaldine [father], Cameron, Lucy (of Lochiel) [mother]
Campbell, Colin of Glenure xi–xiv, 6, 25, 30, 33, 72, 83, 115–18, 128, 157, 207
  career 50–51, 93
  clothing 42–3, 151, 153
  consumerism xi–ii, 142, 144, 147, 149, 157–8, 174–8
  death of xiii, 25, 26, 117–8, 123, 158, 174–8
  education 51
  see also Appin Murder, Campbell, Patrick of Barcaldine [father], Cameron, Lucy (of Lochiel) [mother], Mackay, Janet (of Bighouse) [wife], Campbell, Colina [daughter], Campbell, Louisa [daughter] Campbell, Tibby [daughter] MacPherson, Isabel [daughter]

Campbell, Capt. Colin of Glenure 101–2, 103–4, 106, 110, 143, 175
  see also Campbell, Duncan of Barcaldine and Glenure [father], MacPherson, Mary [mother]
Campbell, Colin of Invernan 22–4, 32, 69, 184–5
  see also Campbell, Alexander of Barcaldine (b. 1647) [father], Campbell, Mary (of Lochnell) [mother]
Campbell, Colina 28, 118
  see also Campbell, Colin of Glenure [father], Mackay, Janet (of Bighouse) [mother]
Campbell, Donald 52, 92–3, 127
  see also Campbell, Patrick of Barcaldine [father], Cameron, Lucy (of Lochiel) [mother]
Campbell, Duncan of Barcaldine and Glenure 23, 59, 72, 76, 77, 83–6, 105, 117–18, 124, 174, 178, 190, 198
  career 73–5, 150
  children 54, 62, 67, 96–8, 101–2, 103–4, 110
  education 51
  see also Campbell, Patrick of Barcaldine [father], Cameron, Lucy (of Lochiel) [mother], MacPherson, Mary [wife], Campbell, Alexander of Barcaldine and Glenure [son], Campbell, Capt. Colin of Glenure [son], Campbell, Maj. Patrick [son]
Campbell, Sir Duncan of Barcaldine and Glenure 20–1, 27, 33, 36, 38, 79, 153, 156, 205, 206
  education 54
  financial problems 110–1, 199, 205
  houses 168–8, 200
  see also Campbell, Alexander of Barcaldine and Glenure [father],

Campbell, Mary ('of the bank') [mother]
Campbell, Helen Maria 36, 63
  see also Campbell, Alexander of Barcaldine and Glenure [father], Campbell, Mary ('of the bank') [mother], Fraser, Rev. Hugh [husband]
Campbell, Isabell 57
  see also Campbell, Alexander of Barcaldine (b. 1647) [father], Campbell, Mary (of Lochnell) [mother]
Campbell, Isobell 59, 60.
  see also Campbell, Patrick of Barcaldine [father], Cameron, Lucy (of Lochiel) [mother]
Campbell, Jean 59, 60.
  see also Campbell, Patrick of Barcaldine [father], Cameron, Lucy (of Lochiel) [mother]
Campbell, John of Barcaldine 23, 26, 84, 105, 120, 143, 147, 168, 184, 191–2
  career 70–3
  children 72, 110, 179, 202
  education 51, 70, 186
  see also Campbell, Patrick of Barcaldine [father], Campbell, Ann (of Kilmun) [mother], Campbell, Col. Alexander [son]
Campbell, Louisa 28, 118, 128, 157–8
  see also Campbell, Colin of Glenure [father], Mackay, Janet (of Bighouse) [mother], Mackay, Col. George of Handa and Bighouse [husband]
Campbell, Mally, 123
  see also, Campbell, Lieut. Alexander (Sandy) [husband]
Campbell, Mary (b. c.1690) 57–8, 127
  see also Campbell, Alexander of Barcaldine [father], Campbell, Mary (of Lochnell) [mother],

Stewart, Duncan of Innernahyle [husband]
Campbell, Patrick of Barcaldine 22–5, 32, 49, 57, 69–71, 73, 74, 114, 168
  children 50–52, 59, 67–8, 92–4, 122
  see also Campbell, Alexander of Barcaldine [father], Campbell, Mary (of Lochnell), [mother], Campbell, Ann (of Kilmun) [wife], Cameron, Lucy (of Lochiel) [wife], Campbell, John of Barcaldine [son], Campbell, Colin of Glenure [son], Campbell, Duncan of Barcaldine and Glenure [son], Campbell, Maj. Archibald [son], Campbell, Maj. Allan [son], Campbell, Lieut. Alexander [son], Campbell, Robert [son], Campbell, Donald [son], Campbell, Isobell [daughter], Campbell, Jean [daughter]
Campbell, Maj. Patrick 67, 96, 99, 100, 101, 106
  see also Campbell, Duncan of Barcaldine and Glenure [father], MacPherson, Mary [mother]
Campbell, Robert 52, 72, 83–6, 95, 96, 99, 105, 124, 145, 149
  see also Campbell, Patrick of Barcaldine [father], Cameron, Lucy (of Lochiel) [mother]
Campbell, Tibby 149
  see also Campbell, Colin of Glenure [father]
Campbell, John of Achallader 58, 72, 114, 118–19
Campbell, Rev. Colin of Achnaba, 35, 78, 121, 127
  see also Campbell, Margaret [daughter]
Campbell, Margaret (of Achnaba) 113

  see also Campbell, Rev. Colin of Achnaba [father]
Campbell, John 'of the bank' xii, 20, 27, 54, 59, 73, 76, 83, 152, 201
  see also Campbell, Mary ('of the bank') [daughter]
Campbell, Mary ('of the bank') 54, 63, 130–32, 201–3
  see also Campbell, John 'of the bank' [father], Campbell, Alexander of Barcaldine and Glenure [husband], Campbell, Sir Duncan of Barcaldine and Glenure [son], Campbell, Helen Maria [daughter]
Campbell family of Glenure *see* Campbell family of Barcaldine and Glenure
  see also Glenure House
Campbell, David of Kethic 26, 48, 71,
Campbell, Ann (of Kilmun) 25, 57
  see also Campbell, Lady Susan of Kilmun [mother], Campbell, Patrick of Barcaldine [husband], Campbell, John of Barcaldine [son]
Campbell, Lady Susan of Kilmun 57, 115, 120–1
Campbell family of Lochnell 119, 161, 167
  see also Campbell, Mary (of Lochnell)
Campbell, Mary (of Lochell) 119–21, 127, 141
  see also Campbell, Alexander of Barcaldine [husband], Campbell, Patrick of Barcaldine [son], Campbell, Colin of Invernan [son], Campbell, Isabell [daughter], Campbell, Mary (b.c.1690) [daughter]
Campbell, John Archibald, W.S. 20, 200
Carlyle, Rev. Alexander 189–90, 203
careers 9, 50, 51–2, 65–86, 91, 99
  commercial 50, 83–6

farming 68–73
  professional 50, 51, 67, 73–7
  women's 98, 107–8, 123–5, 132–3
  see also apprentices, clergymen, legal profession, medical profession, military profession

cattle trade 5–6, 9, 34, 67, 70, 89, 119, 123
Chelsea Pensioners 109
children 22–4, 29, 31, 35–7, 39, 40–64, 127–8, 131, 201, 202, 206
  brothers 48–9, 51–2, 97
  daughters 27, 36, 54–64, 128
    eldest daughters 43, 45, 55, 115, 128
    younger daughters 26, 37,
  illegitimate 32, 56, 68, 72, 99, 108, 123, 149
  sibling hierarchies 43, 55, 115
  sisters 49–50, 55, 107–8, 117
  sons 22–4, 36, 45–54, 48–9, 51–2, 98
    eldest sons 26, 43, 45, 54, 65, 67
    younger sons 48–9, 50, 52, 65, 67, 94, 99, 104
  mortality of 44, 55, 127
  neglect of 44, 45
  orphans 43–4
  parents 43–4, 48, 55
  phases of childhood 44
  wet-nursing 44, 118
  see also babies, childbirth, education, families, fosterage, schools
childbirth 127, 128, 131, 138, 185, 201–2
clans 4,8, 29, 90, 106, 113, 114–15
  chiefs 9, 21, 41, 45–6, 179, 183–4, 211
  clothing 150–2
  retinues 5, 184
  traditions 211–12
  women 114–15, 129
clearances 6
clergymen 22, 33, 34–7, 41, 79–7
  children of 35, 36, 52, 63
  fosterage by 47
  houses of 173, 181
  inheritance 36
  kin networks 34–7
  wives of 35
clothing xii, 2, 42–3, 57, 59, 84, 109, 137, 149–54
  antique 156
  emotions and 152, 154
  gifts of 154
  highland clothes xii, 42–3, 149–53
    arisaid 151, 153
    kilt 42–3, 151–2
    tartan and plaids 42–3, 150–2, 153, 156, 187
    proscription of 150
  lowland clothes, 140, 144, 150, 151 153
  luxury and 153, 154
  men's clothes xii, 42–3, 104, 109, 139, 150, 151, 152–3
    masculinity and 42–3 152
  politeness and 187
  portraits and 152
  status and 42–3, 153
  types of
    aprons 154
    buttons and buckles 109, 140, 150
    gloves 154
    great coat 152, 187
    hats xii
    heraldic costume 10, 138–9
    jewellery 140, 154
    linen, white 153–4
    mourning clothes 59, 138–9
    riding habit 57, 154
    uniforms 103–4, 110, 150, 153
    wigs xii, 151, 153, 154
  women's clothes 124, 139, 147–8, 153–4
  see also consumerism, luxury goods
Coll, Isle of 144
  houses on 181–2
Coll, laird of 68–9, 78, 180

commerce 4–6
conduct books 60, 151, 186–7, 188, 197
   see also *An Essay on Female Conduct* by Alexander Monro, *Rules of Good Deportment and of Good Breeding for the Use of Youth* by Adam Petrie
consumerism xi–iv, 1–2, 8, 12, 14, 54, 79, 86, 108, 124, 131–2, 148–9, 181, 208–12
   military profession and 103–4, 109, 110–11
   pre-modern 137–40
   late eighteenth century 155–58
   romantic 210–12
   women and 112–33, 137, 147–8
   see also 'beneficial luxury', clothing, food and drink, furniture, luxury goods, shops
Crieff 5, 72, 122, 124, 143, 144, 155
civilising the highlands 4–6, 8–10, 41, 182, 192

Dalfuir House *see* Barcaldine House
Dalmally 124
daughters *see* children
Description of the Western Isles of Scotland by Martin Martin 146
Downie, Robert 169
dowries 22, 24–5, 27, 55, 115–16, 119, 123, 141, 208
   see also annuities
Dunvegan Castle 47, 52, 130, 180

economy 3–6, 8
Edinburgh xi, 9–10, 46, 53, 75, 84, 125, 130, 185, 197–203, 212
   Charlotte Square 63, 75, 198–9, 200
   coffee houses 186
   Edinburgh Castle 95–6
   education in 49–52, 54, 57, 59, 63, 148, 195
   George IV's visit to 210–11
   goods from xi–iii, 109, 141, 143, 147, 148, 153, 157, 177, 178
   heraldic processions in 10–11
   leisure in 203–4
   Moray Place 200
   New Town 13, 39, 131–2, 199–200
   Picardy Place 200
   Queen Street 200
   town houses in 45, 75, 111, 132, 169, 192, 199–200
education 9, 41–2, 45–64, 66, 74, 91, 99, 124, 132
   behaviour and 148, 195
   commercial 50
   consumption and 148
   dancing 59
   daughters 14, 54–64, 113, 132, 148, 195
   English 52–4, 98–9, 130, 132
   military 91, 98–9
   music 50, 148, 195
   pastry making 59, 99
   politeness and 186–7
   professional 50, 99
   sons 45–54, 132
   see also children, fosterage, 'governors', governesses, schools
Elgin 74–5, 197
family 19–39
   dependency ratios 208–9
   expenditures of 107, 124, 131–2
   emotions in 125–9
   management of 22–4, 49–50, 52, 106, 115, 208
   tenants 21, 106
   resources of 21–2, 55, 68, 105, 106–7, 127–8
   service families 31–7
   see also children, kin networks, spinsters, wives, widows
farming lairds 67, 68–73, 102–3
Ferrier, Susan 102, 114, 185
Fletcher family of Saltoun 189–90
fosterage 29, 45–9, 53, 56, 68, 124

see also children, education, family, kin networks, 'governors'
Forfeited and Annexed Estates Commission 13, 72,
Fort Augustus 133, 179
Fort George 110
Fort William 143
food and drink 84, 137, 140, 148, 177–8, 183, 184–5, 187–8, 190, 193–6
see also luxury goods, hospitality, social occasions
Fraser, Rev. Hugh 79, 205
see also Campbell, Helen Maria (of Barcaldine) [wife]
Fraser, Simon, Lord Lovatt 183–4, 198
funerals 10, 22–4, 41, 49, 117, 138–9, 177, 184–5, 204
furniture xi, 71, 104, 106, 109, 137, 139, 141, 156, 159, 175–7
  highland made 141–4, 156
  types of
    beds, 146, 176
    chairs, 141, 143, 175–6, 191–2
    curtains, 176
    dining room, for, 106, 141–2
    tables, 174–5
    writing desks, 142, 175

genealogy 10–11.
Gaelic verse xii–xiii, 2–3, 24, 26, 32, 33, 34, 37, 45, 57, 63, 113, 129, 150
gentry culture 66–7, 137–40
Glasgow 34, 51, 83, 93, 94–5, 97–8, 111, 132, 133, 142, 189
Glencoe, massacre of 7, 113
Glenorchy, lord 7, 40–1, 83, 140, 149–50, 163, 180, 186
Glenure House 84, 102, 106, 116–8, 142, 143, 149, 157–8, 161, 174–8, 194
  building of 174
  food and drink in 177–8
  furniture in 175–7
  layout of 174
  room uses 175–7
'governor' 48–9, 61
see also children, education, fosterage, schools
governess 202–3
see also children, education, schools
Graham, James Gillespie 167, 168
Graham, Gen. Thomas of Balgowan, lord Lyndoch 101
Grand Tour 52–3
Grant, Ann (of Laggan) 133
Grant family of Rothiemurchus 75, 113–14, 197, 200, 21
Grant, Elizabeth (of Rothiemurchus) 132–3, 206, 212
see also Grant, Peter of Rothiemurchus [father]
Grant, Peter of Rothiemurchus 75–6, 105–6, 197, 199
see also Grant, Elizabeth (of Rothiemurchus) [daughter]

Hay, George, earl of Kinnoul 10
heraldry 10–11, 138–9
  heraldic costume 10, 138–9
  see also clothing, funerals
Highland Society 6, 102, 111
hospitality 101, 137–8, 177, 183–204
see also social occasions
houses 65, 69, 71, 75, 84, 96, 121–2, 130, 137, 138, 159–82, 198–201
  architects and builders of 161, 163, 166, 167, 173
  Argyllshire houses 164–73
    aristocratic and noblemen's 166–7
    chronology of building 165
    gentlemen's 175
    large lairds' 167–71
    manses 173, 181
    small lairds' 171–2
    tacksmen's 171–2
  buildings process 161–4, 171

Coll, houses on 180–2
'comfort and convenience' in 160, 162, 171
cost of building 161–2, 170, 172, 200
Erray, houses on 181
funding of 161
gardens 162–3, 167, 173
highland houses
  Appin House 169
  Ardmaddy Castle 166–7
  Armadale House 179
  Asknish House 173
  Ballieveolan House 161
  Barbreck House 172
  Cameron House 182
  Castle Downie 183
  Castle House, Dunoon 173
  Coirechatachan 179–80, 194
  Doune 206, 212
  Dregnish House 172
  Duntroon Castle 170–71
  Glengyle House 159–60, 182
  Glenmoriston House 179
  Glenstrae 171
  Governor's House, Fort Augustus 179
  Grishpoll House 180
  Kilchurn Castle 163, 180
  Lochbuie House 182
  Lochnell House 161
  Monymusk 162
  Quarrell 171
  Rarey House 172
  Rasaay House 180
  Stronmagachan House 172
'laird's box' 161, 172, 181
locks and keys, in 158, 174, 178
men and houses 160, 201
pre–modern 139–40
room layouts 160, 161, 167, 168, 170, 171–2, 173, 177, 179–82, 200
style of 162, 166, 168, 171, 173
tacksmen's houses 159, 172, 180, 181
town houses 198–201

types of room
  bedroom 176, 180, 193, 201
  dining room 106, 169, 174, 175–6, 180, 192, 193, 201
  drawing room 169, 175, 193–4, 201
  library 168–9, 206
  parlour 201
visitors to 102–3, 196
women and houses 160, 200–1
see also Barcaldine Castle, Barcaldine House, Dunvegan Castle, Glenure House, Edinburgh, Huntley Castle, Inverary Castle, Taymouth Castle, Poltalloch House
Huntley Castle 152

India 101–2, 132
inheritance 23, 27–8, 34, 36, 106, 108, 115, 119–20, 138, 201
improvement 70, 72, 162
  in manners 183, 186–91
  see also politeness, social occasions
Inverary 23, 83, 141–2, 143, 144, 155, 166, 172, 182, 185, 189
Inverary Castle 161, 166, 182, 188–91
Inverness 52, 57, 122, 141, 143–4, 146, 155, 184, 194, 198, 211

Jacobite Uprisings 6, 26, 37, 72, 150, 207
Johnson, Dr Samuel 54, 62, 63, 66, 78, 179–82, 191
jointure see annuities

Killiecrankie, battle of 7
Kilsyth 57
kin networks 20–1, 22–4, 29, 32, 34–7, 62, 65, 121, 138, 167
  see also clans, family, children
Kirk, Colin 51, 70, 73, 186
knowledge practices 13, 41–2, 55–6, 61, 63, 73

language 8, 41–2, 46, 48, 56, 63
law 8–9
  knowledge of 9, 51, 73,
  training in 51, 53, 73–7, 74
  see also legal profession
lawlessness 4–8, 12–13, 138
legal profession 8–9, 20, 38, 49, 51, 54, 63, 66, 67, 69, 71, 73–7, 100, 101, 126
leisure resorts 203–4
  see also Bath
leisure travel 203–4
literacy 56, 58, 112, 123, 124, 132, 147–8
London 30, 52, 63, 67, 76, 80, 82, 84–5, 97–8, 101–2, 103, 109
  culture of 186, 187
  goods from 109, 140, 143, 147, 149, 155–6
  visits to 109–10, 132, 188, 196, 203
  print culture of 146–8, 151
  town houses in 202–3
Lord Lion at Arms 10–11
luxury 1–3, 12, 14, 103–5, 110–11, 129–33, 153, 154, 187–8, 205–12
  see also auctions, 'beneficial luxury', clothing, consumerism, food and drink, Edinburgh, furniture, London, luxury goods, portraits, shops
luxury goods xi–xiii, 13, 109, 119, 137–58, 174–8, 194
  highland purchased 143–5
  types of
    alcoholic drinks 12, 138, 177, 185, 187, 190–1
    antiques 156–8, 169
    books 11, 49, 51, 59–60, 62, 112, 124, 140, 148, 169, 176
    carriages 196, 199
    china xii, 62, 141, 143, 144, 145, 156, 177, 188, 195
    clocks 119
    domestic linen 154, 177, 187

Dutch tiles xii
glass wares xii, 12, 140, 144, 177
guns and swords 109, 140, 149
mirrors xi, 139, 145, 156, 201
musical instruments 50, 54, 148, 195, 201
pictures and prints xi, xii, 50, 109, 143, 145, 146, 149, 169, 174, 176, 179, 201
silverware xii, 143, 145, 148, 177
sugar 59, 140, 145, 155, 177, 187
tea 59, 140, 145, 155, 177, 187–8
tobacco 140, 145
wallpaper 145, 146
watches 109
see also auctions, 'beneficial luxury', clothing, consumerism, Edinburgh, furniture, London, portraits, shops

magic 40–1
Martin Martin 11–12, 40–1, 47, 50, 140, 146
Macdonald clan 5, 40,
Macdonald family of Sleat 60, 66, 198–9
Macdonald, Alexander of Kingsburgh 46, 53, 74
Macdonald, Sir Alexander of Sleat 53, 54, 62, 66, 179
  see also Macdonald, Lady Margaret [mother]
Macdonald, Flora 43–4, 46, 56, 123, 130, 211
Macdonald, Sir James of Sleat 46, 53, 54, 66
  see also Macdonald, Lady Margaret [mother]
Macdonald, Lady Margaret 46, 53
  see also Macdonald, Sir Alexander of Sleat [son], Macdonald, Sir James of Sleat [son]
Macdonell, Alastair Ranald of Glengarry 211–12
Macintyre clan 23, 32–3, 117, 124

Macintyre, Duncan Ban xii–xiii, 32–3
Macintosh, William of Borlum 2, 187–8, 193, 207
Mackay clan 7
Mackay, General Hugh 7
Mackay family of Bighouse 15, 25, 26, 27–8, 80, 118, 125
Mackay, Elizabeth of Bighouse 26–7
  see also Mackay, Hugh of Bighouse [husband], Mackay, Janet [daughter], Mackay, Marion [daughter]
Mackay, Hugh of Bighouse xi–xiii, 2, 25, 26–7, 28, 34, 70, 80, 116–18, 128–9, 149, 204, 206, 207
  see also Mackay, Elizabeth of Bighouse [wife], Mackay, Janet [daughter], Mackay, Marion [daughter]
Mackay, Janet of Bighouse xi, xiv, 25, 26–7, 115–18, 207
  domestic life 116, 174–8
  marriage 116, 129, 157–8
  widowhood 117–18
  see also Mackay, Hugh of Bighouse [father], Mackay, Elizabeth of Bighouse [mother], Campbell, Colin of Glenure [husband], Campbell, Colina [daughter], Campbell, Louisa [daughter]
Mackay, Lady Dowager of Bighouse 144–5
  see also Mackay, Elizabeth of Bighouse [daughter]
Mackay, Marion of Bighouse 26–7
  see also Mackay, Hugh of Bighouse [father], Mackay, Elizabeth of Bighouse [mother]
Mackay, Col. George of Handa and Bighouse 28, 104
  see also Campbell, Louisa (of Barcaldine and Glenure) [wife]
Mackay, Robert Donn xii, 2, 8, 13, 26, 34, 36, 57, 68, 70, 118, 207
Mackenzie, Henry 126

Mackenzie, John of Delvine 48–9
  children 48–9
Mackinnon of Coirechatachan 146–7, 156–7, 179–8
Mackinnon, Rev. Neil 47
Maclean, Sir Allan 104–5, 130, 181
Macleod, John of Dunvegan 47
Macleod, Roderick 47, 50
Macleod, Lady 130
Macleod, laird of 203
Macleod, Miss 195
MacPherson family of Glenfine 34, 83, 123
MacPherson, Maj. James 83, 84, 94–5, 98, 101, 110
MacPherson, Mary 86, 107, 117
  see also Campbell, Duncan of Barcaldine and Glenure [husband], Campbell, Archibald of Barcaldine and Glenure [son], Campbell, Capt. Colin [son], Campbell, Maj. Patrick [son]
MacPherson, Isabel 32–3, 123–5
  see also Campbell, Colin of Glenure [father]
MacPherson, Lachlan of Badenoch 24
MacPherson, Mary of Badenoch 3, 113
Maclean family of Coll 180
  see also Coll, laird of
Malcolm family of Poltalloch 82, 85, 155–6, 169–71, 206
marriage 23–7, 31, 37, 55, 76, 102, 107, 115–6, 138
  see also annuities, dowries, wives, widows
marriage settlement 55
Marriage by Susan Ferrier 62, 102–3, 114, 185
medical profession 33, 37, 47–8, 52, 79–80, 92–3, 114, 127
  see also Beaton family
mercenaries 7–8, 90–1
merchants 81–6, 94
military control of highlands 6–8
military entrepreneurs 94–8

military highlandism 8, 111, 207
military profession 8, 14, 30, 38, 51–2, 83, 84, 89–111, 125–6, 208–9
   culture of 7, 90
   education of 53, 91, 96, 99
   financial problems of 104
   incomes in 93, 97–8, 100, 103
   labour market 89–90, 96, 110
   luxury and 103–5, 137, 141, 148, 181, 208–9
   majors 92, 95
   patronage in 92, 96, 99, 108
   purchase system 91–2, 95, 99, 107
   recruiting 90, 96, 99, 108
   scandals concerning 105, 110
   sociability in 101–2, 103, 106
   success in 102, 108, 111
   uniforms of 103–4, 110
military tenants 102, 106, 108, 212
Monro, Margaret 60
Morice Rev. James 48–9
Mosman, William xii
Mull, Isle of 104–5, 130
Munro, George Gun of Ponzfield 30–1, 82, 85, 148–9
   see also Sutherland, Col. George of Rearquahar [uncle]
music 50, 54, 61, 63, 129, 138, 183, 195
Mylne, Robert 166

Napoleonic Wars 98, 101, 104, 105, 110, 125
North Queensferry 97

Oban 143
oral culture 9, 47, 56, 79, 113–4

packmen 140, 147
   see also luxury goods, shops
patriotism 6, 12, 162
patronage 4, 46, 51, 72, 79, 90, 92, 101, 102
peddlers *see* packmen
Perth 51, 57, 70, 140, 143, 148, 202

Pennant, Thomas 40, 56
Petrie, Adam 186–7, 192, 197
politeness 12–13, 79, 102, 103, 129–30, 148, 152, 162, 179, 186–91, 209
Poltalloch House 156, 169–71
portraits xi–xii, 11, 110, 146–7, 152, 153
   see also luxury goods
Raeburn, Sir Henry 110, 153
Ramsay, John of Octertyre 69, 153, 207
Reay, lord of 25–6, 28,
Regulations for Chiefs 9, 41,
religion 8, 41, 56, 77, 205
   see also clergymen
romanticism 14, 132–3, 157–8, 210–11
Rose family of Kilravock 29, 80, 113, 126
Rose, Elizabeth of Kilravock 29, 61, 113, 126
Rothiemurchus estate 105–6, 212
royal tours of highlands 9–10
Rules of Good Deportment and of Good Breeding for the Use of Youth by Adam Petrie, 186–7
   see also conduct books

Sage, Rev. Alexander 41
Sage, Rev. Donald of Resolis 36–7, 41, 78
schools 35, 48–9, 51–2, 57, 59, 62, 148
   English 53–4, 96, 98–9, 132, 202
   on forfeited estates 72
   military 96
   see also children, Edinburgh, education, 'governors', governesses
Scott, Sir Walter 127, 132–2, 210–11
second sight 40–1
Sellar, Patrick 69, 74–5, 77
Sellar, Thomas 74–5
sensibility 62, 125–9, 132–3, 157–8, 196

servants 56, 104, 117, 139, 176–8, 184, 195, 196
service families 31–7, 117
Seven Years War 67, 94, 99, 103, 108, 109, 141
shops xii, 140, 141
   shopping xi–ii, 51, 144–5
   see also consumerism, luxury goods, packmen
Sinclair, clan 7, 20–1,
Sinclair family of Brabster 28–9, 38, 139
Sinclair, Ann of Brabster 28–9, 125–6, 142, 146
   see also Sutherland, Robert of Langwell [husband]
Sinclair family of Freswick 31, 38–9
Sinclair, William of Freswick 40–1, 74, 108, 138–9
Sinclair, Dr William of Lochend and Freswick 31, 34, 38–9, 80, 108, 121, 138–9, 146, 149
   see also Sinclair, Dr William [father]
Sinclair, Dr William 31, 34
   see also Sinclair, Dr William of Lochend and Freswick [son]
Sinclair family of Mey 25, 107–8, 125–6
Sinclair, Isabell (of Mey) 125
   see also Sinclair, Capt. John [brother], Sinclair, Whilhelmina [sister]
Sinclair, Capt. John (of Mey) 107–8, 125–6
   see also Sinclair, Isabell [sister], Sinclair, Whilhelmina [sister]
Sinclair, Whilhelmina (of Mey) 29, 126
   see also Sinclair, Capt. John [brother], Sinclair, Isabell [sister]
Sinclair family of Ulbster 25, 198–9
Sinclair, Helen (of Ulbster) 25, 203–4
   see also Campbell, Col. Alexander (of Barcaldine) [husband]
Sinclair, Sir John of Ulbster 79, 155
Skye, Isle of 5, 11, 50, 52, 66, 81, 140, 146, 156–7, 179–80, 195

social occasions 86, 129–30, 177, 183–204
   consumerism and 148, 187–8
   drinking and toasting 190–1, 194
   female 193–4, 195–6, 200–1
   food served at 193–6
   'improvement' in 191–7
   masculine 189–91, 192–5
   meal times 194, 195–6
   pre-modern 137–8, 183–5
   sociability 101, 103, 116, 189–91, 200–1
   types of
      breakfast 189, 193
      card parties 196
      dances 59, 138, 148, 211
      dinner 183, 187–8, 189, 190, 191, 193–4
      outdoor excursions 192–3
      supper 189, 190, 196
      tea parties 59, 148, 176, 187–8, 190, 195–6
   see also funerals
sons see children
spinsters 54, 107–8, 122–5, 129, 199, 203
   costs of 107
spinster problem 107, 122
St Andrews 48–9, 130
state policy on highlands 4–8, 12–13, 138
Statutes of Iona 5, 7, 9, 14
Stewart family of Appin 169
Stewart, David of Garth 205, 207, 209, 210
Stewart, Duncan of Innernahyle 58, 120, 133
   see also Campbell, Mary (of Barcaldine) (b.c.1690) [wife]
Stuart, Baillie John of Inverness 81–2, 83, 145, 147
Stuart, Lady Louisa 107, 196
Stirling 51, 70, 84, 85, 117, 124–5, 133, 145, 202
superstitions 40–1

Sutherland family of Langwell 28, 38, 138–9
Sutherland, Robert of Langwell 28, 139, 142
 see also Sinclair, Ann of Brabster [wife]
Sutherland, Elizabeth, countess of 29, 199
Sutherland, Col. George of Rearquahar 30–1, 82, 108–9, 141, 148–9
 see also Munro, George Gun [nephew]

tacksmen 5, 22–4, 30, 35, 38, 56, 57, 67, 78, 82, 93, 123
Tain 109, 149, 199
Taymouth Castle 140, 161, 163, 188
Telford, Thomas 173
Thurso 57, 80, 125–6, 143, 155
towns, highland 5, 155
 craftsmen in 141–4, 155
 merchants in 144–5, 155
traditional beliefs 41–2, 47, 210
Trapaud, Governor 179

universities 53–4

Waverley by Walter Scott 133, 211

Wealth of Nations by Adam Smith 12
wet-nurses 44, 118
 see also babies, children
Wick 125
widows 22–4, 27, 28, 29, 57, 98, 107, 115–22, 129, 133
 housing for 121–2, 201
wives 25–7, 115–22
women 14, 27–30, 107–8, 112–33, 174–8, 187–8, 195–6, 208–9
 careers of 98, 107–8, 123–5, 132–3
 clanship and 114–15
 consumerism and 112–33, 137, 147–8, 208–9
 education of 54–64
 illiteracy 55, 112, 147
 inheritance 27–30, 37,
 poetry by 113, 114
 property of 27–30, 201
 traditional knowledge of 113–14
 work by 117, 177
 see also annuities, childbirth, clans, clothes, consumerism, dowries, education, families, houses, social occasions, spinsters, widows, wives